Fictions of Sustainability

Also by Boris Frankel

Capitalism Versus Democracy

The Post Industrial Utopians

Beyond the State?
Dominant Theories and Socialist Strategies

From the Prophets Deserts Come:
The Struggle to Reshape Australian Political Culture

When the Boat Comes In:
Transforming Australia in the Age of Globalisation

Zombies, Lilliputians and Sadists:
The Power of the Living Dead and the Future of Australia

Marxian Theories of The State: A Critique of Orthodoxy

Fictions of Sustainability

The Politics of Growth and Post-Capitalist Futures

Boris Frankel

Greenmeadows

A catalogue record for this book is available from the
National Library of Australia

Name: Frankel, Boris, author.
Title: Fictions of Sustainability:
The Politics of Capitalist Growth and Post-Capitalist Futures / Boris Frankel.
Includes bibliographical references and index.
Subjects:
1. Politics of environmental sustainability. 2. Political economy – global inequality.
3. Post-capitalism – post-growth societies. 4. Social reform – alternative policies
5. Disputes over innovation – technological change.

ISBN: (pbk) 978-0-6483633-0-9
ISBN: (epub) 978-0-6483633-1-6
ISBN: (ePDF) 978-0-6483633-2-3

Typeset in Adobe Garamond Pro 11/13.5 by Antoinette Wilson
Cover Design by Emile Frankel

The publisher has endeavoured to ensure that the URLs for external websites referred to in this book were accurate and active at the time of going to press. However, neither the author nor the publisher has responsibility for the websites and can make no guarantee that a site will remain live or that the content has not changed since this book was prepared for publication.

For Julie and Emile

Contents

Preface

This book is an attempt to overcome a pervasive 'analytical apartheid' that characterises so much socio-economic policy on the one hand and so many environmental analyses on the other. I was particularly struck by this in January 2014, when I read a draft copy of Wolfgang Streeck's article, 'Taking Crisis Seriously: Capitalism On Its Way Out' which was published a few months later in the Italian journal *Stato e Mercato* (April 2014) and in *New Left Review* as 'How Will Capitalism End?' (May/ June 2014). The draft was kindly sent to me by Streeck and I found his arguments about the crises confronting capitalist societies simultaneously persuasive and troubling. What troubled me in particular was the complete absence of any mention of the greatest present-day crisis confronting us all, namely, the climate emergency threatening catastrophic climate breakdown. Leaving aside a minority of critical political economists, Streeck's omission of any discussion of environmental issues remains common for both mainstream economists and Left political economists. It is the widespread disregard of crucial ecological issues (or their token inclusion in the odd sentence or paragraph) that motivated me to write this book.

Despite the plethora of publications and unceasing media debate about all facets of eco-system crises, we continue to see many books and articles published by mainstream and radical political economists, as well as by other social scientists, that display what I call a 'pre-environmental consciousness'. Incredibly, regardless of whether they are pro or anti-capitalist, many are almost completely blind to environmental issues. Familiar disputes over the character and functioning of political, economic and social institutions are often approached as if we are living in societies where environmental problems are minor or secondary issues that can be easily solved by markets, governments or radical oppositional movements.

I have been researching topics covered in this book for over a decade. Originally it was part of an earlier manuscript finished in late 2017 (and misnamed *Post Carbon Democracy*) that became too large and insufficiently focused to be contained within one book. I am grateful to John Thompson of Polity Press and to three anonymous reviewers who, in their reports prompted me to rewrite the original manuscript and divide it into two books. This book is a rigorous analysis of the complex policy debates and imaginary socio-political expectations flowing from those who advocate various models of either growth or post-growth. A companion book, entitled *Capitalism Versus Democracy,* focuses on political debates and strategies pursued by various social democratic, green and radical critics of neo-liberalism. These disputes take place within the context of multiple attacks on already limited democratic processes coming from diverse authoritarian governments, businesses and populist authoritarian movements. Both books are self-contained theses but can be read together to gain a more comprehensive understanding of my analysis of the interaction between environmental, socio-economic and political cultural aspects of contemporary capitalist societies.

While writing these books, I have been a member of the Melbourne Sustainable Society Institute (MSSI) at the University of Melbourne. I thank Director Brendan Gleeson for his support. MSSI is a microcosm of contemporary social, scientific and political positions on the environment. Fellow colleagues represent a range of views stretching from ecological modernisation and 'green growth' right through to various strands of eco-socialism, degrowth and radical simplicity. I have also benefited from others at MSSI who are concerned with and active in climate negotiations, decarbonisation strategies, greening cities and the investigation of metabolic processes and the dangers of geo-engineering. In recent years, I have organised with Sam Alexander, MSSI's Political Economy of Sustainability group. I am indebted to Sam and many other participants for their diverse opinions and lively discussion of topics that have both challenged and helped me to clarify my thoughts. Over the years, I have also benefited from stimulating discussions of environmental and political economic issues with my old friends Peter Christoff, Robyn Eckersley, David Spratt and John Wiseman. I also wish to thank Antoinette Wilson for typesetting and helping prepare the manuscript for publication.

Two other people have been very important to me, both in writing these books, and to my life in general. First, I have learnt much from my son Emile Frankel. His own writings, musical compositions and exploration of the interaction between the contemporary arts, digital culture and political movements stimulate us to think beyond familiar categories. Emile's forthcoming new book, *Hearing the Cloud*, is indicative of the need for older analysts to come to terms with the major cultural changes in capitalist societies during the past thirty years. Second, I owe the greatest debt to my long-time companion, intellectual critic and partner, Julie Stephens. Like with my earlier books, Julie has read and discussed each chapter in detail and provided ample criticism, positive suggestions and loving support. I dedicate this book to Julie and Emile.

Boris Frankel
June 2018

Introduction

Let me begin by paraphrasing Max Horkheimer's often-quoted pronouncement, "whoever is not willing to talk about capitalism should
also keep quiet about fascism."[1] Today, one could equally argue that
'whoever is not willing to talk about capitalism should also keep quiet
about sustainability'. Yet, 'sustainability' and 'capitalism' are both specific and amorphous terms that cover many diverse practices and social
and political economic relations.[2] Most people are clearer about what
sustainability means when referring to natural eco-systems and the
desire to prevent these from being destroyed, even though they disagree
about how to achieve this goal. The same is not true of 'capitalism'. A
majority of mainstream and Left economists continue to see it in narrow
terms as an economic system whose intricate dynamics can be analysed
either sympathetically or critically. I share the alternative perspective of
seeing capitalist societies as diverse social systems whereby the so-called
'non-economic' political, social and cultural relations and institutional
practices are absolutely vital and integral to the accumulation of capital
and the sustainability of capitalist markets, as are also the earth's crucial
life-support boundaries and eco-systems.

---

1   Max Horkheimer, 'The Jews and Europe' *Zeitschrift für Sozialforschung*, December 1939, re-
     printed in Stephen Bronner and Douglas Kellner (eds), *Critical Theory and Society: A Reader*,
     Routledge, New York, 1989, p.78.
2   For analyses of historical origins of the concept 'capitalism' and the complex socio-economic,
     political and culture relations and institutions embodied in the term 'capitalism', see the con-
     tributors in Jürgen Kocka and Marcel van der Linden (eds.), *Capitalism: The Reemergence of a
     Historical Concept*, Bloomsbury, London, 2016.

Historically, the ability of capitalist enterprises and governments to subordinate diverse environmental habitats, private household relations, cultures and institutional practices to the processes of profitable production has been phenomenally successful. However, the finely balanced relationship between 'non-economic' social, political and environmental spheres and the capitalist mode of production, distribution and consumption should never be taken for granted. All capitalist societies continue to experience regular conflicts between the needs of businesses and the angry responses of diverse communities, cultural groups and political constituencies affected by capitalist processes. In addition to the endless disputes about what constitutes 'capitalism' and how to control it or even overthrow this system, defenders of market societies argue that without constant change and growth, capitalism will die. The question is: how much change is possible, and at what point do capitalist societies cease being recognisable or viable when compared with their earlier or current historical incarnations?

For the past forty years, critics of capitalism have argued that despite the triumph of the capitalist class over the working class, there are natural limits to growth. According to this perspective, no matter how many innovative products and technologies, new forms of management and marketing, or the expansion of markets beyond the local and the national to the global, capitalism as the incessant accumulation of capital (whether owned privately by families and shareholders, or through managed funds or governments) is unsustainable. Conversely, pro-market policy makers either reject the claim that there are natural limits to growth as mere green ideology, or else proclaim that innovation will soon permit the transcendence of these ecological limits through the absolute decoupling of economic growth from the finite limits of natural resources. These are bold claims and counter-claims, which will be explored in more detail.

Whether pro or anti-capitalist, much is at stake in our future images of both capitalist and post-capitalist societies. German sociologist Jens Beckert has analysed the central role played by 'fictional expectations' or 'imagined futures' in capitalist development.[3] In contrast to literary 'fictional expectations', non-literary 'expectations' are vital to real world capitalist growth. Beckert uses Keynes and many others to show why understanding the dynamics of capitalism requires not just a theory of production, the division of labour and so forth, but also a theory of

---

3   Jens Beckert, *Imagined Futures Fictional Expectations and Capitalist Dynamics,* Harvard University Press, Cambridge, 2016.

social action.[4] Keynes long ago argued that levels of capitalist investment and growth were affected by competing motivations and emotional attitudes. He contrasted two conditions: paralysis and the 'animal spirits'. Potential paralysis occurred when investors feared that their risky investments could lose money or wipe out their whole capital in the future. By contrast, the dynamic and ugly aspects of capitalism were driven forward by the 'animal spirits' of over-confidence, greed and aggression.[5]

According to Beckert, the role of investment, money and credit, as well as innovation and mass consumption depend on the 'fictional expectations' of both individuals and institutional decision-makers. These 'imagined futures' cannot be calculated in purely economic rational terms because the future is unknown and incalculable. A decade before Jens Beckert's broader social analysis, Australian sociologist Jocelyn Pixley, focused not on 'feelings' or personal emotions such as 'animal spirits', but rather on the 'techniques' or specific institutional attempts of the finance sector to manage the unpredictable future. Financial corporations, central banks and the financial press try to counter emotional uncertainty by managing and manufacturing 'trust' to ensure 'predictable' financial strategies that nevertheless eventually fail, as in 2007-08.[6]

We also know that pre-capitalist societies tried to ensure that traditional institutions and social practices endured. Similarly, decision-makers in capitalist social formations have long been committed to preventing political and social revolutions. The difference between most pre-capitalist rulers and contemporary decision-makers is that the latter are also committed to innovation and periodic 'creative destruction' in order to ensure that the market system survives and thrives. "Present-day action" Beckert concludes, "is not to be understood just as the ultimate outcome of past events but rather as an outcome of perceptions of the future: it is not just that 'history matters,' but also that the 'future matters.'"[7]

'Fictional expectations' are equally crucial to the advocates of various alternatives to capitalism. However, Beckert does not explore anti-capitalist 'fictional expectations' or what used to be called 'pre-figurative' images of an alternative society. Like the neglect of environmental issues by his colleague, Wolfgang Streeck, Beckert devotes a whole book to 'imagined futures' but incredibly, says nothing about how our 'fictional

---

4   Jens Beckert, *Capitalist Dynamics: Fictional Expectations and the Openness of the Future*, MPIfG Discussion Paper 14/7, Max Planck Institute for the Study of Societies, Cologne, March 2014, pp.8-10.

5   See discussion of Keynes in *Ibid.*

6   Jocelyn Pixley, *Emotions in Finance: Booms, Bust and Uncertainty*, Cambridge University Press, Cambridge, 2004, second edition 2012.

7   Beckert, *Capitalist Dynamics,* p.17.

expectations' about the threats to environmental sustainability affect the future dynamics of social relations within capitalist societies. After all, how we envisage the future and the possibilities of political change is one of the crucial factors that will determine our social action today. Political paralysis is certainly a common emotion expressed by millions of people who usually invoke their own insignificance and helplessness as a rationalisation for political inaction. Furthermore, 'animal spirits' may be fine for the 'wolves of Wall Street', but hardly the appropriate emotion or motivation for people who wish to bring about caring, co-operative, radical egalitarian and environmentally sustainable societies. Consequently, unless we examine and challenge the feasibility and desirability of various policy proposals and social outlines of alternative societies, our 'fictional expectations' could remain undeveloped, seriously flawed and unable to persuade all those people needed to help bring about desired political goals. There is a pressing need to analyse the character and structure of the 'fictional expectations' of sustainable alternative societies, whether socialist, green post-growth, or some other imaginary society.

Far too many studies discuss contemporary social issues by focussing on the historical origins and details of how we got to our present condition rather than also asking whether what is familiar is also sustainable. Two opposing methods help shape our 'fictional expectations'. One approach is that no understanding of current societies or future options is possible without a detailed understanding of the history of how political economic policies solved or failed to solve earlier crises. Contrast this with future-orientated pop-sociological and ahistorical accounts of rapid technological change. Fifty years of 'future shock' analyses have largely dispensed with understanding the past and focus instead on new innovations and new social institutions and social relations that purportedly will render the past irrelevant.

Caught between familiar everyday practices and the erosion of old public and private institutional relations and values, it is little wonder that so many of us have 'fictional expectations' based on fear and further loss. If we cannot imagine a future different to the present, it is easy to assume that all is pointless as nothing is durable or stable. To put it another way, how do we avoid relying too much on familiar but worn out old ideas, while also not succumbing to the endless, breathless predictions and accounts of the future that have often failed to materialise? For example, all business policy analysts, government intelligence reports and academic books on future scenarios produced in the late 1970s were proved to be wrong. Although scientists in the 1960s calculated that global temperatures would rise a few degrees in the 21st century, all mainstream analysts in the 1970s ignored the threat of climate change. Moreover, none saw the collapse of Eastern European Communism or the rise of China as a major capitalist power, to name just a few developments with profound global impacts that occurred in little over a decade or so after these future scenarios were written.

A rapid change in circumstances can surprise long-time observers. In 2000, *New Left Review* editor Perry Anderson surveyed decades of defeat for the Left and proclaimed: "neo-liberalism as a set of principles rules undivided across the globe: the most successful ideology in world history."[8] Eight years later, the citadels of capitalism were on the brink of chaos. We now know a collapse of the US economy was only miraculously averted in September 2008 when Treasury and Federal Reserve officials belatedly intervened with emergency bailout funds triggering rescue operations in other countries – a stark reminder that the fragility of capitalist markets should never be underestimated.

The Endless End of Capitalism

The end of capitalism has been a long time coming. Proclamations of its impending demise go through alternating cycles and are either debated seriously, ignored or mocked. In 2014, historians marked the centenary of an earlier cycle when many European socialists almost buried, not capitalism, but international solidarity as they embraced the dominant patriotic fervour that engulfed Europe at war. Yet, 2014 also marked the centenary anniversary of the completion of the first draft of *The Decline of the West* by Oswald Spengler. By the time the draft was revised and published in the summer of 1918, the Russian Revolution had toppled Czarism and the Hapsburg Empire and German Reich were on the verge of collapse. These events inspired many in the West to believe that capitalism was ending and that socialist revolution was both possible and imminent. Large sections of the European intelligentsia and middle classes, however, were mired in post-World War pessimism. Spengler's analysis of the rise and fall of Western cultures spoke to these pessimists and became a phenomenal success. By contrast, another contemporary, Theodore Adorno, criticised Spengler for reducing history and cultures to naturalistic, mystical, cosmic laws akin to astrology. Adorno declared caustically:

If one were to characterise Spengler himself in the terminology of the civilisation he denounces and name him in his own style,

8   Perry Anderson, 'Editorial Renewals', *New Left Review*, 1, Jan-Feb, 2000, p.13.

5

one would have to compare the *Decline of the West* to a department store where the intellectual agent sells the dried literary scraps he purchased at half-price at the close-out sale of culture.[9]

On the 30th anniversary of Spengler's death, Adorno reconsidered Spengler in a 1966 essay entitled '*Was Spengler Right?*'[10] Writing within the context of the booming post-war German 'economic miracle', Adorno repeated his critique of Spengler's cosmic naturalism and his role as a forerunner of the Nazis. However, this time he endorsed Spengler's pessimism as more consequential and insightful than the dominant consumer mass culture that had emerged in the decades after 1945.

> In our contemporary mind the recent horror is all too easily repressed; the genuine proportions of the catastrophe are carelessly diminished, and even dismissed as a kind of regrettable traffic accident along the highway of economic-technical progress. Spengler himself might conceivably have argued that the periods of decline from which he drew his analogies, especially the collapse of the Roman Empire, stretched out over centuries, that the deep tragic decline of our own world has only just begun with the passing but symptomatic phenomenon of Hitlerism, that a world split monstrously into two gigantic military blocs, each bristling with atomic weapons, could only promise disaster for the future.[11]

For Adorno, the Western capitalist boom was based on a profound socio-political amnesia and was also geared to social destructiveness and the domination of nature. Attempts to renew and reconstruct culture in the midst of potential nuclear holocaust and narrow instrumental economic rationalism were futile and symptomatic of a culture in denial and decline.

Today, Spengler's work is largely forgotten or unread. Yet, the irrepressible theme of 'decline' continues to stalk the West. The difference today is that whereas the very title *The Decline of the West* shocked and alarmed audiences in 1918-1919, in recent decades 'decline, disaster and collapse' are lucrative staples of popular culture. Now, countless children are raised on a diet of blockbuster disaster movies, speculative dystopias

---

9   Theodore W. Adorno, 'Spengler after the Decline' in *Prisms* trans. By Samuel and Shierry Weber, London 1967, p.62. This essay was written years before it was originally published in German in 1955.

10 Published in *Encounter*, January 1966, pp.25-28.

11 *Ibid*, p.25.

and computer games featuring the collapse of civilisation brought about by terrorists, aliens, environmental catastrophes, unstoppable pathogens and other 'monsters' of the commercial imagination. The sheer volume of current representations of disasters and threats to everyday normality and tranquillity is testimony to the widespread fear that contemporary capitalist civilisation is far from secure.

As decision makers confront deep-seated socio-economic and environmental crises within national and international institutional structures that are ill equipped to overcome political deadlock, their radical opponents now frequently articulate dramatic future scenarios. At the levels of social and cultural critique as well as radical political economy, two trends have emerged in the past decade, especially since the onset in 2007-08 of the Great Financial Crisis or Great Recession. Today, there is an increasing tendency for prominent political economists and sociologists to contemplate what in the early 1990s – particularly after the collapse of Eastern European Communism – would have been considered laughable, namely, the end of capitalism. The other trend, especially in Western art house cinema and television drama series, focuses on themes depicting widespread social malaise and despair, incurable political and media corruption and the high personal price paid by individuals and families for success in the market. It is not that these themes were absent in popular culture in earlier decades. Rather, within the context of major economic and environmental crises, they reinforce pervasive feelings and perceptions that deep-seated cultural decline and social dysfunction are not just temporary aberrations.

Although one could cite numerous examples of cultural and political malaise and despair – from Scandinavian Noir to the dystopias of 'cli-fi', climate fiction – these cultural manifestations do not constitute a threat to the political order. This is largely due to their absorption into and consumption within the global entertainment/consumerist economy, regardless of whether their authors or creators were motivated by anti-capitalist or commercial values. In most countries, political activism and critique is patchy: some have witnessed reinvigorated activism by young people while others display mass disengagement of the populace from public affairs. Unsurprisingly, political consciousness can only have limited development if individuals are isolated from political activism and confined to consuming entertaining TV series, online creations or speculative fiction. In other words, there is no automatic connection between the depiction and cultural critique of political corruption, social inequality or environmental crisis and increased political activism. It may even possibly be the case that widespread cultural representations of these themes themselves contribute to disillusionment, the rejection of political action and the retreat to the private sphere.

Almost a century after Spengler, Slavoj Žižek's *Living in the End Times* (2010) revisits the theme of 'decline' from an eclectic perspective of Marxian, Lacanian and other social theories.[12] The global capitalist system, he argues,

> ...is approaching an apocalyptic zero-point. Its 'four riders of the apocalypse' are comprised by the ecological crisis, the consequences of the biogenetic revolution, imbalances within the system itself (problems with intellectual property; forthcoming struggles over raw materials, food and water), and the explosive growth of social divisions and exclusions.[13]

Žižek is an excellent provocateur, as well as an innovative critic. It is questionable though whether his book delivers a comprehensive understanding of the current global crisis. He begins suggestively by promising to apply psychologist Elisabeth Kübler-Ross' five stages of grief – denial, anger, bargaining, depression and finally, acceptance – to the way various social, economic and political groups try to deal with what he sees as the forthcoming apocalypse.[14] Sadly, there is hardly any analysis of contemporary political economy, only a repeat discussion of Žižek's familiar pantheon of thinkers: Hegel, Marx, Lacan, Badiou and so forth. Similarly, there is no deep analysis of the environmental crisis. By the conclusion of the book, despite covering a characteristically wide range of topics and making numerous provocative digressions, we are little wiser as to why it is that capitalist societies are incapable of dealing with the 'four riders of the Apocalypse'.

Actually, Žižek's crisis symptoms are not too dissimilar from the list provided by his opponents. When one examines what the more far-sighted defenders of capitalism consider to be the most dangerous threats facing countries today, and what radical critics of market society argue are the crisis conditions that may prove to be insurmountable, there is much overlap. Only the causes and the solutions are hotly contested. Each year the World Economic Forum at Davos issues a report entitled *Global Risks* in which it ranks the top 10 risks (out of 30 or more identified) that remain of the highest concern due to their interconnected global impact. For example, in 2014 the ten highest concerns

12 Published by *Verso*, London, 2010.
13 Žižek, Introduction p.x.
14 *Ibid*, p.xi.

included: fiscal crises in key economies; structurally high unemployment and underemployment; water crises; severe income disparity; failure of climate change mitigation and adaptation; greater incidence of extreme weather events; global governance failure; food crises; failure of major financial mechanisms/institutions; and profound political and social instability.[15] As if this weren't enough, *The Global Risks 2017* and *2018* reports added involuntary migration, fraying democracies due to threats from populist movements, terrorism, weapons of mass destruction and other such topics to this grim list.[16]

Although capitalism has always appeared to be in 'crisis', what is new is the growing belief among prominent political economists and sociologists that capitalism, as a social system, is significantly weaker and hence lacking its former capacity to easily overcome serious systemic threats. More dramatically, there is a growing belief that capitalism is plagued with multiple problems that indicate that its condition is terminal. Importantly, one must not confuse the latter analyses with the interrelated but separate debate over the relative degree to which the old Atlantic capitalist powers will suffer economic, military and cultural loss of power to the rising nations in the Asian and Pacific region. Relative loss of power is entirely different to simplistic media stories about how China will shortly surpass the US as the dominant world power. Although the US has lost its former unchallenged position, there is little prospect in the near future that America will cease being the pre-eminent military, economic and cultural power. Hence, the question of whether capitalism has a future is not to be equated with analyses of whether China or India will replace the US as a hegemonic force. The end of capitalism is not a regional or geographical issue that is merely the latest historical instalment of the old 'decline of the West' genre. It is true that China, India and other developing societies continued to grow significantly while developed capitalist countries suffered major economic downturns after 2007. It is also true that developed capitalist countries, especially those in the Atlantic region and Japan currently exhibit advanced and/or different crisis symptoms compared to developing countries. However, given the increasing interdependence of the G20 countries (that account for over 80 per cent of the world economy), any future major crisis of capitalism will be a widespread global crisis rather than a regional crisis.

---

15 World Economic Forum, *The Global Risks Report 2014*, 9th Edition, Geneva, 2014.

16 World Economic Forum, *The Global Risks Report 2017*, 12th Edition, Geneva, 2017; and *The Global Risks Report 2018*, 13th Edition, Geneva, 2018.

Issues and Themes To Be Discussed

A decade after the beginning of the Great Financial Crisis or Great Recession in 2007/8, quite a number of capitalist countries have still been unable to fully recover. While drawing on the rich empirical material documented in the 'Great Recession Literature' of the past decade, my book is not another exposition of neo-liberalism. In fact, we don't need another exposition and critique of neo-liberalism. Instead, this book will focus on two broad but contrasting schools of thought and action. First, to identify the divisions between the various pro-market policy makers and analysts as well as to critique their solutions to the major socio-economic and environmental challenges we face. Second, to examine the strengths and weaknesses of the policies and strategies proposed by a range of moderate and radical socialist, green and other critics of contemporary capitalist societies. I will therefore raise uncomfortable and difficult questions and also probe policies and scenarios coming from a diverse range of political perspectives.

For over one hundred years, reformers have dreamed of 'civilising capitalism' or 'disciplining capitalism' so that the benefits of markets can be preserved within the confines of a strong regulatory state which subjects the economy to the needs of society rather than vice versa. The popularity of the idea of ending the 'disembedded' market economy, especially market globalisation, and 're-embedding' capitalist markets so that social and environmental needs are served, owes much to the revival of Karl Polanyi's ideas.[17] I will leave my discussion of the serious flaws in Polanyi's work to a companion book on *Capitalism Versus Democracy*. In the meantime, this book will analyse contemporary versions of 'civilising capitalism', a dream that continues to be held by advocates of 'green growth', especially by a variety of social democrats, NGOs and mainstream environmentalists.

Over the past few decades, what has become much clearer is that we live in a new transitional period where production-centred capitalism can no longer be considered the *sole* driver of wealth, power and profit. Instead, two parallel realities co-exist. One is characterised by familiar features such as the struggles between industrial workers and capitalists, as well as political disputes over national government budget priorities. The other powerful set of processes that challenge and invalidate both traditional mainstream and radical ways of seeing the world are multiple social, financial and ecological factors. Take, for instance, the increased

---

17 Karl Polanyi, *The Great Transformation: The political and economic origins of our time*, Beacon Press, Boston 1944.

integration of all facets of private household consumption and relations with business and government practices. Similarly, the transformation of educational, health and cultural institutions into key 'industries' vital to capitalist accumulation and social crisis-management makes the old politics of labour and capital centred on the factory a fading memory for many in OECD countries. The sheer scale of all sorts of financial transactions (including derivatives), also make a mockery of national GDP figures, of labour/capital struggles and numerous other traditional political economic relations. It is the continued heavy investment in multiple forms of complex financial instruments and packages that help transform all aspects of social life. Through their circulation and timing, these financial transactions constitute not only very profitable means of exchange but are also quasi-independent powers of their own.

Much has been written about financialisation and, despite the concept sometimes being used in an over-generalised manner, it remains largely mystifying to the public even after they become familiar with it as victims of indebtedness, foreclosure and repossession. Importantly, financialisation today is a much more complex set of socio-economic relations compared with the finance-led capitalism that socialist Rudolph Hilferding analysed over one hundred years ago in 1910.[18] Likewise, most policy makers and electorates are aware of environmental issues but often fail to recognise that the future of their own production and consumption processes are inseparably related to and dependent on the health of remote eco-systems that transcend national borders and political systems. No future social and political developments can ignore these essential ecological relations or merely treat them as expendable and unimportant *external* phenomena. Instead of the usual sentence or two on the environment, a characteristic of many political economy books and articles, I will endeavour to provide a more detailed analysis of whether capitalism is environmentally sustainable or not.

While this book discusses the major threat of climate breakdown and strategies of decarbonisation, it tackles environmental issues that are much, much harder to resolve than climate change. Yet, it is not another outline of all the cultural, moral and ecological reasons as to why we need to safeguard the natural world and biodiversity. It is also not a book for those who seek further moral reasons of why we need a post-capitalist world. These important arguments are largely assumed and are constitutive elements of my analysis of the political debates on

---

18 Rudolph Hilferding, *Finance Capital A Study of the Latest Phase of Capitalist Development*, 1910, English translation by Morris Watnick and Sam Gordon, Routledge & Kegan Paul, London, 1981.

growth and post-growth. So too, are crucial cultural factors and beliefs. Political economy is reduced to a meaningless and ahistorical formula if social relations based on gender, race, or particular religious, secular and popular cultural traditions and practices are ignored or excluded.

One thread that runs through this book is the contemporary preoccupation with growth and innovation. Those who believe in the power of science and technology to transform human and non-human natural processes accept no limits or restraints. In the quest for profitable growth and new markets, many capitalist businesses reject moral and cultural constraints. The question is whether it is possible for corporations to harness new technologies and decouple capitalist economic growth from natural ecological processes? Conversely, can greens and eco-socialists succeed in preventing the potential catastrophes of what they either call the 'Anthropocene' or the 'Capitalocene'?[19] Are they able to help reshape cultural values and practices so that people voluntarily abandon 'consumer capitalism' in sufficient numbers to institute societies based on degrowth or 'prosperity without growth'?

Apart from technological utopians, there is far less optimism about a world of endless growth and post-scarcity that once characterised both Left and Right images of the future. Today, it is difficult for concerned reformers and radical restructurers to ignore climate breakdown, scarcity and massive global inequalities between developed and developing countries. How can societies overcome deep austerity by increasing aggregate demand (consumption) as Keynesians and post-Keynesians desire, and yet not exacerbate ecosystem crises? Why are illusions about seriously flawed policies, such as a universal basic income or a 'steady-state' sustainable society, still so widely shared among alternative green, feminist and socialist movements? These and other fundamental questions are discussed not with the intention of opposing the need for radical solutions to existing capitalist practices but rather with the aim of assisting in the development of more plausible and effective policies. No one person can or should develop a set of detailed policies that needs to be developed by widespread collective public debate. This book will, nonetheless, suggest a number of alternative policies that could be debated and possibly further developed by social change activists and policy makers.

As to whether capitalism is sustainable, this is a question that can be

---

19 See Will Steffen, Paul J. Crutzen and John R. McNeill, 'The Anthropocene: Are Humans Now Overwhelming the Great Forces of Nature?', *Ambio*, vol.38, no. 8. 2007, pp. 614-21 and for a critique of the 'anthropocene' see Jason W. Moore, *Capitalism in the Web of Life: Ecology and the Accumulation of Capital*, Verso, London, 2015. I believe there are major problems with both 'anthropocene' and 'capitalocene' as explanatory concepts – see my discussion in *Capitalism Versus Democracy*.

quickly answered by a 'yes' or 'no', depending on the relevant short or long historical time frame considered. It is an entirely different matter to ask: what will keep capitalist societies viable or bring about their demise? Will their downfall be due to the unintended consequences of their own making or the deliberate result of being overthrown by anti-capitalist socio-political forces? I therefore begin this book with an examination of the conflicting political disputes over innovation and why pro-market policy analysts and governments fervently believe that innovation will ensure that capitalism remains socio-economically sustainable. Innovation is not only supposed to overcome low growth and stagnation, but also to transform capitalism into an environmentally sustainable social order through 'green growth' ecological modernisation. These highly contested ideas are then analysed in relation to low and middle-income countries where 'modernisation as industrialisation' has been the mantra for over one hundred years. Chapter Two identifies the way deep global inequalities affect the ability of developing countries to overcome the numerous domestic and international barriers to becoming high-income countries. Given that most cannot transform their societies through export-led growth as a handful of countries in North East Asia have done, the chapter examines some of the socio-economic and environmental implications of models that advocate modernisation by skipping the industrialisation phase.

In Chapter Three, I explicitly turn to the more future-orientated business and policy-makers who wish to go beyond resolving the threat of climate change and overcome the much larger problem of the natural limits to growth. Whether decoupling economic growth from nature is a myth or the pathway to securing sustainable capitalist societies, there are irreconcilable political differences over decoupling that need to be understood. It is also important to remember that business groups are not the only ones supportive of decoupling. In Chapter Four, I proceed to critically evaluate the various optimistic proposals of the technological utopians and their visions of new forms of capitalist or post-capitalist societies based on the radical application of technology.

Following the analysis of mainstream and radical proposals to overcome the natural limits to growth, Chapter Five focuses on those who promote definancialising society as a necessary part of reforming capitalism. Many of those who favour definancialisation also support degrowing or decelerating credit-driven consumption and production. Can one avoid economic collapse and have the continued smooth functioning of capitalist societies while simultaneously definancialising one of the engines of growth and one of the foundations of contemporary socio-cultural life? Can one have a 'steady-state' or post-growth economy and are these new economies compatible with capitalism? Is there a way forward that does not exacerbate environmental crisis through the Keynesian and post-Keynesian desire to end neo-liberal austerity? After all, definancialisation and degrowth threaten very conservative institutional structures and practices that will invariably be vigorously defended by powerful corporations and governments.

It is not only degrowth that challenges existing forms of capitalism. Chapter Six examines work and income and how new labour processes and competitive pressures are eroding old forms of social mobility. The surge in media and policy discussions of a universal basic income (UBI) from Right, Left, green and feminist perspectives are subjected to a rigorous, reflective analysis. Those who advocate various types of UBI schemes fail to establish how such basic income schemes can solve poverty, let alone stabilise and make capitalism sustainable. Even those who desire that a UBI deliberately destabilise capitalist societies and make possible a radical 'post-work' world, offer only very shaky ground for the claim of political feasibility. In opposition to UBI schemes, Chapter Six argues for the need to transcend individualistic income schemes in favour of a more redistributive and transformative set of social state policies.

Finally, in the conclusion, Chapter Seven, I provide an overview of the issues covered in preceding chapters. I also discuss the controversial issues of how a post-growth social system and new extensive social welfare and care services can be funded from revenue that itself depends on the continued growth regime of capitalist economies. Moreover, are the current theories of state institutions that underpin both reform and radical social movements adequate to the task of realising their political economic and environmental agendas? In other words, this book analyses the politically conflicting fictional expectations of those who wish to either preserve or to replace capitalist social orders in a world constrained by scarcity and deep social inequalities.

While I reject the pessimism of those who argue that there is no way out, this is also not a book based on false hope and rhetorical gestures. There is no avoidance of hard questions and painful choices. Radical social change is not like a business arrangement that glib marketing pronouncements constantly tell us will have a 'win-win' outcome. On the contrary, there will always be winners and losers in most political and social conflicts. Globally, each year approximately two hundred peaceful non-revolutionaries are killed, struggling not for radical change, but just trying to conserve and protect local habitats from deforestation, mining, property development and industrial incursions. The question is whether it is delusional or not to imagine that capitalism can be replaced everywhere in a peaceful manner? As will be discussed, the crucial dependence of business growth on cultural practices underpinning household consumption in OECD countries makes the contemporary politics of growth or post-growth quite different to socio-political conditions one hundred years ago. The possible ways organised politics and crisis management plays out across the world is far from clear or predictable. What can be predicted, nonetheless, is that commitment to existing socio-economic practices or alternative societies is insufficient on its own. Political movements and policy makers alike require an unadulterated and undisguised understanding of the likely obstacles, complications and conflicts resulting from either continued unsustainable growth or the pursuit of poorly conceived post-growth solutions. It is to these issues and problems that I will now turn.

1

Political Economic Fictions: Saving Capitalism Through Innovation

All societies need some level of technological, organisational and cultural innovation to prevent social atrophy. Innovation does not have to take market capitalist forms and it is certainly not equivalent to simply promoting economic growth. In developed capitalist countries, there is a division between those who believe in incessant economic growth and a growing minority who reject conventional growth as environmentally unsustainable. I begin this book with an analysis of why so much emphasis is placed on innovation within capitalist countries and why it remains the sacred cow of pro-market strategic policy. The blind faith in innovation as the panacea to major problems troubling capitalist countries is largely due to the profound lack of choice that has always faced and continues to confront defenders and administrators of capitalism. It is no accident that the unofficial market law 'innovate or die' governs trans-national corporations and local or national industries. Little wonder then that for decades, business schools, think-tanks and supra-national bodies and governments have devoted much time and energy to discussing how innovation and an 'entrepreneurial culture' is instituted and sustained. Globally, government statements, think-tank reports and academic books about innovation have run into the thousands and now face the crisis of how to say something new and innovative about innovation.

This chapter will focus on two interrelated policy disputes that have been conducted at national and global levels in recent years. The first dispute is over how to generate economic growth through innovation and whether or not capitalist countries are now trapped in a long period of low growth and stagnation. Currently, various segments of business as well as governments and labour movements have quite differing hopes and expectations about innovation. Consequently, I initially focus on what global disputes over innovation tell us about how policy-makers and analysts understand and hope to resolve major problems within capitalist societies. Unlike the usual commentary preoccupied with entrepreneurs, start-ups and venture capital, this chapter examines why most governments aim to solve domestic social problems by enhancing national competitiveness and increasing international geopolitical power. Following an analysis of political disputes over how to generate innovation, I analyse the differing mainstream and radical explanations of the causes of stagnation and whether or not leading capitalist societies will experience major crises resulting from low growth.

The second related dispute amongst pro-capitalist policy-makers is over the desirability of 'green growth' and whether this innovation strategy is capable of not only rescuing capitalism from stagnation but also making capitalism sustainable. We live in a historical period characterised by carbon-intensive production and consumption that threatens climate breakdown. Many workers and businesses also fear that low growth/stagnation has become the 'new normal'. They are particularly worried that unemployment or bankruptcy will flow from new technological developments. Hence, a significant section of the liberal social democratic and trade union mainstream Left promotes a different version of innovation, namely, 'green growth', ecological modernisation and social reform as the panacea to unemployment, inequality and economic malaise.

Of course, it is important not to lose sight of the major political struggles over technological innovation between leading economic and military powers. Since 2011, China has become the world's largest applicant of new patents and is second only to the US in terms of expenditure on R&D. However, patents, start-ups and new gadgets are not to be confused with ground breaking basic research. The US and other leading OECD countries spend an average of 20% of research funding on basic research compared with only 5% by China. Yet, by 2014, China had more than 3.53 million science and engineering graduate and PhD researchers – more than the US and the European Union (EU) combined.[1] It is also crucially important to distinguish between the various ideological models of innovation provided for public consumption and

---

1   See World Bank, *China Systematic Country Diagnostic: Towards A More inclusive and Sustainable Development 2017*, World Bank, Washington, February 2018, p.12.

the reality of who funds and carries out the majority of large-scale research and development. The media are particularly susceptible to free market ideology in believing that small entrepreneurs are the main force behind innovation. On the contrary, it is government funding, large research institutions and corporations that account for the bulk of R&D.

To contextualise this uncritical faith in innovation, it is important to recognise that defenders of capitalism are currently in major conflict with one another. Divisions have always been present, but in the past decade, following the impact of the Great Financial Crisis or Great Recession, much fear of prolonged stagnation or even a new major crisis and deeper Depression is regularly expressed within policy circles and business media. Key divisive issues include how to tackle weak economic growth and low productivity in developed capitalist countries, while simultaneously debating how to sustain high growth in some developing countries. In January 2017, almost one hundred years after the Bolshevik Revolution in Russia, it was the leader of the Chinese Communist Party, Xi Jinping, who became the chief defender of global capitalist free trade at Davos while American President-elect Donald Trump (boycotting the World Economic Forum) signalled his preference for 'America first' protectionist measures. President Xi reiterated the religious faith in innovation held by most defenders of capitalism: "The fundamental issue plaguing the global economy" he stated, "is the lack of driving force for growth. Innovation is the primary force guiding development.... We need to relentlessly pursue innovation."[2] Nonetheless, President Xi Jinping voiced a common concern of policy makers that despite patchy and intermittent upswings in growth plus the emergence of various technologies, "new sources of growth are yet to emerge. A new path for the global economy remains elusive."[3]

Many free marketeers located in cutting edge areas such as the 'digital economy' and the 'bio-tech economy' do not share Xi Jinping's concerns. They talk of 'bottom-up', embedded organic innovation rather than conventional, bureaucratic, 'top down' imposed business practices. Opposing what they call 'technocratic and regulatory reactionaries', American free marketeers such as Virginia Postrel, Robert D. Atkinson and Adam Thierer distinguish between 'dynamism and stasis', or between 'preservationists and modernisers', that is, between a future society shaped by security and stability, as opposed to one shaped by a creative,

---

2   Xi Jinping, Speech in Full to Opening Plenary at Davos, *World Economic Forum*, 17 January, 2017.

3   Xi Jinping, *op.cit.*

high growth New Economy.[4] Free marketeers have no direct interest in social outcomes such as greater social justice. In a familiar refrain, they believe that innovation creates greater prosperity, which then 'trickles down' to the rest of society.

Central to these libertarian objectives is the notion of 'permission-less innovation', where creative researchers and innovators on the 'new frontier' learn through errors, calculated risks and experience.[5] Most of these advocates of 'embedded' or 'organic' innovation oppose 'dis-embedded' bureaucrats imposing the 'precautionary principle' (safety controls and ethical research) over self-regulated entrepreneurs.[6] Free market libertarians are diametrically opposed to the 'responsible research and innovation' movement which is particularly growing in European countries. Linking technology and science communities with civil society organisations, businesses and government agencies, 'responsible innovation' favours democratic accountability and the tackling of urgent sustainable environmental issues such as water, food security, health and aged care as well as more traditional developments in product design and urban infrastructure.[7] Like the 'slow food' movement, there has also been a growth in the 'slow science' movement that opposes the rushed, ill-considered application of biogenetics, nanotechnology and other science and technology in the race for all kinds of new market products.[8] Globally, the 'responsible research and innovation' and 'slow science' movements remain minority currents out of favour with the majority of corporations, governments and individual entrepreneurs who prefer minimal or no accountability to society.

Capitalist systems have been subjected to enormous stresses in recent years, which has led to major disputes over the conditions necessary to optimise innovation and the productivity that pro-market policy makers

---

4   See Adam Thierer, *Permissionless Innovation, The Continuing Case for Comprehensive Technolog-ical Freedom*, Mercatus Center, George Mason University, 2014.

5   See for example, Robert F. Graboyes, *Fortress and Frontier in American Heath Care*, Mercatus Center, George Mason Univerity, 2014.

6   For a strong case in favour of the 'precautionary principle' see Andy Stirling, *Towards Innova-tion Democracy? Participation, Responsibility and Precaution in Innovation Governance*, SPRU and STEPS Centre, University of Sussex, November 2014.

7   See Melanie Smallman, Kaatje Lomme, Natacha Faullimmel, *Report on the analysis of needs and constraints of the stakeholder groups in RRI practices in Europe*, RRI-Tools, University College London, March 2015; Richard Owen, John Bessant and Maggy Heintz (eds.) *Responsible In-novation: Managing the Responsible Emergence of Science and Innovation in Society*, John Wiley, London, 2013 and Eva Boxenbaum et al, 'Imaginaries and instruments: conceptual tools for problematizing responsible innovation', *Debating Innovation*, vol.2 no.3, 2012, pp. 84-90.

8   See Jeremy Garwood, 'Good Science Needs Time to Mature and Ripen!' *Lab Times*, no.2, 2012, pp.20-27 and Isabelle Stengers, *Another Science is Possible: A Manifesto for Slow Science*, trans. by Stephen Muecke, Polity, Cambridge, 2017.

hope will flow from this innovation. Moreover, supporters of capitalism lack agreement over how innovation should be funded and what are the acceptable and unacceptable social and political constraints over innovation. These disputes are not just about future business profitability but are crucial when considering the underlying or intrinsic viability of capitalist social formations. Since the Great Financial Crisis in 2007–8, there has once again been renewed discussion of whether capitalism has a future.[9] Defenders of capitalism's resilience dismiss all talk of 'end times' as premature nonsense. In response, some analysts of capitalism's terminal condition argue that it is not a question of 'if', but only a dispute about 'when'.[10] Much is at stake in the varied answers given to the question of whether or not capitalism is close to perishing. While it would be good to have a detailed conception of an alternative society, theorists of 'end times' are not obliged to outline a blueprint for the future post-capitalist society. They merely have to give plausible reasons as to why we have reached or are fast approaching the limits of the ability of existing capitalist countries to reproduce their social orders.

Marx, despite relishing and predicting capitalism's end, was much more sober and cautious. In a now famous pronouncement he argued that: "No social order ever perishes before all the productive forces for which there is room in it have developed."[11] Pro-capitalist policy-makers seem to have taken Marx's comment as a vote of confidence. According to their dominant assumptions, capitalism has ample room to continue developing, precisely because markets supposedly excel at innovation and renewal. Significantly, many pessimistic radicals also share the 'renewal' faith of pro-capitalist policy makers. Long accustomed to political defeats, they believe that capitalists still have more than a few trump cards up their sleeves and that the revolution will not occur in their lifetimes.

However, Marx's comments cited above ignore the political and the cultural. A social order may perish well before it has exhausted its capacity for new productive forces. As Marx put it himself in other writings, capitalism is not an inanimate system based on narrow productive-technological forces. Rather, it is a production system that depends on particular socio-cultural class relations. Currently, a

---

9   See for example, Immanuel Wallerstein, Randall Collins, Michael Mann, Georgi Derlugian and Craig Calhoun, *Does Capitalism Have a Future?* Oxford University Press, Oxford, 2013.

10 See for example, Wolfgang Streeck, 'Taking Crisis Seriously: Capitalism on Its Way Out' in *Stato e Mercato* April 2014 pp.45-68.

11 Karl Marx, *Preface to a Contribution to the Critique of Political Economy,* Selected Works Volume One, Moscow 1950, p.329.

political cultural struggle is being fought between those who believe that capitalism is destroying many facets of natural and social life (or what John McMurtry calls the 'cancer stage of capitalism'[12]) and pro-market supporters who uphold the superiority of the capitalist system. If a majority of people begin to believe that capitalist political economic relations and technological innovation not only cannot solve massive problems of climate breakdown, mass unemployment and increased inequality but actually cause and exacerbate these problems, then the social and political order will enter a period of intense political conflict and possible disintegration.

It is essential to recognise that in many countries there is a razor thin margin between a continuation of 'muddling through' crisis management and political economic disintegration. Some countries will cope much better than others should extreme danger signs become evident. Historical change does not move through uniform stages where all societies of a particular type simultaneously collapse or are overthrown by revolutionary forces. On the other hand, there is no shortage of ideas related to new technologies, new ways of re-organising public services or solving inequality and preventing environmental destruction. Ideas, however, are not enough to meet new challenges. The essential problem is that many of these innovative proposals are simply incompatible with 'business as usual'. As with ruling classes in so many previous social orders, contemporary corporations and small to medium capitalists and their political allies are deeply divided over whether to voluntarily embrace new practices rather than have these imposed upon them in the future by mass political demands. The only certainty is that familiar public policies as well as the character and extent of existing private economic power will not survive intact.

The Conservative Pessimism of the High Priest of Innovation

Such is the blind faith of pro-marketeers in capitalism's ability to survive through incessant innovation, that like other religious disputes, 'scriptural divisions' emerge over what drives innovation. However, this blind faith in the power of innovation to save capitalism did not always exist. In fact, one of the high priests of the religion of innovation, Joseph Schumpeter, was pessimistic about capitalism's ability to survive.[13] In

---

12   J. McMurtry, *The Cancer Stage of Capitalism: From Crisis to Cure*, Pluto Books, London, 2013.

13   See J. Schumpeter, *Capitalism, Socialism, and Democracy*, Harper & Row, New York, 1942 and 2003 edition by Taylor & Francis e-Library with an introduction by Richard Swedberg.

contrast to many present-day analysts who focus on technical issues, the culture of the firm or the availability of venture capital, Schumpeter tried to focus on the broader socio-economic and political conditions that fostered innovation even though his social analysis was inadequate and quite dubious in other respects. In fact, most books, articles and policy reports that refer to Schumpeter usually mention 'creative destruction' and talk about innovation and 'disruption' without any consideration of the historical or political context. They tell us little about Schumpeter's socio-political values and how these related to a particular phase of capitalist development. Importantly, this missing information is crucial to any understanding of his relevance to debates over innovation in contemporary societies.

Very briefly, Schumpeter was born in the Austro-Hungarian Empire in 1883 (the year that Marx died) and settled permanently in the US in 1932. He taught at Harvard until his death in 1950. Although not a Nazi, the deeply conservative Schumpeter detested Roosevelt's New Deal and expressed anti-Semitic and racist views against Jews and blacks while fearing Stalin and the Slavs. In certain respects, he shared the conservative elite theorist Gaetano Mosca's contempt for the masses (Schumpeter called them 'sub-normals') but did not become an open supporter of fascism like the other elite theorists Vilfredo Pareto and Robert Michels. Nevertheless, Schumpeter bequeathed the ideological school of American Pluralism the minimalist definition of democracy. This was a variation of Pareto's theory of 'the circulation of elites': namely, that citizens could not directly run a society but could only exercise a choice of which set of leaders from the two major parties they preferred.[14]

Paradoxically, Schumpeter believed that socialism could succeed. He also greatly admired many of Marx's insights and dismissed the common idea that Marx was an economic determinist who reduced all religion, art, politics and social ideas back to the economy.[15] Marx argued that capitalism was not stationary but an ever-changing mode of production, characterised by lack of planning, periodically leading to over-production and lack of profitable investment outlets, with associated crises manifested in mass unemployment, restricted consumption and a crisis in profitability. This periodic crisis results in the devalorisation or destruction of large amounts of capital and many individual capitalists, followed by renewed investment and growth, the very dynamic process that inspired Schumpeter to coin his famous phrase 'creative

14 See *Capitalism, Socialism and Democracy*, ch.XXII.
15 *Ibid*, p.11.

destruction'.[16]

Consequently, Schumpeter was caustic in his dismissal of many policy makers. They focussed, he argued, on how capitalism administers existing structures, "whereas the relevant problem is how it creates and destroys them. As long as this is not recognized, the investigator does a meaningless job."[17] Today, Schumpeterian buzzwords such as 'disruptors' have become corporate and media clichés. Yet, instead of genuinely taking into consideration turbulent creations and 'disruptions', most think-tanks, governments, supranational agencies and private consultants churn out reports that typically project past trends and present-day institutional relations into the future, thereby arriving at spurious scenarios for the next twenty, thirty or fifty years.

Where Schumpeter disagreed with Marx was over such ideas as the labour theory of value and the role of class conflict in bringing about the end of capitalism.[18] Ironically, Schumpeter argued that capitalism would fail because of its very success. Capitalist growth was driven by innovation (not mere inventions but fundamental changes in technology and production), and it was entrepreneurs who drove the 50 to 60-year Kondratieff Long Waves of technological innovation. Subscribing to Max Weber's theory of rationalisation, Schumpeter believed that the more capitalism evolved into a successful economy, the more bureaucratised large trusts and oligopolies would replace 'heroic' entrepreneurs. These large conglomerates not only lacked the entrepreneurial spirit, but the modern social transformation of the bourgeois family combined with the rise of state administration and large businesses, meant that the innovative engine of capitalism became 'fettered'. Capitalism would therefore not survive and would be succeeded by socialism. The hostility of intellectuals also threatened capitalism as their anti-capitalist views influenced the masses. Schumpeter argued that the bourgeoisie defended intellectuals as a group, because the bourgeoisie protected their own lifestyle and values such as freedom and education. While he concluded that only fascism and socialism could discipline intellectuals, if the bourgeoisie copied fascism or socialism, then this would require

16 Some argue that Schumpeter borrowed the term from Werner Sombart's *War and Capitalism* (1913) who in turn was influenced by Marx and also Nietzsche's *Thus Spake Zarathustra*, see Erik S. Reinert and Hugo Reinert 'Creative Destruction in Economics: Nietzsche, Sombart, Schumpeter' in J. Backhaus and W. Drechsler (eds.) *Friedrich Nietzsche 1844-2000: Economy and Society*, series *The European Heritage in Economics and the Social Sciences*, New York, Springer, 2006, pp. 55-85.

17 Schumpeter, *op.cit.*, p.84.

18 *Ibid*, p.19. For a discussion of Schumpeter's relation to Marx, see George Catephores, 'The Imperious Austrian: Schumpeter as Bourgeois Marxist', *New Left Review*, May/June 1994, pp.3-30.

a change in capitalist institutions and lead to the drastic reduction of individual freedom for all social strata.[19]

Although Schumpeter was aware of the significant growth of educational institutions, he was profoundly mistaken about the role of intellectuals and large corporations. We know with hindsight that socialism did not replace capitalism and that the overwhelming majority of intellectuals and educated strata are not even very critical of capitalism, let alone advocating revolution in most of today's societies. Contrary to Schumpeter, intellectual practices have become the backbone or foundation of many sectors of advanced high-tech capitalism. Moreover, the flaws in his theory of innovation were due to his belief in strong entrepreneurial leaders, who have not proved to be indispensable to capitalism, and also because his theory rested on Kondratieff's highly dubious Long Wave theory.

During the 1920s, Soviet economist Nikolai Kondratieff developed a theory of Long Waves of expansion and decline. These Long Waves have been used by all kinds of analysts, ranging from Trotskyist revolutionaries, Schumpeterian theorists of cycles of technological innovation, to World System theorists and even Wall Street stock market analysts.[20] In recent decades there have been persistent disputes about the differences between Long Waves and Long Cycles as to whether there are recurring internal dynamics made up of shorter cycles (such as Juglar and Kitchin Cycles), or whether Long Waves are caused by external events and phenomena. Comparisons between one Wave with an earlier Long Wave have proved incomplete, inconsistent and dubious due to the lack of comparative statistical data from most capitalist countries (such as time series on profit and production levels in various industries) and the fact that old capitalist powers have declined and new powers have risen over the past 100 years.[21] Technological determinism and analyses of production that reduce class relations, political institutional conflicts and cultural values to secondary phenomena are misguided and also very limited. Integrating socio-political relations into Long Wave theory is speculative at best, as Long Waves and Cycles can only give a vague impression of past developments. Long Waves offer no real explanation of why one society developed in a particular direction rather than another direction.

---

19 *Ibid*, p.150.

20 See my critique of Long Wave theories in *Beyond the State? Dominant Theories and Socialist Strategies*, MacMillan, London 1983, pp.47-55.

21 See the debates over comparative statistics and other aspects of Long Waves in Alfred Kleinknecht, Ernest Mandel and Immanuel Wallerstein (eds.), *New Findings in Long-Wave Research*, Macmillan, Basingstoke, 1992.

As I will later argue in relation to contemporary neo-Schumpeterian advocates of 'green growth', Long Waves and Long Cycles can only be detected with hindsight. The quest to base explanations of socio-economic life on so-called repetitive Long Cycles and Waves owes much to an industrial form of mechanical thinking where non-repeatable social relations and events, not to mention two world wars and numerous civil wars and invasions are all squeezed into cyclical patterns, a form of 'magical thinking' that is little better than trying to read 'the signs' in tea leaves. Whether Schumpeterian Long cycles of technological innovation, Marxian Long Waves of economic crises and the falling rate of profit, or Wall Street brokers forecasting the next boom or slump, all applications of Kondratieff's theory cannot predict the future development of new technologies, let alone the degree of passivity or socio-political conflict that will shape key policies and institutions across the world.

Despite collecting data to support his theory of Long Waves, Kondratieff could not adequately explain why they came into being or recurred and lasted for the length that he claimed. Similarly, Schumpeter made much of technological innovation as the cause of business cycles but given his failure to adequately anchor economic processes within social and institutional relations, could not explain why a number of innovations or 'clusters' occurred at particular historical times. Instead, historical studies of upswings in production and radical technological innovation have not correlated with Kondratieff Long Waves[22] and the corporate sector successfully unleashed a level of innovation since 1945 (mainly without individual entrepreneurs) that would have dazzled even a pessimist such as Schumpeter.[23]

Although Schumpeter failed to correctly prophesise the future of capitalism and socialism, he nevertheless influenced subsequent debates over what drives innovation, especially the relationship between the finance and non-finance sector and the social and political institutional structures and values that, if undermined, could actually result in the decomposition of capitalism. However, Schumpeter's world of old finance and non-finance sectors is now historically obsolete and has been replaced by the dynamics of financialisation (see below and also Chapter Five). It has also been replaced by a world where innovation is not only judged on its benefits to capitalist growth but also on its contribution to, or negation

---

22 See for example, Solomos Solomou's detailed refutation of Kondratieff in *Phases of Economic Growth, 1850-1973 Kondratieff Waves and Kuznets Swings*, Cambridge University Press, Cambridge, 1990.

23 For a critique of the myth that large corporations are not innovators, see Rajesh K. Chandy and Gerard J. Tellis, 'The Incumbent's Curse? Incumbency, Size, and Radical Product Innovation', *Journal of Marketing*, July 2000, pp.1-17.

of environmental sustainability. Politically, moderate social democratic neo-Schumpeterians champion innovation through 'green growth' (see later). Also, contemporary Left non-environmentalists highly influenced by Schumpeter, with Wolfgang Streeck being a notable example, agree with Schumpeter that traditional class conflict will not bring about the end of capitalism. Seventy years after Schumpeter, Streeck argues that capitalism still faces no significant internal opposition from the proletariat. Instead, he believes "capitalism is dying from an overdose of itself."[24] The difference is that whereas Schumpeter feared the loss of innovation due to the emergence of bureaucratic corporate power, Streeck points to unsustainable levels of debt, inequality, corruption and global anarchy. (I critically evaluate Streeck's controversial arguments in *Capitalism Versus Democracy*.)

Contemporary Disputes Over Innovation and Capitalism

If we are to understand the debates over whether capitalism is environmentally sustainable or not, it is first necessary to examine the larger policy debates among pro-marketeers over how to develop and sustain a dynamic 'entrepreneurial culture'. Significant political differences are evident in North America compared with policies in Europe, Asia and other developing regions. It is not just disagreements over the role of state institutions in fostering innovation, but more significantly, over the 'fictional expectations' or what types of capitalist societies are envisaged as both desirable and necessary for long-term growth and social stability. Across the world, the international media reports daily on anxious policy makers worrying about whether their own society has an adequately modernised transport, energy and communications infrastructure, or whether their education system trains sufficient numbers of mathematically and scientifically educated workers, and also whether their investment in research and development is competitive enough. In addition, governments and business groups express concern over the need to sustain a healthy and productive labour force combined with socio-cultural 'strategies' to minimise both the financial and social cost of youth disorder or 'derailment' from a 'productive' life. In other words, innovation is a two-pronged strategy. First, it is hoped that 'heroic' individual entrepreneurs will drive the economy forward. But in their absence, the second prong becomes necessary, namely, the 'economisation' or marketised transformation of all

---

24 Comment made by Streeck at his lecture 'Has capitalism seen its day?' to the British Academy for the Humanities and Social Sciences in London 23rd January 2014.

other social and government institutions into 'servants of the economy' to ensure that a 'entrepreneurial culture' flourishes.

Of course, within individual countries and regions, it is possible to find advocates of a range of policies who disagree with these dominant policy frameworks. Also, within recent decades, the liberalisation of global trade combined with the intensification of competition, characterised by corporate espionage, controversial intellectual property wars,[25] interlocking government and multinational corporate investment, all undermine the purity of respective policy positions and fuel global cross-fertilisation of innovation and crisis-managing strategies. In the decades after 1979, China's enterprises purchased obsolete metallurgical plants in North America, Europe, Japan and Australia for bargain prices and shipped these assets back home. These plants were then reassembled and later emerged as leaders in global competitiveness in the production of aluminium, steel and a range of metals vital to its industrialisation process.[26] From the junk pile to world leading production is a strategy that cannot be repeated by other countries given existing global over-production of key metals and commodities. Now, China faces entirely different problems of how to innovate sophisticated products and processes without purchasing or stealing these as in previous decades. Most non-Chinese multinational corporations pursue innovation and the building of capabilities 'in-house'. By contrast, Chinese businesses actively seek out capacity building, new networks and co-authorship of innovative research with leading partners in the US, UK, Japan and other countries.[27] Nevertheless, Chinese political leaders and enterprises are facing similar challenges and problems to those of other capitalist countries, only magnified tenfold. After the initial phase of rapid industrialisation, it is clear that innovation is no panacea for current and proliferating social and environmental crises.

Despite being the citadel of virulent ideological opposition to any state intervention in 'free enterprise', the US has a long history of major government involvement in innovation (see below). However, those innovation policy analysts opposed to any interventionist role by government usually focus on either the creative individual or the general 'messy' culture of entrepreneurial capitalism that fosters 'heroes' such

---

25   Omar Serrano, 'China and India's insertion in the intellectual property rights regime: sustaining or disrupting the rules?', *New Political Economy*, vol.21, no.4, 2016, pp.343-364.

26   Michael Komesaroff, *Make the Foreign Serve China: How Foreign Science and Technology Helped China Dominate Global Metallurgical Industries*, Centre for Strategic and International Studies, March 2017.

27   Steven Veldhoen, Bill Peng and Anna Mannson, *China's Innovation is Going Global: 2014 China Innovation Survey*, Strategy&, September 2014.

Steve Jobs, Elon Musk and Mark Zuckerberg. As Will Hutton, a critic of the free market, put it: "The neoliberal doctrine is that innovation will happen if there is no state involvement and if it is left to individuals having lightbulb moments, taking risks in free markets in the pursuit of bonanza profits."[28] Adherence to the purported 'lightbulb moment' is deeply entrenched in a range of countries. For example, a study in free-market capitalism by leading business consultancy firm, McKinsey and Company, argued that, "from 10,000 business ideas, 1,000 firms are founded, 100 receive venture capital, 20 go on to raise capital in an initial public offering, and two become market leaders."[29]

Defenders of 'free enterprise' are far from united. They are divided between those who are boosters for self-regulated new industries, such as the 'digital economy' and 'bio-economy', and those like Edmund S. Phelps who ache for the reinvention of the classical economy of creativity and imagination. Worried about falling productivity in America and Europe, supporters of traditional American individual entrepreneurship such as Phelps and Robert J. Shiller criticised former President Obama's project to establish up to 15 National Network for Manufacturing Innovation institutes as corporatism.[30] According to Phelps, President Trump is even worse with his bullying focus on trade and tax, rather than on innovation.[31] The conflicting models of innovation pits those who believe in traditional individual enterprise against those who argue that modern capitalist innovation is impossible without massive state intervention and collaboration between government, academic research institutes and private corporations.[32] Phelps has been fighting a war on two fronts. Like Schumpeter, he opposes corporatism and increasing state involvement. Yet, he also fights against an empty culture preoccupied with the pursuit of money and wealth by those who 'constantly

---

28 W. Hutton, 'British capitalism is broken. Here's how to fix it', *The Guardian*, February 12, 2015.

29 Quoted by Robert J. Shiller, 'Why Innovation is Still Capitalism's Star', a review of Edmund S. Phelps, *Mass Flourishing*, Princeton 2013, in the *New York Times*, August 17, 2013.

30 *Ibid.*

31 Edmund Phelps, ' Trump, Corporatism, and the Dearth of Innovation', *Project Syndicate*, 17 January, 2017.

32 For an outline of Obama's innovation institutes that are modelled on the German Fraunhofer network embracing 66 research institutes, see John F. Sargent, '*The Obama Administration's Proposal to Establish a National Network for Manufacturing Innovation*', Congressional Research Service, January 29, 2014. By 2016, proposed new institutes included those for robotics, advanced tissue biofabrication (bioeconomy and 3D printing), modular chemical process intensification (new fuels and chemicals) and reduced embodied energy and decreasing emissions in materials ('circular economy' techniques reusing man-made materials), see '*President Obama Announces Winner of New Smart Manufacturing Innovation Institute and New Manufacturing Hub Competitions*', White House press release, June 20, 2016.

complain about barriers to social mobility'. Romanticising the old Renaissance and Enlightenment culture of experimentation, exploration, the arts and general education, Phelps calls for a 'mass flourishing' by reimagining and reinstituting the 'good economy' rather than John Rawls's redistributive 'just society'.[33] His hostility to the welfare state and government involvement, reached absurd levels with his claim in 2015 that Greece had not suffered from severe austerity and that only innovation and individual entrepreneurship could overcome the more than 25% unemployment rate![34]

Championing large-scale traditional industries and employers in manufacturing and services (rather than Silicon Valley, finance capital and the media), Phelps seems to long for a bygone world that is fundamentally at odds with the current domination of narrow, commercially-driven values and practices in both public and private business institutions in North America, Europe and Australia. It is common for many Keynesian and post-Keynesian social democrats in OECD countries to also advocate reindustrialisation based on good jobs, instead of what David Graeber describes as 'bullshit jobs'.[35] However, in contrast to Phelps, their definition of 'mass flourishing' necessitates strong state involvement to solve massive inequality and poverty.[36] Phelps is a free marketeer with elite, as opposed to popular cultural tastes, who is light years away from the daily misery and poverty of millions of people. The chances of institutionalising Phelp's entrepreneurial Renaissance culture among fellow pro-capitalists is as remote as reinventing Phelp's highly idealised beloved century (1850 to 1950) in the impoverished cultural commercialism of twenty-first century capitalism.

Although American 'free enterprise' ideology deems it illegitimate for government to be involved in private sector innovation – except for military, aerospace and other 'strategic' areas[37] – the opposite is the case in many non-American capitalist cultures. In Europe, innovation

33 Edmund S. Phelps, 'What is Wrong with the West's Economies?', *New York Review of Books*, August 13, 2015.

34 E. Phelps, 'What Greece needs to Prosper', *Project Syndicate*, August 6, 2015.

35 American anarchist David Graeber's description of millions of meaningless jobs, see 'On the Phenomenon of bullshit Jobs', *Strike! Magazine*, August 17, 2013, and *Bullshit Jobs*, Simon & Schuster, New York, 2018.

36 See for example, M. Jacobs and M. Mazzucato (eds.) *Rethinking Capitalism: Economics and Policy for Sustainable and Inclusive Growth*, Blackwell-Wiley and The Political Quarterly, Oxford, 2016 and William Mitchell and Thomas Fazi, *Reclaiming the State: A Progressive Vision of Sovereignty for a Post-Neoliberal World*, Pluto Press, London, 2017.

37 For an overview of the US government's heavy involvement in R&D, see Fred Block, 'Swimming Against the Current: The Rise of a Hidden Developmental State in the United States', *Politics & Society*, Vol. 36, No. 2, June 2008, pp.169-206.

is increasingly seen as the product of new institutional arrangements and processes that link private businesses with public and private knowledge-based resources, to facilitate learning and research as well as social harmony, co-operation and the distribution of the benefits of new product innovations.[38] The old emphasis on economic competitiveness is now recognised by many European innovation analysts as needing a shift in direction to maximise the productivity and efficiency of resources in the light of concerns about environmental sustainability. This point will be discussed later in reference to advocates of 'green growth'.

In recent years, a debate has been waged on different fronts between exponents of American 'free enterprise' and European 'social democracy'. Economists Daron Acemoglu, James Robinson and Thierry Verdier argue that the cut-throat 'mean streets' of American capitalism produce more innovation and is the model for a globalised world rather than the 'cuddly' social democratic Nordic countries.[39] In response, Finnish economists Mika Maliranta, Niku Määttänen and Vesa Vihriälä detail a range of statistics to show that Sweden, Denmark and Finland have a higher level of innovation than the US, plus more egalitarian and inclusive societies.[40] Like Edmund Phelps, Acemoglu, Robinson and Thierry argue that Europe and the world have benefitted from American innovations and that the Nordic countries are entitled to enjoy their richer domestic life without an American cutthroat social life. Even so, they argue that the world as a whole will be poorer if the 'cuddly' social democratic model is adopted. Beyond the dispute over how many new patents are registered and or new products innovated, the larger questions are:

a) Is the rest of the world doomed to imitate the ruthless 'mean streets' of America in order to save capitalism?

b) Can the currently hybrid social democratic/neo-liberal dominated Nordic countries retain any of their old social democratic features in isolation, or will they eventually end up becoming much more similar to the US 'mean streets' in coming years?[41]

---

38 See for example, Bengt-Ake Lundvall, *National Innovation System: Analytical Focusing Device and Policy Learning Tool*, Swedish Institute for Growth Policy Studies, Ostersund, 2007.

39 Daron Acemoglu, James Robinson, Thierry Verdier, *Can't We All Be More Like Scandinavians? Asymmetric Growth and Institutions in an Interdependent World?*, Massachusetts Institute of Technology Department of Economics, Working Paper Series, Paper 12-22, August 2012.

40 See 'Are the Nordic countries really less innovative than the US?', VoxEU.org. 19 December 2012.

41 For the impact of neo-liberal policies on Nordic countries see Jon Erik Dølvik, Tone Fløtten, Jon M. Hippe and Bård Jordfald, *The Nordic model towards 2030 A new chapter?* trans. by Walter Gibbs, Fafo, 2015; and Luis Buendía and Enrique Palazuelos 'Economic growth and welfare state: a case study of Sweden', *Cambridge Journal of Economics*, vol.38, 2014, pp.761-777.

c)   Is the belief in innovation as the panacea to growth and produc-
     tivity resting upon a serious misrecognition of the wider and
     deeper problems and obstacles confronting capitalist societies,
     especially low and middle-income developing countries?

At the other end of the geo-political debate on innovation is the argument that entrepreneurial individualism is losing out to state capitalism.
Between 2004 and 2009, 120 state-owned companies from various countries made their debut on the Forbes list of the world's largest corporations,
while 250 private companies fell off it. China's largest 121 state-owned
companies control well over $US 3 trillion worth of assets. Moreover,
the 2016 *Fortune 500* shows that the US had 134 of the world's largest
corporations, a decline from 179 in the year 2000. By contrast, China
had 110 companies in 2016, a massive rise from just 10 corporations in
2000[42] (of which only about 20% were privately owned). Also, by 2012,
Chinese state-owned companies already controlled more than $US12
trillion in assets across the world, rivalling private investors.[43]

It is very difficult to gain an accurate estimate of which companies
are fully or part-owned and controlled by the Chinese state as many
are listed on stock exchanges, have mixed management structures and
do not conform to either state-owned or private companies in other
countries.[44] A 2018 World Bank report estimates that in 2017, China
had more than 155,000 state owned enterprises, especially large ones in
the 'commanding heights' of the economy, which accounted for 43%
of domestic industrial assets, 30% of revenues, and 15% of jobs.[45] After
four decades of neo-liberalism, when OECD countries and developing
societies privatised many public enterprises, state-owned enterprises now
account on average for only 5% of developed capitalist economies (as
opposed to employment in public administration and services) and less
than 15% in most developing countries. Strategically, despite the private
sector in China accounting for the lion share of economic activity, the

42 See Ma Guangyuan, 'How the Fortune 500 List Perfectly Mirrors China's Distorted Economy',
    Epoch Times, August 1, 2016 and for analysis of 2015 *Fortune* list see Scott Cendrowski,
    'China's Global 500 companies are bigger than ever—and mostly state-owned', www.fortune.
    com/global500, 22 July, 2015.

43 Joshua Kurlantzick, 'The Rise of Innovative State Capitalism', *Businessweek*, June 28 2012.
    For surveys of SOEs, see Korin Kane, *Size and Sectoral Distribution of State-Owned Enterprises*,
    presentation to OECD Steel Committee, 28 September 2017, and Jan Sturesson et al, *State-
    Owned Enterprises: Catalysts for public value creation?*, PWC report, April 2015.

44 Nathan Richter and Stephan Richter, 'Innovation and Management in China, Germany and
    the US', *The Globalist*, October 1, 2013.

45 World Bank, *China Systematic Country Diagnostic: Towards A More inclusive and Sustainable
    Development 2017*, World Bank, Washington, February 2018, p.9.

Chinese government sees 'command capitalism' as a means of deploying innovation in the service of larger non-economic national objectives – social stability, geo-political strength and tackling massive environmental and social problems.

The media focus on the so-called clash between 'free enterprise capitalism' and 'state capitalism' is particularly visible in the US where many political and business leaders fear the rise of Chinese regional and global economic and military power. Also, for ideological reasons, there has been a concerted campaign by free marketeers who constantly attack the size and strength of state-owned enterprises. However, the distinction between state-owned and privately-owned companies has diverted attention away from the fact that *all* of these companies *exploit their workers*, increasingly display converging management practices and often engage in joint financing and investment ventures.[46]

Despite these similarities, it would be a mistake to overlook the significantly different strategic political interests pursued by authoritarian state regimes in China, Iran, Russia, Saudi Arabia, Singapore and other countries. The heavy involvement of state-owned enterprises in fossil fuel production and exports affect global carbon mitigation policies. It is not only energy policy or military R&D that preoccupies state policy makers. The same is increasingly true for large sectors such as health and information technology, where government strategic interests necessitate regulatory controls (enforcing restrictive controls of the internet or preventing the prices of medicines from exploding) that clash with commercial investments, whether state-run or privately owned. In short, there is no automatic correlation between the desire for greater social justice and particular forms of innovation pursued by governments and state-owned companies. Many state-owned enterprises merely sustain the power of undemocratic governments or are used for domestic or international competitive leverage. If 'green growth' ecological modernisation or improving the living standards of citizens are the outcomes of greater geo-political power, then this must not be confused with common misconceptions that state-owned enterprises are inherently anti-capitalist.

Policy analyst Ian Bremmer argued in 2010 that state capitalists "fear creative destruction — for the same reason they fear all other forms of destruction that they cannot control."[47] Political order is certainly a

---

46 For an overview of state-owned companies in China, see Kellee S. Tsai, 'The Political Economy of State Capitalism and Shadow Banking in China', *Issues & Studies*, vol. 51, March 2015, pp. 55-97.

47 quoted by Kurlantzick, *op.cit.*

paramount concern. However, the bureaucratic personnel in the political apparatuses of these authoritarian regimes are not always identical
to the management running state-owned companies. Hence, market
analysts either ignore the broad socio-political and strategic economic
and military roles played by state-owned enterprises or, conversely, judge
them on narrow market criteria as inefficient and poor innovators. Even
in narrow market terms the reality is far more complex. Many are cush-
ioned and over-bureaucratised. Yet, state-owned, or part state-owned
and state-controlled companies in China and other countries such as
Brazil, India, Norway or Singapore are world leaders in particular industrial sectors as well as sovereign wealth funds, thus disproving the notion
that only 'mean streets' American individualism is the path to capitalist
innovation and wealth.[48]

As to the future role of state institutions, the crisis beginning in 2007-8
showed that major industrial companies such as General Motors and a
raft of financial corporations had to be rescued by American and European governments from bankruptcy. Future economic volatility may
require much greater involvement by state institutions and this necessary
involvement could take a variety of forms. These may include outright
nationalisation of bankrupt corporations or a public-private fusion that
will change the ownership and character of companies as responses to
mass political pressures. The one-sided focus on innovation and growth
underplays the reality that great depressions and recessions have almost
brought capitalist socio-economic orders to the point of collapse.

Stagnation or Growth

The seriousness of disputes over which model(s) of innovation capitalist
firms and governments should adopt or abandon is closely related to a
major crisis of confidence affecting decision-makers. Can developed capitalist societies even grow beyond low levels of growth/quasi-stagnation,
and will developing countries be able to sustain their higher growth rates?
These interlocking fears now plague all countries. There are numerous
corporate executives and politicians who dismiss talk of prolonged crisis
as nonsense. Meanwhile, pessimists cling to hopes that governments will
'muddle through' but dread any new major crisis triggering renewed panic
in markets. Instead, corporate and policy leaders who meet annually at

---

48 For example, see report on innovation in the important chemicals industry by Chinese state
    and private companies, KPMG, *China's chemical industry: The emergence of local champions*,
    KPMG Advisory (China) Ltd, 2013.

conferences such as the World Economic Forum (WEF) at Davos, regularly release platitudinous reports with titles such as *New Growth Models: Challenges and steps to achieving patterns of more equitable, inclusive and sustainable growth*.[49] While these unspecified new growth models called 'entrepreneurial ecosystems' are based upon values of inclusiveness, closing the gender gap, environmental sustainability and 'shared prosperity' for the bottom 40% of income earners, they also endorse fiscal austerity 'where necessary' and 'shared income and wage restraint'.

The emphasis on innovation is more clearly revealed in other WEF reports such as its annual 'Global Competitiveness Report'. Countries are ranked not according to levels of democracy, equality and social justice, but according to such things as favourable tax rates for business, less regulation of product and labour markets and availability of skilled and healthy labour supply. It is no surprise that out of 137 countries in the 2017-18 survey,[50] Qatar, the United Arab Emirates, China, Singapore, Saudi Arabia and Malaysia rate very highly alongside leading OECD members in the top 30 countries. The fact that a country like Qatar has been found to have about 30,000 forced migrant labourers or slaves working on projects such as the 2022 football world cup is no deterrent to a high ranking. As economic journalist, Bernard Keane, caustically observes, the WEF should rename itself "to reflect its agenda more accurately. Something like the World Crony Capitalism and Slavery Forum would be apt. Probably wouldn't get as many celebs to Davos every year though."[51]

Underpinning the quest for innovation and new growth models is the fear of stagnation in many developed countries and the related fear in developing countries that their export-led growth will be curtailed by stagnation in member countries of the OECD. In recent years there has been a new modern twist to the original debate that took place in the late 1930s between Schumpeter and Keynesian economist Alvin Hansen (both colleagues at Harvard). Hansen argued in his famous 1938 speech[52] that a decade after the collapse of Wall Street in 1929, America was facing 'secular stagnation' (a never-ending slump despite brief upswings) creating intractable high levels of unemployment due to low population growth and a lack of new territory and resources to be developed. Within a year or so, Hansen's fears were superseded

---

49 Published by World Economic Forum, Geneva 2014.

50 Klaus Schwab (ed), *The Global Competitiveness Report 2017-2018*, World Economic Forum, Geneva, 2017.

51 Bernard Keane, 'Silliest neoliberal poll champions brutal regimes', *Crikey*, 28 September 2017.

52 Alvin H. Hansen, 'Economic Progress and Declining Population Growth' Presidential address to American Economic Association, 28 December 1938 and published in *The American Economic Review*, Vol. 29, no. 1, March 1939, pp. 1-15.

by the Second World War, which not only absorbed the unemployed masses but also generated a boom in innovation and post-war growth and reconstruction.[53] I will return to the relationship between war and innovation shortly. Schumpeter called Hansen's theory "the vanishing of investment opportunity"[54] but rejected declining population and lack of new frontiers as causing stagnation. Instead, Schumpeter emphasised the need for innovation and the role of individual entrepreneurs, which, as I indicated earlier, he was also sceptical about due to the increasing domination of corporations and the state.

When I began researching this book several years ago, only a few analysts such as Robert Gordon voiced the 'terrifying idea' that America, Europe, Japan and other countries 'might stay stuck forever'.[55] It has long since gained prominence in mainstream policy debates as Gordon predicted that the US economy would suffer very low economic growth and productivity growth for the next 25 to 40 years (dated from 2007).[56] Although disagreeing with the techno-optimists, Gordon argued that stagnation would not be caused by a major decrease in technological innovation which he saw as proceeding at a high pace. Rather, the six headwinds buffeting growth would be: stagnant population growth combined with increasing life expectancy; lower productivity due to no further gains in average education levels; continued social inequality which has witnessed stagnant and falling income for the majority while the top 1 to 10% have increased their share since 1980; the impact of lower foreign labour costs and information technology due to globalisation; higher energy costs due to environmental constraints; and the overhang of high consumer and government debt levels that would restrict consumption and make present-day public services unsustainable.[57]

---

53 Hansen's theory of secular stagnation has become a standard feature of recent economic analysis. Bloomberg Television even ran a commercial for BNY Mellon using Hansen's 1938 theory with a moral tale of how the subsequent boom proves that you need a good finance capitalist institution like BNY Mellon to look after your personal investments.

54 Schumpeter, *op.cit.* Ch.X.

55 This is actually the title of a piece by Matt O'Brien, 'The terrifying idea that the economy might stay stuck forever just got more terrifying', *The Washington Post*, October 23, 2014.

56 Robert J. Gordon, 'Is US Economic Growth Over? Faltering Innovation Confronts the Six Headwinds', NBER Working Paper No. 18315. August 2012. Gordon developed these arguments in *The Rise and Fall of American Growth: The US Standard of Living Since the Civil War*, Princeton University Press, Princeton, 2016. Contrary to Gordon, in 2016 and 2017, life expectancy for white American males declined two years in a row for the first time since the 1960s, due to socio-economic crises and substance abuse, see Olga Khazan, 'A Shocking Decline in American Life Expectancy', *The Atlantic*, 21 December 2017.

57 See Robert J. Gordon, 'The turtle's progress: Secular stagnation meets the headwinds', in Richard Baldwin and Coen Teulings (eds.) *Secular Stagnation: Facts, Causes, Cures*, A VoxEu.org ebook, CEPR Press, London 2014, pp.47-60.

When former US Treasury Secretary, Larry Summers, reminded people in 2013 of Hansen's 1938 views, and leading economist Paul Krugman[58] called stagnation 'the new normal', the stagnation hares were well and truly off and running.[59] Mainstream economists may be engaged in debates about the causes of stagnation but disagree about whether the current mixture of economic malaise and patchy recovery is a temporary phase or a sign of prolonged secular stagnation. Conservative optimists such as Kenneth Rogoff argue that once economies deleverage their post-2007 high debts, growth will return.[60] Others attribute stagnation to ageing populations more concerned with preserving savings rather than high consumption, while others blame falls in productivity growth, lack of available bank finance, restrictive regulations on land use and so forth.[61]

Given the absence of the kind of world war that solved Hansen's fears, mainstream economists appear lost for clear answers or solutions. For example, Summers expressed little confidence that central banks in OECD countries could prevent stagnation or the return of depression economics.[62] By 2017, however, fears of deflation had receded as growth rates picked up in the US and Europe. The truth is that nobody really knows what the global economy will do in coming years and both pessimistic and optimistic predictions are based on constantly fluctuating growth and debt figures. Figures from the Bank for International Settlements figures reveal that between 2008 and 2017, governments in the US, Europe and Japan have boosted central bank holdings by US$8.3 trillion to US$12.9 trillion[63] for use as excess liquidity for private banks. The consequences have been little economic growth but significant boosts to equity markets, property prices and other distortions in global financial markets.[64] A decade after the Great Recession, we live in a

58 Paul Krugman, "Secular Stagnation, Coalmines, Bubbles, and Larry Summers," *New York Times* blog November 16, 2013, http://krugman.blogs.nytimes.com.
59 See Lawrence H. Summers, 'Why stagnation might prove to be the new normal', larrysummers.com, 15 December 2013.
60 Kenneth Rogoff, 'Debt supercycle, not secular stagnation', *Vox CEPR's Policy Portal*, 22 April, 2015.
61 See for example, Alex Gottfries, Colin Teulings, 'Can demography explain secular stagnation?', *Vox CEPR's Policy Portal*, 30 January 2015; Cardiff Garcia, 'Productivity and innovation stagnation, past and future: an epic compendium of recent views' *Financial Times*, March 11, 2016.
62 Lawrence Summers, 'Rethinking Secular Stagnation After Seventeen Months' IMF Rethinking Macro III Conference, April 16, 2015 and 'The Age of Secular Stagnation: What it is and what to do about it', *Foreign Affairs*, March/April 2016.
63 Bank for International Settlements, *Monetary Policy: inching towards normalisation*, 25 June, 2017.
64 Stephen Roach, 'The Courage to Normalise Monetary Policy', *Project Syndicate*, 26 September 2017.

world of unused excess production capacity in many industries, fear of potential bursting debt bubbles in China, debt hangovers in Japan, Europe and the US combined with patchy growth of consumption in the US and Europe. Long-time observer, Stephen S. Roach, argued that Western central bankers have learnt no lessons from Japan's decades of stagnation/deflation.[65]

So desperate are mainstream policy-makers to ensure growth and avoid deep-seated stagnation that many have even advocated anti-neo-liberal policies such as increasing workers' wages and reducing inequality so that the 99% might have more income to spend![66] Bankers are also calling for neo-Keynesian stimulus packages in the form of trillion dollar expenditure packages on public infrastructure to soak up the glut or 'oversupply of labour'.[67] Meanwhile, Right-wing technocrats, ignoring inequality, mass unemployment, and dilapidated public infrastructure and services, opt for innovation projects such as the colonisation of Mars to overcome stagnation.[68]

Since 2008, neo-liberal policy-makers have tried monetary policy such as zero or negative interest rates in order to stimulate business investment and growth. This has produced a global glut of corporate savings due to the lack of profitable investment outlets. Equity markets have become so used to low interest rates that any attempt to substantially increase rates results in a spiralling loss of confidence evident in mass selling of stocks. There are parallels here between the never-ending presence of American and allied troops in Iraq and Afghanistan and central bank policies on interest rates. Just as the inability of American puppet regimes to fend off hostile forces prevents complete US troop withdrawals (for fear of geo-political loss of power and the humiliation of another Vietnam scale defeat), so too, substantial interest rate increases cause market fears of snuffing out weak economic recovery.

Given that between 65 and 70 per cent of households in 25 developed capitalist countries have seen their income fall or stagnate since 2005,[69] potential mass job destruction due to automation will only compound falls in future disposable household income and consumer spending. No

---

65 Stephen S. Roach, 'Another Lesson from Japan', *Project Syndicate*, 26 June 2017.

66 See, for example, Ronald Janssen, 'Central Banks Warm to Collective Bargaining', *Social Europe*, 30 March 2016.

67 Daniel Alpert, 'Glut: The US Economy and the American Worker in the Age of Oversupply', Next, *Third Way*, Washington D.C., April 4, 2016.

68 See Chris Zappone,'Neil deGrasse Tyson's answer to innovation stagnation: a space race to Mars', *The Age*, May 26, 2015. In 2017, Elon Musk also announced an ambitious Mars project.

69 Richard Dobbs et al, *Poorer than their Parents? Flat or Falling Incomes in Advanced Economies* McKinsey & Co Global Institute, July 2016.

wonder leading policy institutions such as the OECD and IMF have in recent years been extremely worried about stagnation. Conversely, economist Bill Mitchell argues that talk of secular stagnation is a hoax because it panders to neo-liberal orthodoxy and assumes that governments lack the power to stimulate growth via a variety of job creating fiscal policies.[70] Mitchell's point may be valid within the context of Keynesian theory, but stagnation is hardly a hoax if many corporations prefer holding large cash reserves to investing in productive ventures, and governments refuse to end austerity measures. It is equivalent to saying that unemployment is a hoax simply because we know that governments have the power to create jobs but they ignore constant calls demanding action to reduce poverty and income inequality.

Despite the return to growth in Atlantic countries, analysts still remain far from convinced that growth is sustainable and that the threat of stagnation has gone. How long will it take governments to heed the call for major fiscal stimulus in the form of renewed public services, new infrastructure and job creation to counter the malaise that Japan has already suffered from since the early 1990s?[71] Any such return to Keynesian policies would spell the end of the neo-liberal era. Yet, neo-Keynesian policies (such as those advocated by Bill Mitchell) are limited in that indiscriminate job creation combined with increasing aggregate demand contradicts desperately needed reforms to prevent dangerous climate change.

Of course, there is no shortage of 'brightsiders' within the global business community. Developing societies or 'emerging markets' (as they are called using the narrow economistic term applied by business analysts) have driven global growth in the 21st century. They accounted for 67% of growth from 2000 to 2007 and 80% of global growth from 2010 to 2014. Developed capitalist societies by contrast, continue to experience low growth rates.[72] China alone accounted for almost 40% of global growth in 2016, or more than the combined contributions of the US, Europe and Japan.[73] Leading corporate consultancy company Price-WaterhouseCoopers (PWC) is one of many corporations bullish about future global growth up to 2050. In their projections, annual growth at 3 per cent will see the global economy double by 2037 and triple

---

70 Bill Mitchell, 'The secular stagnation hoax', *Bill Mitchell-billy-blog*, November 3, 2014.

71 See OECD report, *Escaping the Stagnation Trap: Policy Options for the Euro Area and Japan*, OECD, Paris, January 2015.

72 For growth rates in different regions, see United Nations, *World Economic Situation and Prospects 2018*, United Nations, New York, 2018.

73 Stephen Roach, 'Global Growth – Still made in China', *Project Syndicate*, 29 August, 2016.

by 2050. Global economic power will shift away from North America, Western Europe and Japan with China and India at the top, Mexico and Indonesia becoming larger than France and the UK by 2030 (in purchasing power parity terms), Turkey surpassing Italy, and Vietnam and Nigeria taking the prize for the fastest growing economies by 2050.[74] All these projections are highly speculative. If they are realised by using predominantly fossil fuels and maintaining existing levels of inequality, the end result will spell catastrophe for both the global environment and social justice.

Leaving aside environmental and social justice issues for the moment, there are other valid reasons for believing that the previous rapid export-oriented industrialisation model of countries in East Asia will not be easily replicated in most other developing societies. Putting 25% of the peasant rural workforce into manufacturing will be very difficult in future years, as the competition from existing industrial powers, both in the West and in North East Asia, will resist making room in the global market for major new industrial powers.[75] In 1991, Western Europe was the largest producer of manufacturing value added at 34% of global production followed by North America at 24% and Japan at 18 per cent. Twenty years later in 2011, Western Europe's global share had declined to 25%, America's to 22% and Japan's to 11 per cent while developing economies had doubled from 21% in 1991 to 40% in 2011.[76] Little wonder that any new industrialising countries providing additional competition will be strongly resisted by declining manufacturing powers. For example, in 2012, the EU Commission set the goal of raising the share of the manufacturing sector's share of European GDP from an average of 15% to 20% by 2020. This goal has proved to be very difficult as it required the UK (before Brexit) and France to re-establish manufacturing on a massive scale (from their low rate of 11% of GDP) given that other countries such as Germany, Poland, Sweden, Czech Republic and Austria are unable to expand manufacturing much beyond existing levels of between 17% and 24% of GDP.

Conversely, services are not as easily exported as manufactured goods. The expansion of service sector employment is also based on lower technological development in the 'informal' low-paid sector and will not achieve rapid 7% plus annual growth rates. Meanwhile, the higher

---

74 See PWC, *The World in 2050. Will the Shift in Global Economic Power Continue?* PWC, London Feb.2015.

75 See Dani Rodrik, 'No More Growth Miracles', *Project Syndicate*, August 8, 2012.

76 See figures in Roland Berger Strategy Consultants report, *Industry 4.0 The new industrial revolution: How Europe will succeed*, March 2014.

paid professional workers in services require decades of development in educational institutions in order to compete with skilled, professional workforces in the service sectors of developed capitalist countries.[77]

Low growth/stagnation is now common in 'mature' economies that have long passed their initial phase of industrialisation and rely on the intensive production or importation of consumer goods and services. In short, it is this 'business as usual' model that is environmentally unsustainable. Yet, market proponents are unrealistically expecting that the vast majority of the world's population replicate this disastrous model, both in its highly exploitative initial phase of industrialisation and in its 'mature' phase of consumer-dependent stagnation.

As for all those advocates of 'green capitalism' like Nicholas Stern, Ross Garnaut or Jeffrey Sachs, stagnation poses tremendous problems because it undermines calculations concerning the ability of developed capitalist societies to comfortably absorb carbon mitigation costs up until 2050. If Robert Gordon and others are correct and developed economies will not grow at 2 to 3 per cent for the next 25 to 40 years, then all projections about profitability, productivity and sustainable public services are blown out of the water. Should this scenario eventuate, political volatility could match climate volatility in stagnant, debt-burdened societies suffering from high unemployment and fearful populations. Conversely, if governments embark on massive public job creation programmes combined with increased taxation to supplement over-stretched fiscal resources, will powerful businesses forces undermine these anti-austerity policies as equity markets suffer major losses due to fears of inflation, wage demands and lower profitability rates? Will the end of austerity generate a new boom in corporate profits at the expense of a safe climate, or a new boom without exacerbating carbon emissions via massively funded innovative 'green growth' agendas?

Radical Critiques of the Stagnation Debate

Marxists regard 'the vanishing of investment opportunity' as not due to the factors cited by mainstream economists such as Gordon, Summers and Krugman. Rather, they see stagnation as caused by the over-accumulation of surplus by large transnational corporations faced with a shortage of investment outlets. Paul Sweezy, who was Schumpeter's assistant and close friend, developed the theory of monopoly capitalism with Paul Baran[78]

---

77 Dani Rodrik, 'Back to fundamentals in Emerging markets', *Project Syndicate*, August 13, 2015.

78 P. Baran and P. Sweezy, *Monopoly Capital*, Monthly Review Press, New York, 1966.

partly as a critique of Schumpeter.[79] Later in the decades from the 1980s, Sweezy and *Monthly Review* Marxist colleagues, Harry and Fred Magdoff and John Bellamy Foster, further developed the theory of 'the financialisation of the capitalist accumulation process'.[80] Accordingly, in the absence of profitable investment outlets, corporations increasingly diverted massive accumulated funds into the speculative financial sector thereby creating asset bubbles that periodically burst in the stock market crash of 1987, the 1992 bursting of the Japanese asset/price bubble, the Asian financial crisis of 1997, the 2000 dot-com crash and the Great Financial Crisis of 2007-2008. Without the financial sector dominating production and driving development in speculative areas such as property, they agree that growth rates would have been much lower between 1980 and 2007.

In other words, stagnation is inseparably connected to financialisation. Hence, the tightening of regulations over the finance sector may make asset bubbles harder to emerge but more regulation will not cure stagnation; it may even worsen it by restricting the flow of speculative investment funds.[81] This is because the cause of stagnation lies in the skewed nature of modern capitalist economies, whereby the finance sector is the growth engine that periodically drives asset-bubble growth at the expense of socially useful production and employment. Other Marxists and heterodox economists such as David Harvey and Robert Boyer concur, even though they have different conceptions of financialisation. Harvey denounces endless property development blighting cities across the globe because property investment acts as an essential 'sink' for the investment of surplus corporate capital.[82] French political economist Robert Boyer, and other members of the Paris Regulation School, have long argued that the Fordist regime based on mass production has for the past few decades been subordinated to a post-Fordist accumulation process that prioritises 'shareholder-value' over social needs. Financialisation as a new regime of accumulation is different to earlier forms of finance capital analysed by Rudolf Hilferding or Baran and Sweezy. This is because financialisation is now facilitated by new information technology and global equity markets that help transform the old relationship between financial institutions and non-finance sectors as well as households.

---

79 See John Bellamy Foster, 'The Political Economy of Joseph Schumpeter A Theory of Capitalist Development and Decline', *Studies in Political Economy*, no.15, Fall 1984, pp.5-42.

80 For an overview of their ideas see Fred Magdoff and John Bellamy Foster, 'Stagnation and Financialisation: The Nature of the Contradiction', *Monthly Review*, May 2014. Also see Editorial, *Monthly Review*, April 2016, critiquing mainstream economists for their continued failure to explain the real causes of stagnation.

81 This was argued by Paul Krugman and quoted in *Ibid.*

82 D. Harvey, *Seventeen Contradictions and the End of Capitalism*, Profile Books, London 2014.

While not agreeing with the overgeneralised concepts 'Fordism/ post-Fordism,[83] it is still possible to agree with Boyer that international financialisation promotes short-term boom/busts characterised by the inflation of property, shares and other financial assets. This growth of financialisation leads to high household and company indebtedness, extravagant salary packages for managers and other socially negative practices.[84] However, as Greta Krippner notes, 'financialisation' has itself become a generalised concept that covers too many contradictory meanings.[85] Also, the *Monthly Review* editors developed the concept of financialisation well before derivatives grew to such important and enormous levels during the past twenty years. Although stagnation is linked to the lack of sufficient productive outlets for investment (hence the growth of profitable financial investment in all kinds of debt securities), the explosion of derivatives is now a part of *real capitalist economies* even those that are not stagnating, for instance, the German economy that presides over large trade surpluses. Such is the indispensable role of derivatives to capitalist profit (examined in Chapter Five), that in 2016, Deutsche Bank (the largest single bank holder of derivatives) was estimated to have held between *US$54 and US$75 trillion* worth of derivatives on its books, the upper figure being 20 times the size of Germany's GDP and equal to the entire global GDP![86]

It has been abundantly clear for the past three decades that developed capitalist societies have been stuck in a vicious cycle of asset bubbles followed by busts and stagnation. Governments have either rejected policies to break the dominance of neo-liberal financialisation or lacked the political will and mass support needed for such a fundamental change. As Nomura Bank chief economist and adviser to successive Japanese Prime Ministers, Richard C Koo puts it, "the unfortunate fact is that democracies are ill-equipped" to handle balance-sheet recessions that require deleveraging (reducing) large debts incurred after the bubble bursts, especially if government intervention requires higher taxation that threatens affluent asset holders.[87] Not only have finance experts

---

83 For a critique of Fordism/post Fordism, see Paul Hirst and Jonathan Zeitlin, 'Flexible Specialisation versus Post-Fordism: Theory, Evidence and Policy Implications', *Economy and Society,* Vol. 20 no. 1, February 1991, pp.1-55.

84 Robert Boyer, 'The Present Crisis. A Trump for a Renewed Political Economy', *Review of Political Economy,* Volume 25, Number 1 January 2013, 1–38.

85 Greta Krippner, *Capitalizing on Crisis: The Political Origins of the Rise of Finance,* Harvard University Press, Cambridge, 2011, ch.2.

86 See The Market Oracle, 'Is Deutsche Bank World's Largest Holder of Derivatives in Trouble?', MarketOracle.co.uk, 8th June, 2016.

87 Richard C. Koo, 'Balance sheet recession is the reason for secular stagnation', in R. Baldwin and C. Teulings (eds.), *op.cit.* pp.131-142.

such as Adair Turner admitted that there has been no deleveraging, but according to the Institute of International Finance, in the ten years since the beginning of the financial crisis in 2007, an additional US$70 trillion of debt has been added by households, governments and non-financial corporates taking global debt to a record US$215 trillion or 325 per cent of global GDP.[88]

Critics of financialisation have characterised the present era as 'central bank-led capitalism'.[89] Although central banks have increased their role since the 1980s, the Great Financial Crisis of 2007-8 has seen them play a far greater role than mere monetary policy. They now perform a key role in setting the general economic climate, maintaining financial stability and intervening in the political economic affairs of respective countries. The burning issue of the role of unelected central bank officials in what is called 'capitalism versus democracy' will be discussed in another book. Not only is there increasing electoral hostility to central bank-imposed austerity, but central banks and governments have to deal with mounting debt and new Fin Tech (financial technology) that threatens regulatory control in the form of everything from shadow banking to new forms of privatised money (blockchain) and financial relations.

Radicals such as the *Monthly Review* analysts have been warning about stagnation and the disastrous consequences of monopoly capitalism for over sixty years. Yet, the system continues to survive – through growth and stagnation – while inflicting misery on hundreds of millions who have not secured their comfortable niches. Although I agree with many of the critiques of capitalist practices made in *Monthly Review*, for how much longer can we take comfort in the diagnosis of stagnation without any new political economic breakthroughs? Do we have to wait for another sixty years? It helps us little to recognise that capitalism is in what seems like a state of permanent crisis. We know that its defenders have either been paralysed by policy disputes or continue to 'muddle through' with temporary ad hoc policies. Meanwhile, opponents of existing regimes are currently too weak to replace neo-liberal policies with anti-austerity and environmentally sustainable agendas. The beast seems to struggle from one periodic crisis to another.

---

88 Cited in Nassim Khadem, 'Ten years since the global financial crisis, world still suffers 'debt overhang', *The Age*, 17 June, 2017.

89 Andrew Bowman, Ismail Erturk, Julie Froud, Sukhdev Johal, Adam Leaver, Michael Moran & Karel Williams, 'Central Bank-Led Capitalism?', *Seattle Law Review*, vol.36, 2013, pp. 455–87; and Grahame Thompson, 'The Sources of Financial (In)Security in a Period of Central Bank-Led Capitalism', paper prepared for the 2nd NordSTEVA Conference, University of Stavanger, Norway, December 1-2, 2016.

The Dark Side of Innovation

Any discussion of innovation that does not consider its connection to stagnation and militarism is incomplete. In other words, the past eighty years have been characterised by periodic debates over the causes of stagnation and whether capitalist societies can avoid this fate without resorting to military solutions. There has been a dark side to democracy – from Athenian democracy to the American republic – namely, its long historical association with war.[90] Inadequate attention to the major roles played by war and military expenditure is paid by many of those who currently place their faith in 'green growth' innovation. Remarkably, the US as the largest global power has been continuously involved in domestic and foreign wars for 93% of the 242 years since being founded in 1776. Between 1940 and 2018, there have been only five years of the past 78 years when the US was not at war somewhere in the world.[91] Between 1992 and 2015, the US spent an average of over $600 billion per annum on military expenditure and R &D. At 35% of the estimated total $1,739 billion global military expenditure in 2017, the US military budget dwarfed China's 13% ($228.2 billion), Saudi Arabia's 4% ($69.4 billion), Russia's ($66.3 billion) 3.8%, India's ($63.9 billion) 3.7%, and France's ($57.7 billion) 3.3% as the next five largest spenders.[92] Total annual Department of Defense expenditure in 2017-2018 is nominally $834.2 billion but will exceed approximately $1 trillion when taking into account its property management of more than 555,000 facilities at more than 5,000 sites plus over 700 foreign military bases in more than 100 countries.[93] Furthermore, the longest and most expensive foreign wars in US history in Iraq and Afghanistan are estimated to eventually cost the US more than $6 trillion (depending on accumulating interest on debt), with no end in sight.[94]

When compared with the Second World War, which ended the stagnation of the 1930s, these ongoing regional wars have done little to end

---

90 See John Keane, *The Life and Death of Democracy*, Simon & Schuster, London, 2009.

91 For a chronology of US wars see details www.washingtonsblog.com/2015/02/america-war-93-time-222-239-years-since-1776.html.

92 See SIPRI, 'Global Military Spending remains High at $1.7 trillion', Stockholm International Peace Research Institute (SIPRI), Solna, 2 May 2018. The US military budget has declined from 2011 when it was 41% of total global military expenditure.

93 See latest figures for 'US Defense Spending', usgovernmentspending.com.

94 See report by Sabir Shah, 'US Wars in Afghanistan, Iraq to Cost $6 Trillion', *Global Research News*, Feb.12, 2014 based on a Harvard Kennedy School report estimating that costs of 4 to 6 trillion dollars would continue to accumulate as interest rates and medical costs accumulate in coming years. President Trump claimed in 2018 that $7 trillion had been spent on wars in the Middle East.

the new, current low growth/stagnation. Instead, they have compounded stagnation by adding $2 trillion, or 20 per cent of new US national debt between 2001 and 2012, thus placing constraints on future borrowing for vitally needed domestic public services, new infrastructure and tackling climate change. Also, US military involvement in protracted regional wars has not translated into the same degree of innovative commercial benefits as earlier historical conflicts. One reason for this is that the manufacturing sector in the US is significantly smaller to that of the period from the 1940s to the 1970s. Steel, shipbuilding, automobiles and other industries are now smaller than similar industrial sectors in North East Asian countries and much manufacturing is outsourced abroad. While the US still dominates software, Silicon Valley is a small employer by comparison to the millions employed in the post-war reconstruction and expansion of suburban America between 1945 and 1970.

Equally troubling for those pro-marketeers wishing to counter stagnation with innovation is the long history of the 'dark side of innovation' and capitalism. The strong link between innovation and war and military expenditure bodes ill for humanity and for peaceful capitalist development. Over 57% of US government research and development expenditure has continued to be allocated to military R&D. The massively expensive arms races of the twentieth and twenty-first centuries continue apace. Apart from the US which in recent years has spent near 4% of GDP on defence and related budgetary allocations, of the twenty countries with military expenditure constituting a burden of between 4 and 12% of GDP (compared with between 1% and 3% in other countries), most were, unsurprisingly, to be found in the Middle East, Africa and countries of the former Soviet Union.[95] These countries were importers of weapons and military equipment. In fact, the world has long been divided between a small number of countries capable of producing highly complex weapons systems and the vast majority that have low-level assembly and maintenance capacities. Those countries at the forefront of consumer goods innovation and production are in many instances the same countries capable of partially or wholly synthesising advanced electronics, chemicals, metals, information technology and other industrial processes combined with skilled engineering and machinofacture to produce the latest and most destructive weapons. Where this complex capacity is becoming either too technologically or financially burdensome for former old imperialist powers such as the U.K., France and Germany, then joint European military R&D becomes

---

95 SIPRI, *op. cit.*

an absolute necessity despite the absence of sufficiently co-ordinated EU-wide civilian innovation policy.[96]

The centrality of militarism to innovation and the general health of key capitalist countries have been recognized since 1935 when Michal Kalecki wrote about Hitler's rearmament policies as a method of generating growth and reducing unemployment.[97] Military Keynesianism has been widely practised by many governments. President Obama confirmed the long tradition in 2014 by setting up two new manufacturing innovation hubs in Detroit and Chicago that would be jointly funded by the Pentagon and 143 companies as well as local universities. Economists Moretti, Steinwender and Van Reenen in calculating 'the spoils of war', argue that each dollar of government R&D expenditure generates $2 to $6 of additional private company R&D.[98] However, military R&D is not just a stimulus to commercial innovation. Capitalist growth has depended on the development of general-purpose technologies such as computing or aviation. In his work *Is War Necessary for Economic Growth?*, the late Vernon Ruttan posed the question: "Can private sector entrepreneurship be relied on as a source of major new general purpose technologies? The quick response is that it cannot!"[99] Major new general-purpose technologies that foster hundreds of other spin-off products often require decades of research and development to reach commercial viability. Without heavy state involvement, especially from defence departments, few private companies would have the patience or capital to nurture long-term research projects. Other analysts, such as Fred Block, Matthew Keller and Mariana Mazzucato also argue that the 'entrepreneurial state', especially military R&D, has been central to innovation and growth.[100] Whether capitalist societies are able to transition away from state-directed military R&D to state-sponsored 'green growth' is not a technical question but rather an urgent political question.

---

96 See Paolo Pini and Davide Antonioli, 'We Need an Industrial and Innovation Policy for Europe', *Social Europe*, www.socialeurope.eu 30 January, 2015.

97 Michal Kalecki, 'Stimulating the Business Upswing in Nazi Germany' (1935) reprinted in J. Osiatynsky *(ed.), Collected works of Michal Kalecki,* Vol. VI, Oxford University Press, Oxford, 1996. Also see Peter Custers, 'Military Keynesianism Today – An Innovative Discourse', www.petercusters.nl, April 2009.

98 See Enrico Moretti, Claudia Steinwender and John Van Reenen, 'The Intellectual Spoils of War? Defense R&D, Productivity and Spillovers', emi.berkeley.edu (draft) 2014.

99 V. Ruttan, 'Is War necessary for Economic Growth?', Clemons Lecture, Saint Johns University, Collegeville, Minnesota, October 9, 2006.

100 Fred Block and Matthew Keller, 'Where do innovations come from?' in F. Block and M. Keller (eds), *State of Innovation: The US government's role in technology development,* Paradigm, New York 2010 and Mariana Mazzucato, *The Entrepreneurial State Debunking Public vs. Private Sector Myths,* Anthem Books, London, 2013.

Also, one crucial area where military R&D is playing an important role is unmanned robotics in a multiplicity of land, marine and airborne vehicles.[101] Whereas early forms of general-purpose innovation helped create mass employment as these forms of innovation were transposed to the civilian consumer economy, the opposite is most likely to eventuate from robotics innovation. If advanced automation compounds the low job recoveries currently characterising post-recession countries, then new generation innovation will prove to be a bitter blow to those pro-market analysts hoping for a cure to stagnation and political instability. In Marx's terms, the social order will prove that it has not exhausted innovation and still has room for the development of new productive forces. But if unemployment and poverty increase due to new innovative forms of artificial intelligence and automation, will these only create more social conflict? Furthermore, military expenditure and conflict continues to exacerbate the impact of environmental crises and helps fuel the social production of chaos and misery in parts of Africa, Asia and other regions.[102] Most advocates of 'green growth' focus on civilian infrastructure, technology and employment while paying insufficient attention to the international arms trade, civil wars and the increasing arms race, especially in the Asia-Pacific region and Africa. A 'sea change' in geopolitics is required to drastically reduce militarism and its connection to innovation, if the claims made on behalf of 'green growth' are to have any chance of success.

'Greening' Capitalism: Comfortable or Frightening Conditions

Environmental campaigner, Bill McKibben, reported in 2016 that the new 'climate math' had deteriorated dramatically in the previous four years. In order to have a two-thirds chance of preventing a dangerous additional 2°C degrees rise in global temperature, only a maximum of 800 gigatons of CO_2 can be released into the global atmosphere. Importantly, Norwegian energy consultants Rystad calculated that coal mines, and oil and gas wells *currently in operation worldwide* contain 942 gigatons worth of CO_2![103] Even without any new mines and oil and gas wells, what will be done about the massive existing excess capacity

---

101 See Carl B Frey and Michael Osborne, *Technology at Work The Future of Innovation and Employment,* Citi GPS: Global Perspectives & Solutions, Oxford Martin School, February, 2015.

102 For an overview of conflict and environmental crises in Africa, Latin America, Central Asia and other regions, see Christian Parenti, *Tropic of Chaos: Climate Change and the New Geography of Violence,* Nation Books, New York, 2011.

103 Bill McKibben, 'Recalculating the Climate math', *New Republic*, 22 September, 2016.

of CO2 threatening a safe climate? The forecasts of James Hansen and other environmentalists are one thing.[104] But even leading business consultant PWC pointed out in 2017 that the world needed to reduce carbon emissions by 6.5% annually until the year 2100 in order to keep the temperature rising by no more than 2°C.[105] Yet, as PWC reminds us, 'business as usual' was either increasing emissions or on the most favourable calculations was way off this mark with annual emissions declining by only 1.3% per annum between 2000 and 2015.[106]

For decades, scientists, environmental social movements, such as Greenpeace and Friends of the Earth, or journalists and policy analysts have presented frightening pictures including: melting polar ice caps and rising sea levels; extreme weather volatility becoming the norm; impending food and water shortages due to desertification and lengthy droughts; depleted fish stocks and loss of biodiversity due to destroyed coral reefs and acidified oceans; millions of potential climate refugees from flooded low-level Pacific islands, countries such as Bangladesh, or major cities such as New York, London, Shanghai, Mumbai and Tokyo; higher global warming due to the thawing of the permafrost and release of methane as well as the release of sea-bed methane; urban populations increasingly dying from heat waves; the risk of climate wars and the sixth mass extinction of species since the dinosaurs were wiped out 65 million years ago. Linked to the estimate that in the past forty years, half of all wildlife has been wiped out by human economic development, there is little doubt that without drastic mitigation or adaptation measures, the impact of climate breakdown caused by capitalist development will take on the most catastrophic proportions imaginable.[107]

What is striking is not just the volume of evidence warning us about the extreme dangers of climate breakdown, but just how relatively ineffective those reports have been in altering most forms of 'business as usual'. This is not at all to deny the invaluable preparation of public opinion, the mobilisation of protest movements and the pressure on

---

104 James Hansen et al, 'Young people's burden: requirements of negative co2 emissions' *Earth System Dynamics*, 8, pp.577-616, 2017 (originally submitted in 2016).

105 PWC, *The Long View: How will the economic order change by 2050?*, PWC, February 2017, p.45.

106 *Ibid.*

107 Despite the reactionary position of the Abbott and Turnbull governments, Australia alone has produced numerous reports and analyses of the unfolding dangers of climate change. See for example, Peter Christoff (ed.) *Four Degrees of Global Warming*, Earthscan/Routledge, London, 2013; Paul Gilding, *The Great Disruption*, Bloomsbury press, London 2011, Clive Hamilton, *Requiem for a Species*, Earthscan/Routledge, London 2010 and David Spratt and Philip Sutton, *Climate Code Red*, Scribe, Melbourne, 2008. Also see David Spratt's collation of the latest international news and assessments about climate change at climatecodered.org.

national governments and international climate conferences that various campaigners have contributed to in recent years.[108] It is also not to deny the enormous growth of all sorts of sustainable urban planning, recycling, renewable energy investments and numerous other green public and business ventures and practices brought into being because of warnings about climate change. However, despite all these very positive developments, carbon emissions have not been drastically cut and in most countries continue to rise. A decade after the Stern Review on climate change, Nicholas Stern conceded that emissions were about 41 billion tonnes of carbon-dioxide equivalent in 2005 but had risen on a dangerous upward trajectory of about 50 billion tonnes by 2016.[109]

Despite all the international scientifically-based and rationally argued cases for quasi-war emergency actions, a 'new Marshall Plan' and other similar named global interventions to drastically reduce carbon emissions, surprise, surprise, not a single major national emitter from the G20 governments or a significant business lobby has endorsed adopting such emergency actions.[110] Instead, the world's largest carbon emitter, China, has merely promised to limit peak carbon emissions by 2030 which could be 35% higher than 2010 levels. With the US under Trump abandoning commitment to the Paris Cop21 agreement and the EU yet to show any substantial global leadership in mitigation policies,[111] the loss of momentum for even moderate emissions cuts is disastrous. Should environmentalists continue to advocate mitigation schemes that no government or business group is prepared to endorse? Absolutely. Are these countries able to afford drastic cuts of carbon emissions and does the technical capacity exist to implement such emergency measures? Certainly. Why then is there such complacency and relative lack of action?

Currently, within capitalist countries, a complex battle is being fought

---

108 For an insight into the obstacles and years of coalition building in order to achieve the modest outcomes of the Paris 2015 agreement, see Michael Jacobs, 'High Pressure for low emissions: How civil society created the Paris climate agreement', *Juncture*, IPPR, London, 14, March 2016 and Peter Christoff, 'The promissory note: Cop21 and the Paris Climate Agreement', *Environmental Politics*, vol.25, no.5 2016, pp.765-787.

109 Lord Stern, 'The Stern Review + 10: new opportunities for growth and development' speech given at The Royal Society and London School of Economics and Political Science, Grantham Institute, 28 October, 2016.

110 See for example, Lester R. Brown, Janet Larsen, Jonathan G. Dorn, and Frances C. Moore, *Time for Plan B: Cutting Carbon Emissions 80 Percent by 2020*, Earth Policy Institute, July 02, 2008; Mark Z. Jacobson and Mark A. Delucchi 'A Plan to Power 100 Percent of the Planet With Renewables, *Scientific American*, November 2009; Paul Allan et al, *Zero Carbon Britain Rethinking the Future*, Centre for Alternative Technology, 2013 Machynlleth, Powys.

111 For target figures of leading national emitters see 'What does climate leadership and 'fair share' look like?' *Melbourne Sustainable Society Institute*, Briefing Paper 2, October 2015.

between advocates of the dominant fossil fuels-based, high consumption, high growth model and proponents of an alternative green capitalist 'knowledge society' that it is hoped will be based eventually on zero carbon emissions and sustainable cities and agriculture. Depending on the country concerned, free marketers and various social democrats or communists are to be found on both sides of this divide, as are advocates of either authoritarian or liberal values. In contrast to old forms of class conflict, unusual formal and informal political and cultural alliances have emerged in recent years. A case in point is that it is now possible to see trade unionists and some conservative indigenous leaders joining with businesses and lobbyists to defend their mutual interests in polluting fossil-fuelled industries. In opposition to the old fossil fuels economy, one can also see informal alliances between environmentalists, indigenous groups threatened by mining companies, Left unions representing mainly service sector, especially public-sector workers, all politically aligned with a variety of technocrats and private entrepreneurs geared to new 'knowledge economy' sectors, tourism or industries in the digital economy.

Aside from the active promotion of anti-green policies by the Trump administration and some other governments, 'green growth' or 'green capitalism' has become the dominant ideological viewpoint and policy paradigm within leading national and international policy circles and major business organisations. It is now common to find governments, business groups and supranational organisations such as the World Bank, IMF, OECD, EU Commission plus numerous international organisations and business forums such as the World Economic Forum at Davos, regularly promoting variations of 'green capitalism' such as 'green New Deal', 'green stimulus' and 'green growth'.[112] Yet, there is no policy consistency within international organisations as many are still geared to supporting fossil fuels despite simultaneously advocating 'green growth'.[113] By contrast, a few national governments such as the Swedish government aim to make Sweden the first fossil fuel free welfare

---

112 See for example, Organisation for Economic Cooperation and Development (OECD), *Towards Green Growth* OECD, Paris, 2011; World Bank, *Inclusive Green Growth: the Pathway to Sustainable Development*, World Bank, Washington DC, 2012. For a survey of supporters of green capitalism, see Peter Ferguson, 'The green economy agenda: business as usual or transformational discourse?' *Environmental Politics*, Vol. 24, No.1 2015, pp.17-37. Also see Kyla Tienhaara, 'Varieties of green capitalism: economy and environment in the wake of the global financial crisis', *Environmental Politics*, vol.23, no.2, 2014, pp.187-204 and for a global survey see John Wiseman, *Pathways to a zero- carbon economy: Learning from large scale de-carbonisation strategies*, Visions & Pathways Project, Melbourne, March 2014.

113 See Harro van Asselt, 'Governing the transition away from fossil fuels: The role of international institutions' *Stockholm Environment Institute*, Stockholm, 2014, Working Paper 2014-07.

state. Also, the outright criticism and condemnation by many American and foreign corporations and business leaders of Trump's withdrawal of the US from the Paris COP agreement is indicative of significant splits among business organisations. Nonetheless, the oil and gas lobby is still extremely powerful, especially within the US Republican Party and other conservative parties across the world.

Although there is a growing consensus among decision-makers and businesses over the need for cutting greenhouse gases, climate scientists are alarmed about whether it is possible to keep global warming below 2°C by 2100. Adrian Raftery and colleagues calculated the likelihood of 1.5°C (based on current country-by-country rates of decarbonisation) at an impossible 1% chance, and even 2°C at only a 5% chance.[114] Richard Millar and colleagues are more optimistic but rapid decarbonisation of 4 to 6% per year would have to be sustained for many decades. Such rates of reduction, they caution, would be historically unprecedented. In the past they have been observed globally only for short periods in the 1930s Great Depression and the Second World War, or regionally after the collapse of the former Soviet Union.[115] Rapid decarbonisation requires not only substantial changes in production and consumption, but also the allocation of massive amounts of new capital investment. All this can take place with or without climate justice, and with or without solving mass unemployment and poverty.

Thus, it is important to recognise that climate breakdown and unemployment are related but not reducible to one another. Global warming is occurring despite high levels of unemployment because profitable fossil fuel-based capitalist production and consumption can grow comfortably *without* full employment. It has been abundantly clear for decades that attaining full employment requires abandoning dominant policies in capitalist societies. However, the challenge for opponents of neoliberalism is also to recognise that neo-Keynesian increases in aggregate demand may indeed possibly achieve full employment in many countries, but such conventional economic growth will also destroy a safe climate and deplete finite resources. This will be further elaborated in Chapters Three and Five.

Why is there such a chasm between the ideological endorsement of 'green growth' and the practice of 'green growth' by the majority of

---

114 Adrian E. Raftery et. al, 'Less than 2°C by 2100 unlikely', *Nature Climate Change*, 31 July 2017. The major problem with statistical projections is that they are devoid of politics and how actual policy developments can undermine future projections.

115 Richard J. Millar et al, 'Emission budgets consistent with limiting warming to 1.5°C', *Nature Geoscience*, 18 September, 2017.

corporations and governments? It is true that 'green capitalism' attracts many forms of investment and the provision of new products and services. Leading stock markets such as Wall Street already have companies listed on 'environmental sustainability' indexes. At a political level, Thomas Hale estimates that over 14,000 cities, companies, civil society groups, and other sub- and non-state actors have participated in international initiatives to fight climate change since 1990.[116] Even the titles of recent reports by The Global Commission on the Economy and Climate (co-chaired by Nicholas Stern and former Mexican President Felipe Calderón), *'Better Growth Better Climate'* and *Seizing the Global Opportunity: Partnerships for Better Growth and a Better Climate*[117] (lead author Michael Jacobs) embody the hopes and policies of the social democratic/Third way 'greening capitalism' agenda promoted by many 'civilising capitalism' policy makers, business leaders, labour movement figures and NGOs. Similarly, leading climate change activist Al Gore, explicitly talks about 'sustainable capitalism' based upon extensive forms of ecological modernisation.[118] The latter are to be differentiated from a multitude of cynical businesses and governments across the world that are more preoccupied with 'greenwash' public relations rather than pursuing green practices.

Regardless of divisions among dominant policy makers, especially the resurgence of climate sceptics within the Trump administration, it doesn't require much imagination to envisage a future where substantial parts of future market societies are dominated by all kinds of 'green capitalist' enterprises. For example, Jeffrey Sachs promotes the Deep Decarbonization Pathways Project which claims that:

> …a low-carbon future is within reach, with huge benefits at a very modest cost. In the United States, for example, cutting emissions by 80% by 2050 is not only feasible; it would require added outlays of only around 1% of GDP per year. And the benefits – including a safer climate, smarter infrastructure, better vehicles, and cleaner air – would be massive.[119]

Despite the very low probability of keeping future temperature increases

---

116 Thomas Hale, *Design considerations for a registry of sub- and non-state actions in the UN Framework Convention on Climate Change*, Blavatnik School of Government, Oxford, 24 February 2014.

117 *Better Growth Better Climate, The New Climate Economy report*, The Global Commission on the Economy and Climate, Washington DC, September 2014 and *Seizing the Global Opportunity: Partnerships for Better Growth and a Better Climate*, Washington DC, July 2015.

118 Al Gore, *The Future: Six Drivers of Global Change*, Random House, New York, 2013.

119 Jeffrey Sachs, 'The Clean-Energy Moonshot', *Project Syndicate*, October 11, 2015.

to only 1.5°C, if decision-makers were fully committed to rapid decar-bonisation and switching to renewable energy, these goals could prove to be the easiest objectives to accomplish in coming decades compared with the much harder task of overcoming the natural limits to growth.

Advocates of 'green capitalism' take many forms – from utopian technological entrepreneurs to conservative corporate fund managers promoting infrastructure 'green bonds' and renewable energy.[120] For many Left critics there is no mystery associated with the hegemonic promotion of 'green growth'. Thomas Wanner calls it the 'neo-liberalisa-tion of nature'[121] and describes processes that merely legitimise a slightly modified 'business as usual'. Others conclude that environmental sustainability and preventing climate chaos is incompatible with capi-talism.[122] These are powerful and compelling criticisms. Many capitalist societies, perhaps even capitalism as a global system, may indeed prove to be incompatible with zero carbon emissions and the retention of most existing forms of bio-diversity. Nevertheless, it is important not to dismiss out of hand the fact that the transformation of existing business practices and capitalist societies into new political economic forms of 'green capitalism' is a distinct possibility.

It is crucial to note that what most pro-market analysts understand to be 'green capitalism' is actually a post-carbon economy. This is completely different to another extremely difficult goal of retaining capitalist systems that are based upon decoupling economic growth from natural resources consumption (see Chapter Three). Hence, it would be a serious mistake – regardless of whether one is anti- or pro-capitalist – to conceive the transformation of capitalist societies as an uncontested pre-determined political economic process. Furthermore, the rate and scale of any such 'green capitalist' transitional process will not occur simultaneously in most countries and moreover, it will not follow a uniform process.

---

120 See for example, Al Gore and David Blood, 'A Manifesto for Sustainable Capitalism', *The Wall Street Journal*, 14 December 2011; US SIF Foundation, *Report on US Sustainable, Responsible and Impact Investing Trends*, 10th Edition 2014, Bloomberg, New York 2014; 'Sustainable Reali-ty: Understanding the Performance of Sustainable Investment Strategies', Morgan Stanley Institute for Sustainable Investing, March 2015 and 'The Green Bonds Blockbuster', Macquarie Wealth Management, March 3, 2015.

121 Thomas Wanner, 'The New 'Passive Revolution' of the Green Economy and Growth Discourse: Maintaining the 'Sustainable Development' of Neoliberal Capitalism', *New Political Economy*, no.1, 2015, pp. 21-41 and Steffen Böhm and Maria Ceci Misoczky, 'Greening Capitalism: A Marxist Critique of Carbon Markets', *Organization Studies*, vol.33 no.11, 2012, pp.1617-1638.

122 See for instance, Naomi Klein, *This Changes Everything Capitalism Vs the Climate*, Penguin, London, 2015.

Neo-Schumpeterian Idealists and 'Green Growth'

Contemporary neo-Schumpeterians prophesise a new 'golden age' if only policy makers embrace the lessons of recent booms and busts This is in stark contrast to the stagnation theorists, either mainstream economists such as Gordon and Summers or radical Marxist critics. Two leading neo-Schumpeterians, Mariana Mazzucato and Carlota Perez have fused Schumpeter's innovation theory with a mixture of social democratic Keynesianism and 'green growth' policies, combined with radical critiques of financialisation and its link to neo-liberal austerity policies. Straddling conventional 'Third Way' and Keynesian social democratic traditions in Europe,[123] they are seen as Left-wing by American conservatives and free marketeers, even though they advise the World Economic Forum and the EU.[124] In a Europe dominated by neo-liberal austerity, Mazzucato sided with former Syriza Finance Minister, Yannis Varoufakis, in criticising the Eurozone's governments for their harsh treatment of Greece as no solution to the economic crisis.[125] Perez has long been a leading analyst of innovation policy and her interests also extend to innovation policy in developing societies.[126] She has worked for many Latin American and European governments as well as for leading multinational corporations and supranational organisations such as the UN and OECD. Like Schumpeter, Perez subscribes to Kondratieff's highly problematic theory of Long Waves of innovation.[127]

---

123 Mazzucato originally published *The Entrepreneurial State* as a pamphlet for the 'Third Way' think tank *Demos* in 2011 and has written for the Fabian Society, see her contribution 'Lighting the Innovation Spark' in Andrew Harrop, *The Great Rebalancing How to fix the Broken Economy*, Fabian Society, London, 2013.

124 See for instance, Tyler Kublik, 'The "Entrepreneurial" State is Anything But', *Mises Daily*, July 29, 2014.

125 Both Mazzucato and Perez endorsed Varoufakis's approach to the Greek crisis well before things turned nasty in the middle of 2015. See their paper, *Innovation as Growth Policy: the challenge for Europe*, Science Policy Research Unit, Working Papers Series, University of Sussex, July 2014, p.17. Alongside five others, including Jeff Sachs and Larry Summers, Mazzucato was part of the Board of International Advisors, advising the Minister of Finance on the Greek government's *Policy Framework for Greece's Fiscal Consolidation Recovery and Growth*, Green Working Paper, Athens, May 2015, which was submitted by Finance Minister Varoufakis and rejected by EU Ministers. While Mazzucato advises the European Commission and World Economic Forum on innovation and growth, she has also become one of seven anti-austerity economic advisors (including Joseph Stiglitz and Thomas Piketty) to UK Labour leader Jeremy Corbyn, see Mazzucato, 'Jeremy Corbyn's Necessary Agenda', www.socialeurope 1ˢᵗ October 2015.

126 See Carlota Perez, *The new context for industrializing around natural resources: an opportunity for Latin America (and other resource rich countries)?*, Working Papers in Technology Governance and Economic Dynamics no. 62 May 2014, The other canon foundation, Norway and Tallinn University.

127 See for example, Carlota Perez, 'Finance and Technical Change: A Long-term View', *African Journal of Science, Technology, Innovation and Development*, Vol. 3, No. 1, 2011, pp. 10-35;

Synthesizing their respective analytical approaches, Mazzucato and Perez argue that innovation policy must take central place in any 'green growth' revival of capitalist economies. No amount of tax breaks, quantitative easing to help the financial sector, or toxic debt can expand the real economy, only investment in innovation-led growth. As markets alone cannot return societies to prosperity, the state must be heavily involved in 'mission-oriented' innovation just as governments have been heavily involved in military R&D. Just as the Cold War and suburbanisation generated innovation and prosperity after 1945, Mazzucato and Perez argue that a new 'golden age' based on heavy state-sponsored investment in 'green growth' can lead the next technological and market opportunities.[128] These would include new types of energy, major productivity increases from natural resources, new sustainable lifestyles and forms of production that will transform cities, transport and many other society-wide work, education and social relations.

Significantly, Mazzucato and Perez caution that this new 'golden age' will not materialise unless governments rectify their past mistakes. Stagflation of the 1980s, they argue, was not driven by too much state regulation but by a lack of innovation. By contrast, the booms and bubbles from the 1990s until 2008 were caused by inadequate financial regulation.[129] Financialisation manifested itself in two principal negative forms. First, the finance sector lent to itself (to generate higher profits through all sorts of toxic derivatives and speculative investments) instead of funding productive investment in the real economy. Second, the corporate sector concentrated on short-term boosts to profits through mergers and acquisitions, which also boosted share prices and extravagant

Carlota Perez, *Technological Revolutions and Financial Capital: The Dynamics of Bubbles and Golden Ages*, Edward Elgar, Cheltenham, 2002 and her earlier work with Christopher Freeman, 'Structural crises of adjustment: business cycles and investment behavior, in G. Dosi, et.al (eds), *Technical Change and Economic Theory*, Columbia University Press and Pinter, New York, 1988, pp. 38–66. For a critique of Freeman and Perez's use of Kondratieff's Long Waves (which also applies to her later work and also to Mazzucato's reliance on Long Waves), see Paul Hirst and Jonathan Zeitlin, *op.cit*. pp.15-17 who argue that Freeman and Perez succumb to a high degree of technological determinism.

128 In Chapter Three I will examine the advocates of 'green growth' in more detail. The belief in green industrial innovation is now becoming quite orthodox among prominent economists. See for example, Dani Rodrik, 'Green Industrial Policy', *Oxford Review of Economic Policy*, Volume 30, Number 3, 2014, pp. 469–491 and Mariana Mazzucato, Mario Cimoli, Giovanni Dosi, Joseph E. Stiglitz, Michael A. Landesmann, Mario Pianta, Rainer Walz, Tim Page, 'Which Industrial Policy Does Europe Need?' *Intereconomics Review of European Economic Policy*, May/June 2015, pp.120-155 and Mazzucato's EU commissioned report, *Mission Oriented Research and Innovation in the European Union: a problem solving approach to fuel innovation-led growth*, EU Publications, February 2018.

129 See M. Mazzucato, 'Financing innovation: creative destruction vs. destructive creation', *Industrial and Corporate Change*, Vol. 22, Number 4, 2013, pp. 851–867.

executive salary packages.[130] Meanwhile, over the past decade companies also divested from long-run R &D and engaged in over $3 trillion of share-buybacks in *Fortune* 500 companies alone.[131] Crucially, finance capital abandoned its role as the 'ephors' (Spartan leaders) of innovation to use Schumpeter's description. Instead, venture capital became risk-averse and opted out of long-term, large-scale technological innovation (which takes at least 15 to 20 years) by funding short-term gadgets and then cashing in via initial public offerings (IPOs) on share markets.

In short, Mazzucato and Perez employ radical critiques to argue that financialisation has proved to be disastrous for both society and for innovation. Private corporations continue to focus on the short-term and are hoarding trillions of dollars in leading OECD countries thus starving innovation of long-term funding. Europe has massively under-invested in science while over-emphasising the commercialisation of innovation and product marketing. Accordingly, to remedy this situation, governments should re-regulate and definancialise the economy via new tax policies and incentives, reorient investment to productive, long-term major technological innovation and earn revenue by charging private companies for the profits they have derived from government-sponsored innovation. The EU should also issue investment bonds to fund 'mission-oriented' R&D, especially in the weak periphery countries of the EU that need massive capital investment rather than punishing austerity. As Mazzucato put it: "The EU needs a common innovation and investment policy, not a common (and idiosyncratic) austerity policy as it does now."[132]

Apart from their endorsement of some radical critiques of financialisation and the futility of austerity policies, there is a significant part of Mazzucato and Perez's approach that is attractive as a policy strategy for achieving post-neo-liberal socio-economic change within the constraints of capitalist political economies. On the other hand, there is a strong sense of déjà vu in their 'Third Way' attempt to appeal simultaneously to the progressive corporate sector and green and social movements. It is worth

130 Mazzucato and William Lazonick, 'Innovation: let the good risk-takers get their reward', *The Guardian*, 29 November 2012.

131 See Mazzucato and Perez, op.cit.; also see chapters by Perez, W. Lazonick and others in M. Mazzucato and Caetano C.R. Penna (eds.) *Mission-oriented Finance for Innovation: New ideas for Investment-Led Growth*, Rowman & Littlefield, London 2015; M. Mazzucato and L. Randall Wray, 'Financing the Capital Development of the Economy: A Keynes-Schumpeter-Minsky Synthesis', Levy Economics Institute of Bard College, Working paper 837, May 2015; and M. Jacobs and M. Mazzucato (eds.) *Rethinking Capitalism: Economics and Policy for Sustainable and Inclusive Growth*, Blackwell-Wiley and The Political Quarterly, Oxford, 2016.

132 See Mazzucato's response to *The Guardian's* question: 'Greece's rescue package: utter humiliation or disaster averted?', July 14 2015.

recalling that New Labour rejected both laissez faire and 'Old Labour' solutions, such as the nationalisation of industry. In reality, Tony Blair and Gordon Brown presided over neo-liberal inequality and financialisation that culminated in the great crisis of 2007-8. Mazzucato and Perez recognise that one cannot go back to New Labour's love affair with financialisation. Yet, to imagine that governments will voluntarily definancialise the most powerful sector of existing economies without either mass radical mobilisation or as a response to a future major economic depression is to live in fantasyland. Any such definancialisation would require at a minimum a detailed plan of how the transition to alternative industries, public employment and revenue and fiscal policy could fill the potential massive economic slump caused by definancialisation (see Chapter Five).

Like other advocates of ecological modernisation of capitalism or 'green growth', Mazzucato and Perez promote a very positive emphasis on the necessity of state-led innovation policies but seriously underemphasise the need to change existing forms of consumption and a redistribution of wealth.

As to Mazzucato and Perez's subscription to Kondratieff's flawed Long Wave theory (see above), this is entirely unconvincing both in terms of dates and the character of the next new big innovation period. Perez argues that the beginning or 'installation period' of the next technological Long Wave can be dated around 1971. During previous 'installation periods', she observes, new innovation, such as autos, co-existed with frenzied financial bubbles (the 'Roaring Twenties') and was then followed by the Depression; after that there was a transition period and the large-scale 'deployment period' of new technology post-1945. The recent new Wave is characterised by innovation technology such as the internet, which has also been accompanied by financial frenzy in the form of the dot.com bubble caused by internet mania, as well as by emerging markets, the financial casino and property speculation. The 'turning point' is dated by Perez as somewhere between 2000/7 and an unknown 20??. From this 'installation' and 'turning point period' we are supposed to enter the 'new golden age' based on a sustainable global knowledge society.[133] By contrast, Russian economists Askar Akaev and

---

133 See Perez, *op.cit*, 2002 and modified Long Wave schema in Perez, *op.cit*. 2014. Australian neo-Schumpeterian, John Mathews, *Greening of capitalism: how Asia is driving the next great transformation*, Stanford University Press, Stanford, 2015, uses Perez and an eclectic mixture of degrowth and green growth theorists to argue that we are entering a period of green capitalism fuelled by China and other Asian countries. In the German context, Ralf Fücks, *Green Growth, Smart Growth: A New Approach to Economics, Innovation and the Environment*, Anthem Press, London 2015, also uncritically subscribes to a Schumpeterian 'Green Kondratieff Wave' without questioning the periodisation of Long Waves and innovation and what brings about social change.

Andrey Korotayev are brimming with mathematical confidence and predict the sixth Kondratieff Long Wave to begin in 2018 and last till 2050. Plotting Long Waves with mathematical formulas and technical innovations, Akayev and Korotayev's positivist defence of Kondratieff is totally bereft of any socio-political explanations. It's as if economic fluctuations are driven by technology and detached from actual social conflict or disputes over day-to-day policies.[134]

One of the many difficulties followers of Kondratieff overlook is that political economic change is not driven by recurring waves. Mazzucato and Perez and others argue that 'green growth' will lead the new Long Wave boom of the future. Yet, if Long Waves or Cycles are supposed to predict future expansion or contraction but cannot tell us which new technologies will become dominant or whether there will be more or less ecological sustainability, or less or more social equality and so forth, what is the point of trying to detect their existence? Moreover, R&D green innovative technology (apart from ICT developments) did not begin in the 1970s as Perez claims and is still years away from emerging and underpinning a new world of 'green growth'. Mazzucato and Perez list some of the potential 'green growth' that is desperately needed aside from whether it generates a Long Wave boom or not. However, the absence of this new innovation (and the long R &D time lines needed) gives supporters of 'green growth' little hope that their claim is feasible to quickly end decades of low growth/stagnation in OECD countries in less than twenty years.

Can pro-market policy makers afford to wait twenty years for the innovation 'known unknowns' that may or may not solve socio-economic and environmental problems? Actually, what pro-market 'green-growth' think-tanks such as The Global Commission on the Economy and Climate tell us is that the world needs a conservatively estimated budget of between $US 90 trillion to over $US 105 trillion (about $US6 to 7 trillion per annum) spent on new infrastructure and renewable energy and other measures by 2030.[135] Pause to consider that this is almost four times the 2017 annual global military budget of approximately $US1.7 trillion!

---

134 Askar Akaev and A. Korotayev, 'Global Economic Dynamics of the Forthcoming Years: A Forecast', *Structure and Dynamics*, vol.10, no.1, 2017, pp.1-23 and Andrey Korotayev and Sergey Tsirel's positivist attempt to verify Kondratieff's long waves, 'A Spectral Analysis of World GDP Dynamics: Kondratieff Waves, Kuznets Swings, Juglar and Kitchin Cycles in Global Economic Development, and the 2008–2009 Economic Crisis', *Structure and Dynamics*, vo.4, no.1, 2010, pp. 1-57.

135 These figures are calculated by The Global Commission on the Economy and Climate, see their report *Seizing the Global Opportunity: Partnerships for Better Growth and a Better Climate*, Washington DC, July 2015.

If most of the green expenditure required was broken down into about $US300 to $US400 billion upfront capital expenditure and the rest was new debt, then the additional global level of debt could be $US 85 to $100 trillion higher by 2030 on top of existing massive debt levels. The figures would be much higher if funded by private corporate debt or expensive public-private ventures rather than cheaper government borrowing. These large debt levels are financially manageable, but politically unlikely.

Raising tens of trillions of dollars for a new green global economy constitutes an enormous political act of faith given the prevailing dominance of many hostile neo-liberal decision-makers. Furthermore, most of this required infrastructure and renewable energy programme is based on already existing technology rather than new innovation. Although 'green growth' could stimulate renewed capitalist growth, once the infrastructure and renewable energy projects are built, it is questionable whether it would generate sustainable mass employment and profitable production.[136] After all, new innovation, whether in the manufacturing sector or services sector, will have to *reverse or abandon dominant innovation trends* of recent years which are nearly all geared to *labour-saving technology* rather than job creation.

Those who over-emphasise innovation as the necessary policy solution to kick-start ailing capitalist economies misunderstand the fact that for a whole host of environmental, employment and social stability reasons, the old era of 'general purpose' and 'mission led' innovation can fulfil few of the hopes nourished by the neo-Schumpeterians. It is clear that Mazzucato and Perez represent the 'civilised' wing of capitalist development. They want a green, socially just and harmonious society that deploys innovative technology in the interests of the majority at the expense of the short-term carpetbaggers and financial vultures. Lacking an overall transformative politics, their solutions veer between belief in innovation policy as the panacea to contemporary global crises or faith in more traditional social democratic reform.

Mazzucato and Michel Jacobs (a leading neo-Schumpeterian proponent of 'green growth' and former advisor to British Prime Minister Gordon Brown) argue that:

> Public policies are not 'interventions' in the economy, as if markets existed independently of the public institutions and social

---

136 For an analysis of the difficulties in estimating new 'green jobs', see Alex Bowen and Karlygash Kuralbayeva, *Looking for green jobs: the impact of green growth on employment*, Grantham Research Institute on Climate Change and Global Green Growth Institute, London and Seoul, March 2015.

and environmental conditions in which they are embedded. The role of policy is not one simply of 'correcting' the failures of otherwise free markets. It is rather to help create and shape markets to achieve the co-production, and the fair distribution, of economic value. Economic performance cannot be measured simply by the short-term growth of GDP, but requires better indicators of long-term value creation, social well-being, inequality and environment sustainability.[137]

Whether focussing on innovation or a broader social democratic Keynesian 'green growth' strategy, the neo-Schumpeterians rely heavily on top-down policies that are based on businesses changing direction under state-led policies rather than actions responding to mass political movements from below. Importantly, their 'entrepreneurial states' are still largely geared to capitalist markets. For decades we have endured neo-liberal propaganda about wealth creation and how the 'trickle down' effect would benefit all. Now Mazzucato gives a social democratic version of this so-called cure to inequality and poverty. She wants to "change the narrative of the left from one of 'redistribution' to one that champions value creation".[138] This is a utopian notion of entrepreneurial states where governments are supposedly able to extract sufficient revenue from joint public/private innovation to fund egalitarian public services and create social equality.

The neo-Schumpeterians do not have blind faith in the romanticised 'capitalism' depicted in glossy corporate public relations brochures about 'shared prosperity' and 'inclusive growth' and environmental sustainability. Nevertheless, they fail to adequately address how innovation and reform-orientated state-led capitalist production can substantially transform a situation where the corporate sector thrives on inequality and injustice and remains the major engine of growth. It is entirely unclear how their preoccupation with technological and organisational innovation could prevent recurring historical crises stemming from the over-accumulation of capital or how the 'entrepreneurial state' could begin to overcome the major socio-economic inequalities between developed and developing countries. As to fundamental changes in existing forms of consumption, or solving massive problems of poverty and creating employment in an era of labour-saving innovation, Schumpeter's heirs

---

137 Michael Jacobs and Marianne Mazzucato (eds.) *Rethinking Capitalism: Economics and Policy for Sustainable and Inclusive Growth*, Blackwell, Oxford, 2016, p.23.

138 M. Mazzucato, ,The Entrepreneurial State – Towards an Innovation and Investment-led Recovery in Europe', *Journal For a Progressive Economy*, 8 October 2016, p.17.

offer few solutions to these major problems. Neo-Schumpeterians can either be viewed as the wave of the future in advocating more-publicly controlled and planned 'civilised capitalism' or as Pollyannas, ignoring the significant obstacles to changing the direction of capitalist societies away from their well-worn paths.

Unresolved Aspects of Innovation and Stagnation

One of the crucial factors cited by Alvin Hansen as a cause of stagnation was the decline in population growth and the end of new frontiers or new markets. The wealthiest countries in Europe, Japan, North America and Australia have already witnessed low birth rates and an ageing population over the past few decades. Now China and other Asian countries are heading in this direction, as are many global regions except sub-Saharan Africa, which has more than double the birth rate of Latin American, South Asian and South East Asian countries. The relationship between demography and capitalist growth and savings is complex. Some, but not all aged populations, save less yet require greater expenditure on health and other public services. Neo-liberals are always quick to use ageing populations as an excuse to cut public services as unaffordable, even if there are weak demographic reasons to justify these cuts. Whether population factors compound the likelihood of stagnation in coming years depends on a series of contested political and socio-economic factors. What we do know is that world population growth will impact negatively on environmental sustainability and the possibility of keeping carbon emissions below a very dangerous level. Clearly, the faith of those who believe that innovation will solve the crises facing capitalist societies will be keenly tested by the combined challenges of demography, inequality, environmental resources and stagnation.

Two important caveats are necessary. First, whether analysts are pro-market conservatives or anti-market radicals, there is a common reliance on Gross Domestic Product (GDP) as the ultimate indicator of the level of growth or stagnation. It is almost impossible to write about capitalist societies without recourse to statistics about GDP. Yet, for several decades, many critics of GDP – ranging from feminists,[139] environmentalists and advocates of social wellbeing – have argued that national accounts and measurement indicators are irrational and misleading in that they value destructive activities such as military production

---

139 See Marilyn Waring, *Counting for Nothing: What Men Value and What Women Are Worth*, originally published 1988, second edition, University of Toronto Press, Toronto, 1999.

or pollution from manufacturing but exclude highly valuable work that improve the quality of life and sustains communities such as unpaid housework and most caring activities.[140] French economist Michael Aglietta notes that in the US the high cost of health insurance and education boosts GDP performance but only at the expense of appalling levels of life expectancy, morbidity, obesity and indebtedness.[141] Others such as David Pilling call for a 'GDP 2.0' that recognises the need to exclude environmental and social negatives and that the 'growth delusion' has to be counter-balanced by measures that reduce poverty and enhance wellbeing.[142]

Similarly, critics argue that GDP as a metric was devised for economies where raw materials and manufactured goods dominated. Most growth in developed capitalist countries in recent years has come from technological innovation in information and other technologies, but that 'intangibles' in the dominant 'knowledge economy' or service sector make productivity difficult to evaluate. Hence, there is no clear idea of what 'output' means and that many services have no material form (as units of goods) in everything from administration, health care, educational use of the internet and so forth.[143] Also, there has been a staggering decrease in the cost of computerisation while the processing power of IT has increased exponentially over recent decades. Consequently, the actual size of 'Silicon Valley's' contribution to national and global GDP has fallen, even though in real terms IT constitutes an ever-increasing part of everyday production and social life. Could it be that capitalist economies have not slowed as much as mainstream and radical stagnation theorists believe because conventional measures of growth are not equivalent to real growth, decline or stagnation?

While I also rely on GDP statistics, this book takes a critical view of any policy that is primarily geared to growth – particularly policies promoting market innovation. Regardless of whether we accept or reject current definitions and measurements of GDP, we know that corporations are sitting on massive cash assets because of the lack of profitable

140 On disputes over GDP, see Diane Coyle, *GDP: A Brief but Affectionate History*, Princeton University Press, Princeton, New Jersey, 2014. For an analysis of the role of the OECD in promoting GDP as the pre-eminent measuring tool for economies, see Matthias Schmelzer, *The hegemony of growth: the OECD and the making of the economic growth paradigm*, Cambridge University Press, Cambridge, 2016.

141 Michael Aglietta, 'America's Slowdown', *New Left Review*, 100, July/August 2016, pp.119-29.

142 David Pilling, *The Growth Delusion: Wealth, Poverty, and the Well-Being of Nations*, Penguin Random House, New York, 2018.

143 See Catherine Colebrook, *Measuring What Matters: Improving the indicators of economic performance*, IPPR Commission on Economic Justice, London, April 2018.

productive investment options (outside the speculative finance and property sectors). Moreover, we lack more comprehensive data about the real cost of natural resources to establish what is the actual scale and character of growth or stagnation. It is very important to replace 'GDP' with more socially and environmentally sensitive measurement tools. Yet, on their own, these new measurement devices would not alter the quantity of finite natural resources used or the level of domestic labour performed by women unless there were also corresponding changes in production processes and social relations.

Crucially, the concept 'GDP' also affects advocates of degrowth or post-growth. For how can we know what to degrow (see Chapter Five) without more accurate estimates of existing levels of production, the real environmental costs of resources use and acceptable measures of socially-enhancing or wasteful forms of consumption? Nonetheless, what we do know is that the pressures and objectives of financialisation, such as short-term increases in shareholder value (resulting in such things as labour-shedding, costly mergers and acquisitions or plant closures) have skewed the relationship between the real value and performance of companies and their nominal, often inflated, value on stock markets.

As to whether major capitalist societies succumb to prolonged stagnation, this is not in itself a predictor of future political volatility. We know that Japan has survived decades of stagnation without major political upheaval. Similar political tranquillity will not necessarily be repeated in other countries. How particular socio-political groups and movements react to prolonged social and economic malaise is not something that one can deduce from unfavourable economic growth statistics. After the Russian revolution of 1917, Keynes feared that capitalism had to be not just successful but very successful if it was to satisfy the masses by 'delivering the goods' as otherwise, workers with falling standards of living, would look to anti-capitalist movements to improve their life chances. Currently, most capitalist societies face no major internal or external socialist or revolutionary threats. They have, nonetheless been seriously challenged by Right-wing protectionist and anti-immigration movements threatening the free movement of capital and labour.

In a world where official figures tell us that the average output growth rate in developed capitalist countries *declined* by more than 54% since 2008 as well as by 32% in developing countries, any future major recession could well stretch crisis-management capacities to their limit.[144] It has been clear for a number of years that every major capitalist country

---

144 See United Nations report, *World Economic Situation and Prospects 2016, New York, 2016, p.11.*

faces a crisis as to which new industries or new sectors can be created to generate employment or soak up idle investment capital. One has to be a super-optimistic Schumpeterian to imagine that new general-purpose technologies – innovations that take at least twenty years to develop – will not only be the magical panaceas to global problems, but will also prevent escalating crises in a volatile and precarious world where the next twenty to thirty years may be equivalent to an eternity.

One of the hallmarks of capitalist societies is the relative absence of long-term planning. As we know, state planning is anathema to many business groups. Limited planning exists in some sectors of society, such as the delivery of military weapons or aspects of urban planning and infrastructure. Yet, there is a distinct lack of vision about long-term goals displayed by most business leaders and governments. Without major political change, the proponents of large-scale social innovation will continue to be held prisoners of the narrow, self-interested decisions made by existing market forces. The more that advocates of innovation call for the intervention of governments to overcome stagnation and address climate change, mass unemployment and inequality, the more that some form of planning and regulation of economic resources and capital must take centre stage. Politically, this shift to long-term goals and greater planning is extremely controversial among business groups and very difficult to achieve. Hence, in a world characterised by greater integration yet political fragmentation and competing national and regional interests, the prospects of shared long-term goals and innovation targets remains as remote as ever. It is true that international agreements such as the need to limit carbon emissions are a sign of global co-operation. Yet, how these necessary agreements can be delivered, and the role of innovation and/or regulation in future long-term visions of capitalist societies, remains unresolved.

We must not forget that Keynesians promoted the measurement of GDP in earlier decades as a way of using national accounts to achieve full employment. Since the 1940s, the US and other governments preferred measuring national product instead of inequalities in national income regardless of levels of employment. Measuring 'growth' takes precedence regardless of whether or not it achieves more employment or improves the quality of life. Politically and socially, the goal of 'growth' has always historically been disconnected from environmental sustainability; for more than forty years it has also been disconnected from full employment and social justice.

Equally importantly, the dominant notions of what constitutes 'innovation' (whether driven by 'heroic' entrepreneurs or the 'entrepreneurial state') invariably relate to those new practices that will increase productivity and profits in capitalist systems. The Schumpeterians of the Right fail to recognize that the very dynamic of 'creative destruction' is a process that is geared to incessant growth, namely, the temporary but wasteful deployment of massive resources in new industries and ventures followed by obsolescence and destruction. This inherent process is itself historically redundant because it is driven by the twin myths of unlimited progress and unlimited resources, thus making it largely incompatible with environmental sustainability. While the social democratic neo-Schumpeterians do recognise the crisis of eco-system sustainability, they are nevertheless committed to incessant growth.

Conclusion

This Chapter has discussed how the major disputes over innovation, growth and stagnation are closely tied to ideological frameworks supporting free market, social democratic, statist or radical socialist and green positions. The current social democratic focus on innovation and 'green growth' is infinitely preferable to either neo-liberal austerity policies or authoritarian government controlled capitalism. However, new 'green growth' policies ignore and downplay the fact that earlier Keynesian policies failed to prevent major recessions. Similarly, any future neo-Keynesian strategy (at national and global levels) will also suffer from these weaknesses so long as private capitalist sectors are not fully controlled and remain the engines of international economic growth. Despite the positive aspects advocated by 'green growth' policy strategists, the neo-Schumpeterians are significantly compromised by the failure to advocate policies that seriously challenge the deeply destructive connection between state expenditure, innovation and military systems – a crucial foundation of geopolitical power conflicts and an enduring cause of human misery. Finally, and crucially, the advocates of 'green growth' neglect three other vital policy areas that will be discussed in later chapters. First, they fail to promote fundamental changes and reductions to unsustainable forms of consumption that are the backbone of capitalist economies. Second, when neo-Schumpeterians do address the need for definancialisation, they grossly underestimate the serious political economic ramifications of this policy. Third, ecological modernisation in its 'green growth' form fails to tackle profound global inequality within and between countries, as I will now proceed to discuss.

2

Global Development Crises: Modernisation as Industrialisation

In the previous chapter I discussed the policy conflicts over innovation between defenders of existing capitalist systems and those who favoured 'green growth' socio-economic reform. Mainstream notions and applications of innovation are very limited as urgent solutions to major forms of social inequality, or to ongoing violent conflicts and threats to our eco-systems. It is also necessary to go beyond familiar national debates over innovation if we are to better understand why profound inequalities within and between countries are perpetuated by dominant political economic policies promoting industrial development, consumerism and trade. Currently, there are two parallel debates over the desirability and the viability of a 'sustainable capitalism'. Remarkably, they exist relatively independently of each other, with most participants rarely acknowledging the other's conflicting ideas and policies, let alone debating them. The dominant debate between governments, a range of business policy makers, international agencies, such as the World Bank, IMF or OECD, and NGOs and assorted analysts, covers recognisable crisis-management topics ranging from trade, investment and conflict resolution to financial and climate policies. Meanwhile, many environmentalists and alternative social movements are engaged in quite a different political discourse. They oppose capitalist economic growth and instead promote degrowth for affluent nation states alongside local self-sufficient communities, such as transition towns and eco-villages. Most of these local community alternative models are strong on how to organise small-scale activities but weak on detailed conceptions of how local communities connect to larger regional, national and international political, economic, legal and socio-cultural institutions.

Advocates of alternative sustainable societies are familiar with the many negative local, national and global consequences of decades of capitalist development but are far from united on what should replace market capitalist practices. This chapter will therefore outline why it is necessary to understand how the legacy and practices of capitalist development in both developed and developing countries challenges both Right and Left arguments for national sovereignty and local self-sufficiency. It focuses on the reasons why dominant models of industrialisation are both socially and environmentally unsustainable and further discusses whether developing societies can skip the industrialisation stage while simultaneously protecting eco-systems and combatting poverty and inequality. Once these fundamental issues are evaluated, we are in a better position to understand some of the complex problems associated with the ambitious goal of decoupling economic growth from natural resources use and the political feasibility of degrowth and definancialisation. The issues of deep global inequalities covered in this chapter are also highly relevant to the later assessment of the problems associated with various popular policies like a universal basic income.

In recent years, a reinvigorated protectionism or anti-free trade nationalism in the US combined with hostility to the European Union (EU) has produced Right-wing 'populists' as well as Left leaders, such as Jeremy Corbyn in the UK and Jean-Luc Mélenchon in France. Attacking President Trump at the Glastonbury Festival in June 2017, Corbyn called for the building of bridges rather than walls, while simultaneously supporting (or failing to strongly oppose) the newest wall called Brexit. The question that needs to be addressed here is how anti-neo-liberal policies are to be accomplished at national and local levels without dismantling existing secluded and privileged walls in a world already suffering from extensive and deep inequalities? Similarly, are the goals of self-sufficiency or national autonomy compatible with the building of socio-economic and cultural bridges?

Like earlier generations of social change activists, many present-day social movements mainly focus on their own national societies. Yet, constructing domestic alternative policies and institutions can be myopic and ineffective if vital global interactions are ignored. The future ability to manage domestic and external factors itself depends on dubious notions of national sovereignty that when probed often reveals the limits of partial or full independence. Sadly, many people preoccupied with social change at the local grass roots level pay insufficient attention to how their local futures are connected to the outside world. Even those mainstream political economists who devote their careers to global analysis, often also subscribe to these fundamental misconceptions. Various caricatures and ideal typical models dominate comparative analyses of capitalism. In the following sections I will examine why it is necessary to question these models if we are to better understand the possibilities and limits of social change strategies across the world. Too many of these 'Varieties of Capitalism' and similar international relations models are still based on divisions between countries in the Atlantic region and fail to comprehend a world that has dramatically changed in recent decades.

Ants and Grasshoppers – Rethinking Independence and Pseudo-Sovereignty

At the height of the Great Financial Crisis in 2010, prominent *Financial Times* columnist, Martin Wolf, reworked Aesop's fable about the industrious ants who stored away food while the lazy grasshopper played away the summer but begged the ants for food when winter came. According to Wolf, in today's complex world, the industrious ants are Germans, Chinese and Japanese while the grasshoppers are American, British, Greek, Irish and Spanish. The frugal ants deposited their surplus earnings in supposedly safe banks that relent their money to grasshoppers that are very good at building houses, shopping malls and offices but don't produce much that the ants want to buy. As grasshoppers' debts skyrocketed, the banks of the ants demanded fiscal discipline and repayment of their deposits and loans. Austerity policies in grasshopper countries led to unemployment and a fall in consumption that also produced unemployment in the ants' nests because exports to grasshopper countries declined. The ants realised that their surplus deposits were not worth much, especially as the grasshoppers and their governments kept on increasing their debts. Wolf's moral lesson: "If you want to accumulate enduring wealth, do not lend to grasshoppers".[1]

As a fable about relations within global capitalism, Wolf's division of countries into ants and grasshoppers appears at first sight to explain a great deal. In fact, such parables can further distort and obscure real life political economic relations. To have a better chance of changing existing connections between the local and the global, we must have a more complex understanding of the world we share. First of all, 'ants' and 'grasshoppers' cannot signify the complexity of whole countries. It

---

1   Martin Wolf, 'The grasshoppers and the ants – a modern fable', *Financial Times*, 25 May 2010.

is worth remembering that tens of millions of workers in so-called 'grass-hopper' countries are no less industrious than workers in 'ants' countries. Wolf's half-humorous/half serious analysis ignores class divisions. As history has shown, millions of victims of the Great Recession – especially unemployed workers – had little or no power compared to governments, businesses, central banks and so-called financial regulators and ratings agencies in creating the crisis.

Secondly, the fable overlooks the fact that Japan had a 'grasshopper' debt-fuelled bubble of property and equities between 1985 and 1991 that crashed by 1992 and has resulted in near stagnation for more than two and a half decades. By the end of 2015, the same year that the EU imposed brutally harsh conditions on the Syriza government, Greece's public debt was 176% of GDP, while Japan's debts were much higher at 248%.[2] The main difference here was that most Japanese debt was owed internally, while Greek debt was owed to other European governments, international agencies and foreign banks. Similarly, at the time Wolf was writing his article, China, perhaps the greatest of 'ants', through a mixture of local regional governments and private speculators managed to counter a serious fall in exports to Europe and America by fuelling dangerously overheated domestic property and equity market bubbles. Between 2007 and 2014, China's total debt quadrupled and was higher as a proportion of GDP than debt in the US, UK, Australia and other 'grasshopper' countries.[3] A large part of this debt was due to real estate. China had seventeen companies involved in real estate on the 2016 For-tune 500 world's largest companies, more than any other country.[4] So much for Wolf's claim that 'ants' were not into houses, shopping malls and offices.

Thirdly, and equally importantly, classifying countries as 'ants' or 'grasshoppers' homogenises national economies. What is needed instead is recognition of the complex and diverse sectors in capitalist countries, some of which are export-driven while others are consumption and import-based. The US might be regarded as a 'grasshopper' because of its bloated financial, property and equity markets, but it still leads the world strategically in terms of advanced software for information and communication technology as well as high-tech military R&D.

---

2   Adair Turner, 'Greece and Japan: A Tale of Two Debt Write-Downs', *Social Europe*, 16 June 2016.

3   McKinsey & Company, *Debt and (Not Much) Deleveraging*, McKinsey Global Institute, Febru-ary 2016, p.76.

4   Ma Guangyuan, 'How the Fortune 500 List Perfectly Mirrors China's Distorted Economy', *Epoch Times*, August 1, 2016.

Investment in software or intellectual property, for example, is steadily growing. Maintaining its world dominance, the US by 2013 had invested 3.9% of GDP in the 'knowledge sector' while investment in residential property had dropped to 3.1% of GDP.[5] In 2016, software companies spent US$ 63.1 billion on R&D, or almost 20% of total US business investment and employed 2.9 million workers directly and another 10.5 million people indirectly.[6] American companies are still the dominant force in the global software sector that is crucial for high tech manufacturing and services but are being challenged by companies in China, South Korea, India, Taiwan, Israel and Northern European countries. As for manufacturing industries, those in the UK, Japan, US, France and other countries have all fluctuated in terms of dominance or relative decline compared with financial and other sectors. The same is already happening in China as it moves to more service sector growth. Also, there is no guarantee that Germany's large export-led surplus will continue in coming years, as it depends on the health of importing countries. In the Eurozone, the interdependence of so-called strong 'ant' banks in Germany, France and the Netherlands with weak 'grasshopper' banks in Greece, Ireland and Spain has meant that the EU has had to bail out all of them.

The political struggles over tariff reductions, liberalising capital flows, privatising public enterprises or lack of government industry policies have all played a disproportionate role in deindustrialising whole sectors and shifting capital offshore. All the while local businesses went begging for funds. These factors helped create the appearance that some countries were 'grasshoppers' rather than anything to do with so-called national industriousness or laziness. Also, very importantly, the reorganisation of multinational corporate production into cross-country interlocking value chains now affects many industrial sectors. Take for example, automobile production involving 'ants' such as Germany as well as 'grasshoppers' such as the UK. These corporate value chains distort national GDP figures and definitions as to what is a 'national economy'. So too, important factors such as currency fluctuations, tax evasion and especially deregulated capital flows all impact government revenue and the proportionate size of public and private sector activity and debt levels. It is therefore difficult to sort out nominal 'national economic' GDP from real production and services that continually cross borders.

---

5   See Macquarie Research report, 'Software: An Invisible Growth Engine', Macquarie Private Wealth, 1 April, 2014.

6   See 'Software Industry Growth Far Outpaces US Economy, Hits $1.14 Trillion', software.org BSA Foundation, 26 September 2017.

One of the challenges for social change activists pursuing a political strategy that aims for national sovereignty or self-sufficiency in capitalist or in future post-capitalist societies is how to disentangle interlocking value chains and financial flows if the aim is a 'steady-state' degrowth economy or some other form of post-carbon democracy. It is short-sighted to assume that current 'surplus' or 'deficit' countries reveal a full or accurate picture of international exchanges. Importantly, aiming for a trade surplus can come at a very high social price. As economist John Weeks observes, "generating trade surpluses reduces the welfare of a population and in extreme cases impoverishes households. This is especially the case when a surplus derives from depressing wages and output."[7]

If the classification of 'ants' and 'grasshoppers' is quite distorting, comparative examination nonetheless has a very important role to play in the development of future macro socio-economic policies. This is especially true when comparing the different ways nation states deal with the impact of global inequality and climate change and whether they have the capacity to develop adequate solutions.

Political Consequences of the Uneven Global Monetary System

During the Cold War period, most analysts recognised that America dominated the global capitalist monetary and financial system through its economic and military power. Only the Soviet Union and other Communist countries in Eastern Europe, Asia and Cuba stood outside this system. Today, the question of American hegemony has been re-evaluated within the context of rival powers in Asia and Europe. None of these other capitalist powers have replaced US economic and military hegemony. However, their challenges to US global dominance have prompted new models of comparative capitalist strength and questions about the ability of small and medium countries to survive or thrive in the midst of greater multi-polar uncertainty. Shortly, I will discuss what modernisation as industrialisation means for most developing countries. In the meantime, it is important to understand the uneven nature of the global monetary system and how few countries are able to exercise 'national sovereignty' beyond the level of political rhetoric.

Belgian political economist, Mattias Vermeiran, has provided a very useful survey and critique of the conflicting international debates over

---

7   John Weeks, 'Eurozone Stagnation: Wrong Diagnosis, Wrong medicine, No Recovery', *Social Europe*, 2 September, 2016.

the global monetary system.[8] I will draw on his work as well as discuss the strength and weakness of his alternative analytical framework. Vermeiran begins by arguing that 'realist' analysts assume that nation states strive to preserve their national policy autonomy within an anarchic international system where, following the collapse of the Bretton Woods system of fixed exchange rates and the removal of capital controls, countries either have the strength or lack the capacity to protect their domestic policy agendas. In other words, a country that has weak exports and depends on the heavy importation of goods and services will soon run up a large current account deficit. As Vermeiran notes,

> Excessive imbalances automatically generate mutual pressures to adjust, representing an intrinsic threat to a nation's macroeconomic autonomy: because adjustment can be costly in both economic and political terms, no government likes to compromise its key domestic macroeconomic objectives for the sake of restoring the external balance. As such, the main foundation of a nation's international monetary power is its capacity to avoid the burden of adjustment to payments imbalances in order to realize its key domestic macroeconomic goals.[9]

The ability of each nation-state to 'delay' international demands that its government implement domestic 'adjustments' (expenditure cuts and austerity) to get its 'domestic house in order' (either made directly by other governments or through agencies such as the IMF), is a sign of its relative strength in the international market order. Similarly, some countries have the power to 'deflect' monetary and financial crises onto other countries and thereby avoid painful domestic adjustments. The US is a notable example where despite large current account deficits it has been able to get the world to continue depositing capital (in such things as US Treasury bonds) and selling goods to it because it is the 'consumer of last resort', especially for North East Asian countries.

Several policy questions flow from the realist school's account of international trade, finance and politics. First, are China, Japan and the EU as economic competitors to the US still subject to American hegemony because they depend on propping up the US dollar to sustain their exports to America, or do they pursue their own domestic and EU-wide agendas in an autonomous manner? Second, if most

---

8   Mattias Vermeiren, *Power and Imbalances in the Global Monetary System: A Comparative Capitalism Perspective*, Palgrave MacMillan, Basingstoke, 2014

9   *Ibid*, p.22

developing countries lack the power of China, how does this affect their ability to modernise their societies and transition from low and middle-income to high-income countries? Third, how can governments that lack political economic strength implement reform agendas such as definancialisation and capital controls? Fourth, if social change movements succeed in implementing anti-austerity social policies or degrowth policies to prevent climate breakdown and resource depletion, will these post-neo-liberal governments be resilient enough to 'delay' and 'deflect' international demands and sanctions given the prospect of major currency devaluation and other trade and financial pressures? I will return to the third and fourth questions in Chapter Five.

The US may have lost some of its power in recent decades, but its powerful financial sector, its continued domination via the dollar as the reserve currency, and its massive global military reach has helped it avoid domestic 'adjustments' to its finance-led economy. Meanwhile, China has built very large foreign currency reserves thus enabling it to avoid international control over its own domestic economic development programme. Vermeiren is critical of the 'realist school' and those that focus on systemic international state-centric power relations between nations as an explanation of monetary imbalances. He observes that this type of analysis pays insufficient attention to the domestic institutional context within which macroeconomic policies are embedded. Accordingly, Vermeiren argues that the 'monetary power literature' has to explain why the American domestic economy and society has not implemented sweeping reforms to unsustainable financial imbalances and profound social inequality that has led to the destabilisation of the global monetary system. Second, he also claims that neglect of domestic relations prevents an understanding of why since the onset of the banking and sovereign debt crisis of 2008, the Eurozone is a site of struggle. The international monetary power system cannot fully explain why the crisis of the Euro has necessitated that some EU countries (especially Southern European members) have incurred more of the burden of domestic adjustment (austerity) than others in the Eurozone. Third, China's trading and currency relations to the dollar, Euro and Yen cannot explain why China has accumulated foreign exchange reserves. Rather, it is the domestic strategy of economic and social national development pursued by the Chinese government which helps explain China's external relations to the international monetary system.[10]

While Vermeiren develops a detailed and insightful analysis of

---

10 See *Ibid*, chs. 2,3 and 4 on the US, EU and Chinese domestic relations.

American, Chinese and European domestic economic policies, one major weakness of his approach relates to his subscription to a modified version of the Varieties of Capitalism (VoC) theory of capitalist societies. Instead of just talking about Anglo-American liberal market economies (LME) such as the UK and co-ordinated market economies (CME) such as Germany and Austria, Vermeiren adds mixed market economies (MME) such as France and Southern European countries. As Asian countries industrialise, the European Central Bank and EU Commission have imposed one policy favouring export-orientated monetary and fiscal policies that benefit EU countries such as Germany at the expense of the domestic socio-economic relations in MME Southern European countries that have trouble competing with cheaper imports.[11] This undoubtedly constitutes part of the explanation for the crisis in the Euro zone but ignores a range of other contributing socio-political factors too complicated to discuss here.

Later I will discuss why the VoC approach is severely restricted by a narrow economistic approach to social, environmental and cultural relations and political institutions. The emphasis on 'drivers of growth' assumes that one can categorise countries according to whether they are export-led, consumption-led or investment-led. The reality is that most countries have more than one driver of growth. The other big problem is that because the VoC approach was formulated with Atlantic region countries in mind, there has been a tendency to add to the list of 'varieties' as Southern European, Eastern European, Asian, African, Middle Eastern, Central Asian, Latin American and other developing capitalist countries fail to fit the original Atlantic mould or typologies. The old division between social democratic, liberal and conservative social welfare economies is long gone. Hybrid mixtures of neo-liberal, social democratic and authoritarian statist non-Western developments have emerged that render the old typologies redundant. Global monetary and fiscal imbalances affect the whole world. Importantly, adherence to old development models no longer provides explanations for the crises troubling so many low and middle-income countries.

Pro-market policy makers have reached a dead-end in trying to explain, let alone do anything substantial about the failure of the vast majority of countries to make the transition to high-income societies. Few Left and green anti-capitalist globalisation movements and theorists

---

11 Mattias Vermieren, *Rising Powers and Economic Crisis in the Euro Area*, Palgrave Macmillan, Basingstoke, 2016 and M. Vermeiren, 'One-size-fits-some! Capitalist diversity, sectoral interests and monetary policy in the euro area', *Review of International Political Economy*, vol.24, no.6, 2017, pp. 929-957.

(apart from those working in development studies or campaigning NGOs), pay much attention to these mainstream development debates. This is a serious mistake given the momentous political economic consequences of modernisation strategies for the vast majority of the world's population. All advocates of rectifying the massive global imbalances between countries and classes, especially those aspiring to construct post-carbon democracies or post-growth societies, could learn from the sobering evidence of decades of failed but paradoxically still dominant modernisation strategies.

Lessons From Exhausted Market-Driven Models of Development

It is worth recalling that during the Cold War, decision-makers and political economic theorists in capitalist and Communist countries differed on issues such as ownership, political control and social values while sharing a belief in *industrialisation* as the pathway to modernisation. Armed with this faith, it was not only leading Western governments and businesses that pursued models of state-capacity building in order to foster new markets and industrialisation. The constituent elements of the old global Left may have espoused anti-imperialism, but they also advocated industrialisation via reform or revolution. New socialist state institutions would encourage industrial development or modernisation thereby supposedly raising people out of poverty and ending inequality by transforming peasants, indigenous peoples, tribal and caste groups into modern workers and citizens. Today, much of this old homogenising global industrialisation model is incompatible with a safe climate and the need to sustain finite natural resources; it is also incompatible with the survival of diverse cultural practices and identities. Unfortunately, many activists and leaders of labour movements have not received this message and continue to pay lip service to environmental sustainability. Too many still believe that restoring or attracting new manufacturing industries is the main pathway to social and economic health.

It is sobering to be reminded of the consequences of undemocratic planning and industrial homogenisation at national or urban levels. Generations of people suffered, and still suffer from the legacy of well-intentioned socially concerned urban planners (such as Le Corbusier and members of the International Congress of Modern Architecture) who from the 1920s on wanted to end capitalist-created social squalor by designing sun-filled, hygienic cities with modernist towers surrounded by gardens and linked by highways. Governments in the East and West tore down both slums and diverse thriving neighbourhoods and created dehumanised, high-rise blocks (most without adequate surrounding gardens), many which subsequently became the new slums. For more than seventy years, capitalist developers also adopted this functionalist conception of modernity and urban space, for cost-saving rather than socially progressive reasons to maximise profitable investment. Complexity, diversity and the human scale are still the enemies of most businesses and governments that thrive on the logic of the profitable 'bottom line' and authoritarian values, rather than community decision-making to enhance social and environmental wellbeing.

In opposition to dominant practices, a new generation of urban planners promote designs for cities that simultaneously recognise the importance of social diversity, small environmental footprints and accessibility to cultural and material resources for low-income people. 'Principles for Better Cities'[12] and many other proposals have been put forward to create sustainable cities based on numerous economic, environmental, cultural and democratic political guidelines. While these guidelines are sensible and socially inclusive, they say little or nothing about the actual structure and ownership of the political economy that is compatible with these guidelines. Some guidelines could be implemented in capitalist systems and many others would meet strong opposition from private businesses and conservative political forces. The fundamental problem is that cities are *the* industrial and consumer-driven growth machines of capitalist accumulation. Thus, for nations, and for the world as a whole, *new environmentally sustainable cities presuppose new alternative political economies.*

The question remains: what are the obstacles facing the development of new political economies? Above all, scarcity and environmental constraints prevail. It is no longer a matter of claiming to be more radical or more ambitious in one's goals of material equality for all. The whole world simply cannot attain equal levels of material prosperity enjoyed by majorities in Australia and New Zealand, Europe, Japan, North America and some other countries, regardless of whether the world remains capitalist or becomes socialist or adopts another type of social formation. Disregarding utopian pronouncements, no one seriously believes that majorities in rich countries would voluntarily distribute most of their wealth and material possessions to poor, developing societies. Keep in mind that we live in a world where 60% of the world's

---

12 These principles for better cities were developed within forums in Berlin, Buenos Aires and Mexico City during 2015 and 2016, see circlesofsustainability.org.

population receives between $US1 and US$5 per day, while 91% of the global population receives less than the median income of people in rich countries. In this respect, dramatically increasing essential services and provisions of the 'social state' is a much more radical strategy, as I will explore in Chapter Six, in comparison to the utterly naive goal of trying to equalise profoundly unequal global wages, pensions and other incomes. Three decades after the collapse of discredited Soviet central planning, anti-capitalist movements regularly promote various forms of non-central planning, mixtures of state and market mechanisms or moneyless exchanges. De-globalisation may be widely championed, but few agree on what kind of political economic framework could make this goal a viable reality.

Those who subscribe to a total redistribution of material possessions from rich to poor usually overlook the impossibility of equally 'redistributing' established infrastructure, housing stock, or health, education and other facilities from rich countries to poor countries. Given these significant constraints, what forms of development or radical social redistribution could replace the old modernising panacea of industrialisation?

In recent years, technocratic debates over how to enhance industrial market competiveness have fused with updated models of the old modernisation theories of the 1950s and 1960s. Recall that during the Cold War, modernisation theorists advised American and other Western governments on the political-legal administrative institutions and socio-economic and cultural 'structures and functions' necessary for Asian, African and Latin-American countries to become more like 'Western' parliamentary market societies rather than Eastern Communist countries. The Vietnam War and other national liberation struggles revealed the political agenda and limits of old modernisation theory and policies. In opposition to liberal modernisation strategies, an outpouring of radical critiques of imperialism emerged during the 1960s and 1970s in the form of 'dependency' and 'under-development' strategies; namely, how Western governments and corporations maintain their dominance at the expense of 'Third World' countries. With the rise of neo-liberalism, the opening of China to market forces and the collapse of Eastern European Communism, most anti-imperialist struggles have ceased.

The old 1950s and 1960s modernisation models were updated within the new context of globalising market developments. In Eastern Europe, for instance, debates focussed on how much 'shock therapy' these middle-income countries needed and which prerequisite laws and institutions of advanced liberal market societies (such as property rights, contract law, efficient communications and administrative systems) could transform Communist societies into capitalist countries. Parallel policy debates thrived in Asian, Latin American and African countries, all designed to transform low and middle-income countries into possible contenders for sustained market growth. Instead of leaving it mainly to private businesses, non-liberal statist solutions were sought, particularly in East Asian countries, in the form of effective state-run industry policies or bureaucratic reforms that could counter corruption and harness both market and non-market resources to promote capitalist industrial growth.

By the 1980s, as 'Third World' socialist development models were consigned to the historical dustbin, many radicals and reformers were caught floundering. They still actively challenged the 'Washington consensus' on a number of fronts: battling to wipe out the burden of massive financial debts crippling developing societies; focussing on development and environmental sustainability, as well as criticising the character and effectiveness of foreign aid such as the Millennium Development Goals to relieve poverty and social neglect.[13] These actions were no substitute for the articulation of models of development that developing societies could genuinely pursue as alternatives to capitalist globalisation. The same is particularly true of the 'post-development' and post-colonial critiques of Eurocentric models of modernisation that argue against the imposition of external homogenous 'Western' standards of 'development' on a variety of indigenous, local cultures and communities.[14]

However, 'post-development' criticisms of capitalist modernisation remain largely confined to the cultural level, rather than setting out clear paths of how alternative non-Western states or grass roots communities can preserve their identities while still meeting their needs. 'Post-development' critiques of 'Western' science and technology and universal needs for food, shelter and health have in turn been strongly criticised by anti-capitalist development theorists. Twenty years ago, Ray Kiely criticised 'post-development' for unintentionally promoting neo-liberal ideas of a level playing field where supposedly local communities and developing nation states all have sufficient local resources and capacities, if only they were left alone to pursue their own development.[15] In a world of numerous impoverished communities, autonomous

---

13 For an overview of development policies and debates see Philip McMichael, *Development and Social Change A Global Perspective* Sixth Edition, Sage, London, 2017.

14 See for example, Gustavo Esteva and Arturo Escobar, 'Post-Development @ 25: on 'being stuck' and moving forward, sideways, backward and otherwise', *Third World Quarterly,* May 2017.

15 Ray Kiely, 'The Last Refuge of the Noble Savage? A Critical Assessment of Post-development Theory', Journal *of Development Research,* June 1999, vol.11, no.1, pp.30-55.

development, free of 'Western' aid and universal values, rather is a recipe for perpetuating deprivation under the name of cultural 'independence'. Rejecting market globalisation does not mean uncritically adopting the post-colonial romanticisation of local grass roots communities that can often comprise complex mixtures of conflicting practices including fundamentalist and oppressive ones.

If cultural autonomy is an elusive goal for indigenous populations in the face of market modernisation, national self-determination and national sovereignty are equally elusive. National independence movements continue in a world where the borders and character of many nation states have been drawn arbitrarily by victorious powers or former colonial governments. Today, the concept of national sovereignty has been hollowed out by the reality of economic interdependence and loss of full control by governments due to multinational corporate value chains and declining control over capital inflows and outflows. Cultural and individual sovereignty and autonomy are also increasingly emptied of meaning in a world of mass surveillance, data collection and the mass marketisation of cultural products and services.

We have now come a long way from the ideological certainties of modernisation models 'exported' globally by both Western and Soviet governments in the 1950s. Today, we witness a situation of profound failure and widespread doubt as to the efficacy of any of the dominant models of development designed to transform low and middle-income countries into rich capitalist countries. These models are still promoted by international agencies, major governments and policy analysts.

Visitors to many capital cities in developing countries are often struck by the gleaming office towers, extensive shopping malls and gridlocked highways choked with private cars – all signs of how markets have seemingly had success in raising all people's living standards. Outside the corporate city towers and lifestyle of the new urban middle classes, mass poverty tells another story about low and middle-income countries. According to Andy Sumner, in 1990, it was estimated that 93% of very poor people were living in low-income countries. Now, three-quarters of the world's poorest people are to be found in middle-income countries.[16]

There have been several definitions in recent years of what constitutes lower middle-income and upper middle-income countries that range widely from those with per capita incomes of US$1,050 right up to

16 Andy Sumner, *Global Poverty and the New Bottom Billion: What if Three-quarters of the World's Poor Live in Middle-income Countries?*, Institute of Development Studies, Working Paper 349, University of Sussex, 2010.

US$16,000.[17] If industrialisation is the long-recommended pathway for countries to become modernised and achieve high-income status, the historical record tells quite a different story that is both disastrous and very sobering for all concerned. An oft-cited 2013 World Bank study, tracked 101 countries identified in 1960 as middle-income. Only 13 countries reached high-income status (above US$12,736 per capita) by 2008, and only nine of these were 'non-European': Equatorial Guinea, Puerto Rico, Hong Kong, Japan, Mauritius, South Korea, Singapore, Taiwan and Israel.[18] What the study omitted to mention was that most of the latter countries were highly integrated with, or dependent on American or British military strategy and/or financial investment that helped boost growth sectors. Also, countries such as Equatorial Guinea and Puerto Rico are in the 'high-income' club due to averaging per capita figures that disguise shocking degrees of poverty and inequality at levels that make comparison with the standard of living in Japan or Singapore look ridiculous.

Similarly, a 2015 IMF report examined how a wider range of 167 low and middle-income countries in 1970 had fared in subsequent decades. Only nine countries reached high-income status by 2010 (or the equivalent of 46% of US GDP per capita income) and of these, only Taiwan and South Korea were not small European countries: Cyprus, Czech Republic, Greece, Ireland, Malta, Portugal and Slovenia.[19] Very importantly, of this tiny number of nine countries, high-income status was not always achieved through industrialisation. Moreover, a 2018 report on 100 countries[20] showed that China, India, Brazil and Indonesia that ranked 1st, 5th, 9th and 11th respectively, as having the largest manufacturing sectors in the world, still belonged to the classification of lower-middle income countries. This confirms that industrialisation does not propel the vast majority of their populations into the global high-income club.

Leaving aside future industrialisation and its negative impact on climate change and natural resources, it is abundantly clear that *over the past seven decades industrialisation has failed as a strategy to end global inequality*. Not that most businesses and governments promoted

---

17 See Indermit S. Gill and Homi Kharas, *The Middle-Income Trap Turns Ten*, World Bank, Policy Research Working Paper 7403, August 2015, pp.8-9.

18 World Bank, *China 2030: Building a Modern, Harmonious, and Creative High-Income Society*. Washington DC, 2012, p.12.

19 Reda Cherif and Faud Hasanov, *The Leap of the Tiger: How Malaysia Can Escape the Middle-income Trap*, Working Paper 15/131, IMF, Washington DC, 2015, p.2.

20 World Economic Forum and A.T. Kearney, *Readiness for the Future of Production Report 2018*, WEF, Geneva, 2018.

industrialisation because they wanted to reduce inequality. Industrialisation has conspicuously failed to even end the interminable problem that World Bank analysts, Indermit S. Gill and Homi Kharas, coined, 'the middle-income trap'.[21] For more than a decade, mainstream economists and policy makers, including many from the World Bank, the Asian Development Bank and the IMF, have debated whether there is a 'middle-income trap', its possible causes, and ways developing countries can escape and join the rich countries' club. Why should this debate about how to generate and sustain capitalist growth be important to all Left and green radicals and reformers, even though they may desire quite different social and environmental objectives to those promoted by capitalist globalisation? One major reason is that the 'middle income trap' debate simultaneously focuses on the failures of existing policy solutions and highlights crucial issues that are largely absent from debates among opponents of capitalism at local, national or international levels.

Since 1945, most Latin American, Asian, Middle Eastern and African countries have been unable to move beyond their low or middle-income status. This is a massive problem, as more than six billion of the world's population now live in broadly defined low and middle-income countries. According to Gill and Kharas, middle-income countries are "squeezed between the low-wage poor country competitors that dominate in mature industries and the rich-country innovators that dominate in industries undergoing rapid technological change".[22] It was therefore extremely difficult, they admitted, for the World Bank to recommend growth strategies that could be adopted by such a diverse range of developing countries. In fact, the concept 'middle-income country' embraces societies that have completely different historical institutional structures and political economic and cultural profiles. Some resemble poor countries while others appear wealthier but have been stuck in low growth or stagnant situations lasting between three and more than six decades.

For the vast majority of developing countries, the chances of achieving rapid industrialisation are both remote and judging by the historical record of middle-income countries, will retain middle-income status even if they manage to industrialise. The type and level of industrialisation is what is crucial. As a strategy, 'imitation' of old industries such as textiles and clothing has had a degree of success in various low-income countries. However, once a certain level of labour-intensive industrialisation

21 Indermit S. Gill and Homi Kharas, *The Middle-Income Trap Turns Ten*, World Bank, Policy Research Working Paper 7403, August 2015.
22 Indermit S. Gill and Homi Kharas and Others, *An East Asian Renaissance: Ideas for Economic Growth*, World Bank, Washington, DC, 2007.

has been achieved, 'imitation' loses much of its effectiveness for middle-income countries competing in the elaborately manufactured global goods markets. Complex value-added, high tech production and services require advanced education systems, R&D investment and many other socio-political institutional support structures and capital resources. Notably, these conditions and resources are either completely or significantly absent in most middle-income countries.

Although the dispute over the 'middle-income trap' is mainly relevant to businesses and policy makers preoccupied with profitable economic growth and social mobility in a global capitalist world, key socio-economic issues also affect the ability of countries to adopt alternative paths of development. For example, if so few developing capitalist societies escape the 'middle-income trap', are the barriers to joining high-income countries largely domestic or external? Is it because the initial phase of plentiful cheap rural labour underpinning urban industrial development is exhausted, thus resulting in higher wages in both urban and agricultural sectors thereby eroding competitive advantage?[23] Or is it because many 'middle' countries have education systems that ill-equip workers and managers capable of competing with major technological powers, that is, technical competences and general management skills that take decades to develop?[24] We know that various authoritarian regimes have found it easier to deal with low-wage, poorly educated labour. By contrast, the transition to new high-tech, 'knowledge economy' industries poses direct threats and challenges, as these require more open and critical education systems and political cultures antagonistic to authoritarian government repression.

Moreover, debates over how to create sustainable growth policies seriously neglect the negative aspects of market activity. Take the polluted and chaotic quality of giant cities in Asia, Africa and Latin America which are evaluated more in terms of how detrimental they are to productivity growth, but less in terms of the health and wellbeing of populations and their natural environments. In their preoccupation with policies of how to move from low-wage to high-tech production, in the form of various investment, labour training of 'human capital' and other institutional conditions, these market-focussed strategies acknowledge a range of issues to do with inequality. However, they generally lack interest in or

23 Pierre-Richard Agénor, Otaviano Canuto, Michael Jelenic, 'Avoiding middle-income growth traps', *Vox*, 21 December 2012.

24 Barry Eichengreen, Donghyun Park, and Kwanho Shin, Growth Slowdowns Redux: New Evidence on the Middle-Income Trap, NBER Working Paper No. 18673, Cambridge MA, January 2013.

pay insufficient attention to social protection policies and ways governments can combat poverty.

Importantly, what all these debates about the so-called 'middle-income trap' ignore or downplay are the crucial external global obstacles that make it extremely difficult if not impossible to surmount for most of these countries. Take for instance, the fact that countless middle-income countries depend on external investment finance that is often available for property and other speculative investment but scarce when it comes to funding crucial social projects. Investment and production are also interrupted when multinational corporations change their supply chains or completely bypass many countries as 'unattractive' investment options. The old 'Third World' debt-burdened developing countries continue to constrain development proposals that are out of favour with powerful supranational funding bodies and private market forces.[25] Given this history, anti-capitalist development strategies are faced with a major dilemma: in a world of precarious jobs increasingly threatened by new labour-saving technology, what alternative forms of development to the old industrialisation model do radical greens or socialists propose?

Compounding dilemmas of development is the important factor that many business groups and policy makers, as well as workers in developing countries are divided over the desirability and the benefits of moving to a high-tech economy. Existing businesses are reluctant to invest in expensive new technology and fear losing their current labour-intensive profitable enterprises. Workers also worry that they will be unemployable due to lack of education and greater automation. Domestic employment fears are all exacerbated by the opposition of existing global industrial powers to creating extra market room for new businesses in those sectors that they currently dominate, not to mention room for whole new competitive countries.

Above all, as we have long known, the development game is rigged and stacked in favour of dominant players. Given that so few countries have been successful in transitioning to high-income status, it is no surprise that despite all the decades-long policy recommendations there is virtually no escaping this 'trap' in the contemporary capitalist world. It is not just that the structure of global economic and military power dominated by a handful of countries allows for few new entrants. Even though big players China, India, Indonesia, Mexico, Brazil, Russia and Turkey may now be part of the G20, they are also stuck in 'middle-income' land with high levels of poverty. At least four of the latter have

---

25 Robert H. Wade, 'Industrial Policy in Response to the Middle-income Trap and the Third Wave of the Digital Revolution', *Global Policy*, Vol.7, no.4, 2016, p.474.

large military machines and China has had the fastest and largest level of industrialisation in human history.

Consulting firms such as McKinsey and Co or PwC may predict that countries such as Indonesia, Mexico, Nigeria, Turkey or Vietnam will become major economic powers by 2050 (see Chapter One). However, this does not mean that they will also eradicate massive domestic poverty and become high-income countries as measured by the World Bank or IMF. Market ranking in the global pecking order is a far cry from development strategies that drastically reduce inequality and poverty. The lesson from the 'middle-income trap' debate is that the so-called 'trap' is less a trap and more a deliberate refusal of powerful political elites and business groups to pursue policies that threaten their power and privileges.

For instance, there is little or no mention by conventional development analysts about the replacement of old forms of colonialism by new rapacious methods whereby wealthy classes and corrupt individuals in combination with foreign corporations, strip *trillions* of dollars from low and middle-income countries. According to a 2015 report carried out by international researchers, far more money in the form of illicit money transfers to tax havens, interest payments or falsely priced invoices is used by subsidiaries of multinationals to disguise capital flight, avoid tax, and conceal flows out of developing societies than the combined total of foreign aid, investment and other income received from developed capitalist countries.[26] In the last year of recorded data, between 1980 and 2012, this 'reverse aid' is estimated to be a massive US$16.3 trillion, or more than enough to eliminate the worst forms of extreme global poverty. For example, in 2012 alone, multinational and local businesses, corrupt officials and wealthy individuals in developing countries sent out US$2 trillion more than the poor populations in these countries received.[27]

There is no doubting that various researchers in international institutions such as the World Bank desire a reduction in poverty and an increase in environmental sustainability. Nonetheless, what appears as a 'middle-income trap' is more reflective of the impasse in which global and national policy makers are caught as they pursue only those policies that are non-threatening to market values and entrenched political

26 Global Financial Integrity, the Centre for Applied Research at Norwegian School of Economics, et al, *Financial Flows and Tax Havens: Combining to Limit the Lives of Billions of People*, Washington DC, 5 December 2016.

27 Jason Hickel, 'Aid in reverse: how poor countries develop rich countries', *The Guardian*, 28 March, 2017.

hierarchies. Within these restrictive pro-market-growth parameters there is no agreement about what kind of policies should be explored next. Whether they be specifically tailored policies for particular countries or general socio-economic strategies applied across many low and middle-income nation states, the results speak for themselves: *the overwhelming failure of more than 90% of countries* to breach the more than seventy-year-old barriers to high-income status.

It should also be remembered that it is not just approximately 160 low and middle-income countries floundering in their quest for viable policies. All high-income countries are equally fearful of how they will be able to maintain their status and juggle the incompatible goals of social justice and environmental sustainability with market competitiveness. A minority of policy makers are slowly recognising that the old social pillars of former growth and stability are eroding in this new phase of globalisation, as I will examine in Chapter Six.

Tellingly, mainstream analysts still assume that the ability of governments to prioritise economic growth while satisfying demands for greater social justice and environmental sustainability is a problem largely related to the operation of *domestic* political institutions. Take for example, Daron Acemoglu and James Robinson's controversial book *Why Nations Fail.*[28] The authors attribute economic growth to 'inclusive' political and economic institutions as opposed to 'extractive' political systems run by undemocratic elites that rule over others and exclude people, especially entrepreneurs, from decision-making. Acemoglu and Robinson are typical of mainstream political economists who have very limited notions of democracy or 'inclusive' political orders. They promote a truncated conception of democracy that largely excludes workers and citizens from any real say in the crucial every-day socio-economic decisions in parliamentary democracies carried out by managers in private businesses, 'machine bosses' in parties or senior state bureaucrats. In addition, even if a country had the most 'inclusive' democratic *domestic* institutions, this would still be inadequate on its own to counter the *external* global barriers to economic growth determined by dominant corporations and geo-political powers.

Maximising democratic control should never be abandoned as a major political goal. Nevertheless, it is also necessary to recognise the limited power of domestic democratic control. Take the fact that there is little doubt that greater democracy could see the imposition of higher taxes to alleviate poverty. Chris Hoy and Andy Sumner argue that it is no longer

28 Daron Acemoglu and James Robinson, *Why Nations Fail: The Origins of Power, Prosperity, and Poverty*, Crown, New York, 2012.

tenable to assume that most developing countries lack domestic financial resources to tackle extreme poverty of millions living on between US$1.90 and US$5 per day. Higher taxes on the rich, redirecting current military expenditure and ending regressive subsidies on fossil fuels are some of the important funding suggestions they make.[29] Although they do not discuss levels of democratic power, they imply that these policies would either require greater democratic domestic power, in the absence, of course, of benevolent dictators prepared to undermine their own oligarchic power base. Nevertheless, Hoy and Sumner recognise that once it comes to tackling the inequality and poverty of all those on US$10 or more per day, domestic resources are insufficient, and global rather than domestic solutions are unavoidable.[30]

The quest for magical domestic, market-based recipes so that countries can become high-income societies is futile in a world where powerful multinational corporations and governments have set the rules of the game. Alongside the inequality of global power are the domestic ruling classes in dozens of countries harvesting wealth and enjoying privileges while colluding in the exploitation and oppression of their fellow citizens. Social reformers who oppose radical change have long ignored this fundamental fact. This is particularly true of many 'green growth' advocates who desire new post-carbon paths of development in low and middle-income countries while saying little or nothing about countless corrupt and authoritarian regimes.

How more equitable post-carbon democracies are supposed to emerge in opposition to both external corporate forces and domestic exploiters is the burning issue that is too easily ignored. Some feeble options are occasionally offered. For instance, economist Dani Rodrik is a leading advocate of a more 'moderate', nationally regulated globalisation rather than a free-market or deregulated hyper-globalisation. In 2001, he observed that America, Europe and Japan each took different paths to high-income development:

> Policy makers in developing countries should avoid fads, put globalization in perspective, and focus on domestic institution building. They should have more confidence in themselves and in domestic institution building, and place less faith on the

---

29 Chris Hoy and Andy Sumner, *Gasoline, Guns, and Giveaways: Is There New Capacity for Redistribution to End Three Quarters of Global Poverty?* Centre for Global Development, Washington DC, Working Paper 433, August 2016.

30 *Ibid*, p.25.

global economy and blueprints emanating there from.[31]

Although it is a truism to declare that countries need to pursue strategies that are appropriate to their unique circumstances, Rodrik's general advice glosses over the highly unequal and imbalanced global order within which any 'home-grown' strategy is situated. Without fundamental radical reforms to this unequal global order, analysts in 2100 will themselves be caught debating why 90% of low and middle-income countries repeated the twentieth century's dismal record and failed to escape the so-called 'middle-income trap'.

Incomplete Maps of Global Inequality

It is undeniable that due to industrialisation, there have been massive improvements in the standard of living for hundreds of millions of people in China and several other countries over recent decades. Pro-market globalisation perspectives claim that humanity has had its 'best 25 years ever' with extreme poverty falling from 47% to 14% of the world's population since 1990 and life expectancy increasing on average from 48 to 71 years.[32] Despite highly uneven global benefits, there is no doubt that many improvements in health and living standards have occurred in the past fifty years. While the statistics and character of poverty can be disputed, any improvement is welcome news. My argument is a different one. Not that industrialisation has had no substantial benefits but rather that as a future strategy to attain social equality and prevent eco-system disasters, capitalist industrialisation has proven to be both a failure and very dangerous. Even leading advocates of global industrialisation have established that social *inequality* has dramatically increased in all those developing countries currently undergoing industrialisation.

To get a snapshot of increasing inequality, the *World Inequality Report 2018* documents that between 1980 and 2016 inequality rose in almost all regions of the world.[33] Also, each year Oxfam maps and records the extent of injustice globally. We have become quite familiar with these annual confirmations of extreme inequality. In 2017, just eight of the richest billionaires had the same wealth as 3.6 billion of the world's

---

31 Dani Rodrik, *Development Strategies for the Next Century*, Economic Commission for Latin America and the Caribbean Seminar, Santiago, Chile, 28 August 2001, p.45.

32 See Carl Bildt, 'Restoring Faith in Globalization', *Project Syndicate*, 19 February, 2017.

33 Facundo Alvaredo et al, *World Inequality Report 2018*, World Inequality Lab, Paris, December, 2017.

poorest people, eight times worse than the 62 individuals Oxfam identified in 2015. Moreover, the 1,810 US dollar billionaires on the 2016 Forbes list (89% men), own US$6.5 trillion, or as much wealth as the bottom 70% of humanity and all this before one even factors in the trillions of dollars in tax havens.[34] Theoretically, one would think that such obscene forms of extreme inequality would mobilise millions to the barricades. Practically, these types of reports appear to have little or no direct political affect. Instead, staggering figures wash over us, perhaps causing momentary alarm, but then we return to business as usual. At the level of rhetoric, the recognition of inequality has become a standard item of inclusion in government and business reports and forums – an empty signifier that elicits condemnatory language but is rarely matched by any substantial reforms to reduce levels of inequality.

On the issue of extreme poverty, Bill Gates, one of the aforementioned eight richest billionaires, believes there will be no very poor countries by 2035, except perhaps Haiti and some coastal African countries.[35] Likewise, the 2014 and 2016 World Bank reports[36] also stated that it is possible to reduce the world population living on less than US$1.90 per day to a mere 3 per cent by 2030. This would, however, require higher growth rates in developing countries and more 'sharing' of benefits. Why do these approaches to extreme inequality sound so reasonable on the one hand but on closer analysis are so very problematic?

First, the so-called elimination of extreme poverty by raising people to between US$2 and US$3 per day may make the figures look good, but still leaves the world with over four billion very poor people by comparison with all those in affluent OECD countries on US$50 plus per capita per day. Development analysts Peter Edward and Andy Sumner divide the world's 'geography of inequality' not into classes, but rather into four consumption 'layers': the 'global absolute poor' (US$0 to $2 per capita per day); the 'global insecure' (US$2 to $10); the 'global secure' (US$10 to $50); and the 'global prosperous' (US$50+ per day).[37] This description of consumption 'layers', however, gives us no analysis of the causal dynamics of poverty and inequality. Also, one could certainly quarrel with their definition of the 'global secure' on US$10 to $50 per day. Significantly,

34 See Oxfam, 'An Economy for the 99%', *Oxfam Briefing Paper*, 16 January 2017.

35 See report in *The Independent*, January 21, 2014.

36 Nobuo Yoshida et al, *'Is Extreme Poverty Going to End?'* Policy Research Working Paper 6740, World Bank, January 2014 and *Poverty and Shared Prosperity 2016 Taking on Inequality*, International Bank for Reconstruction and Development/The World Bank, Washington, 2016.

37 Peter Edward and Andy Sumner, *'The Geography of Inequality: Where and by How Much has Income Distribution Changed Since 1990?'*, Centre for Global Inequality, Working Paper 341, September 2013, p.21.

Edward and Sumner provide no analysis of sources of income, especially income from precarious employment in private businesses.

Second, Edward and Sumner confirm that the top 5% of the 'globally prosperous' enjoyed most of the benefits of global growth since 1990 compared with the bottom one third of people in extreme poverty.[38] While China is responsible for the lion's share of the reduction of global poverty, it continues to have massive poverty and inequality. Yet, China's phenomenal economic development skews global figures. As they note, "in the rest of the world outside China between-country inequality rose in the 1980s and 1990s but has then stayed relatively constant since 2000. Throughout this entire period within-country inequality has overall been remarkably constant – as some countries have become less equal, others have become more so."[39]

David Woodward from the United Nations Conference on Trade and Development produces even more dramatic figures about the ineffectiveness and lack of distribution flowing from global growth.[40] In 2010, 62.3% of the global population received less than US$5 per day. Assuming a continuation of the 'trickle down' impact on poverty eradication of pre-2008 economic crisis global growth rates (achieved between 1993 and 2005), it would take between *123 and 209 years* for global growth to deliver a very austere US$5 per day poverty line income. Such is the lack of redistribution and ineffectiveness of 'trickle down' global growth, that it would require an astronomical *US$11,500 trillion* (I repeat, *trillion not billion!*) increase in global GDP to reach the relatively tiny 'trickle down' sum of an additional US$4.57 trillion. This is the figure that would be needed to deliver a US$5 per day income to the two thirds of the world's population that is currently below this miserly level.[41] In addition, another overlooked factor is that the consequences for climate change of such an enormous, almost impossible to imagine level of growth would be disastrous if propelled by fossil fuels.

Inequality is not just a problem for defenders of capitalist industrialisation. The sheer scale of global inequality and poverty seriously challenges the parochialism and the strategies pursued by various local self-sufficiency and inward-looking national-based alternative programmes. I agree with leading analyst of inequality, Branko Milanovic, that one cannot understand inequality within nation-states in isolation from understanding

---

38 *Ibid,* p.31.

39 *Ibid* p.36.

40 David Woodward, 'Incrementum ad Absurdum: Global Growth, Inequality and Poverty Eradication in a Carbon-Constrained World', *World Economic Review*, no.4, 2015, pp.43-62.

41 *Ibid,* p.59.

changes in global inequality.[42] My reservations and disagreement with Milanovic relate to his application of the Kuznets Curve to explain inequality as well as his solutions to inequality. It will be recalled that it was Simon Kuznets who began arguing in the 1950s that as countries industrialised and agrarian populations urbanised during the nineteenth and early twentieth centuries, these developments produced an inverted Curve of rising inequality.[43] The Curve supposedly began to decline once developed economies saw better jobs flow from mass education and the benefits of technology and greater social protection. However, this reduction in inequality ceased a few decades ago. Thomas Piketty, for example, argued against the Kuznets Curve by showing that the decline in inequality, especially in the three decades after 1945, was an anomaly and that inequality has continued to rise since the 1980s as the owners of capital continue to take a greater share of income.[44]

It is political struggles that determine levels of inequality, a basic fact frequently omitted from economic analyses. We know, for example, that during the twentieth century military coups in various Latin American countries reversed earlier social gains made by workers. Milanovic agrees with Piketty and most other critics who argue that the application of neo-liberal policies since the late 1970s has not only halted the decline of inequality, but *significantly increased inequality*. The difference is that Milanovic adheres to Kuznet's theory and claims that since the 1980s, a new or second Kuznets wave of inequality has emerged in the US, UK and other OECD countries. He attributes this modified or second curve of inequality not to industrialisation but rather to its opposite, namely, neo-liberal deindustrialisation and globalisation. Today, he argues, China, India and other industrialising developing countries are experiencing a rise in inequality between urban and rural populations as they go up the original Kuznets Curve, while developed capitalist countries are also in a phase of rising inequality due to the second Kuznets Curve or wave. According to Milanovic, this renewed increase in inequality shows no sign of having reached its peak for the following reasons: there has been a distinct increase in both the concentration of capital and also the share of capital and income going to the top 1% to 10%; higher educated and high-income individuals tend to inter-marry; and the rich also maintain inequality by determining political outcomes, especially

---

42 Branko Milanovic, *Global Inequality: A New Approach for the Age of Globalization*, Harvard University Press, Cambridge, 2016, p.2 and ch.1.

43 Simon Kuznets, 'Economic Growth and Income Inequality', *American Economic Review*, vol. 45 March, 1955, pp. 1–28.

44 Thomas Piketty, *Capital in the Twenty-First Century*, pp.14-16.

in the US where money buys elections and policies, in short, plutocracy.

Milanovic also documents the impact of place and class. Despite a world full of mass migration and refugees, only about 3% of the world's population live in countries where they were not born. For 97% of the world's population, half of a person's income is pre-determined as soon as they are born living in either a rich, middle-income or poor country; a further 20% is determined by the income level of their parents, and a further amount is pre-determined by race, gender and other criteria – over 80% of the future personal income of most people in the world.[45] The notion that the US has high inequality but high social mobility is a myth, Milanovic and Roy van der Weide argue, as figures reveal low mobility for low-income people.[46] Some Nordic countries have relatively lower levels of inequality and high mobility, but many countries have high inequality and low mobility. No country currently has low inequality and low mobility.[47]

The main beneficiaries of globalisation in the past thirty years, argues Milanovic, have been the top 1% in developed capitalist countries and urban workers and middle-class people in China and other East Asian countries. The main losers have been low and middle-income people in developed capitalist countries as well as the poorest people in less developed countries and a mixture of rural and urban social classes in stagnant middle-income countries largely by-passed by foreign capital.

However, if Milanovic's so-called second Kuznets Curve confirms rising inequality in OECD countries since the 1980s, he tells us little about how global inequality can be overcome for the numerous poor country 'losers' in this scenario. Just as the Kuznets Curve is an inadequate theory to explain the causes of inequality, so too, is the application of the 'Environmental Kuznets Curve' by economists. The thesis that environmental degradation initially increases with economic growth but then declines as per capita income increases, has been strongly criticised as lacking consistency or causal relations between levels of income and different types of environmental pollutants.[48]

---

45 Sean McElwee, 'On Income Inequality: An Interview with Branko Milanovic', *Demos*, 14 November, 2014.

46 Roy van der Weide and Branko Milanovic, *Inequality Is Bad for Growth of the Poor (But Not for That of the Rich)*, World Bank, Policy Working Paper 6963, July 2014.

47 Branko Milanovic, 'The Schumpeter Hotel: Inequality and social Mobility', *Social Europe*, 13 April, 2016.

48 See for example, David I. Stern, 'The Rise and Fall of the Environmental Kuznets Curve', *World Development*, vol.32, no.8, 2004, pp.1419-1439 and Richard T. Carson, 'The Environmental Kuznets Curve: Seeking Empirical Regularity and Theoretical Structure', *Review of Environmental Economic and Policy*, vol.4, no.1 2010, pp.3-23.

Interestingly, Milanovic believes 'place' will cease to be the main determinant of global inequality because he optimistically assumes the gap between countries will close in coming years. As this occurs, internal country divisions along class lines will become much more important. Tellingly, Milanovic does not explain how major environmental constraints as well as market barriers on any new national entrants to industrialisation can be overcome. Rapid industrialisation (or a repetition of the China model) is a highly unlikely possibility for countless less developed countries. In fact, during the past thirty years many developing countries, especially in Latin America and Sub-Saharan Africa have experienced the opposite, or what Dani Rodrik calls 'premature deindustrialisation'.[49] Having built up modest manufacturing sectors and employment behind protectionist walls, these countries have witnessed declines in manufacturing due to 'free trade' policies and the shift of manufacturing to China and East Asia since the 1980s. What Milanovic fails to explain is why the enormous gap between the economic and geopolitical power of the top G20 countries and the rest of the world would close, if existing patterns of trade and investment continue.

Milanovic is illuminating in regard to mapping the 'winners and losers' from globalisation since the 1980s, but his Kuznets waves are more descriptive rather than analytical tools. They fail to explain why some classes within particular nation states have lost less or won more than other similar classes within comparable nations. Like Kondratieff Long waves, the problem with relying on Kutznets Curves (or waves) is that they are too economistic and assume almost predictable outcomes from large developmental processes such as industrialisation or globalisation. Milanovic says little on how the varying strength or weakness of particular political forces and trade unions in capitalist countries determine the rate and scale of inequality. In other words, Milanovic's use of the Kuznets curve implies that politics is either irrelevant or at best secondary in explaining particular levels of inequality. For instance, in recent decades, what role did the presence of weak or strong parliamentary democracy as opposed to authoritarian one-party command policies or de facto military regimes with parliamentary veneers play in levels of inequality in developing and developed capitalist countries?

While globalisation remains a contested term, what does it actually mean in this context? Is the level of industrialisation and rising inequality in developing countries due mainly to the *internal* economic response to 'external' developments? Or, given that most Asian countries are

---

49   Dani Rodrik, 'Premature deindustrialization', *Journal of Economic Growth*, no.1 2016, pp.1-33.

heavily dependent on the export of manufactured goods (over 70% of their trade[50]), would industrial development in China and other Asian countries have either been severely delayed or much less rapid and intensive without the *external* decision of multinational corporations and finance capital to shift production and capital flows to developing countries? Furthermore, was 'offshoring' (or industrialisation in developing countries) only made possible by the political allies of business in most *developed* OECD countries first defeating labour movements and dismantling high levels of protectionism, as well as removing tight regulations on capital flows between countries? Neither the Kuznets Curve nor Milanovic's use of Kuznets adequately answers these and other important questions.

Not only are Kuznets curves inadequate and vague in apportioning causality to politics, wars and regional struggles, but also Milanovic arrives at feeble solutions to inequality. He is a progressive liberal social democrat who favours higher taxation on the rich and a utopian 'egalitarian capitalism' based on 'shareholder democracy'. Crucially, Milanovic favours even more capitalist globalisation in order to bring poor countries into what he calls the 'international capitalist division of labour' (or industrialisation).

Milanovic devotes little or no space to crucial environmental issues and also avoids the highly negative consequences of financialisation in both exacerbating and perpetuating inequality. Instead, he is resigned to major inequality being with us in the future despite favouring social reforms. Fearful of Right-wing nationalism and anti-globalising 'localism', it is the second Kuznets Curve that Milanovic sees as contributing to Donald Trump's victory and the rise of populists in Europe.[51] What he fails to explain is why and how the former parties of social protection (social democrats, Labour parties and American Democrats) introduced and presided over policies that increased inequality for over thirty years and laid the conditions for Right-wing populists.

The lesson from various studies of inequality is that without a theory of what political, socio-economic and environmental factors encourage or impede capitalist growth – nationally and internationally – then we are left with little else other than nice curves and waves. After all, where would those countries on the second or first Kuznets Curve be today if the Great Financial Crisis of 2007-8 had developed into a Great

---

50 See Richard Baldwin and Masahiro Kawai, 'Multilateralizing Asian Regionalism', *Asian Development Bank Institute*, Working Paper 431, August 2013, p.3.

51 Vincent Bevins, 'To Understand 2016's Politics, Look at the Winners and Losers of Globalization: An interview with economist Branko Milanovic', *New Republic*, 21 December 2016.

Depression that enveloped China and other developing societies rather than the Great Recession of the Atlantic region? We still do not know if political leaders will be able to overcome quasi-stagnation within most OECD countries and at what cost to the environment or to workers and all other segments of societies interconnected by the global 'geography' and class structure of inequality.

Most snapshots of global inequality compare levels of per capita income and so forth. They tell us little about the significant social inequalities based on race and gender, or the multiple disadvantages experienced by families and individuals still experiencing the traumas of colonial uprooting from traditional lands or other forms of traumas caused by war or ethnic and religious persecution. No statistical comparison of household income can capture the global levels of discrimination experienced by women who suffer from extensive forms of disadvantage well beyond mere income inequality. Similarly, non-white people may acquire similar incomes to white working-class people or middle-class professionals in Western countries but they are constantly reminded of their unequal status due to pervasive levels of racism. The glaring gap between statistical facts about per-capita and household income on the one hand, and the reality of quite different lived lives in crowded households (with poor support services and non-existent infrastructure) in many parts of the developing world, and the much more advantaged life of households in developed countries is never really captured in many official reports. Fewer snapshots of inequality are needed and instead more dynamic cultural and political economic analyses of both its causes and proposed solutions.

This being said, Milanovic's work is still the most detailed study of global inequality to date and should be read by all proponents of post-capitalist democracy, especially by the advocates of universal basic income (UBI) schemes. As we shall see, UBI schemes are unable to produce major reductions in inequality or prevent more inequality. This is because inequality is not related to income alone. Even the late Tony Atkinson, who devoted a lifetime to social democratic reforms to alleviate poverty, recognised that full employment and more progressive taxes were insufficient on their own to eliminate inequality.[52] No future post-carbon democracy or post-growth society will successfully combat inequality and environmental crises unless it moves beyond conventional policies that consistently over-emphasise income at the expense of a raft of other solutions.

---

52 See Anthony B. Atkinson, *Inequality What can be Done?*, Harvard University Press, Cambridge, 2015.

Can Countries Leapfrog Industrialisation?

As mentioned earlier, it was Dani Rodrik who popularised the concept of 'premature deindustrialisation' and its negative ramifications for developing societies in Latin America and Africa. Without reaching levels of industrialisation and high-income enjoyed by rich capitalist countries, developing countries now confront the extremely difficult task of how to generate sufficient national income to combat poverty and maintain social stability. A less severe dilemma faces those OECD countries that have witnessed significant deindustrialisation but lack natural resources for commodity exports or have few globally competitive high-tech companies. High and middle-income countries all seek solutions to unemployment and national income by trying to expand various consumer-led service sector industries such as tourism, retailing, hospitality and leisure, health services and gambling. The problem is that in a highly unequal world, developed countries always start with well-established institutions and infrastructure, higher wages and higher formal levels of education, better social protection and head starts in the delivery of professional services. Conversely, a majority of developing societies are disadvantaged by poor education levels, much lower wages, a lack of complex infrastructure and a lack of corruption-free, efficient public institutions.

If most low and middle-income countries cannot change the unequal global order on their own, what other options might be possible? Can less developed and middle-income countries successfully skip or leapfrog the industrialisation stage and generate prosperity through consumption-led growth or other strategies? Or can they sidestep inequality and industrialisation by exporting their low-wage and unemployed populations to developed countries? Mainstream and radical analysts put forward the following options:

1. Immigration as a solution?

In a world characterised by displacement, where unprecedented numbers of refugees and migrants are forced to seek safe havens in affluent countries, one solution advocated is to open borders in OECD countries as a way to alleviate persecution and inequality. Giving refuge to desperate people fleeing war-torn countries and oppressive regimes could certainly reduce persecution and misery for a minority and all countries should play a role in this effort. As a solution to global inequality, however, it is a different story, particularly in a world still dominated by capitalist markets. Harvard academic, George Borjas, simulated models to enquire how wages could be equalised in a free market world with completely free labour mobility. Such is the level of global inequality that he estimated that 2.6 billion workers from developing societies (or 96% out of a total labour force of 2.7 billion) would have to move to developed capitalist countries for global wages to be equalised.[53] Leaving aside the upheaval and multiple social and environmental problems for both developing societies and developed capitalist host countries, Borjas' exercise is an insight into what the free market would look like if taken to its logical extreme. In Europe, North America, Australia and Japan, where very small numbers of migrants and refugees have already fuelled historically deep-seated manifestations of racism, the notion of exporting hundreds of millions, let alone billions of low-waged or unemployed populations to solve income problems in developing societies is clearly dystopian.

From a purely market efficiency perspective, Borjas argues that moving billions of low-income people to high-income countries would result in migrants importing the very negative organisational and socio-cultural values that created poor economic conditions in developing countries in the first place. Note, he does not mention colonialism and imperialism as playing a large historical contributing factor to their existing conditions, nor does he blame the current global barriers to development operated by major capitalist countries. Dani Rodrik and Branko Milanovic also favour greater labour mobility through immigration but believe that national equality requires economic growth in developing societies.[54] How this capitalist domestic economic growth in developing societies can be generated and the consequences for a safe climate and environmental sustainability are not revealed in this policy scenario.

Advocates of post-carbon democracy and degrowth are also deeply divided on these issues. Many in affluent societies reject capitalist consumption and focus primarily on local issues or their own national problems. A certain proportion favour population controls on environmental grounds, rather than concerning themselves with detailed solutions to global inequality and refugees. Others try to simultaneously change local communities while pursuing conflict resolution and social justice for the poor in developing societies. Calls for global revolution continue to be made. Yet, environmentalists and radical socialists provide

---

53 George Borjas, 'Immigration and Globalization: A Review Essay', *Journal of Economic Literature*, vol. 53, no. 4, December 2015, pp.961-74.

54 Dani Rodrik, *Is Global Equality the Enemy of National Equality?* January 2017, see Dani Rodrik's weblog, rodrik.typepad.com.

few clear and persuasive policies that link the possibility of post-capitalist democracy to the resolution of the burning issues of transmigration, global inequality and environmentally sustainable alternatives to capitalist growth.

2. Can consumers replace factories?

If resolving global inequality of wages is not on the mainstream political agenda, what about increased consumption enabling developing societies to skip the industrial stage? There are three broad conceptions of consumption: first, increasing growth through consumer capitalism; second, a variation of private and public sector consumption mainly supported by Keynesians and post-Keynesians who favour increased public services and employment rather than heavy reliance on consumer capitalism as the driver of aggregate demand; third, ecological sustainability or degrowth as an alternative to existing conceptions of consumption (see Chapter Five for a discussion of degrowth).

Turning to consumer capitalism, market optimists such as Tomáš Hellebrandt and Paolo Mauro do not discuss the possibility of skipping stages but imply that economic development will thrive via what they see as an explosion of consumers by 2035. According to their projections,

> ...the number of people earning between US$1,144 and US$3,252 per year in 2013 prices in PPP terms will increase by around 500 million, with the largest gains in Sub-Saharan Africa and India; the number of people earning between US$3,252 and US$8,874 per year in 2013 prices will increase by almost 1 billion, with the largest gains in India and Sub-Saharan Africa; and the number of people earning more than US$8,874 per year will increase by 1.2 billion, with the largest gains in China and the advanced economies.[55]

Whether these new consumers will obtain their income from manufacturing, mining, agriculture, or from services is not clear. It is also entirely unclear how greater domestic consumption can be self-generating for low and middle-income countries in the absence of export-income, or new domestic service industries and larger public sectors driven by higher borrowing or taxes. How can very poor households obtain credit finance

---

55 Tomáš Hellebrandt and Paolo Mauro, *The Future of Worldwide Income Distribution*, Peterson Institute for International Economics, April 2015, p.4.

for higher consumption given their existing low incomes of US$1 to $5 per day? Also, how can governments and businesses borrow from international financiers given their existing debt levels and their present inability to fund new infrastructure and services? Should they manage to borrow additional funds, how can a consumption-generated leapfrog-ging of industrialisation avoid a balance of payments crisis, debt-default and other calamities in the absence of massive foreign aid? Crucially, even Hellebrandt and Mauro concede that the Gini coefficient of global inequality (the lower the number, the less inequality) will only decline marginally from 65 in 2013 to 61 in 2035, still much higher than very unequal countries such as the US with a Gini coefficient of 40.5 in 2013. Critics of the Gini coefficient such as Robert Wade also argue that this relative measurement fails to reveal the real level of inequality.[56] Equally importantly, Hellebrandt and Mauro acknowledge that increased con-sumption will have serious negative impacts on natural resources but say nothing about this massive problem.

It is not surprising that most mainstream political economic debates tend to ignore the majority of developing societies and instead focus overwhelmingly on the prospects of G20 countries. These major cap-italist countries, including members of the G20 classified as 'emerging markets', account for over 80% of global GDP. There is little or no discussion of leapfrogging the industrial stage for G20 countries. The nearest one comes to this issue is whether India and other countries can generate sufficient exports in services given that few if any countries in the future will replicate China and 'Factory Asia'. In a 2016 report, McKin-sey and Co sub-divided new consumers into nine urban demographic groups ranging in ages from under 14 to over 75 and spread across all developed and developing countries. They project that over 70% of new consumption by 2030 will occur in developed capitalist countries and amongst urban consumers in China. Poor regions with large populations such as South Asia, South-East Asia and Sub-Saharan Africa would only increase consumption by small amounts of 6.60%, 4.98% and 3.56% respectively.[57] In other words, conventional consumption will be too low to leapfrog industrialisation in low and middle-income countries.

We thus live in a world where images of the mass expansion of cap-italist consumerism go hand-in-hand with persistent high inequality and environmental destruction. This is particularly true of prominent

56 Robert Wade, 'Our misleading measure of income and wealth inequality: the standard Gini coefficient', *Triple Crisis*, 6 May 2013.

57 Richard Dobbs et al, *Urban World: The Global Consumers to Watch*, McKinsey Global Institute, April 2016, p.7.

G20 members such as the BRICS countries (Brazil, Russia, India, China and South Africa) and Indonesia, Argentina, Mexico and Turkey where combatting poverty through non-market policies is unfortunately given very low priority by governments. In Chapter Five, I will discuss the different component elements of household consumption (durable and non-durable goods as well as services) and why conventional consumption has to be abandoned in favour of new sustainable combinations of goods and services.

3. New technology solutions

Apart from the huge populations of poor people in large G20 developing countries, it is sobering to remember that more than 600 million people live in small developing societies. The prospects of these societies successfully combatting poverty and inequality by skipping the industrial stage are no better than their failure to escape low to middle-income status for the past seventy years. Premature deindustrialisation combined with inadequate education systems and insufficient national income all constitute major domestic roadblocks to sustained socio-economic development. Alongside low-wage manufacturing, agriculture and mining sectors, their service sectors are often based on unregulated 'informal sectors' with highly exploitative labour conditions and corrupt political institutions. This does not deter neo-Schumpeterians such as Leonardo Burlamaqui, Rainer Kattel[58] and Carlotta Perez[59] or technological utopians like Jeremy Rifkin from creating images of leapfrogging old industrial models of development on the road to a market-based high-tech, well-paid 'green growth' economy.

There is no doubt that new technologies such as mobile phones are helping leapfrog old communication systems. Or, as Rifkin argues,

> ...the electrification of the developing world makes it possible to power 3-D printers and for distributed manufacturing to proliferate. In poor urban outskirts, isolated towns and rural locales – where infrastructure is scant, access to capital spotty at best and technical expertise, tools and machinery virtually non-existent

---

58 Leonardo Burlamaqui and Rainer Kattel, 'Development as leapfrogging, not convergence, not catch-up: towards schumpeterian theories of finance and development', *Review of Political Economy*, vol.28, no.2, 2016, pp. 270-288.

59 Carlota Perez, *A Green and Socially Equitable Direction for the ICT Paradigm*, Chris Freeman Memorial Lecture GLOBELICS 2012, Hangzhou, P.R. China, Revised and updated March 2014.

– 3-D-printing provides a desperately needed opportunity for building a Third Industrial Revolution infrastructure.[60]

It is also true that all kinds of visionary and tantalising innovations in the areas of essential needs (water, energy, transport, food production) or health, education, housing and social welfare could dramatically alter the conditions of everyday life for billions of poor people. In fact, without the introduction of new innovative technologies, the task of solving a multitude of social problems will be much harder. However, many technological proposals to leapfrog industrialisation are often disconnected from political power relations and the realities of deep-seated inequality and deprivation. The importation of high technology, for instance, will do little to benefit the majority of people in developing societies without first overcoming appalling authoritarian regimes, entrenched domestic class privilege and corruption; all factors requiring major political change. Regrettably, most G20 governments are more interested in arms sales and advancing their geo-political interests rather than supporting the removal of authoritarian and corrupt political allies or puppet regimes.

Leapfrogging strategies such as the importation of new technology particularly fail to address the pressing issues of whether growth from high technology or increased numbers of consumers can effectively be decoupled from the depletion and destruction of finite natural resources, as I will explore in the next chapter. Other than pursuing self-sufficiency, these high-tech strategies also say little about how developing societies can sustain and grow their national incomes, especially given that global financial, trade and market barriers have been so effective in preventing middle-income countries from becoming high-income societies.

High technology is a double-edged sword. On the one hand, it is quite possible that new technology could help foster local production and eventually erode or make redundant trade barriers erected by developed industrial powers. On the other hand, in developing societies with massive unemployment, the introduction of labour saving technology could also exacerbate poverty without national government counter-strategies to simultaneously increase essential health and education 'social state' services as well as infrastructure such as housing, water, energy and transport. It is still too early to ascertain whether new technology can assist in the partial or full leapfrogging of old industrialisation strategies. Without a transformation in the quality and quantity of foreign aid

---

60 Jeremy Rifkin, 'How Developing Nations Can Leapfrog Developed Countries with the Sharing Economy', *The Huffington Post*, 2 November, 2015.

from developed capitalist countries (especially much existing aid that is wasteful or benefits businesses and corrupt governments rather than poor people), the vast majority of poor countries lack the financial means to import these technologies. Should this foreign aid be forthcoming in future years, if it is not combined with the radical political overhaul of existing authoritarian and corrupt regimes, the application of innovative schemes will fail to reach their full potential.

4. Illusions of self-sufficiency

Whether utilising various market mechanisms or promoting statist conceptions of post-capitalism, it is not enough to be narrowly focused on immediate problems. Policy analysts and social movements also need goals and a sense of direction. Note that many socialists and greens have long had predominantly static conceptions of a post-capitalist society. These future imaginary socialist or environmentally sustainable societies are frequently conceived of as being free of class-conflict and undemocratic politics. For many socialists, wealth is imagined as having already been redistributed in a planned economy. Simultaneously, the alienation pervading capitalism is somehow relegated to history with all the negative social consequences of competitive individualism making way for co-operation in an egalitarian society. Many greens are just as utopian and imagine decentralised, face-to-face sustainable communities, living at one with nature and obliterating the waste and destructiveness of growth-obsessed consumer capitalism. Other socialists and greens, however, do not see post-capitalism as the 'end of politics' or the 'end of social conflict and change', but rather envisage open-ended projects to be constructed by active individuals and groups. Instead of some mythical return to an authentic human nature, post-capitalist societies are conceived as inaugurating the first historical phase of 'conscious' participatory democracy, in contrast to all hitherto existing repressive societies, where tiny minorities make decisions and policies 'behind the backs' of the population: a feature of societies whether they have been called feudal, capitalist or one party Communist states.

What is the urgent relevance of whether socialists or greens conceive their future societies in static, harmonious terms, or as the dawn of a dynamic, creative era? Any move toward developing a post-carbon democracy or post-growth society, that is, a society not based on the idea of 'steady-state' harmony or planned equilibrium, requires addressing which social and economic institutions or community structures are capable of new forms of innovation to meet unforseen social and environmental challenges. Also, moving away from export-led or consumption-led growth typically used in capitalist societies requires alternative models of political economy suitable for post-capitalist social formations.

It could be argued by radical environmentalists that importing new technology would enable countries to disengage from the global economy and become self-sufficient societies rather than high-income economies. This is certainly a technical possibility, especially for a number of naturally well-endowed countries in the short-term. However, most self-sufficiency models ignore the problem of overcoming technological stagnation, once new technology became obsolete and domestic levels of specialised knowledge and lack of export-income proved inadequate to sustain standards of living. In a post-carbon world, it is assumed that some form of information and cultural exchange between diverse societies would continue through the internet and perhaps other media. It is entirely unclear how supposedly self-sufficient, post-capitalist democratic societies could satisfy most citizens able to see higher standards of living enjoyed in other countries, especially the desire for foreign products (either not affordable or available) if imports have largely ceased. Few alternative communes in the past have been able to reproduce the toil and enthusiasm of the original founders, and in current alternative green or socialist models, this problem could be magnified. As the post-World War One song asked: 'how ya gonna keep 'em down on the farm after they've seen Paree'?

Semi-autarky or substantial rather than full self-sufficiency is difficult but possible with controlled levels of imports and balancing increased local production of needs. However, in my view, the aim of *full* self-sufficiency would be a regressive step, largely closing off the external world. An alternative self-sufficient society would not survive long as a democracy, or self-sufficiency itself would not last within a democratic framework where citizens desired material exchanges with other countries.

Any self-sufficient society, even one substantially based on rural/agricultural life and rejecting capitalist consumer growth values, would still need to ensure the viability of urban residents (constituting the majority of the world's population) unable to fully produce their own sustenance. Increasing urban food production in transformed green cities, in combination with less reliance on foreign imports are indeed possible future options. Yet, it is not only the lack of food security that is very worrying in this scenario. Over 80% of global populations currently live in countries unable to fully provide local needs or renew vital resources without imports. Hence, there is a high likelihood of increased poverty and political conflict in many societies unable to become self-sufficient. Rather than think of self-sufficiency in all sectors of production – from food to minerals and high technology goods – it is more helpful to identify which parts of production and consumption in a particular society could or could not become self-sufficient. For example, we know that the more energy and a range of goods are produced locally, the less is lost or wasted through transmission and transport. Even if we allowed for reduced material consumption and radical organisational innovations and production techniques to enhance self-sufficiency, these might possibly reduce the 80% of global populations currently not self-sufficient to perhaps 50% or 30% of people in the world. Unfortunately, at this stage it is guesswork as to a possible reduction of import-dependent populations. Even realising the best-case scenario would still leave billions of people unable to be self-sufficient and reliant on varying levels of external resources.

Advocates of self-sufficiency and stateless local communes, especially in affluent countries, promote so-called universally applicable ideas that have little chance of being sustainable in all parts of the world. Equally importantly, the illusion of self-sufficiency is quite threatening to the current welfare of billions of people lacking the environmental and technical resources to provide anything but the most meagre forms of subsistence for themselves.

Defenders of self-reliant communities like environmentalist George Monbiot, argue that these communities (rather than atomised large societies) will be more sympathetic to helping desperate refugees fleeing their environmentally degraded homelands.[61] This may well be the case for a certain proportion of self-sufficient communes, depending on their caring values and available natural resources. Currently, about 3% or 225 million of the global population of 7.6 billion live in countries where they were not born (and many of these were not refugees). It is most doubtful that self-sufficient communities would cope with an additional 5% to 10% of the impending 9 billion global population by 2050 (an extra 450 to 900 million people) possibly forced to flee their uninhabitable home regions or countries due to war, poverty and current and future climate catastrophes.

Only significant multi-government intervention to ensure a safe climate, conflict resolution and major foreign aid can prevent these potential unfolding human and environmental catastrophes. Currently, 'public goods' aid from OECD countries primarily takes the form of aid to refugees in donor countries (rather than aid to the source of refugees

---

61   George Monbiot, 'On Neoliberalism: "A self-serving racket", *Verso Blog*, 15 March, 2017.

in poor countries), as well as narcotics control, infectious disease control, peace-keeping, dealing with HIV/AIDS, or environmental management and clean energy generation.[62] We are yet to see trillion dollar 'public goods aid' in the form of mass housing, public health and education facilities, clean running water, sewage systems and electricity for all, just to name a few areas of desperate need without which food production, employment and income will be severely constrained.

Those who believe that export-led industrialisation can be skipped through mass immigration, adopting consumer-led development, implementing advanced new technologies or pursuing full self-sufficiency are delusionary. Some aspects of these latter solutions may work, but only in combination with massive external aid. The possibility of multi-government intervention, in turn depends on the rise of new forms of national and supranational democratic political economies in combination with reinvigorated decentralised local public institutions, rather than the illusion of stateless, self-sufficient communities.

Export-led Growth, 'Peak Trade' and Environmental Challenges

It is difficult to shake the faith that many policy-makers have in international trade and export-led industrialising strategies. Those who want 'grasshopper' countries to become savers and imitate exporting 'ants', or others who worry about how developing societies can escape the 'middle-income trap' and premature de-industrialisation, as well as those who advocate an end to low growth and neo-liberal austerity via co-ordinated mission-orientated innovation, all assume that export-led growth is one of the key paths to future problem-solving. Yet, it is highly possible that we have already reached 'peak trade' and this is without even taking into account threats of trade wars and the future impact on global trade of policies to combat climate change and natural resources depletion.

In recent years, the IMF, the World Trade Organisation and numerous other analysts of the centrality of trade to capitalist globalisation have all expressed deep concern that trade has ceased growing at former rates. Even in the mainstream *Time Magazine*, Rana Foroohar sums up these broad concerns:

Until the financial crisis of 2008, global trade grew twice as fast

---

62 For figures, see Robin Davies, *Public enemies: the role of global public goods in aid policy narratives*, Development Policy Centre Discussion Paper 57, Australian National University, March 2017.

as the global economy itself. ...According to the World Trade Organisation, average global trade flows grew around 10% a year from 1949 to 2008. But those numbers slumped to 1.3% from 2009 to 2015 and show no signs of picking up, even as the global economy has partially recovered from recession. Meanwhile, flows of financial capital have become balkanised – which is to say that after decades of coming closer together, global markets and banking systems are pulling apart. While cross-border goods, services and financial flows represented 53% of the world economy in 2007, they are a mere 39% now. And there is a drastic political pushback against the free flow of people across national-borders – globalisation at its most human.[63]

The IMF is also alarmed at the fall in 85% of product lines of traded goods since 2011 due to a range of factors, especially weak economies.[64] Linked to related deep concerns with the prolonged decline in productivity,[65] the IMF places its hope in kick-starting growth and trade with typical neo-liberal additional measures. These include further trade liberalisation – something that major economic powers have not been able to agree upon for years. Another indicator of the concern by free marketeers about 'the end of the liberal order' is that between 2008 and 2018 there has been a doubling of outstanding cases with the World Trade Organisation (about 50,000 cases) of complaints against member states introducing all sorts of restrictions in the form of non-tariff measures and anti-dumping duties.[66]

The decline in trade growth takes on new significance when combined with the fact that in recent years China has accounted for almost 40% of world GDP growth dwarfing the US at only one fourth of China's contribution.[67] China's contribution to global growth has been 50% larger than the combined contribution of America, Europe and Japan! However, regarding trade, as opposed to growth of total world GDP, the EU was the largest global importer and exporter of goods in 2015 accounting for 36.2% of imported merchandise goods (down from 45% in 2003) and 37.3% of merchandise exports (down from 45.9% in 2003) compared with Asia 34.2% (up from 26.1% in 2003)

63 Rana Foroohar, 'We've Reached the End of Global Trade', *Time*, 12 October, 2016.
64 IMF, *Global Trade: What's Behind the Slowdown?*, International Monetary Fund, October 2016, p.65.
65 Gustavo Adler et.al, *Gone with the Headwinds: Global Productivity*, International Monetary Fund, April 2017
66 See 'The end of liberal order', *Macquarie Wealth Management Research*, 28 March, 2018.
67 Stephen Roach, 'Global Growth – Still made in China', *Project Syndicate*, 29 August 2016.

and North America at 14.4%.[68] It is an illusion to think that trade liberalisation could dramatically boost world trade as long as the EU and
other important trading regions are unable to overcome their sclerotic,
stagnant low-growth domestic economies.

Whether 'peak trade' has been reached is by no means an established
fact. Those who disagree, point to the cyclical economic downturn in
OECD countries since 2007, with corresponding falls in oil and commodity prices that they hope will eventually turn the corner.[69] Conversely,
advocates of 'peak trade' cite the widespread falls in productivity, the
onset of stagnation, high debt and the limits to credit-fuelled household
consumption as all contributing to reduced import levels. Although
world trade has returned to modest growth figures in 2017/2018, it is still
substantially below the growth figures achieved before 2008.[70]Moreover,
the inability of services to generate as much export-growth as manufacturing and natural resources affects trade levels. Nonetheless, there are
other compelling reasons to suggest that former trade growth rates may
be very hard to revive. First, natural resources constitute almost 20% of
merchandise trade and *fossil fuels make up almost 80% of natural resources
exports and imports*. This level of trade simply cannot continue if carbon
emissions are reduced either gradually or drastically in coming years.
There will be extremely serious consequences for 21 countries that have
80% of their exports made up of natural resources.[71]

For leading producers of goods and services, the future need to
switch to renewable energy will affect each country in different ways
depending on their capacity to reduce renewable energy costs in production, transport and other sectors thereby minimising loss of export
competitiveness. Shipping, for example, accounts for about 2% of
global carbon emissions apart from its massive contribution to ocean
pollution. Currently, thousands of ageing ships are registered in poorly
regulated countries such as Panama, Liberia and the Marshall Islands.
Employing low-wage crew such as about 250,000 from the Philippines
alone, shipping owners and governments from major trading nations
have resisted the International Maritime Organisation's call to modernise ships so they run on liquefied gas (still emitting carbon emissions) or
wind power. Should modernisation and regulation succeed, the cost will
amount to hundreds of billions of dollars and moreover will lift freight

68   World Trade Organization, *World Trade Statistical Review 2016*, pp.92-93.
69   See Ian Tomb and Kamakshya Trivedi, "Peak trade' is premature', *Vox*, 6 January, 2017.
70   See *World Trade Outlook Indicator*, World Trade Organization, February 2018.
71   Michele Ruta and Anthony J. Venables, *International trade in natural resources: practice and policy*, World Trade Organisation, Working Paper ERSD-2012-07, March 2012.

107

or export costs significantly. Without these reforms, carbon emissions from shipping are projected to increase to 17% of global emissions by 2050. [72] However, these projections are unlikely to eventuate if trade continues to stagnate and decline.

Secondly, if the uptake of new technology such as 3-D printing escalates, the upswing in local production will cut the need for imports and shift total global production away from current export leaders such as Germany, China and so forth. It is unclear if these new technologies will undermine regional value chains spread over various countries or whether the market dominance of existing multinational corporations will survive relatively unaffected. The crucial challenges posed by climate change and finite natural resources will not be simply whether new technology *reverses* decades of 'offshoring' production to Asian and other developing countries. Rather, it will be whether the need to secure a safe climate also leads to tariffs and other cost penalties on fossil fuels and manufactured exports such as chemical products containing fossil fuels. If so, will these penalties and restrictions curb global trade growth and alter the relationship between developed and developing countries in ways that are currently unforseen?

Conventional debates on export-led strategies concentrate on all the government and private factors such as infrastructure, educational levels, financial resources, currency and wage rates or technological innovation that enhance or impede trade. Most businesses, governments and consultancy firms have yet to fully comprehend that this old way of thinking about production and trade has been rendered environmentally unsustainable in the medium to long run. Crucially, the past seventy years has taught us a very clear lesson: export-led growth strategies have been overwhelming failures for all but a handful of low and middle-income countries. Given that most countries will not be able to imitate China, South Korea and a few others, it is imperative that export-led market strategies be abandoned in favour of domestic development, assisted by foreign aid that focuses on providing employment through the provision of essential social infrastructure and services. In the short to medium term, this strategy would entail shifting policies away from an emphasis on market-driven consumption-led investment that primarily benefits high-income minorities in developing countries. Instead, what is required is raising the standard of living, education and elementary facilities for the majority of low-income populations.

---

72 Marin Cames et al, *Emission Reduction Targets for International Aviation and Shipping*, European Parliament's Committee on Environment, Public Health and Food Safety, Brussels, November 2015.

Direct Government Action and Regional Pacts

In later chapters, I will discuss more fully the relationship between future economic development and environmental constraints. In the meantime, it is important to briefly note how trade and development strategies are affected by both authoritarian and parliamentary systems. It is possible to identify non-market policies on climate change that vary according to whether they are advocated by pro-market conservatives as opposed to radical Left and green movements in OECD countries, and also whether they are proposed and implemented by authoritarian governments in countries without free elections such as China. An example of conservative direct action is the Australian government's 'direct action' (since 2014) under the Abbott and Turnbull Right-wing governments. In reality, it is legislation designed by a government wishing to protect the fossil fuels industries. It is a 'greenwash' gift to polluters, an expensive public relations act that avoids and delays deep cuts to carbon emissions.

By contrast, the inadequate character of market solutions has led to various Green and Red direct action policies. These radical proposals of direct action concede some room for market solutions but are overwhelmingly geared to emergency action. Preventing climate change is conceived along war lines and emphasis is placed on governments intervening directly in all forms of large-scale renewable energy, public transport, new green R &D and many other aspects necessary to construct a 'new economy'. Planning is given high priority rather than leaving mitigation to the relaxed and comfortable, but contemptible obstructive pace of market forces.[73] Penalties are advocated for fossil fuels via stringent regulatory measures to decommission fossil-energy power stations, reduce fossil fuel inputs into agriculture and ban various types of deforestation and land clearing. In contrast to conservative forms of 'direct action', these 'direct' policies prioritise a safe climate over a profitable future.

Part of the non-market solution to carbon emissions involves carbon rationing, thus directly affecting market forces and household consumption via restraints on the consumer economy. Direct action proposals also challenge fossil fuel exports and imports through the imposition of carbon trade sanctions and tariffs and quotas. How these extensive non-market mitigation processes could be enacted without the mass support of electorates in parliamentary democracies or the overturning of World Trade Organisation rules is the unanswered question here.

---

73 A good example of direct emergency action is David Spratt and Philip Sutton, *Climate Code Red the case for emergency action*, Scribe Books, Melbourne, 2008, Part Three.

Given that hostile business groups would mobilise massive resources and wage a virulent campaign to defeat any such emergency measures, the alternative would have to be a replication of an all-party 'wartime' cabinet to impose such dramatic policies. Excluding climate catastrophes, the likelihood in the next decade of either democratic support or an all-party 'war' cabinet adopting radical decarbonisation is currently remote.

No such concerns for the electorate affects direct action policies in countries with authoritarian regimes. This is particularly evident in newly industrialised countries like China, where a broader environmental agenda beyond decarbonisation preoccupies government policies. Given the shocking levels of air pollution,[74] degradation of land and rivers and numerous other environmental hazards from toxic waste and polluting production processes, the Chinese and other governments in Asia, Africa and Latin America are slowly recognising that direct government action may be necessary to curb private and state-owned enterprises for the sake of public health and economic productivity.[75] If decarbonisation through green technology simultaneously reduces emissions and helps restore polluted environments, then this strategy will be imposed by government diktat. However, authoritarian governments are far less powerful than is often imagined. China is the world's largest emitter of dangerous greenhouse gases but the Chinese central government relies heavily on regional and local authorities to implement central directives. These are often undermined by corruption or exaggerated claims to have fulfilled planning targets. We simply do not know the real state of decarbonisation or what may be inflated Chinese public relations claims about moving from the old 'industrial civilisation' to 'ecological civilisation' articulated in the 13th Five Year Plan (2016-2021).[76]

Authoritarian regimes are not immune to competing interests and must juggle these pressures even without the obstacles of free elections.[77] On the one hand, their own populations are increasingly upset at everything from the health costs of immense urban pollution, to dangerous toxins

---

74 Alex Wang, Orville Schell, Elizabeth Economy, Michael Zhao, James Fallows, Dorinda Elliott, *Airpocalypse Now: China's Tipping Point? A ChinaFile Conversation*, Asia Society, February 6, 2013.

75 For an overview of the the state of the environment in China, see Judith Shapiro, *China's Environmental Challenges*, Polity, Cambridge, 2012.

76 See Melbourne Sustainable Society Institute, *A new starting point: China's eco-civilisation and climate action post-Paris*, Briefing Paper 6, MSSI, University of Melbourne, June 2016.

77 Arthur Mol, 'Chinese Sustainability in Transition: Which direction to take?' *in* Michael Redclift, Delyse Springett (eds.), *Routledge International Handbook of Sustainable Development*, Routledge, New York, 2015, ch.23 and Mark Beeson, 'The coming of environmental authoritarianism', *Environmental Politics*, vol.19, no.2, 2010, pp. 276–294.

in food production and general environmental degradation. Countering this is the demand of domestic and foreign investors concerned that non-market measures and increased environmental protection will reduce profitability and thus affect the rate of economic growth. Dealing with international carbon treaty negotiations is relatively easy in comparison to negotiating the contradictory demands of a 'strong and healthy nation' on the one hand and 'strong and powerful economic growth' on the other.[78] Whether developing countries can 'skip a stage' and move directly to low carbon production will depend on the mindset of authoritarian rulers, international pressure, the depth and extent of environmental and human damage from climate change, and the ability to control the direction of foreign investment and domestic business activity. In dozens of countries such as Indonesia, Pakistan, Mexico, India, Nigeria, Brazil or Russia, widespread corruption and violation of sustainable environmental development goals go hand in hand with the outright failure of governments to prevent environmental destruction by regulating unacceptable foreign and domestic business practices.

In the era of globalisation, many radicals have misconceptions about the existence of a 'global ruling class'.[79] Not only is there no cohesive 'global class', but also there is no global state that can enforce the will of any so-called 'global ruling class'. Some argue that the prevention of dangerous global warming would be much easier to achieve if only one government ruled the world. Such an undemocratic 'top-down' administrative nightmare remains the fantasy of authoritarians and technocrats. Unfortunately, the real world is no less nightmarish, as it is riven by deep regional and global military and strategic political economic tensions. The misconception made by those who believe in the existence of a 'global capitalist class' is to assume that the old US deployment of military and foreign policy strategy to ensure a world safe for capitalist trade and investment *is* the model imitated by other states, whether China, Russia, Japan, Iran, Saudi Arabia, through to India, Nigeria or Brazil. Some of these ruling classes may want the protective umbrella of US power because they are too weak to go it alone on the global or regional stage. Others pursue their own political agendas which corporations must accept if they wish to keep their investments viable. It is this divided world that affects the contradictory pace and scale of industrialisation, decarbonisation and trade strategies.

---

78 See for example, panel report *'What Action Is China Taking on Climate Change?'*, Environmental and Energy Study Institute and the China FAQs Project of the World Resources Institute, July 14, 2015.

79 Leslie Sklair, *The transnational capitalist class*, Blackwell, Oxford, 2001.

Even though the European Union constitutes the largest regional market in the world, its fractious member states may not agree on future deep decarbonisation strategies. Like many other countries in the Asian-Pacific and African regions, the member states of the EU are torn between maintaining their military alliances with the US while not jeopardising their investment and trade interests with both the US and China. Consequently, in recent years we have witnessed the possible development of new blocs. These include the formation of new regional free trade pacts and investment coalitions such as the rejigged Trans Pacific Partnership (minus the US after being rejected by President Trump). Initially formed by the US and allies, the TPP excludes China and omits the other BRICS countries as well as South Korea. Meanwhile, the Chinese-driven Asian Infrastructure Investment Bank excludes the US, Japan and Canada but includes leading EU countries as well as Australia, South Korea, Saudi Arabia and other US military allies. Like the Trans-Pacific Partnership, it remains to be seen whether the proposed Transatlantic-Trade and Investment Partnership between the US and the EU ever re-emerges and becomes operational. If so, it would exclude all other states and business rivals outside the US and EU. A number of countries are members of more than one of these proposed or actual regional supranational and business coalitions. Given the widespread opposition to these Trans-Pacific and Trans-Atlantic trade pacts by many social, labour and business organisations, it is currently unclear whether they will be ratified, modified or abandoned.

The dramatic implications for climate breakdown and environmental depletion flowing from these developing regional blocs can be seen, for example, in China's massive 'One, Belt, One Road' ('Silk Road') infrastructure proposal. This proposal is the greatest development project in human history and aims to create a complex new Eurasian economic zone linking Central Asian, South Asian and Middle Eastern countries to Europe and North Asia via numerous rail, road and marine ports and industrial developments. If fully completed, it may either consolidate market forces or lead to European and Asian countries adopting significantly new modes of internal and external social and political relations with one another. These hypothetical future outcomes are overshadowed by the division within EU countries over whether 'One, Belt, One Road' constitutes a threat or an opportunity. Similar concerns are expressed by the other major Asian powers such as India and Japan, who fear Chinese expansion and its massive leverage of power in the Asian-Pacific region. Nevertheless, India, Pakistan and other Asian, Middle Eastern and Central Asian countries are hedging their bets by attending the Shanghai

Cooperative Association (founded in 1996 by China and Russia) as new members or observers of a powerful bloc which rivals the G7 Western powers.

Crucially, 'One Belt, One Road' and the other major free trade pacts are being proposed or established with minimal concern for environmental sustainability and global warming. The end result could well be an exacerbation of future environmental disasters. Despite governments paying lip-service to environmental values, it is most unlikely that these regional and global trade developments can be successful and at the same time decarbonise and decouple economic growth in order to preserve fragile ecosystems. The architects of these new trade blocs are not only environmentally short sighted, but also reflect the desperate desire of so many businesses and governments to do anything to sustain or revive economic growth. It is also possible that if 'peak trade' does become a reality rather than a snapshot of what may only be a temporary downturn, then the massive construction of new ports, railways and other infrastructure may turn out to be underused or obsolete white elephants.

Conclusion

This Chapter has argued that long-held development models based on modernisation as industrialisation have not only failed to end global and domestic inequality but have produced even higher levels of social injustice. Alternative domestic political movements must reject export-led industrialisation that is largely incompatible with global decarbonisation targets and finite natural resources. Instead, political development strategies should aim to cultivate only those necessary forms of limited industrialisation geared where possible to the provision of domestic production needs as well as renewable energy, housing, public transport and various other necessary infrastructure and social facilities. This is not a strategy of self-sufficiency but rather one that combines domestic priorities with international exchanges in order to shift the emphasis away from export-dependent market development. Most countries cannot become export tigers. Such a social strategy will encounter much opposition from many domestic and foreign businesses long committed to promoting private market growth. The old political economic models and policies – including those driven by private capitalist investment, World Bank and other market institutional modernisation goals for developing societies, or labour and social democratic wage-led and consumption-led increases in aggregate demand – all need to be reconceived or replaced. Similarly, naïve beliefs in stateless forms of local self-sufficiency are equally inadequate and delusional as solutions to the magnitude of the systemic socio-economic and ecological crises we confront.

3

Banking on Decoupling: Politics, Technology and Ecosystems

Capitalist societies face a situation where the implementation of familiar crisis-management policies by governments and central banks are becoming less and less effective. To add to the worries of defenders of capitalist markets, a minority of far-sighted business and political leaders now recognise that decarbonisation and the switch to renewable energy constitutes only a very small part of the solution to ongoing environmental crises. These business leaders and policy makers now believe and hope that science and technology will make it possible to avoid the need for profound social reform, thus enabling capitalist economies to overcome the 'natural limits to growth'. How feasible is decoupling economic growth from nature and other radical technological solutions to natural constraints? Will they simply sustain existing levels of inequality or provide affluent material standards of living for the vast majority of humanity currently mired in poverty and deprivation? Radical socialists and technological utopians may espouse oppositional social agendas, but they also share with corporations and defenders of capitalism a strong faith in the power of science to reconstitute nature. I will discuss the Left Prometheans in the next chapter.

In the meantime, the rate of decarbonisation continues to create numerous disagreements among businesses and political groups. It is no secret that political parties and business groups are divided over whether moderate decarbonisation strategies are necessary and affordable, let alone emergency measures. Even the internal political struggles within the fossil-fuels sector (coal, oil, gas) is leading to divisions whereby oil and gas companies jettison coal as the sacrificial lamb in order to preserve other fossil fuels. Coal is still heavily used in economically powerful Asian countries such as India, Japan, China and South Korea and phasing it out in less than 15 to 20 years will be difficult.

This chapter will first examine some of the political and economic strategies that businesses and governments are likely to adopt in dealing with the relatively easier goal of decarbonisation. Secondly, I will then go on to discuss the technological, political and social complexities of the highly ambitious goal of absolute decoupling of economic growth from nature.

Decarbonisation and the 'Political Aspects of Innovation'

Most national governments and parties favour varying degrees of defence of existing fossil fuel industries while at the same time, phasing in post-carbon energy systems and carbon neutral industries. This is combined in many countries with the development of infrastructure for 'green cities'. Recently, there have been quite different approaches taken to 'disruptive innovation' in the area of low-carbon energy transformation. Analysts and policy makers are divided between those who pursue 'Schumpeterian' business approaches to innovation and others who see energy transformation in larger socio-political terms.[1] Many businesses are mainly interested in new niche product markets and 'disruptive' technologies to enhance profitability or their own survival. Policy analysts, on the other hand, argue that renewable energy and new technologies cannot be understood adequately at the level of the firm or corporation without grasping the larger systemic social and political aspects of decarbonisation.

In contrast to these debates over energy transformation, post-Keynesian Jerry Courvisanos, rather than turning to Schumpeter, has instead applied the insights of Polish political economist, Michal Kalecki,[2] on the 'political aspects of full employment' to what he calls the 'political aspects of innovation'.[3] Although he has not produced a detailed

---

1   See for example, Charlie Wilson and David Tyfield, 'Critical perspectives on disruptive innovation and energy transformation', an introduction to contributors in the special issue of *Energy Research & Social Science*, vol.37, 2018, pp.211-15.

2   Michal Kalecki, 'Political Aspects of Full Employment', *Political Quarterly*, no.4, October 1943, pp.322-330.

3   J. Courvisanos, 'Optimise versus satisfice: Two approaches to an investment policy for sustainable development', in R.F. Holt, S. Pressman and C.L. Spash (eds.), *Post Keynesian and Ecological Economics: Confronting Environmental Issues*, Edward Elgar, Cheltenham, 2009, pp. 279-300 and J. Courvisanos, 'Political aspects of innovation', *Research Policy*, vol. 38, 2009, pp. 1117–1124.

Kaleckian analysis of political divisions over 'green capitalism' and decarbonisation, Courvisanos argues that in recent decades capitalists have had *three fears* about innovation and each of these fears has instigated government attempts to alleviate these threats:

(i) Loss of economic control with respect to their individual market power as innovation encourages new entrants that have the potential to reduce the incumbents' market share and ability to control the market.... Governments have various innovation policies to support the incumbents; notably, R&D subsidies and tax concessions for incremental innovations, patent protection and other intellectual property rights.

(ii) Loss of policy control as innovation becomes distributed across society through the public institutions and public infrastructure that create the national innovation system. Governments have developed various strategies that support incumbents to regain some policy control, notably deregulation, privatisation, public–private infrastructure programs and public contracting.

(iii) Loss of industrial control of the workforce if governments maintain industrial relations policies that reflect the full employment-type high-union membership structure of the first 20 years after WWII. Governments have introduced new industrial relations policies aimed at supporting and encouraging 'flexibility' in the workplace in the name of innovation.[4]

Building on Courvisanos' analysis, it is possible to show why business leaders fear that government intervention to implement decarbonisation, given strong demands of climate justice for low-income people, could lead to expenditure and public investment in areas normally dominated by, or neglected by the private sector. If decarbonisation were linked to anti-austerity measures such as full employment, this could also deliver what businesses have always feared – the loss of what Kalecki argued was the disciplinary power over workers, namely, the threat of 'the sack'.[5]

---

4 Coursinavos, 'Political aspects of innovation', p.1121.

5 In his famous observation in 'Political Aspects of Full Employment', p.326, Kalecki argued that, "under a regime of permanent full employment, the 'sack' would cease to play its role as a disciplinary measure. The social position of the boss would be undermined, and the self-assurance and class-consciousness of the working class would grow. Strikes for wage increases and improvements in conditions of work would create political tension. It is true that profits would be higher under a regime of full employment than they are on the average under laissez-faire; ... But 'discipline in the factories' and 'political stability' are more appreciated than profits by business leaders. Their class instinct tells them that lasting full employment is unsound from their point of view, and that unemployment is an integral part of the 'normal' capitalist system."

Now, imagine the even greater and unforseen impact on profitability and threat to business survival arising from government intervention to prevent climate chaos. Just as businesses prefer lower profits to full employment, *many companies prefer to live with the risk of global warming* rather than face the consequences of government action on decarbonisation. This is a sobering realisation.

Nonetheless, there are also many other non-carbon-intensive businesses that have little or no fear of decarbonisation and indeed, as 'green innovators', welcome government policies that encourage 'green growth'. But, if we take Kalecki and Courvisanos to their logical conclusion, there are additional multiple political threats to the power of many private businesses that flow from decarbonisation. Past governments have often protected 'incumbents' in particular industries with a range of measures. This will prove to be much harder as governments are now increasingly pressured to decarbonise, not just particular enterprises but *whole societies*. Unsurprisingly, the result is widespread business angst and hostility, especially from those sectors least able to innovate and adjust to a low or post-carbon economy.

As no self-regulating market economy exists, and given that action to mitigate carbon emissions, or even a carbon emissions market requires some form of government legislation or regulation, the critical issue becomes: *how much higher are the global temperatures* that business and political leaders *are prepared to risk,* and what type of government 'green' policies are acceptable to old or new market forces? The answers will vary from country to country and will depend on three factors. First, the prevailing political culture and whether there is widespread support for government action on climate change or intense hostility to deep decarbonisation policies; second, the degree of authoritarian control or the level of democratic contestation of environmental policies; and third, a preference for either market-based solutions, or direct action in the form of legislation or decrees, or a hybrid mixture of market and government interventions. A majority of businesses in countries across the world are aware that each of these options either disadvantages their own business or disadvantages the interests of their national and international competitors.

Many business and political decision-makers are equally concerned that both national legislation and international mitigation treaties will almost certainly open the door to a range of other social and environmental demands. For example, even though a return to pre-1970s industrial relations is remote, it is politically possible that anti-austerity policies combatting precarious work, poor wages and unemployment could be legislated in future years, precisely during the same period where businesses were required to bear the additional costs of decarbonisation. It is the cumulative impact of environmental and socio-economic demands that will place increased pressures on profitability and shareholder value.

Hypothetically, if full decarbonisation were something that merely involved narrow technological adaptation without any other social, economic, political and environmental considerations and consequences, then many of the existing political divisions over climate change might disappear. However, in the real world, carbon mitigation involves social justice issues within and between developed and developing countries. It also necessitates new agricultural, urban and water policies, new trade and tax policies, new measures to raise massive amounts of finance for green industry and infrastructure, new crisis-management budgetary allocations to assist those businesses and communities affected by the reduction of fossil-fuel production, and new government measures to readjust economies from current high consumption levels to new forms of 'sustainable' production/consumption. These and a raft of other policy problems confront businesses and governments already saddled with high government and household debt, stagnant or low growth economies and inadequate public services. Instability and unpredictability are despised by both small and large businesses. Few if any governments welcome the challenge of decarbonisation, especially those elected governments facing angry and discontented business groups, the power of the fossil fuels lobby and fearful electorates.

Although renewable energy production has grown, the pro-fossil fuels International Energy Agency 2017 World Energy Outlook report forecasts that fossil fuels (coal, oil and gas) will still supply 75% of energy by 2040 – a decline of only 6% compared with 81% use in 2016.[6] Whether this forecast eventuates is highly speculative and depends on a range of political and financial factors such as the comparative cost of implementing renewable energy. Radical greens are justified in wanting emergency measures to deal with carbon emissions. Unfortunately, the moral and scientific case for emergency action fails to persuade most businesses and governments. The latter will never agree to drastic mitigation policies, unless there is a massive drop in the cost of renewable energy or an environmental catastrophe makes it impossible to halt mass demands for the reform of 'business as usual'. The latest climate change research throws serious doubt on the Paris 2015 agreement to limit the

---

6   International Energy Agency, *World Energy Outlook 2017*, OECD/IEA, Paris, November 2017, p.648.

global temperature increase to no more than 1.5°C.[7] This target may be near impossible, if such an increase is expected to take place as soon as between 2026 and 2030 while decarbonisation rates are not expected to fall significantly until well after 2030. Yet, in the absence of environmental catastrophe, many business and political leaders will fight strenuous battles to *prevent* greater state intervention necessary to achieve a safe climate in the *shortest time* possible.

As to advocates of moderate decarbonisation, a majority of businesses concede the potential threat of climate change. Regardless, many fear the broader socio-economic consequences of greater state intervention which deep decarbonisation requires. Some major carbon emitters will stall and adopt whatever measures are necessary to preserve their market share. Like tobacco companies, each decade that can be secured for 'business as usual' is worth the price of denial, deception and fraud.[8] When no accurate price is placed on the value of environmental resources, it is common for many businesses to squander and abuse non-renewable natural resources without facing any immediate negative impact on their balance sheets. Hence, socially responsible accounting reports are often meaningless examples of corporate 'greenwash'.

Even corporations committed to tackling climate breakdown can rely more on 'spin' than substantive change. In a study of managers and other decision-makers in 25 leading corporations to ascertain their commitment to decarbonisation, Christopher Wright and Daniel Nyberg demystify three prevalent myths in market societies: the myth of corporations as the saviours of the environment; the myth of 'corporate citizenship' as the moral leaders and 'representatives of the people' that gives 'us' a voice (which, however, can only be heard through consumption); and the myth of corporate omnipotence which renders them as efficient and capable of taming nature itself.[9] While Wright and Nyberg make many important observations as to why we should not rely on corporations to prevent dangerous climate change, their study remains somewhat limited in that it captures attitudes of corporations in Anglo-American countries rather than of those corporations in countries

---

7   For a survey or recent scientific research, see David Spratt, '1.5°C Just a Decade Away', *Break-through*, April 5, 2018.

8   For a survey of spin and deception in regard to corporate climate change action, see David Miller and William Dinan, 'Resisting meaningful action on climate change: Think tanks, 'merchants of doubt' and the 'corporate capture' of sustainable development' in Anders Hansen and Robert Cox (eds.) *The Routledge Handbook of Environment and Communication*, Routledge, New York, 2015, ch.7.

9   Christopher Wright and Daniel Nyberg, *Climate Change, Capitalism and Corporations: Processes of Creative Self-Destruction*, Cambridge University Press, Cambridge, 2015.

like Sweden, Germany or China where the political culture and state intervention demand deeper emissions cuts.

There are also many radical critics of capitalism who have an instrumental view of the relationship between business groups and state institutions. The tendency in many radical analyses of capitalism and climate change is to emphasise the way in which states help *reproduce* the prevailing conditions of capitalist production and social relations. The prevalent radical view of 'the state', as simply an instrument of capital or the 'executive committee' of diverse segments of capital, has never been able to explain adequately how it is that progressive social change has occurred in the past one hundred years. If the emphasis is exclusively on how states *reproduce* favourable conditions for capitalists, the role of political contestation is devalued and historical improvements in social conditions remains inadequately explained. It is no secret that anti-capitalist revolutionary and reform movements have suffered major defeats in many countries since the 1970s. But this does not justify seeing 'the state' as permanently, irredeemably, exclusively a tool of capital and unchangeable, not just in the area of environment policies but also in relation to political conflict over key social and economic issues.

One can never take politics out of climate change or assume that the vast range of quite different types of businesses have the same interests. Corporate responses to climate change cannot be reduced to one simple policy that requires an equally simple affirmative decision by governments. Hence, divisions and conflict are by-products of the multiple economic, legal, social and scientific aspects of ensuring comprehensive measures for a safe climate. Consequently, policy responses are likely to become much more fluid, urgent and unpredictable as existing and projected mitigation measures fail to arrest an increase in global temperatures. Political pressures will most certainly mount within the decade, as the mitigation commitments for 2030 prove to be difficult to achieve for a number of major emitter countries, let alone the next and much more significant 80% cuts to carbon emissions that are required in the period after 2030.

Despite Kalecki's insightful account of why business leaders oppose full employment, he viewed capitalists in far too homogenous a manner. We know that the millions of individual businesses and corporate giants do not speak with one voice. His insights about why business leaders are prepared to suffer lower profitability in order to stop full employment undermining worker discipline needs to be modified significantly when applied to the politics of climate change. We will continue to see massive fiscal pressures to resolve a range of social welfare issues in coming years. The likelihood is also very high of increases in unemployment, underemployment and precarious work. These looming socio-economic crises coincide precisely with the period 2025 to 2050 when the need for major CO_2 mitigation will be unavoidable, short of destroying a safe climate. Hence, conflicting interests and policy agendas pursued by leading corporations, disparate local and national business associations as well as political parties and state administrators will continue to erupt and sharpen in coming years.

Examining the response of European businesses to perceived environmental regulatory pressures and whether these new policies add new cost burdens or benefits, Jonas Meckling argues that corporations adopt four types of political strategies in environmental politics:

> ...*opposition* – firms trying to veto a regulatory initiative; *hedging* – firms seeking to minimize compliance costs or level them across a global industry; *support* – firms aiming to create or expand markets for environmental products and services; and *nonparticipation* (my emphasis).[10]

If we expand Meckling's discussion of business strategies to include local, national and international political leaders and organisations, then policy outcomes become less predictable in future crisis scenarios. Just as there are many business and political leaders who are simultaneously culturally liberal but economically conservative, or vice versa, so too, climate change and broader environmental issues cut across traditional class interests and are likely to produce unexpected political decisions. Crucially, we must cease thinking of 'capitalism' or the 'capitalist system' as dominated by the US presiding over a 'global corporate elite'. We live in a much more fluid world with interconnected policy makers who have divided loyalties and interests. The old 'world system' model is broken. This does not mean that the old 'core' (based on North America, major European countries and Japan) is not still extremely powerful in comparison to numerous 'semi-peripheral and peripheral countries', whether in Southern Europe, Africa, Latin America or Central Asia. However, it is the new political economic powers in Asia and elsewhere that increasingly pursue their own agendas.

There is also no doubt that the top 100 to 1000 corporations play a significantly disproportionate role in all key sectors of the international

---

10   Jonas Meckling, 'Distributional Effects, Regulatory Pressure, and Business Strategy in Environmental Politics', *Global Environmental Politics* vol.15 no.2, May 2015, pp.19-20.

economy. The traditional Left response has been to draw attention to the power of dozens of multinational corporations that have revenues larger than many nation states. I do not wish to deny this glaring fact of concentrated capitalist economic power. Yet, despite the existence of these immense corporations, the ability to shape and control future national and international economic policy is far from pre-determined. Today, there are millions of small and medium businesses across the world. No accurate estimate exists of all the listed and unlisted large businesses. Eelke Heemskerk and Frank Takes, for example, point out that in 2013 there were 968,409 distinct large firms in almost 200 countries with over 3.2 million directors and board members. Leaving aside all the shelf companies and other artificial entities, many of these listed directors serve on the boards of multiple companies and clusters of connecting firms.[11] Allowing for significantly fewer distinct businesses, this would still leave tens of thousands of directors in thousands of large firms with separate company, industry sector and local or national political economic agendas. There are simply too many firms and directors of private and public companies to predict accurately how they will respond strategically to looming environmental challenges.

If we take Meckling's four strategies adopted by European businesses (opposition, hedging, support, or non-participation) and apply these to decision makers across the world, the outcome of business policies on climate change and related political economic objectives is far from predictable and pre-determined. Quite different scenarios are produced if we qualify and sub-divide Meckling's two strategies of 'support' or 'opposition' into varying degrees of mild, moderate or strong 'support' as well as mild, moderate or strong 'opposition'. Business and political leaders, as well as industry lobby groups and a range of national and international organisations will formulate their strategies of opposition, hedging, support or neutrality complicated by the following issues and areas of contestation:

- Whether the transition to renewable energy will penalise their company, related industry sectors or their local and national economy very little, moderately but still amount to manageable costs, or constitute an unaffordable and ruinous imposition.
- Whether the character and scale of non-market forms of state involvement in promoting 'green growth', such as infrastructure, renewables, sustainable urban planning, or safe food production,

---

11 Eelke M. Heemskerk and Frank W. Takes, 'The Corporate Elite Community structure of Global Capitalism', *New Political Economy*, vol.21 no.1, 2015, pp.98-118.

undermines markets or advantages particular businesses at the expense of others.

- Whether support for 'green growth' also entails support or opposition to neo-liberal austerity measures especially the role, form and rate of taxation as well as level of public debt in any 'green transition'.

- Whether government policies should curb the power of the private finance sector in order to prioritise new 'green growth' investments, for example, deny all businesses the right to buy or sell carbon offsets in other countries thereby forcing greater domestic decarbonisation.

- Whether support for 'green growth' also requires new World Trade Organisation or bi-lateral and multilateral trade rules that penalise or restrict trade in fossil fuels or manufactured goods and agricultural commodities highly embodied with or dependent on fossil fuels.

- Whether 'direct action' by governments to bring about 'green growth' in developing countries requires similar state interventions in developed countries phasing out dependence on the fossil-fuel economy.

- Whether support for 'green growth' also necessitates government policies that tackle social inequality such as raising income support for welfare constituents and higher wages for low paid workers.

- Whether there is a need for new consumer and manufacturing laws that implement tough environmental standards or require restrictions on the purchase or use of high carbon emitting forms of consumption such as road and air transport.

- Whether governments should implement strict carbon rationing in the likelihood that carbon pricing and tax measures fail to reduce carbon emissions at a sufficient rate to prevent the destruction of a safe climate.

None of the current options on each of these controversial issues remains frozen in time. Each one of the above, together with many other policies on water, agriculture, marine life and endangered land habitats will prompt either opposition or support from different segments of business and various governments. We can, however, be certain of only one thing: the *inability* of market forces to control the global climate and environment. Of necessity, this means that *greater state intervention by governments* will be required across the globe. Whether business groups demand the less financially and socially destabilising option of dangerous geo-engineering solutions rather than the social volatility of deep decarbonisation, is a political struggle that is yet to play out.[12] What forms and what levels of new state intervention unfold will be determined by both the balance of political forces in each country and the ability/inability of particular countries to withstand global pressures for change.

At global and regional levels, most optimistic policy-makers in business or government assume, mistakenly, that existing market solutions and hybrid policy frameworks will be adequate to avoid catastrophic climate change, despite the high probability of even greater and more destabilising future climate challenges. The world, however, is characterised by deep imbalances and contradictions, discussed more fully in Chapter Two. It is not just the profound inequalities of wealth and income, or the deep geopolitical consequences of resource rich and resource poor countries. The old imperial powers in Europe and the US can no longer largely determine unchallenged the pattern of global political economic change as they did in the past. The consequences of former and current military and economic domination produces spill over effects (mass refugees, terrorism and political instability) to name just a few of the intractable problems we face. These have entered the metropolitan bastions of the Atlantic countries formerly relatively immune from volatility in the 'colonies'. Market solutions to climate change will be inadequate without solutions to all these other global imbalances in wealth, resources, finance and military conflicts. Throw all these global and regional crises into the policy mix and one begins to get a sense of why the preference of many businesses to *minimise* state intervention in decarbonisation strategies is delusional. It is neither a viable medium-term nor a long-term option.

We know that Kalecki's generation of economists prior to the 1970s never dealt with climate change and environmental crises, but what are the excuses of most contemporary economists, whether neo-classical, heterodox post-Keynesians or radical Marxists? They seem confounded by the new reality that environmental challenges are entirely different

---

12 See 'Climate Intervention Is Not a Replacement for Reducing Carbon Emissions; Proposed Intervention Techniques Not Ready for Wide-Scale Deployment', Statement issued by National Academies of Sciences and Engineering, Institute of Medicine and National Research Council, Washington, April 2, 2015; Jesse Reynolds, *The International Legal Framework for Climate Engineering*, Working Paper, 24 March 2015, geoengineeringourclimate.com; David Keith, Gernot Wagner and Claire Zabel, 'Solar geoengineering reduces atmospheric carbon burden', *Nature Climate Change*, September 2017 and Andreas Sieber, 'How not to save the world', *International Politics and Society*, 5 April 2018.

problems to the old issues of labour and capital. Many effectively dismiss or relegate climate breakdown to a second order problem because they put their faith in technological solutions. This belief that Science or the Market has all the answers to climate change is completely misplaced. Neo-liberal austerity, old distributional socialist planning models, or Keynesian and post-Keynesian policies generating aggregate demand to overcome recession and stagnation will simply not suffice when it comes to climate change and finite environmental resources. Rather, these growth-orientated policies are likely to exacerbate the crisis.

Disputing Decoupling: Aims, Methods and Politics

Decarbonisation will remain a highly contentious political issue for years to come. However, relatively little attention is paid to the ambitious goals of decoupling put forward by a range of business and political groups. As mentioned earlier, far-sighted business and policy strategists have argued in recent years that future capitalist economic growth will only be sustainable if the 'natural limits to growth' can be overcome. Does this mean that business and political leaders have adopted the old 1970s Club of Rome's warning on natural limits[13] that was widely criticised and supposedly debunked by pro-market analysts?[14] Not entirely. Most businesses continue to operate as if there are no natural fetters on growth. Why the change in attitude by forward thinking pro-market analysts?

Since the dire warnings about climate breakdown, a significant proportion of corporate and government decision-makers now implicitly or explicitly factor in the need to overcome the natural limits to growth. But how can this goal be achieved without acknowledging the decades-long critiques of capitalist growth made by environmentalists or, alternatively, adopting green and socialist ideas about the necessity of major social change? It is true that a sizeable number of decision-makers would prefer various forms of technological geo-engineering 'quick-fixes' to global

---

13 Dennis L. Meadows et al, *The Limits to Growth: A Report for The Club of Rome's Project on the Predicament of Mankind*, Universe Books, New York, 1972.

14 Herman Kahn, William Brown, and Leon Martel, *The Next 200 Years: A Scenario for America and the World*, William Morrow and Company, New York, 1976. For an analysis of how the Club of Rome report has stood up to developments since the 1970s, see Graham Turner, *Is Global Collapse imminent?*, Melbourne Sustainable Society Institute, University of Melbourne, Research Paper 4, 2014, and Tim Jackson and Robin Webster, *Limits Revisited: a review of the limits to growth debate*, All-Party Parliamentary Group on Limits to growth, London, April 2016.

warming rather than widespread socio-economic reforms necessary to achieve zero carbon societies. Even if all the very high risks associated with geo-engineering worked, it only deals with the symptoms rather than the cause of global warming.[15] Very importantly, technological solutions to climate change are not in themselves a solution to the related but far greater problems associated with the natural limits to growth.

As I discussed in Chapter One, innovation has become an over-hyped sacred cow by techno-disciples who believe in its capacity to solve current crises such as mass unemployment or lack of profitable investment outlets. Existing innovation policies, whether of the free market, post-Keynesian or hybrid variety, are incapable of preventing future environmental restraints on capitalist growth. This major constraint is a dilemma that also faces all those old-style socialists, anarchists and other radicals who are guilty of ignoring environmental limitations. With some notable exceptions, these alternative approaches assume that in a post-capitalist society, the level of industrial technological production and consumption achieved by capitalists will be managed differently and somehow miraculously not run into finite natural resources limits.

Leaving aside imaginary post-capitalist societies for the moment, the inescapable question remains: if old and conventional economic theories and solutions are inadequate, how can capitalist systems overcome the natural limits to growth? These days much more is hoped for from future innovation than simply creating new industries, new jobs and higher consumption. In fact, future-orientated business and political leaders are now aiming for something overwhelmingly staggering in its ambition and historical novelty – a fantastic technological revolution that aspires to detach or decouple the accumulated global processes of material production from the finite limits of natural resources.

At present, the notion of 'decoupling' or 'dematerialisation' has an almost utopian or science-fiction quality to it. As a goal, various radical anti-capitalists also embrace it (see discussion in the next chapter). At the centre of visions of both ecologically modernised capitalism and radical post-capitalism stands the promise of 'decoupling'. Decarbonisation may drive key aspects of decoupling, but *absolute decoupling* is a much larger, more diverse and quite profound ambition. What is to be decoupled? The following sample list gives us a sense of the utopian hopes embodied in the proposed break with the past and the present:

---

15 See survey of scientific and social positions on geo-engineering in Jonas Anshelm and Anders Hansson, 'Battling Promethean dreams and Trojan horses: revealing the critical discourses of geoengineering', *Energy Research & Social Science*, no.2, June 2014, pp.135–144.

- economic growth will be *absolutely* decoupled from the limits of
  nature;
- goods and services will be decoupled from material forms;
- income and wellbeing for all will be decoupled from paid labour;
- life, knowledge and intelligence will be decoupled from biological
  processes and social relations.

Not all of these beliefs in decoupling are simultaneously held or shared
across the political spectrum. Those who still cling to various traditional
Right and Left political economic theories – whether corporations, social
reformers or policy institutes – support particular forms of decoupling
in more conventional but ambitious forms. Within policy debates it is
possible to see the following qualifications made to the above utopian
ideas:

- economic growth can be *relatively* decoupled from nature;
- a growing part of the economy, rather than all goods and services, can be decoupled from material forms;
- a very limited basic income rather than universal basic income as
  well as social welfare can be relatively decoupled from economic
  growth and provided to those not in the labour market;
- the techno-sciences such as robotics and bio-genetics can partially decouple life, knowledge and intelligence from biological
  processes but within highly constrained political and moral
  contexts.

During the past four decades, new technologies harnessed by businesses and governments have helped to severely weaken old forms of
labour solidarity that underpinned earlier social change movements. It is
unclear whether the tables will be turned and similar fates await dominant business and political classes. Will the unintended consequences of
new technologies and intractable political economic problems become
too difficult to manage? Or will the achievement of new goals of
decoupling only compound the lack of power and security experienced
internationally by most workers, recipients of welfare benefits, villagers,
slum dwellers and other marginalised groups? Before analysing these
issues, I will first focus on the crucial issue of decoupling economic
growth from nature.

The old debate over decoupling economic growth from natural
constraints tends to avoid political issues and instead focuses primarily
on whether it is technically feasible or whether decoupling is a myth.

Much is at stake. The very character and viability of future capitalist or post-capitalist societies depends on answers given to these fundamental questions. Unsurprisingly, supporting economic growth via 'decoupling' is contrasted with anti-growth policies often called 'degrowth' (see Chapter Five). Such conflicting positions usually tell us where people stand in contemporary environmental debates.[16] The most common meaning given to decoupling in policy discussions is whether the material production underpinning economic growth can be absolutely or only relatively decoupled from both carbon emissions and the depletion of finite natural resources.

Absolute decoupling assumes that economic growth can be achieved without any negative despoiling or depletion of natural resources. Relative decoupling acknowledges that negative environmental impacts occur, but are less, or far less than the rate of economic growth.[17] Pro-growth analysts argue that technological innovations and organisational efficiencies will make absolute decoupling a reality in years to come. For example, statistics are cited to show that since 1980, the major economies such as the US and China have doubled and tripled energy intensity thereby needing far less energy to produce infinitely more material goods. There are several critical problems associated with energy intensity and general resources use or intensity. Firstly, the ability to decouple economic growth from natural resources is not just an abstract, mathematical problem. Both proponents and opponents of material economic growth muddy the waters of the decoupling debate by acknowledging that *no growth limits exist* on immaterial socio-economic activity such as the 'knowledge economy' or on all those aspects of culture and care that enrich wellbeing in societies. Secondly, as to material consumption and economic growth, it partly depends on whether the objective of absolute decoupling is to bring the whole world's population up to the standard of consumption enjoyed by most people in a minority of rich countries, or whether it is based on maintaining the status quo of profound global inequality. Even the maintenance of existing inequality makes absolute decoupling a technological myth. Despite relative decoupling through energy and resources intensification, as Tim Jackson notes (citing a 2015

---

16 See for example, the debate 'Green Growth vs. Degrowth: two irreconcilable visions of the green economy?' between Ralf Fücks and André Reichel (both members of the German Greens) and organised by Zeppelin University and the Heinrich Böll Foundation, 26 March 2014.

17 For detailed explanations of what criteria determine absolute and relative decoupling, see Katharina Umpfenbach et al, *How will we know if absolute decoupling has been achieved?*, Dynamix Project, European Union, September 2013 and OECD, *Indicators to Measure Decoupling of Environmental Pressure From Economic Growth*, OECD, Paris, May 2002.

United Nations report), "the 'material footprint' of the OECD nations as a whole still rose by almost 50 per cent between 1990 and 2008. There was no absolute decoupling of GDP from resource use over this period."[18] Thirdly, the debate on decoupling is sanitised without considering the crucial political issue of what type of society is decoupling aiming to uphold or replace.

It is clear that the majority of reports on decoupling from organisations such as United Nations Environmental Programme (UNEP), the OECD or business consultancy firms accept the political power and practices of market capitalism and focus on technical issues such as scientific, organisational and implementation frameworks.[19] After acknowledging a range of environmental resources issues and social problems such as inequality, the prevalent approach of mainstream reports on decoupling is technocratic: how can existing businesses and governments in different countries maximise productivity and technological innovation in order to cope with finite environmental resources. By contrast, a parallel radical discourse on post-capitalism embraces the wider socio-economic, technological and political aspects of decoupling. Whether we desire a 'green capitalism' or a post-growth or post-carbon democracy based on various forms of socialist or green post-capitalist social relations, it is important to first recognise the constraints and possibilities associated with different notions of decoupling.

While I am yet to be persuaded that the absolute decoupling of economic growth from natural limits is feasible, I remain open-minded about new possibilities, if not necessarily in all spheres of production and economic activity.[20] Materials analyst, Vaclav Smil, identifies many of the possible new technologies (electronics, nanotechnology, polymers and other synthetic processes) that will *relatively* dematerialise a range of producer goods and consumer products in coming years. Yet, he also argues that the prospect of absolute decoupling or dematerialisation is extremely unlikely given the incessant demand for resources and materials by growing populations, the limits of efficient production methods

---

18 Tim Jackson, *Prosperity Without Growth: Foundations for the Economy of Tomorrow*, Second edition, Routledge, London, 2017, p.93.

19 See for example, International Resource Panel, *Decoupling Natural Resource Use and Environmental Impacts From Economic Growth*, United Nations Environmental Programme, March 2011.

20 For example, it appears that various technologies such as non-fossil fuel for aviation (a significant contributor to global warming) and various synthetic substitutes for construction materials and other everyday materials are being developed with a good chance of success. See for example, Robbert Kivits, Michael Charles and Neal Ryan, 'A post-carbon aviation future: Airports and the transition to a cleaner aviation sector', *Futures*, 42, 2010, pp.199-211.

and the rise in standards of living.[21] The preservation of the biosphere's integrity therefore demands that we will have to reduce absolute levels of material consumption. One thing is certain, absolute decoupling will not occur while 'business as usual' remains the dominant approach. Moreover, placing our faith in the goal of absolute decoupling could become a dangerous fantasy if an inadequate cut to carbon emissions means that it is too late to prevent the destruction of a safe climate.

The argument against absolute decoupling does not need to rely heavily upon abstract statistical projections of future global growth rates, population size, carbon intensity and so forth. For example, Tim Jackson and Robin Webster argue:

> Since the middle of 20th Century, the global economy has expanded at around 3.65% each year. If it were to continue to expand at the same rate, it would be more than 200 times bigger in 2100 than it was in 1950. A world in which everyone around the world achieved the level of affluence currently expected in the west would mean global economic output growing by 30 times by the end of 2100, related to current levels. Meeting carbon targets in such a world would demand quite astonishing rates of decoupling – much higher than anything that has been observed historically.[22]

While I am very sympathetic to Jackson's concept of 'prosperity without growth', his projections are quite inconsistent, as he has also said that the world economy will be 17 times bigger in 2100 than it is today if average growth rates continue.[23] Whatever the correct figures, the problem with these statistical scenarios is that they ignore the effect of actual political economic conflicts. Calculations are based on 'business as usual' remaining dominant until 2100, or a convergence of incomes so that the rest of the world is going to live like the small affluent minority of today's world's population.[24] Hence, both scenarios can appear absurd for a variety of political and environmental factors that will impact well before we get to 2040, let alone by 2100.

Importantly, the ability of societies to absolutely decouple economic

---

21 Vaclav Smil, *Making the Modern World Materials and Dematerialization*, Wiley, Chichester, 2014.

22 Jackson and Webster, *op.cit.* p.14.

23 Tim Jackson, 'The Case for Slower Growth', *The World IfIA compilation of scenarios*, September 2015.

24 Jackson, *Prosperity Without Growth*, pp.99-100.

growth from nature should not and cannot be understood as a battle between competing abstract statistical projections. Scientists have made estimates, but there are still disputes about the precise impact of carbon emissions on the biosphere, hydrosphere and other vital interrelated life-enhancing systems. Statistical models calculating the impact of carbon dioxide emissions on temperature change arrive at their conclusions, regardless of whether these emissions were caused by different political regimes or types of economy. By contrast, decoupling economic growth from nature is much more than decoupling growth from carbon emissions. It requires societies to be able to decouple economic growth from *the continued destruction and depletion of a wide range of non-renewable natural resources* as well as the future adequacy of renewable resources.

Since 1970, alarming evidence has shown that half of all land animals, marine animals and fish stocks have been decimated by overfishing, illegal hunting and destructive capitalist development or environmental devastation in Communist countries.[25] Environmentalists such as George Monbiot argue that industrial fishing and industrial farming are greater threats than climate change in terms of their ecological destructiveness.[26] Furthermore, we do not have to uncritically accept the metrics behind 'ecological footprints' in order to recognise that 'business as usual' cannot continue without a further mass extinction of species and depletion of natural resources. Global Footprint Network regularly tracks national and international bio-capacity levels.[27] Far from decoupling economic growth, there is more rather than less demand on natural resources. Various critics argue that there are serious and valid methodological disputes concerning what is included or excluded in the measurement of 'ecological footprints'.[28] Despite these criticisms, there is a moral and political imperative to significantly improve and retain a more comprehensive and rigorous measurement of 'ecological footprints' if we are to have any idea of what level of production and consumption needs to be significantly reduced or transformed to achieve sustainable societies.

---

25 Damian Carrington,' Earth has lost half of its wildlife in the past 40 years, says WWF', *The Guardian,* 1 October, 2014.

26 George Monbiot, 'Insectageddon: farming is more catastrophic than climate breakdown', *The Guardian*, 20 October 2017.

27 'August 13th is Earth Overshoot Day this year', *Global Footprint Network*, footprintnetwork. org, 26 October 2015.

28 See for example C. J. M. van den Bergh and Fabio Grazi, 'Ecological Footprint Policy? Land Use as an Environmental Indicator', *Journal of Industrial Ecology*, vol.18, no.1, 2013, pp.10-19 and response by Mathis Wackernagel of Global Footprint Network in *Journal of Industrial Ecology*, vol.18, no1, 2014, pp.20-22.

Methodological issues are always political and never merely technical. Both promoters of decoupling, such as UNEP and the Intergovernmental Panel on Climate Change (IPCC), as well as prominent critics of decoupling tend to partially or fully rely on Paul Ehrlich's and John Holdren's I=PAT formula, that is, the human Impact on the environment equals the product of Population size, level of consumption or Affluence, and application of Technology.[29] Unfortunately, the problematic political and socio-economic assumptions underlying I=PAT risk distorting and clouding future policy development. H. Patricia Hynes and others have demolished the validity of I=PAT on feminist, class and anti-colonialist grounds. This is due to the fact that the model ignores the gross inequalities between social classes in terms of unequal consumption, the role of patriarchal power and population growth in developing countries and the disproportionate use of up to 80 per cent of natural resources by less than 20 per cent of the world's affluent population and businesses in developed economies.[30] The formula fails to elucidate how doubling technological efficiency, or reducing population and levels of consumption actually reduces overall impact due to the possible stimulation of additional production and consumption, named the Jevons rebound factor. Consequently, I=PAT has been rejected by many as even mathematically meaningless. It focuses primarily on total individual consumption rather than quite different types of consumption according to socio-economic and political systems, for instance, rural versus urban consumption, transnational rather than just national production and consumption, especially the vital role of multinational corporations and also government military budgets.[31]

The various IPCC reports have been weakened not only by the use of the 'Kaya identity' (a modified I=PAT model named after Japanese energy analyst Yoichi Kaya) but also by the inclusion of highly problematic pro-market socio-economic concepts and generalisations. These ideologically flawed assumptions about everything from individual consumption and the positive role of GDP growth seriously detract from the analysis in the scientific chapters of IPCC reports dealing with the impact of greenhouse gas emissions. Yet, even the scientific analyses

---

29 Paul Ehrlich and John Holdren, 'Impact of Population Growth', *Science*, 171, 1971, pp.1212-1217. For UNEP's use of I=PAT see *Global Material Flows and Resource Productivity Assessment Report for the UNEP International Resource Panel*, United Nations Environment Programme, 2016.

30 H. Patricia Hynes, *Taking Population Out of the Equation: Reformulating I=PAT*, Institute of Women, North Amherst, 1993.

31 Ben Courtice, 'I=PAT means nothing, proves nothing', *Climate & Capitalism*, March 17, 2010.

produced by the IPCC are very conservative and seriously underestimate the rate and scale of climate breakdown. IPCC reports are cumbersome compromises that fail to include the latest scientific research. They also reflect pressures coming from governments in high fossil-fuel producing countries.[32] Overall, like other United Nations reports, the 2014 IPCC report (published in 2015) promotes pro-market 'green growth' mitigation and adaptation solutions.[33]

The major flaws in I=PAT means that it is impossible for social change activists to determine with any certainty that absolute decoupling is a myth, as Tim Jackson and others have argued.[34] Additionally, and very importantly, I=PAT is a very poor socio-political tool capable of telling us what potential level or rate of *degrowth* of production and consumption will be necessary or sufficient to ensure comfortable, conflict-free human habitation on this planet. Therefore, the continued use of I=PAT by environmentalists is politically and scientifically counterproductive. It only serves to weaken otherwise extremely important proposals about the need for a safe climate and a sustainable future.

Recent growth rates that have required fewer resources or resulted in lower carbon emissions is used by advocates of absolute decoupling as evidence that decoupling is feasible. These findings are then projected forward to create optimistic scenarios for 2050 and beyond. Unfortunately, like most future projections they are notoriously unreliable. This is true whether they come from governments and central banks, business consultancy firms or from environmentalist critics of the system. Optimists also point to the significant cheapening costs of renewable energy and battery storage, although they admit that little progress has been made in major industries such as steel, chemicals, concrete and transport. Importantly, one should not confuse cheaper renewable energy with decoupling or dematerialisation. It is possible, however, to empirically examine specific industries and practices such as manufacturing, energy, mining or transport, and compare levels of resource use and decarbonisation with actual rates of production and consumption. Likewise, one can evaluate whether increased food production is achievable without deforestation, deteriorating soil nutrients and water resources, thus ascertaining whether there has been significant or negligible progress in

---

32 See critical analysis of IPCC reports in David Spratt and Ian Dunlop, *What Lies Beneath: The Scientific Understatement of Climate Risks*, Breakthrough – National Centre for Climate Restoration, Melbourne, September, 2017.

33 See Intergovernmental Panel on Climate Change, *Climate Change 2014 Synthesis Report*, WMO and UNEP, Geneva 2015, pp.93-112.

34 See T. Jackson, *Prosperity Without Growth*, Ch.5 and Ted Trainer, 'Eco-modernism?', *Arena Magazine*, no.143, August-September 2016, pp.36-38.

decoupling. The trouble is that decoupling in each major industry sector is not a mere 'technical' problem but involves highly contentious political economic struggles over policies on unemployment and inequality.

What is perhaps insufficiently recognised by both advocates and critics of decoupling is that the more that some or all of the desired socio-political goals of decoupling economic growth become mainstream practices (such as decoupling income from work or dematerialising goods), the more that conventional crisis-management frameworks become ineffective. Key institutions and socio-economic practices of existing social orders simply cannot continue as before.

Contradictory futures are therefore highly likely to flow from most types of decoupling. This is because the potential to radically decouple a range of material and food production processes, communication technologies, biological or various income generating processes is quite unlike the innovations of earlier historical phases. Some will enhance ruling powers. Others will undermine secrecy and control. Hence, the double-edged swords of new technology on social reproduction have the potential to explode long familiar forms of corporate control and the accumulation of wealth. Those clinging to old nineteenth and twentieth century liberal or radical political economic theories of industrial capitalism are already heavily dated. They will be truly redundant in the next few decades as explosive social, environmental and technological changes transform our familiar world.

From the point of decoupling and degrowth, let me simply cite the future of 3D printing as one example of something highly unpredictable and far from the romantic image promoted by Left and Right technological utopians.[35] On the one hand it may facilitate decentralised community production and control by disrupting mass production and decoupling it from its current narrow corporate ownership base.[35] It is already creating significant advances in life-saving areas of surgery and health care. On the other hand, it could quickly lose its democratic potential, as was the case with the internet which ended up largely controlled by giant businesses such as Google and protected by restrictive government (especially US backed) intellectual property law. It is possible that 3D printing could reduce environmental damage caused by current poorly regulated toxic production methods in factories, especially in developing countries, as well as carbon emissions caused by transporting international trade in resources and manufactured goods. Nonetheless, 3D printing technology will have to surmount several environmentally dangerous features.

---

35 See Guy Rundle, *A Revolution in the Making: 3D Printing Robots and the Future*, Affirm Press, South Melbourne, 2014.

Many 3D printers consume 50 to 100 times more electrical energy than conventional injection moulding to make an item of the same weight.[36] If 3D printers become as ubiquitous as home computers, then without stringent government regulation, they could lead to increased lung disease through the emission of fine particles, not to mention more waste and carbon emissions. The local transportation of 3D products and input materials will increase the circulation of hazardous chemicals throughout cities and in residential homes, thus constituting dangerous environmental waste disposal problems.[37] Moreover, if consumption of fossil fuels (oil in polymers) increases, the consequences of 3D printing could be highly negative. Finally, the ability to print guns, medicines and other items requiring safety regulations will all test whether the social benefits of 3D printing outweigh its negatives.

For the sake of improving living conditions for the vast majority of the world's population without drastically depleting natural resources, one hopes that the goal of decoupling growth from nature is realised. Yet, even if various types of decoupling prove to be technologically feasible, let us not confuse decoupling with the burning issue of *redistribution*, especially combatting inequality and poverty. Without either profound decoupling or a radical decline or transformation of consumption by affluent populations, the future looks extremely bleak, especially for the poor majority of the world's population. Paradoxically, many who believe in disengagement from consumer capitalism continue to support other aspects of decoupling. Advocates of degrowth believe, for instance, that a universal basic income can be decoupled from paid work thereby reducing material consumption through lower incomes. This ties in with the socio-economic agenda of redefining 'prosperity' and assumes that social life will increasingly take a dematerialised form by shifting from material goods to services. Both of these scenarios will be discussed in Chapters Five and Six.

Whether decoupling is feasible or not, prominent environmental scientists[38] have highlighted the dangerous vulnerability and high-risk

---

36 Lyndsey Gilpin, 'The dark side of 3D printing/10 things to watch', *TechRepublic*, 5 March, 2014.

37 For a report on the implications of 3D printing see Thomas Birtchnell, John Urry, Chloe Cook and Andrew Curry, *Freight Miles: The Impacts of 3D Printing on Transport and Society*, Lancaster University, 2013.

38 See Johan Rockström et al. 'Planetary Boundaries: Exploring the Safe Operating Space for Humanity', *Ecology and Society*, Vol.14, no.2, 2009, pp.1-33 and updated version 2.0. Will Steffen et.al. 'Planetary Boundaries: Guiding Human Development on a Changing Planet', *Science*, January 16, 2015. Although these reports blame business activity for much of the damage to the planetary boundaries, they are not anti-capitalist and believe that business can remedy dangerous transgressions.

threat to between four and eight of the Earth's nine planetary boundaries or 'life support systems', in short, the interconnected bio-geophysical system, such as atmosphere, biosphere, hydrosphere and so forth. However, advocates of degrowth not only believe that the possibility of absolute decoupling of material resources is a dangerous myth,[39] but that the whole logic of incessant economic growth should be rejected in favour of alternative social values and practices. I agree with Tim Jackson when he argues that:

> There is no simple formula that leads from the efficiency of the market to the meeting of ecological targets. Simplistic assumptions that capitalism's propensity for efficiency will allow us to stabilise the climate or protect against resource scarcity are nothing short of delusional.
>
> The truth is that there is as yet no credible, socially just, ecologically sustainable scenario of continually growing incomes for upwards of nine billion people. And the critical question is not whether the complete decarbonisation of our energy systems or the dematerialisation of our consumption patterns is technically feasible, but whether it is possible in our kind of society.[40]

Given the 'brutal numbers' concerning not just carbon emissions but the other planetary boundaries affecting oceans, forests, nitrogen cycles, genetic diversity, fresh water and other forms of life and resources, the feasibility of absolute or relative decoupling becomes much more than a speculative exercise in futurology.

Having Your Cake… Obstacles to Decoupling Economic Growth

The dominant business and political discourse about decoupling growth from nature is characterised by technological innovation and investment solutions, rather than profound systemic changes to market-driven social production and consumption.[41] Some see decoupling as either advanced forms of miniaturisation or dematerialisation in which all

---

39 See for example, Tim Jackson, 'The myth of decoupling', in *Prosperity Without Growth: Foundations for the Economy of Tomorrow*, Second edition, Routledge, London, 2017, Ch.5.

40 Jackson, Prosperity Without Growth, p.102.

41 Paul Hawken and a team of 'natural capitalists' have produced ideas for 100 different types of decarbonisation and efficiencies in energy, food production, urban living and so forth. See Paul Hawken (ed.), *Drawdown The Most Comprehensive Plan Ever Proposed To Reverse Global Warming*, Penguin Random House, New York, 2017.

types of goods can either be drastically reduced in size or produced in a form that no longer require existing amounts of material inputs. It is also hoped that recycling and re-use through the 'circular economy', or efficiencies gained through new production methods combined with new synthetic technologies and artificial substitutes can achieve incredible productivity gains without needing to reduce drastically high utilisation of either material resources in the form of producer goods or household consumption. This pro-market discourse on decoupling is expressed in two forms: first, a propaganda version mainly promoted by industry lobbies and corporations for public consumption to counter criticisms from environmentalists; and second, a genuine belief in ecological modernisation as the pathway to profits, political stability and social improvement.

A stark example of decoupling as propaganda is the World Resources Institute (WRI) 2015 report which cites that 21 countries have managed to significantly increase their GDP between 2000 and 2015 while reducing their CO2 emissions.[42] Although the WRI heavily promotes renewable energy and green infrastructure in both the US and developing countries, a closer inspection of the WRI figures casts serious doubt on both the rate of decoupling and even its actuality. First, no account is taken of imported carbon content embodied in both manufacturing and fossil fuel imports. Second, the report acknowledges that industrial production declined in all of these 21 countries as a proportion of their national GDP. This confirms that decoupling rates were artificial and were either due to declines in consumption and production due to the Great Recession or to the outsourcing of production to other countries. Finally, and crucially, the WRI acknowledges that the rate of decoupling would have to escalate dramatically, simply because the current rate is grossly inadequate to prevent dangerous increases in global warming.

Decoupling as propaganda plays a limited strategic political role in trying to postpone the inevitable, namely, full decarbonisation. Ultimately, it is self-deluding as businesses either survive through implementing genuine decoupling measures or succumb to a crisis of unsustainability as governments are forced to impose more stringent decarbonisation targets and other emergency environmental restrictions. The divisions among political and business leaders as to the desirability and feasibility of achieving deep decarbonisation *completely preclude any smooth or comfortable political road* to serious decoupling. When we add all the other planetary boundaries that are seriously polluted, eroded or stressed by decades of highly destructive economic growth, then business

---

42   Nate Aden, 'The Roads to Decoupling: 21 Countries are Reducing Carbon Emissions While Growing GDP', *World Resources Institute*, Washington, April 5, 2016.

and political leaders are cutting their own throats with short-term evasive measures. No wonder other decision-makers are opting for the panaceas of ecological modernisation or 'green growth' technological break-throughs. Some of these breakthroughs will undoubtedly materialise if sufficient R&D funding is allocated in addition to massive trillion-dollar global 'green economy' expenditure initiatives.

Even if we concede all these efficiencies, innovations or massive green infrastructure projects, something has to give in a future world of nine to possibly as many as sixteen billion people, if current consumption in OECD countries is not only to be sustained but also increasingly enjoyed by all across the world.[43] In reality, conventional business and political decoupling goals are thinly veiled agendas to maintain profound inequality enjoyed by majorities in rich OECD countries and affluent middle classes who still remain minorities in developing countries. Even so, the challenges confronting tacit advocates of continued inequality are enormous. For instance, more than 1.8 billion people will shortly be living in water-scare regions by 2025 (less than a decade away), and this without even thinking about attaining high consumption growth rates. Solutions such as pumping water from desalination water plants to inland areas or developing new cereal crops that are able to grow in deserts may or may not prove feasible.[44]

Unfortunately, most of the pro-market neo-Schumpeterians are primarily focussed on innovation as a means of reviving growth rates in OECD developed countries. Some neo-Schumpeterians like development policy analyst Carlotta Perez, is genuinely concerned about poverty and climate change. However, she advocates policies for Latin American and African countries that will exacerbate climate breakdown.[45] These countries, she argues, should pursue a natural resources led industrialisation strategy by hitching their economies to Asian growth developments, adding value to minerals processing and agribusiness in combination with biotech industries. Moreover, these policies could be funded by government subsidies and investment from multinational corporations

---

43 In India alone, the ecological footprint of the richest 1% is 17 times greater than the poorest 40%. See Development Alternatives Group and Wuppertal Institute, *Decoupling Growth from Resource Consumption*, Backround Paper to 2nd Indo-German Expert Group Meeting on Green and Inclusive Economy, New Delhi, 3-4th February, 2014.

44 See Steve Wylie, 'To future-proof our crops from drought, look to the Australian deserts', *The Conversation*, August 19, 2016.

45 See Carlota Perez, *The new context for industrializing around natural resources: an opportunity for Latin America (and other resource rich countries)?*, Working Papers in Technology Governance and Economic Dynamics no. 62 May 2014, The Other Canon Foundation, Norway and Tallinn University; and Carlota Perez, 'Finance and Technical Change: A Long-term View', *African Journal of Science, Technology, Innovation and Development*, Vol. 3, No. 1, 2011, pp. 10-35.

like BHP Billiton – the very corporation which in 2015 caused one of the largest environmental disasters in Brazil's history. This is hardly 'green growth'. China's future need for resources is not likely to continue at the previous rate of the past two decades of rapid development. Recent domestic economic changes in China have already caused recessions in countries such as Brazil. Importantly, Perez's strategy is a problem-ridden policy based on rapid global industrialisation or regional economic growth – the very goal that threatens planetary 'life support systems'. Like other corporate strategists of 'green growth', Perez pins her hopes on technological innovation, the 'circular economy' and other yet unproven conventional decoupling strategies.

Another neo-Schumpeterian, John Mathews, believes China will decouple its economy through 'green growth' innovation, the circular economy and biomimcry.[46] Mathews provides little evidence that absolute decoupling is taking place other than the boost to investment in renewable energy and some forms of recycling. Sadly, he is probably correct to argue that Asian countries will continue to industrialise come what may. But his Pollyannish optimism that capitalist innovation can successfully combine with degrowth 'steady-state' economic futures remains a pure fantasy. How a consumption-led and export-led economic system could be compatible with degrowth and still remain profitable is the miracle we await to see. As for tax revenue in the decoupled economy, like Mazzucato and Perez, Mathews favours switching from taxing labour and capital to taxing resources. This sounds logical as an environmental policy but we don't know whether the revenue raised from this fundamental tax switch will match or exceed existing sources. Also, like numerous proposals for various financial transaction taxes such as the Tobin tax, little has transpired because of fierce resistance by business groups.

Overall, few adequate answers have been given by pro-business analysts to dispel the arguments (provided by Tim Jackson and others) that absolute decoupling of economic growth from nature is a myth. Two types of responses are common. The first type of response from 'prosperity *with* growth' proponents Cameron Hepburn and Andrew Bowen

---

46 John Mathews, *Global Green Shift*, Anthem Press, London, 2017. Mathews' work is full of detail about how China and other Asian countries are promoting 'green growth' rather than actual decoupling. His work displays an uncritical celebration of industrialisation, plus no real analysis of how massive global inequality could lead to major policy conflicts in coming years. As a perspective that is largely technologically determinist, Mathews presents a rose-tinted future for humanity where technology triumphs over scarcity and threats to the earth's life support system.

argues that zero economic growth is neither necessary nor desirable. [47] As for a 'steady state' economy, they argue that this may be possible in the very distant future. It would limit material production but permit unlimited intellectual or dematerialised economic growth (a version of the 'knowledge economy'). Ultimately, they hope that by 2050 new technological innovation will make current scepticism about absolute decoupling look out-dated.[48] Anthony Giddens and many other prominent policy analysts also share a faith in 'utopian realism' or 'human ingenuity'.[49] Ralf Fücks, self-proclaimed German 'Green Ordoliberal'[50], articulates this quasi-religious faith, a belief that "humanity will find ways out of its environmental predicament: as the danger grows, so too does the chance of salvation."[51] This is the modern version of the blind leading the blind as all hope is now invested in technological utopianism.

The second type of rebuttal takes the form of projections based on scientific computer modelling. It is important to note that few studies have been made of actual real industry decoupling. Also, these computer models are represented as deliberately 'apolitical' and we know that any so-called 'value-free' approach to social issues is inherently highly political. One study undertaken by Heinz Schandl and academic colleagues recently modelled three future scenarios and concluded that both OECD economies and developing countries such as China have significant potential to reduce material throughput and carbon emission with little impact on economic growth.[52] Despite this optimistic computer modelling of future relative decoupling, when it came to analysing *actual* decoupling of productivity from global material flows, Heinz Schandl and fellow researchers (as part of the UNEP 2016 team report) concluded the opposite, namely, that since 2000, decoupling had *not*

---

47 See Cameron Hepburn and Alex Bowen, 'Prosperity with Growth: Economic growth, climate change and environmental limits', *Centre for Climate Change Economics and Policy*, LSE, Working Paper no.109, October 2012.

48 *Ibid* p.20. Also see A. Bowen and C. Hepburn, 'Green growth: an assessment', *Oxford Review of Economic Policy*, vol.30, no.3, 2014, pp.407-22 for an overview of some of the macro-economic policy issues and problems that will be system-wide and necessitate strong state involvement if inequality, financial crises and other negative developments are to be avoided.

49 Anthony Giddens in conversation with Ralf Fücks, 'We Need a Radicalism of the Centre', Heinrich Böll Stiftung, The Green Political Foundation, 3 May 2010.

50 See interview with Ulf Poschardt, 'Yes, I am a green Ordoliberalismus', *Die Welt*, 7 September 2015. Fücks co-wrote the German Greens policy program which states: "As much state as necessary, as much market as possible."

51 Ralf Fücks, *Green Growth, Smart Growth: A New Approach to Economics, Innovation and the Environment*, with an Introduction by Anthony Giddens, Anthem Press, London 2015, p.210.

52 Heinz Schandl et.al 'Decoupling global environmental pressure and economic growth: scenarios for energy use, materials use and carbon emissions', *Journal of Cleaner Production*, 132, 2016, pp. 45-56.

occurred.[53] In other words, computer modelling is one thing, but it will require a revolution in resources use, the application of new technology and other social strategies over the next twenty to thirty years for significant relative decoupling (rather than absolute decoupling) to be realised in the large G20 economies, let alone in all other countries.

Another great doubt about the possibility of absolute decoupling is the serious underestimation by governments and business groups of what is needed in the form of future resources to sustain growth industries. Take for example, one of the largest environmentally destructive global industries, automobiles and related tyre and petro-chemical industries. It is difficult to think of another conglomeration of key industries revolving around road transport that has had a greater negative impact on the shape of cities, consumption and the growth of capitalist societies in the past one hundred years. If decoupling is to prove feasible, it must either include these pivotal industries of past and present capitalist growth or replace them with new modes of transport and new types of sustainable cities.

A concrete and sobering example is that of the Bridgestone Group, the world's largest producer of tyres and rubber. It is a business that believes in decoupling and proclaims that it follows the United Nations sustainable guidelines on decoupling. In its *2015 Environmental Report*, Bridgestone envisages 2.4 billion cars in the world by 2050, much more than double the total number of cars currently in the world.[54] While Bridgestone claims to take sustainability seriously, it displays no fundamental concern about the massively negative consequences of environmentally destructive road building, carbon emissions from road paving, blighted urban centres due to traffic congestion, more than a million annual road deaths and millions of serious injuries, plus numerous other undesirable social and environmental impacts of the automobile industry. Fifty-six per cent of the pollution and negative impact on natural resources caused by vehicles takes place in their manufacture *before* they even hit the road.[55] One could argue that all roads of the future could be converted into 'solar roads' for cars similar to the

53 See *Global Material Flows and Resource Productivity Assessment Report for the UNEP International Resource Panel*, United Nations Environment Programme, 2016.

54 'Looking Ahead to the World in 2050' *Bridgestone Group Environmental Report 2015*.

55 As Richard Smith notes: "A life cycle study of the automobile by the Umwelt-und Prognose-Institut of Heidelberg Germany in 1993 found that only 40 percent of an average car's pollution is emitted during the car's "driving" life stage... Most of the pollution any car will ever cause is generated in the production process ... in the production of all the steel, aluminium, copper and other metals, glass, rubber, plastic, paint and other raw materials and inputs that go into every automobile, and in the manufacturing process itself." – 'Green Capitalism: The God that failed', *real-world economics review*, no.56, 2011.

experimental 'solar road' for bicycles tested in the Netherlands in 2015. This might reduce post-construction automobile carbon emissions but it could be prohibitively financially and socially costly to construct across the world where funding for green infrastructure is already desperately short of investment finance.

Politically, the battle to construct car-less, sustainable cities will be extremely difficult to win, at least in China, India, the US and other countries where car production and ownership either proceeds at a phenomenal pace or there is little government funding or commitment to alter the dominance of private vehicle road transport. Unless car sharing pools, driverless cars and new and more extensive forms of public transport undermine private ownership, we are heading for a doubling and tripling of cars. Taking the next twenty years as a critical time frame for decarbonisation and decoupling, the prospect of politically reversing the deep-seated trend to grow the automobile industry is currently remote. Leaving aside the disastrous social and environmental consequences of a dramatically expanded automobile industry, there is still the major problem of the resources available to build the billions of cars that will use tyres. Moreover, it is estimated that just two billion cars equipped with fuel cells would require 6000 tonnes of platinum, that is 30 times more than total mine production in 2008. If these billions of cars had electric motors, then two to four million tonnes of neodymium would be needed which is 100 to 200 times current annual mine production.[56] Neodymium is heavily used in electronic devices and wind power turbines. Forecasted peak production is 2060 and already the mining of neodymium (in major producer China) is associated with extremely serious environmental pollution.[57] Bridgestone's plan leaves key environmental questions unanswered and this is even truer of the 2016 World Energy Council scenarios which forecast between 2.8 to 3 billion cars by 2060![58] Decoupling will have to be extraordinarily and miraculously productive, not to mention extracting sufficient old or new minerals or moving to hydrogen vehicles or salt-based batteries to build so many cars. Perhaps, the scarcity of minerals may curb automobile production and lead to new human scale and liveable cities.

Meanwhile, it is not just a simple matter of global equality between

---

56   Figures quoted by Development Alternatives Group and Wuppertal Institute, op.cit., pp.18-19. Also see World Platinum Investment Council Journal *Platinum Quarterly*, 8 September 2016 for recent levels of platinum production and industry sector consumption.

57   Yiying Zhang, *Peak Neodymium – Material Constraints for Future Wind Power Development*, Masters Thesis, Department of Earth Sciences, Uppsala University, 2013.

58   World Energy Council in Collaboration with Accenture Strategy and Paul Scherrer Institute, *World Energy Scenarios 2016*, London, 2016, p.94.

rich and poor countries. Today, *more than 80 per cent of the world's population lives in countries that use more resources than can be renewed and available within their own national borders.*[59] Recent struggles over globalisation and free trade directly affect the future capacity of countries to meet resource needs from outside their own borders. It is disputable whether we need two or four earths for the world's population to live like most North Americans, Australians, Japanese or Europeans. Not open to dispute is the fact that if existing profound social inequalities are to be even moderately let alone drastically reduced, the privileged affluent minority of the world's population will need to either significantly decrease or decouple their disproportionate use of natural resources. Conversely, the vast majority of the world's population will also have to abandon the goal of aiming for existing affluent standards of living, even if decoupling proves moderately successful. These restrictive choices are likely future options if catastrophic degradation of the earth's 'life support systems' are to be avoided.

Denying or trying to cope with these potentially catastrophic scenarios, pro-market environmentalists such as Michael H. Smith, Karlson Hargroves and Cheryl Desha favour various methods of securing growth over degrowth. Proposals include substituting non-renewable resources by renewable resources, reducing to zero the rate of release of toxic substances that cannot be assimilated without harm, and avoiding irreversible adverse effects of human activities on ecosystems.[60] While these guidelines may sound fine as aspirational 'environmental' goals, overcoming inequality as a goal is either ignored or barely mentioned. Also, the latter pro-market idealistic environmentalists, like so many others, neglect or minimise the unpleasant reality of capitalist production. A substantial proportion of businesses either have no interest in adhering to 'safe' environmental criteria or have enormous difficulty decoupling their own specific production processes without incurring the high costs of new technology and precipitating steep falls in profitability. Consequently, decoupling as propaganda is adopted by many businesses in the form of 'greenwashing' so change remains superficial or else is pseudo-decoupling in the form of outsourcing environmentally damaging production to those developing countries with weak regulatory structures.

Nonetheless, decoupling is much more than propaganda or ecological

59 See national footprint figures and charts provided by *Global Footprint Network*, April 11, 2016.
60 Michael H. Smith, Karlson Hargroves and Cheryl Desha, *Cents and Sustainability: Securing Our Common Future by Decoupling Economic Growth from Environmental Pressures*, Routledge/Earthscan, London 2010, ch.2.

modernisation. It must be also understood as a process that if successful needs to occur within two very specific and very different political economies of time. What does this mean? The first 'time framework' clearly rules out a casual and complacent political attitude to achieving decoupling over a very long period. If major technological breakthroughs are not achieved within the next ten to twenty years, then climate breakdown and resource depletion will force governments to take emergency action and scale back production and growth. Yet, decoupling cannot simply be confined to the short-term time frames or the seemingly brief attention spans of CEOs and businesses. Millions of small to medium size businesses have short and very limited life expectancies of between less than 12 months to 3 years. Many large companies disappear within 20-year time frames. Cumulatively, the gap between long-term commitment to decoupling and short-term business survival strategies are fundamentally out of sync and must be taken into account when considering the practical feasibility of decoupling policies. Ultimately, all the optimistic hype about venture capital and start-ups may sound good in free market innovation theories. In reality, it is major corporations that governments pin their hopes on to achieve decoupling in combination with large research institutes and government departments. As it is only too clear from recent history, corporations are highly unreliable partners with quite mixed agendas.

Depending on the industrial sector they are in, corporate giants promote quite different images and methods of decoupling. The American Petroleum Institute, for instance, attributes decoupling of economic growth from carbon emissions to the switch from coal to gas. This is hardly a decarbonising or decoupling panacea even though gas emits less carbon than coal. [61] One of the favourite business strategies is the promotion of the 'circular economy'. [62] Much is to be gained by reuse and recycling. One recent report estimated that a shift to a 'circular economy' in just three areas of food, mobility and built environment could reap the EU economies an annual benefit of $2 trillion. [63] So far, the technical reality is that very few parts of electronic goods, whether smart phones

---

61 See American Petroleum Institute, 'Natural Gas and the US Model for 'Decoupling', *Energy Tomorrow Blog*, April 12, 2016.

62 For example, electronics giant Philips promotes decoupling through PR publications such as 'Rethinking the Future: Our Transition to a Circular Economy', Philips.com 2016.

63 See Ellen MacArthur Foundation, SUN and McKinsey Centre for Business and Environment, *Growth Within: A Circular Economy Vision for a Competitive Europe*, 10 December 2015. Also see Bio Intelligence Service and Social Ecology Vienna, *Analysis of the Key Contributions to Resource Efficiency*, European Commission, March 2011, for a breakdown of resource savings in a range of industry sectors.

or computers, can be re-used, especially components made of rare earth minerals. The truth is that large parts of manufacturing and mining are incredibly polluting and toxic. They use all kinds of chemicals, smelt a range of metals and other environmentally dangerous materials that are not capable of being 'dematerialised'. This is a far cry from what the technological dreamers of a clean 'green capitalism' would have us believe. Take the case of the shocking environmentally polluting mining conditions for rare metals, and the human misery and exploitation of these industries in countries such as China and the Congo. In order to produce thousands of industrial scale wind turbines, large amounts of coal-fired steel, concrete and rare metals are required. These renewables are currently not as advocates of 'green growth' claim, the clean sources of energy they are cracked up to be.[64]

Certainly, the point here is not to rule out the capacity to 'clean-up' a great deal of production. Rather to highlight that great savings from a 'circular economy' are not equivalent to absolute decoupling. Take, for example, electronic and engineering corporate giants Philips and Siemens pursuit of ecological modernisation strategies that have increased revenue from 'green' products to 52% and 46% respectively. Of course, these impressive figures have to be adjusted given that Siemens builds heavy industrial equipment for the fossil fuel industries such as gas and oil. Comparatively, the European giants have embraced renewables and new green manufacturing techniques at a faster rate than similar American corporations such as General Electric (31%) or Caterpillar (18%).[65]

Nevertheless, the gap between future projections and the reality of international business practices has always been profound. For instance, major environmental problems are caused by the widespread presence of synthetic chemical polymers and plastics. Earlier proclamations about how biodegradable plastics would eliminate global pollution of land and oceans have simply not eventuated. Now the plastics industry hopes that the 'circular economy' will deliver feasible decoupling of growth from the disastrous leakage of plastics blighting oceans, waterways and land. There is no doubting that producers in Asia accounting for 80 per cent of current ocean pollution, can clean up their production processes by adopting reduced European levels of leakage. So far, this goal has not been a political priority. Future growth of plastics is also estimated to

---

64 Alexander Dunlap, 'End the "Green" Delusions: Industrial-scale Renewable Energy is Fossil Fuel+', *Verso Blog*, 10 May 2018.

65 See comparative industrial figures in Thomas Singer, *Driving Revenue Growth Through Sustainable Products and Services*, The Conference Board and Investor Responsibility Research Institute, April 10, 2015.

account for 20% of global oil production by 2050 (15% of the world's carbon budget) unless major new production techniques are implemented. Moreover, even the ambitious goal of a 'circular economy' to reduce negative leakage to an incredibly low target of a mere 1% of annual global plastics production is of major concern. This would still be equivalent to one million tonnes of plastics dumped in fragile natural systems each year.[66] Marine biologists are already alarmed at the scale of micro-plastic carcinogenic elements inundating oceans – dangerous elements entering all levels of the marine and human food chain.

A possible decoupling solution for businesses or future green societies would be to develop petroleum-free materials such as fungal mycelium for products ranging from building materials, clothing and numerous other items of daily use.[67] Seaweed is another very promising multi-purpose material that is currently being developed into everything from clothing, building materials and stock feed for livestock industries right through to all kinds of medicinal products. It is possible that 90 per cent of the approximately 310 million tons of petro-plastic produced globally could instead be derived from plants or especially seaweed. Whether chemical giants switch to oil-free polymers and other new renewable materials is not a technical issue but either a commercial or a political decision that will require government intervention.

Imagine if decoupling growth from nature were merely an issue of voluntary compliance and the desire of each industry sector to achieve maximum productivity with minimal use of resources. Even this end goal would be extremely difficult enough on its own. However, when one considers the enormous gulf between nation states and their industries in terms of their various manufacturing, mining, transport, energy and food production practices – relatively clean, efficient production versus waste-creating and environmentally dangerous industries using old technology and toxic chemicals – then the possibility of decoupling is highly uneven. Those businesses and nations reliant on cheap labour-intensive production, or antiquated technology and heavy income dependence on commodity exports will have little incentive to voluntarily adopt decoupling technologies.

One could argue though that decoupling is not difficult because the G20 countries account for over 80 per cent of global production and it

---

66 Figures provided by plastics industry to World Economic Forum report, *The New Plastics Economy Rethinking the future of plastics*, Geneva, January 2016.

67 A preview of the potential product developments from mycelium R&D was displayed at the *Fungal Futures/Growing Domestic Bio-landscapes* exhibition, Universiteit Utrecht, March 24-May 16, 2016.

is much easier gaining consensus within this small group than among 193 nation states. Sadly, the gap between the political will and the technological capacity of G20 nations is huge. The ability of India or Brazil to even relatively decouple growth is quite constrained compared to other G20 countries such as Germany, the US or Japan. More advanced technological powers such as the US confronts major political obstacles to decoupling production and consumption. These obstacles possibly exceed the lack of technical capacities evident in developing countries within the G20. For instance, the largest fossil fuel producing US states such as Texas bitterly resist environmental initiatives in comparison to California and other 'green growth' states. Importantly, it is crucial to acknowledge the environmentally destructive production methods and resources currently required for 'green growth' and renewable energy, not to mention the human costs.

Irreconcilable Political Differences Over Decoupling

The failure of leading G20 governments to commit to massive environmental R&D expenditure is indicative of the gap between the rhetoric and commitment to decoupling. The reason many business groups, governments and international agencies think that absolute decoupling is preferable to major social change is perfectly understandable. Yet, decoupling is far from cost-free. It requires massive government funding of innovative pure research and applied scientific and technological R&D, the very policy solution that is either paid lip service to or strongly opposed by many G20 governments who actively prefer low taxes and minimal government expenditure budgets.

Technical possibilities of decoupling are secondary to ongoing political conflicts over limited fiscal and material resources as well as related struggles over levels of inequality in consumption, income and social infrastructure. Tellingly, no major government has as yet presented a detailed and coherent plan at national level, of how decoupling could be achieved over a specified period, or what particular decoupling indicators and measurement devices could be used to effectively monitor progress. The closest case would be the Swedish government's announcement in November 2015 that it aims to make Sweden a fossil-free country by 2030.[68] This is an admirable objective but is only partial decoupling of

---

68 See press releases from Swedish Minister for Strategic Development, 24 November, 2015 and Swedish government press release for 2017 budget, 'Government presents historic climate and environment budget', 13 September, 2016.

economic growth, as there is no clear plan outlined to decouple economic growth from all other non-fossil-fuel natural resources.

At an international level, organisations such as the United Nations Environmental Programme (UNEP) and the OECD are far too integrated with leading corporations and other pro-market agencies to offer independent views that are critical of market approaches to decoupling.[69] According to UNEP, "actual progress towards sustainable development will ultimately depend on how responsibly the planet's natural resources are managed."[70] What at face value may sound plausible is instead the pursuit of wrongheaded solutions. While UNEP has done much good work over the years promoting environmental awareness, its endorsement of technocratic resources management is a superficial solution that ignores the necessity of fundamental socio-political change. Without concerted political intervention to prevent market forces from driving incessant wasteful growth for profit, sustainability will remain an impossible goal. If technocratic solutions based on absolute decoupling prove to be impossible, what alternative is there other than to pursue some form of degrowth and major socio-political change?

As to 'responsible natural resources management', it is true that there have been comparative studies of how nation states can pursue the narrower issue of decarbonisation pathways.[71] Apart from international data on material footprints[72] such as the use of natural resources by different nations, there have been almost no globally integrated analyses stipulating how each developed or developing country can contribute to strategies necessary for decoupling economic growth from natural constraints. Specifying which industries must be closed, scaled back or drastically remodelled to become more sustainable is too controversial politically for international agencies and most national governments. Therefore, little confidence in achieving absolute decoupling goals can be had in market systems with minimal or non-existing government strategic guidelines. This creates a situation where, apart from some limited forms of co-operation, each business or industry group pursues their own agenda.

---

69 See e.g. UNEP's sponsorship of the 2015 *Natural Capital Declaration*, November 2015 and the numerous forums and publications produced in conjunction with leading finance sector corporations and other private industry bodies.

70 International Resource Panel, *Managing and Conserving the Natural Resource Base for Sustained Economic and Social Development*, UNEP, 7 February, 2014, p.7.

71 See for example, *Pathways to Deep Decarbonization 2014 report* undertaken by The Deep Decarbonization Pathways Project 15 DDPP country research partners and published by Sustainable Development Solutions Network and Institute for Sustainable Development and International Relations, New York and Paris 2014.

72 See UNEP, *Global Material Flows and resource Productivity*, 2016.

Meanwhile there are numerous failed states or borderline failed states affected by civil wars, deep-seated corruption and violence that are aided and encouraged by geo-political power rivalry and trillion-dollar global military budgets. Decoupling presupposes a population that is sufficiently literate and numerate to understand the necessity and complexity of sustainability measures. Unfortunately, in failed and semi-failed states, mass unemployment and social instability flourish and approximately 900 million of the world's 1.4 billion children of school age will reach adulthood without acquiring basic literacy and numeracy skills.[73] There is also a powerful argument against promoting decoupling of material processes in countries where brutalised, suffering populations live in some of the harshest and most desperate environments without even the basic necessities like running water.

Of course, the popular idea of a failed or borderline failed state in places equivalent to Iraq, Haiti, Somalia or Pakistan, is far too narrow a designation. Regardless, the political ability of governments to implement decoupling strategies across their own national territories via technological innovation, stringent environmental regulation and the socio-economic co-operation of citizens and businesses depends vitally on nation states being free of endemic corruption, civil war or repressive authoritarianism. Powerful G20 members such as Turkey, Russia, Saudi Arabia, Brazil, Mexico, Argentina, Indonesia, India and China, not to mention non-G20 countries Nigeria, Thailand, Egypt and numerous other African, Latin American, and Asian states fail the test on at least one or more criteria. It would also be very naïve to think that just because countries such as the US, Canada, Australia, Japan and the UK are 'officially' free of civil war and authoritarian regimes, or have less corruption than Italy or Indonesia, that their governments and business groups are honestly and vigorously committed to the active pursuit of environmental decoupling objectives.

In the minds of liberal idealists, a capitalist version of post-carbon democracy presupposes innovative entrepreneurial 'new economy' start-ups and corruption-free market competition. The fact that President Obama's Council of Economic Advisers issued a report in 2016 showing that between 1997 and 2012 there had been a significant increase in criminal price-fixing and other forms of corporate corruption in addition to increased monopoly market power in key sectors and industries, is testimony to the widespread abuse within capitalist

---

73 See *The Education Commission report, The Learning Generation Investing in Education for a Changing World,* educationcommission.org 2016.

markets.[74] The year 2015 also witnessed the highest level on record of acquisitions and mergers totalling more than $US5 trillion worldwide and $US 2.5 trillion in the US alone – a concentration of power that will consolidate more abuse of economic power rather than promote the so-called 'competitive market' road to environmental sustainability.[75]

Serious political divisions continue within the corporate sector regarding their degree of commitment to a 'green growth' model of development as I have illustrated earlier. The goal of absolute decoupling is extremely difficult even with the full support of business groups. It is almost impossible without definancialisation, as argued in Chapter Five. Consequently, the goal of decoupling is itself a political struggle between two unofficially aligned groups. First there are those hostile and complacent business and political leaders (especially in the US, Australia, Canada and various oil producing countries) who oppose more concerted government 'green' action. They either reject decoupling or erroneously believe that it can be achieved with current inadequate rates of financial investment in green innovation. Essentially, they believe in retaining existing non-green forms of finance sector activity and profitability. Opposed to these decision-makers are mixtures of other pro-market and anti-market socio-political forces that, for different reasons, demand far greater investment in a 'green capitalist' or a green post-capitalist economy.

Perhaps the political winds of change will soon be whipped up by alarming carbon emissions or economic crisis. In the meantime, most mainstream talk of decoupling needs a political reality check in order to move beyond the familiar mixture of optimistic corporate public relations or hopeful but ineffective pronouncements by 'green growth' think-tanks listing trillions of dollars of potential spending priorities by 2030 or 2050. Overwhelmingly and regrettably, these lists of possible spending priorities lack necessary funding and political commitments by governments.

Apart from modifications in personal and business behaviour such as recycling in the 'circular economy', decoupling is essentially envisaged as the capitalist technological version of ecological modernisation per se. It is also important to distinguish mainstream notions of decoupling from those defenders of fossil fuels who have long promoted ideological arguments for 'greening/decarbonising' strategies of 'business as usual' based upon carbon capture and sequestration or 'clean coal' – strategies that

---

74 Council of Economic Advisers Issue Brief, *Benefits of Competition and Indicators of Market Power*, whitehouse.gov April 2016.

75 *Ibid* p.7.

have little or no technological developments to support such dangerous and spurious claims. Similarly, decoupling has to be distinguished from last-resort forms of climate geo-engineering such as solar radiation management. Geo-engineering is the option that comes into play precisely because relative and absolute decoupling has failed to make any major impact on carbon emissions and global warming. The current level of scientific knowledge confirms that many forms of geo-engineering are extremely risky options that could go terribly wrong and unleash irreversible harm to fragile earth 'life support' eco-systems.

Conclusion

This chapter has focused on the politics of innovation with specific reference to major divisions within business groups and governments over decarbonisation and 'green growth'. It has also analysed the ambitious business goals of absolutely decoupling economic growth from nature and why this mainstream goal is either a myth or, at the very least, highly improbable. To sum up, the dominant discourse about decoupling presupposes no major change in political administrative systems, ownership of wealth or dominant forms of profit derived from consumerism. Consequently, most policy makers are in for a rude shock in the coming decades once the failure to achieve little more than relative decoupling of economic growth registers and political options begin to narrow or evaporate. It is important to re-emphasise that linking decoupling to major social reform is anathema to most contemporary business and political leaders. Without cultural and social change, dominant decoupling policies are reduced to technocratic panaceas or 'green wash' avoidance strategies, and once again, we witness the triumph of short-term politics over long-term sustainability.

4

Technological Fantasists
in the Realm of Scarcity

The business goal of decoupling economic growth from nature discussed in Chapter Three has been directly and indirectly influenced by technological futurists. In recent years, technological utopianism has taken several forms. These include a market utopian capitalist approach characterised by the desire to introduce new profitable production and communication technologies, as well as to decouple the life cycle from biological processes through cryogenics or by significantly extending life expectancy. The market utopians also desire to transform and deepen control over eco-systems and human nature, and to colonise distant planets. All these technological transformations are proposed without an accompanying interest in altering existing hierarchical and concentrated structures of unequal social and political power. Technocratic solutions are represented as preferable to messy and 'inefficient' forms of existing political processes. Other utopian capitalist approaches are based on a combination of market and non-market practices in the hope of solving environmental problems and a range of social issues. Finally, there are radical post-capitalist or socialist utopian thinkers who envisage new technologies as heralding and underpinning egalitarian non-class societies. This chapter will focus predominantly on those technological utopians who favour 'sustainable capitalism' via hybrid mixtures of market and non-market solutions as well as on those who promote different types of post-capitalism. It will conclude with an analysis of the politics of food production systems, a crucial area that is often ignored by most technological utopians. It is a vital issue needing far greater attention by reformers and radicals committed to addressing our environmental crisis.

A mixture of entrepreneurialism and anti-capitalist politics drives alternative technological notions of decoupling. America is the home of what I call 'airport lounge' technological 'faction' in the form of never-ending best sellers (consumed by business travellers and 'aspirationals') about how the 'facts' of new technologies will create the 'fiction' of profound changes to socio-economic life. Characterised by a combination of surveys of scientific and product innovation, business strategies and popular sociological insights, technological 'faction' is a tradition that goes back to the 1950s and blossomed after the 1960s with writers such as Alvin Toffler.[1] Futurism has morphed from Cold War tensions[2] to present-day responses to environmental crises. In a time of widespread scarcity, writers such as Peter Diamandis and Steven Kotler promise 'abundance'.[3] Also, in a world saturated with all sorts of crises and dystopian scenarios, market 'rational optimists' such as Matt Ridley[4] and Steven Johnson offer visions of a better, 'future perfect' world.[5]

Outside North America, the appetite for such books now extends globally, especially in Europe and China. This genre revolving around future high-tech imaginaries is characterised by magnifying, exaggerating and projecting various socio-economic trends. It takes a few empirical examples that are then transformed into images of new futuristic societies, which on closer analysis are unlikely to eventuate. These days, high-tech books, TED talks and numerous online sites, as well as the old print media contain a heavy dose of references to 'peer-to-peer' technology, 'disrupters', the 'internet of things', the 'sharing economy' and other buzz terms. Apart from the obligatory mention of Airbnb, Uber or a few big internet companies, little evidence is provided on how Uber and other marketing companies can 'dematerialise' production let alone lead to the wholesale decoupling of all other industries and economic processes. This is not at all to deny the proliferation of networked devices or the introduction of all kinds of new technologies and connectivity.

1   For a critical analysis of Toffler, see my book *The Post Industrial Utopians*, Polity Press, Cambridge, 1987.

2   For a survey and analysis of futurism, see Mark Solovey and Hamilton Cravens (eds.) *Cold War Social Science: Knowledge Production, Liberal Democracy, and Human Nature,* Palgrave Macmillan, New York, 2012.

3   See for example, K. Eric Drexler, *Radical Abundance: How a Revolution in Nanotechnology Will Change Civilization*, Public Affairs, New York 2013 and Peter H. Diamandis and Steven Kotler, *Abundance: The Future Is Better Than You Think*, Free Press, New York, 2014.

4   Matt Ridley, *The Rational Optimist: How Prosperity Evolves*, Harper, New York, 2010.

5   Steven Johnson, *Future Perfect: The Case for Progress in a Networked Age*, Riverhead/Penguin, New York, 2012.

Fusing environmental concerns with visions of dramatic technological decoupling is a particular characteristic of the work of futurologist Jeremy Rifkin. Like Toffler and others before him, Rifkin is in high demand as a conference speaker and consultant to international corporations and to European, Chinese and other governments. He simultaneously appeals to corporate and government desires to decouple economic growth from nature and yet also attracts those interested in post-capitalist utopianism. As the super-salesman of the 'zero marginal cost society', Rifkin also partially influences some of the anti-capitalist 'Accelerationists', as I will go on to discuss. Importantly, Rifkin has consistently embraced a range of technological trends and has long promoted a radical form of decoupling in all spheres of life. Take for instance, his 1998 visions about the 'biotech century'. In coming decades, he claimed, genetic engineering will free much food production from farmers and the soil, as it will be grown indoors in giant bacteria baths. According to this scenario, animal and human cloning will be widespread, deadly diseases will be eliminated and our mood, behaviour and intelligence will all be affected by biogenetic changes, including birth in artificial wombs.[6] Rifkin's 'bio-economy' imagines decoupling in the form an 'abundance' of artificial food production. This contrasts with predictions by those fearful of food shortages and diseases due to climate breakdown. Rifkin's work is part of a trend in recent decades of promoting 'biomimicry', that is, the technological copying of natural processes which would supposedly enable capitalist production to continue and escape the limits of nature.[7]

Thirty years before Rifkin's pronouncements, Right-wing futurologists Herman Kahn and Anthony Wiener[8] also listed all the biotech changes in the pipeline, changes that would decouple biology and behaviour from language, socialisation and inter-subjective communication. In response, Jürgen Habermas called this trend towards man-made biogenetic machine control, one more example of how technology and science had become a central force in capitalist production. Technology and science become a new ideology by assuming the appearance of an independent force separate from the capitalist class. The new technological processes of production were seen to render ineffective Marx's critique of bourgeois ideology. It was no longer just a matter of explaining and

---

6   Jeremy Rifkin, *The Biotech Century: Harnessing the Gene and Remaking the World*, Tarcher/ Putnam, New York, 1998.

7   See for example, Jesse Goldstein and Elizabeth Johnson, 'Biomimicry: New Natures, New Enclosures', *Theory, Culture & Society*, Vol.32, no.1, 2015, pp.61-81. Also see OECD, *The Bioeconomy to 2030: Designing a Policy Agenda*, OECD, Paris, 2009.

8   Herman Kahn and Anthony J. Weiner, *The Year 2000: A Framework for Speculation on the Next Thirty Years*, Macmillan, New York, 1967.

demystifying how capitalists exploit workers, as 'technology and science as ideology' now occluded the ability of individuals to self-reflectively interpret and comprehend the modern relationship between the 'knowledge economy' and socio-political power relations.[9] Interestingly, some of the scientific and technological forecasts by Kahn and Wiener in 1967 have now become reality. Even the late 1960s critique of 'technology and science as ideology' by Habermas has itself been taken much further by radical Accelerationists in their justifiable attempt to decouple radical political change from reliance on the now diminished industrial working class.

Today, most radicals accept that capitalist production and Communist industrialisation have been based on the 'domination of nature'. The abuse and destruction of eco-systems is the direct consequence of treating nature as the mere 'stuff' essential to capitalist production and consumption. Yet, radicals are either divided about, or less alarmed by those aspects of the techno-sciences that constitute the 'knowledge economy' – that is, those scientific developments that are driving the reconstitution and reconfiguration of nature. Whether in the form of AI, biotech or other R&D promoting the post-human or the development of artificial substitutes for food and natural resources, the techno-sciences are on the cusp of altering traditional natural settings and historical political economic disputes over social distribution, such as old conflicts between capital and labour.[10]

If Rifkin's coming 'biotech century' looks half dystopian/half utopian, his excursion into the hydrogen economy, the 'internet of things' and 'distributive capitalism' is definitively utopian, despite his own rejection of this label. Rifkin heavily promotes what is called the 'Third Industrial Revolution' in his lectures and consultancies to governments, businesses and not-for-profit social institutions.[11] The paradox of capitalism, he argues, is the quest to reduce the marginal cost of production and so increase profits which in turn will lead to zero marginal costs that now threaten to transcend the market system and bring about the end of capitalism. Up until now, capitalists have reduced marginal costs by

---

9   Jürgen Habermas, *Towards a Rational Society: Student Protest Science and Politics* translated by Jeremy J. Shapiro, Beacon press, Boston, 1971, ch.6.

10   The critique of the techno-sciences and the new stage of capitalism based on the reconstitution of face-to-face social relations and former notions of human and non-human nature have been developed over the past thirty years by Geoff Sharp, John Hinkson, Alison Caddick, Paul James and other members of Arena editorial group in Melbourne, see e.g. Geoff Sharp, 'Constitutive Abstraction and Social practice', *Arena*, no.70, 1985, pp.48-82.

11   Jeremy Rifkin, *The Third Industrial Revolution: How Lateral Power is Transforming Energy, the Economy, and the World,* Palgrave MacMillan, Basingstoke, 2013.

integrating production under one vertical roof. But the 'Third Industrial Revolution' is a lateral system. Zero marginal cost production has already happened in publishing, music and information and it is now possible to extend this to all goods through the development of the 'internet of things'. The new system will be based on three operating engines: 1) a communication network based on the internet; 2) a sustainable energy system based on renewables; and 3) a new mobility and logistics system based on driverless vehicles circulating goods made by 3D printers. By 2030 there will be 100 trillion sensors in the world facilitating these three operating engines of the new 'collaborative commons'. Any consumer can become a *'prosumer'* (Toffler's concept) and use big data via apps to produce and consume their needs.

One key aspect of the 'super internet of things' linked by 100 trillion sensors is that it will purportedly connect the entire human race so that they can by-pass corporations and governments and engage directly with one another as a 'collaborative commons'. Rifkin optimistically assumes that the radiation emitted from 100 trillion sensors (connected by wi-fi) will not result in an epidemic of cancers and neurological illnesses. Hundreds of millions of buildings (191 million homes, factories, offices, shops and warehouses in Europe alone) will produce their own decentralised energy from renewable sources, solar and wind, for example. As Rifkin puts it:

> Market capitalism will be transformed into 'distributed capitalism'. Just as the internet led to the democratisation of information, the Third Industrial Revolution will lead to the democratisation of energy. The required changes to infrastructure are going to create massive amounts of jobs and a whole new economy. But when you have peer-to-peer sharing of energy across an intelligent grid system, you no longer have the top-down, centralised economic system. Distributed energy requires distributed capitalism, and that relies on the opposite view of human nature than that of market capitalism. But the politics isn't right or left – its centralised, top-down versus collaborative commons. You don't hear people say, I'm going onto a social networking space because I'm a socialist – it's just a different frame of reference.[12]

---

12 Amanda Gefter interview with Jeremy Rifkin, *New Scientist*, 17 February 2010. Rifkin develops these ideas in *The Zero Marginal Cost Society: The internet of things, the collaborative commons, and the eclipse of capitalism*, Palgrave Macmillan, London, 2014.

Many of Rifkin's ideas are very attractive in comparison to the existing irrational, destructive and wasteful practices of present-day capitalism. Yet they also fit comfortably with social democratic 'green growth' capitalism and espouse a heavy measure of 'Third Way' social and market entrepreneurialism. Underpinning Rifkin's new society is the belief in 'free'. Using digital online services and products (music, publishing and video files) as the base model for the 'Third Industrial Revolution', it is only one small theoretical step to link renewable energy, 3D printers and biotech to a whole world of self-generating products and collaborative social relations. Despite being well aware of climate change and natural resource depletion, especially the critical shortage and extensive waste of water, Rifkin's new 'Third Industrial Revolution' is a world unconstrained by scarcity and based on an absolute decoupling of production from natural limitations. Like many utopian market entrepreneurs, Rifkin glosses over major problems of how the natural resources and the labour needed to construct the hardware for the globally connected human race such as metals, rare minerals, polymers for 3D printers and electric cars can be provided cost-free. Zero marginal cost production needs the myth of 'free' in order to function. This myth assumes not only that the cost of producing the original product is zero or near zero, but that all subsequent copies can be produced free by digital and other reproductive technologies such as 3D printers. Even critics using conventional theories of marginal economics[13] let alone Marxists and radical environmentalists, reject the premises of zero marginal cost.

Consequently, Rifkin himself has several guises that range from radical environmentalist, social democrat to business insider. One is Left-wing, as he argues that capitalism creates unemployment, inequality and environmental crises. Rifkin is also anti-nuclear, pro-unions and pro-social justice and animal welfare. Yet, the other guise adopted by Rifkin is the high-flying corporate and government consultant as well as 'guru' to mass readers yearning for a world free of scarcity. The zero marginal cost society is simultaneously a mixture of ecologically modernised capitalism and post-capitalism brought into being by technological innovation rather than by mass political action. Rifkin recognises that existing corporations can hijack the 'Third Industrial Revolution'. Tellingly, his new society requires neo-liberal governments and capitalists to commit suicide by investing in technologies and social processes that lead to their own replacement by a 'collaborative commons'. This is a

---

13 See for example, John M. Newman, 'The Myth of Free', *Social Science Research Network*, 25 August, 2016 and Eric Raymond (who inspired Rifkin), 'Zero Marginal Thinking: Jeremy Rifkin gets it all wrong', 3 April, 2014, http://esr.ibiblio.org/.

'distributive economy' where profitable enterprise will cease after the initial decentralised energy and reproductive grids have been constructed. The question that remains is how can profit and tax revenue survive in a society where most goods and services will be free?

Unchained Radical Prometheans

Those on the radical Left of Rifkin are also seduced by the promise of new technology. It is precisely at a time when the socialist Left is extremely weak in developed capitalist countries that utopian thinking flourishes to fill the gap created by the absence of strong mass movements. This is particularly true of the UK and US where a sense of hopelessness about radical change has produced unusual or spectacular flights of fancy. When major thinkers, such as Fredric Jameson contemplate that the American army as an institution could be transformed into the vehicle of radical change, one knows that despair has well and truly manifested itself in utopian escapism. [14] Utopian theorists fleetingly talk about the whole world, while remaining firmly focussed on developed, affluent capitalist countries. Schooled in Marxist, anarchist and feminist debates, they recognise that most of the old Left strategies revolving around the industrial working class as the principal agent of social change belongs to an era long passed. Disappointingly, most say little about the environment or decoupling. Rather they appear so mesmerised by the promise of new technologies that they assume a 'cheer squad' and form an unofficial 'united front' with capitalists in wishing to accelerate its progress.

One of several current utopian movements that embrace rapid technological innovation is Accelerationism.[15] Its theorists claim that the sooner labour-saving technology and all kinds of digital, biogenetic and other dematerialising technologies are introduced the sooner capitalism will come to an end. Just as Lenin argued in 1917 that the Bolsheviks needed to 'give history a push' (rather than first wait for the bourgeois revolution and then the socialist revolution), so too, for quite different reasons, the Accelerationists see new technology as a force that will

---

14 See Jameson's vision and responses in Slavoj Zizek (ed.), *An American Utopia: Dual Power and the Universal Army*, Verso, London, 2016.

15 Benjamin Noys gave the term a political meaning in 2010, see Benjamin Noys, *'Futures of Accelerationism'*, academic. edu 23 October 2016; also see B. Noys, *Malign Velocities: Accelerationism & Capitalism*, Zero Books, Winchester, 2014; Nick Srnicek and Alex Williams wrote the manifesto 'Accelerate Manifesto for an Accelerationist Politics', *Critical Legal Thinking*, 14 May 2013. Also see Robin Mackay and Armen Avanessian (eds), *#The Accelerationist Reader*, Falmouth, Urbanomic, 2014.

topple capitalist social orders. Combining philosophers such as Deleuze and Guattari, radical political theory and avant-garde art, Accelerationism has assumed many different forms since the 1970s and has become more visible in recent years, especially in arts colleges, online blogs and magazines.[16] It is revealing that Accelerationism has no real presence in labour or green movements.

Journalist Paul Mason has done much to popularise the notion of post-capitalism[17] in the media and has himself been influenced by Accelerationist ideas. Utilising the work of Rifkin, Paul Romer and others, Mason also subscribes to the zero marginal cost society. Neo-liberalism, he says, is broken and cannot solve existing problems let alone the impending threats posed by automation and climate change. A former Trotskyist, Mason now rejects not only the Leninist vanguard party but also the old Left model of centring social change on the industrial working class. This is a familiar position that goes back to Herbert Marcuse's 1964 analysis of the incorporation of the working class into the destructive logic of capitalism.[18] In the late 1970s and early 1980s, mass unemployment and the restructuring of capitalism produced variations of the 'farewell' to the revolutionary industrial working class by people such as Andre Gorz.[19] Similarly, the rise of the cognitive worker and the reliance of capital on collective forms of exploitation beyond the factory led Antonio Negri (in his fusion of Marx, Foucault, Deleuze and Guattari) to focus on the transition from struggles in the factory to resistance in the 'social factory'.[20]

Mason builds on these earlier political critiques of orthodox Marxism and takes them one step further. He argues that the historical values of collectivism centred on the factory have dissolved and need to be replaced by a new social collectivity based on the digital information society or 'collaborative commons' (Rifkin, Michael Bauwens, Elinor Ostrom, David Bollier and others). Consequently:

The main contradiction today is between the possibility of free,

---

16 For a variety of cultural sites and socio-political publications including a list of publications by Accelerationists, see for example, Monoskop.org and Charlie Mills, *Towards a Future Post-Capitalism: Accelerationism and its Aesthetics*, Dissertation for the Department of Visual Cultures, Goldsmiths College, University of London, 2016.

17 Paul Mason, *PostCapitalism: A Guide to Our Future*, Allen Lane, London, 2015.

18 Herbert Marcuse, *One Dimensional Man: The Ideology of Industrial Society*, Routledge & Kegan Paul, London, 1964

19 Andre Gorz, *Farewell to the Working Class: An Essay on Post-Industrial Socialism*, trans.by Michael Sonenscher, Pluto, London, 1982.

20 Antonio Negri, *From the Factory to the Metropolis: Essays Volume 2*, Edited by Federico Tomasello and trans. by Ed Emery, Polity, Cambridge, 2018.

abundant goods and information; and a system of monopolies, banks and governments trying to keep things private, scarce and commercial. Everything comes down to the struggle between the network and the hierarchy: between old forms of society moulded around capitalism and new forms of society that pre-figure what comes next.[21]

There is much that is valuable in Mason's account of historical strug-gles, crisis theories and cultural changes. His work is also imaginative and suggestive in outlining some of the new social relations promised by post-capitalism. One problem is that Mason's alternative vision is founded on the highly dubious theory of Kondratieff long waves.[22] This is combined with his failure to spell out, much like Rifkin, how a zero marginal cost society can prevent major environmental crises. Importantly, nearly all Mason's new technology examples come from digital media and simply fail to translate adequately when applied to key areas of mining, manufacturing and food production. Mason accepts the ecological modernisation ideology of the 'circular economy' which is a far from proven solution to decoupling growth from nature. These and other gaps in his work are just some of the fundamental weaknesses that make his analysis of natural limits (scarcity) and the transition from neoliberalism unconvincing. The fact that half of the world's population is not online, especially the global poor in developing countries, where in some countries less than 15 per cent of the population have online access is a case in point. To hundreds of millions of people who don't even have electricity or running water, the zero marginal cost society is like pure fantasy.

Since publishing *Post Capitalism* in 2015, Mason has changed his tune. He is now concerned about combatting the rise of 'nationalist neo-lib-eralism' associated with Brexit, Trump, Alternative for Deutschland and other movements. Following the 2017 British election, Mason argues that we need to counter the rise of 'nationalist neo-liberalism' with 'national Left' strategies – a 'radical social democracy' or an updated 'spirit of 45' (Ken Loach) such as a Corbyn-led Labour government that manages or 'civilises' capitalism.[23] This position contradicts his thesis in *Post Capitalism* that the old Left strategies are dead and that 'post-capitalism' could be a 500 year-long transition. In short, Mason

---

21 P. Mason, 'The end of capitalism has begun', *The Guardian*, 17 July 2015.

22 P. Mason, *PostCapitalism*, ch.2.

23 Paul Mason, 'Neoliberalism has destroyed social mobility. Together we must rebuild it.' *Open Democracy*, 2 February 2018.

veers between conventional Left politics and utopian visions, both of which demand a massive leap in faith to become convincing transitions to high tech post-capitalism.

Other influential radical utopians such as Nick Srnicek and Alex Williams, authors of the Accelerationist Manifesto,[24] also place their hopes in high tech 'mission-oriented' innovation (following Marianna Mazzucato).

> A forward-thinking government could support mission-oriented projects such as decarbonising the economy, fully automating work, expanding cheap renewable energy, exploring synthetic biology, developing cheap medicine, supporting space exploration and building artificial intelligence.[25]

Most of these objectives sound straight from 'boys own' manuals and would be quite compatible with the wish lists of capitalist entrepreneurs even though they are paraded as the foundation of "fully automated luxury communism".[26] A few objectives such as space exploration and synthetic biology, betray either a lack of environmental priorities or an uncritical acceptance of bio-tech values. Media blogger Aaron Bastani goes further and adopts 'fully automated luxury communism' (FALC) as his manifesto. Accordingly: "new technologies will liberate us from work, providing the opportunity to build a society beyond both capitalism and scarcity. Automation, rather than undermining an economy built on full employment, is instead the path to a world of liberty, luxury and happiness. For everyone."[27] This is a pre-environmentalist perspective that combines simplistic political sloganeering with the technological determinist illusion of utopian abundance. Similarly, some feminists influenced by Accelerationism, such as the extreme postmodern

---

24 See Srnicek and Williams, 'Accelerate Manifesto for an Accelerationist Politics', *Critical Legal Thinking*, 14 May 2013. They have since rejected being called 'accelerationists' as they see the term as too confusing given that it embraces a diverse range of Right and Left thinkers.

25 N. Srnicek and A. Williams, *Inventing the Future: Postcapitalism and a World Without Work, revised and updated edition*, Verso, London, 2016, p.147.

26 This phrase is used by a supporter of degrowth, Aaron Vansintjan, to describe Srnicek and Williams proposals after attending a 'Future Society Forum'. See his *'Accelerationism… and Degrowth? The Left's Strange Bedfellows'*, Institute for Social Ecology, social-ecology.org 28 September 2016. He also criticises Aaron Bastani's disregard for environmental sustainability in Bastani's *Fully Automated Luxury Communism* in media presentations, see A. Vansintjan, 'Where's the "eco" in Ecomodernism', *Red Pepper*, January 2018.

27 See promotion material for Bastani's *Fully Automated Luxury Communism*, (Verso, London, 2018, forthcoming). Also see Aaron Bastani, 'Fully Automated Luxury Communism', *Novara Media and Youtube*, November 10, 2014 where he outlines what he calls FALC.

Xenofeminists, see nature as the enemy and desire that bio-technology and other technologies facilitate a reconfiguration of human biology where there are no limits to the human or natural world.[28] The total decoupling of gender is neither nurture nor nature but rather a 'feminist' technological determinism that bends the stick in the opposite direction until humans are eviscerated in favour of infinitely plastic, malleable 'post-human' creatures. The Xenofeminists begin positively by rejecting conservative ideological notions of 'male' and 'female' but end up supporting the anti-environmental notion that everything can be transformed, re-engineered and manipulated technologically.

In terms of political programs, if one attempted to identify the counter-hegemonic alternative to the ecologically destructive, consumption-led accumulation of capital, the answer would not lie in the re-distribution of the existing *unsustainable* pie. Redistribution remains absolutely central to social change but it must be based on ecologically sustainable socio-economic policies. Take away private ownership of wealth and power and there is little difference between corporate capitalist technological hopes placed in the absolute decoupling of economic growth from nature and the technological promises of Accelerationists, Trotskyist groups such as Socialist Alternative[29] or a group of Left Promethean writers published in the radical journal *Jacobin*.[30] These ecomodernists attack a wide range of environmentalist 'doomsdayers' for offering nothing but 'eco-austerity'. Instead, they promote hyper-technological solutions including nuclear power, dangerous geo-engineering, discredited carbon capture and the old Promethean goal of controlling nature.

If social redistribution combined with technological innovation facilitates significant improvements in the standard of living of the impoverished masses of the world without environmental destruction, then this will indeed be very welcome news. However, naïve and misconceived technological expectations of delivering Western consumption and affluence to nine to sixteen billion people through decoupling economic growth from the limits of natural resources is based on the old discredited politics of technology. The dangers and political

---

28 Laboria Cuboniks, *Xenofeminism A Politics for Alienation*, laboriacuboniks.net 2015. Helen Hester develops XF *as* "a technomaterialist, anti-naturalist, and gender abolitionist form of feminism" in *Xenofeminism*, Polity, Cambridge, 2018, p.6.

29 See for example, Pete Dickinson, Planning Green Growth A Socialist Contribution to the Debate on Environmental Sustainability, *Socialist Alternative* pamphlet, 2017.

30 See Peter Frase, Angela Nagle, Leigh Phillips and Michal Rozworski, Christian Parenti, et al in special issue of *Jacobin*, no. 26, 2017. For a critique of this Left hyper-technology perspective, see John Bellamy Foster, 'The Long Ecological Revolution', *Monthly Review*, November 2017.

misconceptions of Promethean utopians is due to the fact that they alternate between seeing science and technology as politically neutral, and yet also according technology an active role as the agent or driving force of social change. They ignore the need for radical materialists to once again confront and absorb the old lessons produced by decades of environmentalist critiques of dangerous technologies and production levels. This requires that radicals abandon their simplistic belief that a change in ownership from capitalists to workers will remove most environmental constraints on everyday life.

Srnicek and Williams share much of this love of new technology. Their central thesis rests on how capitalism is creating a surplus population, a mass precariat of the underemployed and workless. Hence,

> The utopian potentials inherent in twenty-first-century technology cannot remain bound to a parochial capitalist imagination; they must be liberated by an ambitious left alternative. Neoliberalism has failed, social democracy is impossible, and only an alternative vision can bring about universal prosperity and emancipation.[31]

Most of Srnicek and Williams' book is devoted to critiquing the historically obsolete political strategies of the Left and social movements. In key respects they share a view of technology that is similar to the ecological modernising platforms of pro-market technological entrepreneurs and 'green growth' think-tanks such as the Breakthrough Institute. If they wish to rescue the future from 'capitalism's version of modernity', their fundamental lack of analysis of environmental limits reveals much that is illusory in their version of a post-scarcity world. After incurring strong criticisms, Srnicek and Williams have had to proclaim that they are aware of environmental issues and believe a reduction of the working week and the introduction of a universal basic income (UBI) will foster reduced forms of consumption.[32] Given the enormity of the environmental challenges we face, these feeble answers are far from adequate.[33]

Nonetheless, their discussion of old and current Left strategies contains valuable insights. Paradoxically though, Srnicek and Williams have no developed politics of their own. Their vision of an anti-capitalist movement largely depends on capitalists automating production and

---

31 Srnicek and Williams, *op.cit*, p.3.

32 See Srnicek and Williams, *op.cit*, Afterword to updated edition.

33 Nick Srnicek, Response to Symposium discussion on Inventing the Future, disorderof things. com November 15, 2015.

creating the socio-technological conditions for the future socialist society. 'Inventing the future' amounts to little more than a few slogans: full automation and a reduced working week (a contradiction in terms); *full unemployment* – an inversion of Kalecki on full employment; a global universal basic income (UBI); a modernised Left that recognises the liberating power of technology; and a new 'Left populism' that helps construct a post-work society. I will leave discussion of mass unemployment and a UBI to a later chapter. Suffice to say that 'Inventing the future' is a poorly developed thesis that cannot advance a post-work society until capitalists have eliminated most jobs through 'accelerated' automated production and implemented a UBI.

Srnicek and Williams convey no sense that they have wrestled with any of the environmental complexities of achieving absolute decoupling or how an automated capitalism or post-capitalism can avoid the natural limits to growth. Similarly, they fail to discuss fiscal and monetary policies, international trade or a range of issues from development politics to welfare services. These and many other socio-economic and political institutional issues are not addressed because they place their hopes in full automation and the UBI delivering socialism. Their vision and strategy is yet another example of intellectuals from affluent developed capitalist countries playing theoretical games. Their political slogans fail to address the multiple challenges of how a fully automated, but low-growth and absolutely decoupled high tech, post-work society can be economically and environmentally sustainable in developed OECD countries, not to mention the many low-income countries in the rest of the world. Crucially, the 'cart' of post-capitalist technological society is put before the 'horse' of anti-capitalist politics. Why the vast majority of service, manufacturing, mining and agricultural sector workers would stop being very fearful of losing their jobs, which also means loss of access to consumer goods, and rush to join the post-work political movement so that they can enjoy austerity living on a meagre global UBI, is perhaps something that only politically detached utopian theorists could imagine.

Mason, Srnicek and Williams straddle the worlds of scarcity and post-scarcity. They are vaguely aware of natural limits and yet are driven by visions of abundance in information technologies that supposedly translate into material abundance. Post-capitalism is also envisaged as different types of dystopia unless a Left high-tech society is brought into being.[34] Peter Frase, editor of *Jacobin*, also spells out how if socialism

---

fails to triumph, automation could lead to a modern version of 'social-ism or barbarism' based on scenarios of exterminism, policing, racism, new forms of colonialism and environmental crises.[35] Leaving aside these speculative dystopias, Paul Mason's advocacy of the 'collaborative commons' stands closer to other post-capitalists such as Belgian philos-opher Michel Bauwens (author of the Peer to Peer Manifesto[36]) rather than to the high-tech Leftism of Srnicek and Williams. According to Bauwens, contemporary political economy is based on the fundamen-tally false idea of material abundance and immaterial scarcity. Material pseudo-abundance fuels debt-driven growth which is unsustainable given finite natural resources. Conversely, the false idea of immaterial scarcity enforced by intellectual property laws, monopolies and patents restricts and discourages social innovation and co-operation (similar to Mason's 'hierarchies' versus 'networks'). Thus, pseudo material abun-dance destroys the biosphere while pseudo immaterial scarcity prevents social justice and human learning.[37]

Utopian Neglect of the Political Ecology of Food Systems

Rifkin, Mason, the Accelerationists and many other devotees of tech-nological solutions differ significantly from business advocates of decoupling economic growth from nature. However, all seem to gloss over the fundamental difficulties of achieving food security in a future world of at least nine, and possibly as many as twelve to sixteen billion people facing the continuing deterioration of eco-systems. Decoupling food production from nature is not just an extremely problematical technological goal in the present world of 7.6 billion people but is par-ticularly difficult when fully taking into account the obstacles posed by conflicting political and social power relations and cultural values.

Each social formation throughout history has been defined by the way it produces and consumes food. The same will be true of future societies whether capitalist or post-capitalist. Agribusinesses and those engaged in the commercial processing and retailing of food continually look to technological innovation and labour market restructuring to increase profit margins by saving on production and exchange costs. By

---

35 Peter Frase, *Four Futures: Visions of the World After Capitalism*, Verso, London, 2016.

36 Michel Bauwens, The Peer to Peer Manifesto: The Emergence of P2P Civilization and Political Economy, *P2P Foundation*, November 2007.

37 Michel Bauwens and Franco Iacomella, 'Peer to Peer Economy and New Civilization Centered Around the Sustenance of the Commons' in David Bollier and Silke Helfrich (eds), *The Wealth of the Commons: A World Beyond Market & State*, Levellers Press, Amherst, 2016.

contrast, most urban social change activists desire social reform and care for eco-systems. Yet, many still ignore or have only a dim awareness of crucial aspects of food production, despite greater recognition of the centrality of food to all kinds of environmental, political economic and cultural processes. This low priority given to food production is unfortunate, as no viable post-carbon or post-capitalist economy is possible without the transformation of dominant forms of commercial food production, distribution and consumption. My purpose here is to briefly signal some of the important political and technological aspects of food production that will need to be abandoned or surmounted if business images of 'sustainable capitalism' are to become viable. Similarly, faith in technological solutions put forward by advocates of 'green growth' social democracy and radical socialist post-capitalism (Accelerationists and others) ignore food production at their own peril.

Rural populations have historically been the major victims of social transformations, especially rapid industrialisation. The legacy of brutal nineteenth and twentieth century assaults on peasants, tenant farmers, indigenous people and small farmers is all around us – from the millions killed by forced collectivisation in Communist countries to the vast areas of the world where rural populations have been uprooted, starved and driven into desperate poverty by capitalist market forces. Most residents of OECD countries enjoy sufficient food and comforts and tend to block from view the daily reality of hundreds of millions of malnourished, starving and suffering fellow human beings. Global inequality occasionally rears its many heads in trade negotiations, foreign aid reports, the individual consumption of fair trade goods such as coffee, or regular news bulletins briefly featuring a montage of starving children and appeals for charity. Few people in OECD countries are aware of the millions in developing societies forced to live under the harsh rule of large landholders, (regularly documented by the International Peasants' Movement La Via Campesina) and the continued impoverishment of countless rural populations who are nominally free, but barely survive. Each year, numerous resisting villagers, environmentalists and rangers are killed trying to protect their land from deforestation and ruin by agribusiness, mining and logging.[38]

Given the large contribution made by chemical agribusiness and processed manufactured food to carbon emissions and environmental destruction, it is safe to say that all present-day societies that fail to begin seriously tackling the existing commercialised processes and character of

---

38 John Watts and John Vidal, 'Environmental defenders being killed in record numbers, new research reveals', *The Guardian*, 13 July 2017.

food production will only reap far more despoiled environments in the future.

It is paradoxical that the wide range of books, articles and reports on all component elements of the food chain – from land and sea, through to processing, consumption and waste – remain inadequately attuned to the socio-political implications of transitioning to a post-carbon political economy. This is not to deny that many environmentalists promote agroecology as part of their larger vision of green societies. Radical critics of agribusiness have also long advocated socialist and other types of post-capitalist societies. All share the goal of preventing dangerous climate change. Each investigative area has made significant and invaluable contributions to our understanding of the larger ecology of food. [39] However, without linking various component elements, the overwhelming majority of analyses and activities tend to be compartmentalised into the following studies and messages:

1. Major environmental damage affecting the future of food. This alarming message is the product of countless scientific and technical studies of soil and fresh water and marine ecologies ranging from nitrogen cycles, impact of temperature changes on arable land, fertility and crop yields, fish stocks, scale and causes of deforestation and desertification, species extinction, water quality, bio-energy, and numerous other aspects of human interaction with natural resources and cultivated agriculture and marine habitats.

2. Political and social campaigns about the relationship between agribusiness and its impact on dietary practices and the environment. These include increasingly familiar issues such as amounts of water and grains needed to produce a kilogram of various meats, or energy and freight costs embodied in transporting processed food over long distances. It also includes environmental and social costs of packaging, marketing and disposing of food waste as well as the increasing focus on the connection between food industry businesses and deteriorating health such as obesity and chronic illnesses.

3. Social awareness flowing from methods of food production, especially the focus on chemical agriculture and aquaculture

---

39 Numerous studies have popularised the centrality of food production, see Michael Pollan, *Omnivore's Dilemma*, Penguin, New York, 2007; Michael Carolan, *The Real Cost of Cheap Food*, Routledge Earthscan, London, 2012 and Joel K. Bourne, *The End of Plenty: The Race to Feed a Crowded World*, W.W. Norton & Co, New York, 2015.

versus organic farming and hunting and gathering. Studies of capital-intensive agriculture and fish farming analyse how and why capitalist food production invests in particular crops and livestock, the economic as opposed to environmental cost of fertilizers, pesticides, machinery and feedlots for caged animals. Moreover, the scale of production and market size includes the competition between large international producers and small farms, and the financialisation of agriculture through greater debt due to financing expensive machinery, the role of futures contracts, trade agreements and the subordination of many farmers to prices set by supermarkets and fast food chains. In addition, the treatment of farm labourers and poor villagers is highlighted plus taxpayer subsidies for fossil fuels and the over-production of various crops. All these issues now form part of a growing literature on the political economy of food.

4. Demystifying commercial 'organic' food and combining social change with food sovereignty. Organic farming, slow food and farmers' markets receive more positive treatment in recent analyses and campaigns. However, important aspects of various forms of organic food production adopt agribusiness methods, hide behind loosely redefined marketing criteria of 'organic' food which are not necessarily equivalent to sustainable agriculture. Increasing proportions of 'organic' food is imported from other countries and disguised as home grown or processed sustainable food. By contrast, the growth of agroecology movements especially in Latin and Central America (pioneered by people such as Miguel Altieri) combines social change with food sovereignty, that is, emphasising ecological sustainability, restoring local self-reliance and embracing diverse traditional and modern food production methods.[40]

5. The application of biotech and other techno-sciences to market-driven food production such as conflicts over genetic engineering and the impact of losing seed varieties is quite familiar. Less well known are the unknown costs and dangers to human health and environmental sustainability of nanotechnology and pharmaceuticals when used to increase yields and new

---

40 See Miguel A. Altieri and Victor Manuel Toledo, 'The agroecological revolution in Latin America: rescuing nature, ensuring food sovereignty and empowering peasants', *The Journal of Peasant Studies*, Vol. 38, No. 3, July 2011, 587–612 and C. Francis, M. Altieri, et al. 'Agroecology: The Ecology of Food Systems, *Journal of Sustainable Agriculture*, vol.22, no.3, 2003, pp.99-118.

hybrid species in the face of natural pests, climatic changes and reducing cost of commercial livestock feed.

6. On the positive side, increased preoccupation with the mitigation of carbon emissions and repair of damaged environments in relation to food production. This activity focuses on new measures to reverse a century of environmental damage. It includes co-operative work between farmers, villagers and environmentalists. Attention also focuses on how to 'green' cities by expanding urban food production, cleaning and restoring waterways and marine ecologies as well as minimising food waste and the promotion of 'slow food' networks of producers and food consumption outlets.

Considering all the different facets of food production just mentioned, it remains entirely unclear how decoupling growth from nature in a capitalist world or aiming for a post-capitalist egalitarian society can resolve most major environmental constraints if the form and scale of industrialised, chemical agriculture and dietary cultures continue. Above all, we face a major crisis in food production sustainability due to systematic eco-system destruction and breakdown. The United Nations Food and Agriculture Organization estimates that chemically-based, industrial agriculture causes over US$3 trillion worth of natural damage each year, a catastrophic price that is clearly unsustainable.[41] Such is the loss of soil nutrients and mass extermination of insects through pesticides that current agribusiness harvests and levels of production *may only last for approximately another sixty years.*

Given the short time frame, of about sixty years to solve major food security problems, how could decoupling capitalist food production growth from nature or a new post-capitalist food system be simultaneously environmentally sustainable, and compatible with social justice goals while also being founded on post-carbon democratic organisational and institutional structures and values? For example, can small-scale farms feed the world in the absence of industrialised agriculture? Are the interests of producers in self-managed food cooperatives and local communes compatible with the needs of low-income consumers? What level of private land ownership and commercial control of food production and distribution is compatible with social justice in cities and rural areas?

It is not merely accidental that most governments have avoided tackling the use of fossil fuels in agriculture or curbing dangerous emissions

---

41 See Nadia El-Hage Scialabba et al, *Natural Capital Impacts in Agriculture*, FAO, Rome June 2015

such as methane from livestock excreta and fertilisers. Greenhouse gas emissions from food production account for approximately 15% of total global emissions, or more than the combined total emitted by road, rail, shipping and air transport. Politically, rural constituencies and agribusiness lobbies are very powerful and many political parties are reluctant to antagonise these socio-economic forces. It is difficult enough getting support for reform policies affecting urban-based businesses, let alone threatening existing practices and control of land by millions of farmers.

Land has always been much more than mere property and embodies significant cultural, religious and social meanings for families, communities and individuals. This is particularly true in developing societies. Even in developed capitalist countries, where banks and governments classify farming and other aspects of agricultural production as just another form of business activity, rural communities retain significant local traditions and resist change, unless persuaded by government subsidies or new production techniques that there is more income to be earned. Hence, several inescapable political economic problems associated with both food production and sustainability need urgent resolution through the implementation of new practices and techniques.

First, critics of decoupling economic growth who promote organic food production as a sustainable alternative for a future world of more than 9 billion people have to overcome some major hurdles. Currently, organic food constitutes a tiny proportion of existing global production (only 2% of total agriculture in the US, one of the world's largest food producers). Hence the recurring question: can organic food feed the world? Some environmentalists assert the capacity of organic production to meet future world need by emphasising *distributional* and *consumption* rather than production issues; these include 40% of existing cereals are fed to livestock, up to 10% is used in biofuels, high-fructose syrup and other processes, while up to 40% of food produced and purchased in many OECD countries is unused or thrown out as waste. As Damien Carrington reported recently, "new research shows that without meat and dairy consumption, global farmland use could be reduced by more than 75% – an area equivalent to the US, China, European Union and Australia combined – and still feed the world. Loss of wild areas to agriculture is the leading cause of the current mass extinction of wildlife. The new analysis shows that while meat and dairy provide just 18% of calories and 37% of protein, it uses the vast majority – 83% – of farmland and produces 60% of agriculture's greenhouse gas emissions."[42]

---

42 Damien Carrington, 'Avoiding meat and dairy is 'single biggest way' to reduce your impact on Earth', The Guardian, 1 June, 2018.

Despite these alarming figures, a dramatic decline in meat and dairy foods production and consumption is easier said than done in a non-authoritarian society with freedom of choice.

Second, the old historical dispute between the competing interests of producers and consumers is also a key social justice issue. Currently, farmers in OECD countries earn higher incomes from producing organic food which compensates for the fact that yields from organic production tend to be on average 9 to 20 or more per cent lower than conventional farming. While farmers receive higher prices, unfortunately, the price of organic produce is unaffordable for most low and middle-income people compared with agribusiness food. Many people on welfare or minimum wages cannot even afford non-organic fruit and vegetables and rely on cheaper fast food and processed manufactured food. Switching to organic food production requires more labour-intensive farming yet wages for farm labourers are very low in market economies. How would a post-carbon or post-growth democracy reorganise agricultural labour to ensure that urban residents could afford to buy food while maintaining price and income incentives for farmers to switch to organic production? Is large-scale organic food production viable in regulated capitalist 'mixed economies', or does it require profit-regulated co-operatives, state planning and the distribution of land to become socially just and sustainable?

Third, it is no accident that the future political economic and environmental sustainability of both agribusiness, organic and agroecological food production is closely tied to how class divisions between rural and urban regions of developed nation states are resolved. Conversely, millions of poor villagers and rural residents in less developed capitalist societies are struggling to prevent agribusiness destroying their traditional food producing methods. Different trajectories of food production and consumption are thus visible in advanced capitalist countries as opposed to developing societies. In OECD countries, there has been greater consciousness of the environmental and health benefits of organic, 'slow food' despite the vast majority of people in these countries still consuming food made and sold by businesses who put the environment and public health a firm second to profits. This growing 'food' consciousness is also partly visible in developing countries where amongst the growing urban middle-class there is a demand for clean food (especially in highly polluted countries such as China) even if 'clean' is not necessarily equivalent to organic. A case in point is the importation of agribusiness food from less polluted countries such as Australia, Canada and New Zealand to meet the growing consumer tastes for processed food.

Fourth, the imbalance between the production and consumption patterns of *capital-intensive* food production in advanced capitalist countries and *labour-intensive* farming in developing countries is a major obstacle to any smooth transition to organic production and agroecology alternatives to agribusiness. For instance, 85% of the world's approximately 570 million farms are very tiny family farms, producing food on less than 1 to 2 hectares. This constitutes control of only about 12% of all agricultural land. Millions of women produce a substantial proportion of food for populations in developing societies on highly productive plots of one hectare or less, but over 815 million people suffer from chronic undernourishment. These tiny farms are distinct from the other small farmers on land that is between 3 and 10 hectares in size. By contrast, only 2% of all farms in the world ranging from 20 hectares to thousands of hectares, control 65% of the world's agricultural land.[43]

With urbanisation and a dramatic increase in processed food production in Africa and Asia, plus an additional 2 billion mouths to feed in the next twenty to thirty years, the shortage of agricultural land, class inequality and environmental pressures make food production an explosive and crucial problem in coming decades. A familiar pattern of environmental destruction of food-producing land and marine habitats by market predators (from cash crop agribusinesses to mining companies, loggers, property developers and manufacturers) is met with numerous forms of local resistance. There is little, however, that connects diverse urban and rural food and land movements in developing and developed capitalist countries. The regular anti-Davos conferences of alternative movements in Porto Alegre may bridge some of these differences momentarily, but the global Left and greens still lack detailed food production and consumption policies that address the needs of quite diverse social and political constituencies.

Fifth, in the event that successful political coalitions emerge, the wholesale global replacement of chemical food production by organic and agroecological production could not be accomplished democratically in less than two or three decades. The enormous task of cleaning and restoring polluted soils or eliminating genetically modified crops while reorganising production and distribution methods with sufficient non-exploited labour are just a few examples of why any transition would take time. So too would the channelling of public services and resources into deprived rural areas to rectify social neglect and also make rural life attractive to young urban residents, given the need to replace

---

43 See, '*The State of Food and Agriculture 2017, In Brief*', Food and Agriculture Organization of the United Nations, Rome, 2017.

ageing farming populations (if the cost of robots is prohibitive). Reversing the rapid urbanisation of global populations will be no easier than the difficult task of changing cultural patterns of food consumption to make food production sustainable. In order to guarantee food security and prevent possible starvation due to lower yields from organic food in various global regions, industrial agriculture will still be needed in any transitional process toward sustainability.

Alternative farming methods could incorporate new scientific research methods and the deployment of robots and labour-saving machinery if they are compatible with environmental sustainability. Technocratic options such as synthetic food production, the eating of insects as a new food staple or the harvesting of new plants and marine species (presently not part of the popular diet) are also part of some new food production agendas being explored. Currently, countries such as South Korea and Australia are at the forefront of developing seaweed into multiple forms of nutritional food for humans and also for cattle.[44] Hypothetically, seaweed could also possibly help expand fish farming by cleansing pollutants, store carbon emissions and provide sufficient new food to feed growing global populations. Yet, these alternative food sources offer false promises if their output proves to be very limited due to the fact that these new food sources are also strictly bound by the same metabolic processes of land-based agriculture (such as rates of photosynthesis) in a world of damaged ecological life-support systems. The same is true of business investment in 'artificial meat' substitutes. It remains to be seen whether reducing the environmental damage from meat production and distribution can be accomplished without artificial food substitutes requiring similar levels of intensive energy. Futuristic images of mass food production in urban or rural greenhouses may or may not be technically possible should desertification or flooding become permanent features due to climate breakdown. Whether decoupling food production from land will be possible without chemical inputs, or whether it will be privately or collectively owned remain future issues of major policy conflict.

Food and the Politics of Private or Communal Property

Whatever the future mode of food production adopted in different countries, each will depend on the type of political institutions, forms of property ownership or level of global trade or self-sufficiency that

---

44 Tim Flannery has uncritically explored the new promising developments of seaweed in an Australian documentary for *Catalyst* screened on ABC television on 22 August 2017.

prevail in any transition to post-carbon or post-growth societies. Crucially, the relationship between food production and political economic institutions will depend on the degree to which market or non-market mechanisms prevail. We know from the Soviet experience, that it took three decades for livestock and food production to return to pre-1929 levels following the horrific bloodshed of collectivisation and the Second World War. Command planning targets from the 1960s to the 1980s failed to feed the population and relied on internal markets and large amounts of imported grain. On the other hand, we also know that conventional agribusiness or organic food based on prevailing market systems are *fully compatible* with massive social inequalities, including starvation alongside enormous waste and highly exploitative conditions of work.

Importantly, the level of democracy or the change in ownership of land and urban property (whether in the form of co-operatives, local control of the 'commons' or other collective initiatives) will not automatically translate into environmentally sustainable food production and consumption systems. It is the form and character of larger social and macro-economic co-ordinating processes, that is, the degree of planning or market mechanisms that will shape future outcomes. So too will the amount of conflict or the degree of interests shared by producers and consumers as well as their concern for the wellbeing of strangers in other regions or countries. Almost three decades after the collapse of the Soviet Union, there are no fully developed and persuasive ideas of how to avoid the disastrous Soviet model or how to transition to post-capitalist societies without the use of either some form of state planning or some use of market mechanisms. All we have are vague abstract models of degrowth, 'doughnut economies', eco-socialist transitions, zero marginal cost societies and other theoretical models. These models advance valuable ideas but have little to say about the necessary organisational forms that will be needed for a sustainable food production system.

Transitional strategies and policies remain crucial. Radical technological utopians provide few answers. If old social change politics based on the vanguard party or social movement models are rejected, is it possible for a 'social bloc' or coalition to emerge that supports a post-carbon or post-growth democracy in a form that is durable beyond a few elections? One must not, however, confuse the contemporary attempts to construct a 'social bloc' with Gramsci's 1920s' notion of an 'historic bloc' of the working class and the peasantry. Given the colonial treatment of the peasantry and urban poor in the Italian South by both Northern capitalists and Northern trade unions and Left parties, Gramsci recognised that a revolutionary strategy could not be forged without an alliance of workers and peasant movements.[45] No alliance could counter bourgeois hegemony, Gramsci argued, unless it was also recognised how ruling class values were tied to folklore, popular culture and religion in both the north and the south.

Today, *La Via Campesina* campaigns on many important issues related to the negative impact of global marketisation on farmers. However, its claim to be a global peasant movement[46] is a misnomer, as there is little in common between the cultural traditions of Latin American, African or Asian villagers (aside from hardship and exploitation). It is also questionable to rename the social conditions, cultures and conservative political affiliations of small business farmers in Australia, Europe, North America and New Zealand as equivalent to those experienced by 'peasants' even though they are often in a dependent position vis-a-vis large agribusiness corporations. Constructing a 'historic bloc' between workers and peasants in China, India, South East Asia or Latin American and African countries is ambitious but equally remote politically. During Gramsci's day it was even difficult to forge alliances between northern Italian industrial workers and southern peasants, let alone building a global alliance between contemporary villagers, service sector and manufacturing workers and other social groups. While cash crops and export markets are vital to many farmers in agribusiness-dominated countries like Australia, Argentina, the U.S and Canada, they nonetheless constitute a threat to hundreds of millions of villagers surviving on small plots in developing societies. Another major obstacle to forming a new political 'bloc' or alliance, would be the division between urban workers and other consumers reliant on low-cost manufacturing and cheap food imports and other rural and urban sections seeking protectionist trade policies.

Hence, it is the level of democracy permitted in existing and alternative societies which will obstruct or encourage the development of sustainable agriculture and the institutionalisation of an equitable global distribution of food. As yet, no collectively owned land system has succeeded at national levels during the past century, for a range of reasons not least due to the lack of freedom and democracy in particular countries. There are plenty of successful co-operative farming enterprises but these are mainly integrated into national and global capitalist food markets.

---

45   See Rjurik Davidson, 'Between Como and confinement: Gramsci's early Leninism', *Marxist Left Review*, no.14, Winter 2017.

46   See Salena Tramel, 'Global Peasant Movement Assesses and Responds to a Heated Political Moment', *HuffPost*, 28 July, 2017.

One solution put forward by advocates of the 'commons' such as Elinor Ostrom, David Bollier, Michel Bauwens, George Monbiot and others is for local communities to take back both urban and rural land via government regulation, land taxes and so forth.[47] How one combines non-private land ownership with non-agribusiness practices and sustainability is a crucial issue in urgent need of further discussion. Radical reformers like George Monbiot claim that too many policy debates focus on either more state intervention or more market freedom. Instead, he emphasises taking back the 'commons' – restoring control of public resources like land, forests, water, minerals, or research and knowledge embodied in software and hardware – that have been privatised and 'enclosed' by wealthy individuals, corporations and the state.[48] Monbiot imagines that the 'commons' is a sector separate from the state or the market. It both is separate and it is not. In order to return all the resources back to 'the people' one needs state intervention to break the power of private corporate rentiers controlling the internet, intellectual property and so forth. Land, water, minerals and forests are also impossible to protect against capitalist abuse and control without government intervention and legislation. Monbiot is also drawn to the participatory planning model of Porte Alegre. However, this is a model of a more democratised public sector rather than a separate 'commons'. Participatory budgeting has spread to hundreds of cities across the world. Its many positive features are currently constrained by the lack of participation of the poorest residents in cities and more particularly by the lack of funding for popular neighbourhood priorities – a revenue deficit problem affecting all public sectors in capitalist countries.

Taking back the 'commons' is an essential component element of any transition to an alternative food production system and post-carbon democracy as long as enforceable state laws that protect both the use of, and the benefits of the 'commons' for *all* people are fully enacted. Otherwise, local people claiming exclusive proprietary rights over 'their' commons could undermine the democratic management of the 'commons' for all.

Even with the existence of an extensive democratically controlled 'commons', socially and politically, it is a recipe for conflict to leave

---

47 See for example, David Bollier and Silke Helfrich (eds.), The Wealth of the Commons: A World Beyond Market and State, Levellers Press, Amherst, 2012; Elinor Ostrom, *Governing the Commons: The evolution of institutions for collective action*, Cambridge University Press, Cambridge, 1990; Michel Bauwens and Jurek Onzia, 'A Commons Transition plan for the City of Ghent', *Commons Transition*, 8 September, 2017.

48 George Monbiot, 'Don't let the rich get even richer on the assets we all share', *The Guardian*, 27 September 2017.

one important sector of society (rural production for example) in the hands of private farming businesses, while urban social life in a post-capitalist society is based on collective ownership of former corporations and medium-sized businesses. This socio-political dilemma has to date never been solved satisfactorily. Regardless, the capacity of an inefficient and inequitable food production system to undermine the viability of post-capitalist and potential post-carbon societies should not be underestimated. Most urban radicals and most of the recent growing literature on food, avoids or fails to discuss adequately the politically explosive issue of land ownership, even though many people simultaneously advocate radical anti-capitalist urban policies. Currently, we have highly unequal land and property-owning systems, plus the vested interests of large food and drink manufacturers, supermarkets and corporations that are dominant in the international trade of cereals and other essential foods. How the prevailing private forces in land, food production and distribution can be overcome is vital to the shaping of post-carbon as well as post-capitalist societies. Hence, the very positive ideas and practices explored by theorists of the 'commons' need to be developed much further, especially how local 'commons' initiatives tie in with larger national and international macro-political economic alternative models relating to food sustainability and social equality.

Conclusion

This chapter has focused on the technological utopians who dream of a post-scarcity world where poverty and inequality are overcome. These goals are both ambitious and socially just. However, many of the technologies designed for market societies are not all appropriate for post-capitalist social formations. Food production is one of many crucial areas where these unrealistic visions of decoupling growth from nature remain vague and largely unconvincing at both the technological and political levels. Without deep-seated changes in production, consumption and distribution, Left technological fantasists will both continue to promote visions which ignore the fragile health of our eco-systems and the finite limits of natural resources, as well as the deeply entrenched cultural notions of private land and the significant ecological challenges that lie ahead.

5

The Promise of Definancialisation and Degrowth

In the previous chapters I focussed on how the political conflicts over innovation were connected to three conceptions of the future. First, those businesses, governments and policy analysts who still see a long and profitable role for fossil fuels. This group largely rejects the growing emphasis on innovative forms of decarbonisation and 'green growth' or, at best, only pays lip-service to it by engaging in deceptive and delaying forms of 'greenwash'. Second, in contrast to all those with a vested interest in protecting existing modes of production and consumption, a significant number of future-orientated businesses and policy makers increasingly promote technological solutions to make capitalism sustainable, based upon the absolute decoupling of economic growth from the constraints of nature. Third, radical technological fantasists also believe in absolute decoupling and the zero marginal cost society, but for quite different socio-political reasons to those goals promoted by business. These radical Private Private Private Private wish to unchain science and technology in order to create a post-capitalist society characterised not only by the decoupling of income from wage labour, but also to realise the dream of post-scarcity based on a desire to end global inequality.

At this point, two other broad Left and environmental tendencies need to be identified and analysed. Both internationalists as well as those who favour local and national solutions to economic and environmental crises call for the de-globalisation of market capitalism. This chapter will analyse two important aspects of de-globalisation: definancialisation and degrowth. In contrast to the technological fantasists promoting either capitalist or post-capitalist forms of absolute decoupling, the goals of definancialisation and degrowth can be accomplished without the development of a futuristic science and technology. The crucial question is whether these goals can be achieved within the context of existing national and local political institutions, or whether they are no less utopian than the ambitions of the technological fantasists? In other words, can the separate but related goals of definancialisation and degrowth be accomplished without mass radical political movements that require the prior rejection of the deep-seated culture of consumer capitalism? If so, can these difficult goals be achieved without also creating secluded social enclaves behind privileged walls in a world already suffering from profound inequalities?

It is important to remember that degrowth is not possible without a substantial degree of definancialisation. However, it would be a major mistake to assume that most of the supporters of definancialisation also advocate environmentally sustainable degrowth. In fact, a wide variety of policy analysts and movements endorse some degree of definancialisation (that is, curbing the power of finance capital) but not all of them advocate degrowth or 'steady state' sustainable societies. As I will later discuss, just as there is no agreed use of the term 'austerity' or of the inevitable relationship of financialisation to neo-liberal 'austerity', so too, there is no agreement as to whether degrowth constitutes a new form of austerity or the necessary foundation of wellbeing. I strongly support both definancialisation and degrowth. However, as these are both over-generalised concepts, I am critical of how some aspects of these goals are characterised and the inadequate understanding of their likely impact on existing growth-orientated societies. This chapter aims to provide a fuller analysis of this potential impact.

To get a better sense of what the advocates of degrowth oppose, it is first necessary to identify and analyse those neo-Keynesians, post-Keynesians and Marxists who advocate anti-neoliberal policies but remain essentially trapped in a 'pre-ecological' mindset. Apart from a growing minority, most contemporary economists and policy analysts – whether neo-classical, heterodox post-Keynesians or radical Marxists – either ignore or seem confounded by the new reality that environmental challenges are entirely different problems and not reducible to the old solutions and debates about deciding how the social dividend is to be distributed between labour and capital. Secondly, I will proceed to discuss the major problems associated with definancialisation as part of an integrated socio-economic and environmental solution to existing crises. Thirdly, I will examine degrowth and why some see it as a new form of sustainable capitalism whereas most champion it as a profoundly anti-capitalist social philosophy and practice. I will conclude with a discussion of why the issues bundled under the term degrowth constitute a litmus test that will increasingly divide people on whether they will continue to support or oppose destructive capitalist social formations.

Obsolete Neo-liberal and Post-Keynesian 'drivers' of Growth

The majority of conservative economists and their Keynesian, post-Keynesian and Marxist critics continue to fight old battles. It is as though climate breakdown and finite environmental resources were either minor-issues or marginal problems that could be comfortably solved by price mechanisms, or 'green growth' innovation and investment in renewables, or the redistribution of wealth and power. Regrettably, only a minority of anti-neoliberal critics devote more than the obligatory sentence or two to climate breakdown and other eco-system crises. Even those mainstream policy responses that treat it in more depth, generally desire to decouple production from natural resources in order to maintain the old 'drivers' of economic growth such as increased exports and consumption.

Recent discussion of 'drivers of growth' among neo-Keynesians and post-Keynesians illustrate some of the difficult choices facing both reformers and radical social change activists. More importantly, this debate confirms why both mainstream neo-liberal policies as well as oppositional Keynesian and Marxist policies need to be radically overhauled. Critics of neo-liberal austerity argue that up until the late 1970s, the Keynesian growth model was driven by productivity growth which drove wage growth. It was wage growth which then fuelled consumption or demand growth. After 1980, the neo-liberal growth model was based on increased financialisation as debt (especially household and business debt) and asset price inflation (such as increased property values) drove demand growth instead of wages growth.[1]

Similarly, post-Keynesian political economists Lucio Baccaro and Jonas Pontusson observe that mid-twentieth century political economist Michal Kalecki espoused only one growth model "based on consumer demand stimulated by real wage growth, deficit spending, or

1   Thomas Palley, *Inequality, the Financial Crisis and Stagnation: Competing Stories and Why They Matter*, Macroeconomic Policy Institute, Hans-Böckler-Stiftung, Dusseldorf, Working paper 151, May 2015, p.10.

redistribution of income."[2] While being admirers of Kalecki, they never-theless argue that since the demise of the Fordist corporatist model in the 1970s, the post-Fordist or neo-liberal era is no longer driven solely by one growth model. Instead, there are now "three different alternatives to the traditional Fordist model of wage-led growth: consumption-led growth financed by credit, investment-led growth and export-led growth."[3] Baccaro and Pontusson also cite 'state-led growth' as another conceivable growth model where government consumption and invest-ment would be the primary drivers of economic growth but the rate of state investment would not be determined by the profit share going to either capital or labour. However, no country, not even China, is cur-rently driven by 'state-led growth'. Instead, China has had a combination of investment-led and export-led growth which is now slowing down.

Leaving aside their problematic acceptance of the concepts 'Fordism' and 'post-Fordism',[4] Baccaro and Pontusson survey several OECD coun-tries to make important comparisons between export-led countries like Germany with credit-financed household consumption-led economies such as the UK and Sweden. Instead of confining their analysis to a study of comparative economies, Baccaro and Pontusson are interested in what the growth model adopted in particular countries tells us about the 'social bloc' or coalition of socio-political forces that underpins a dominant growth strategy. For example, they argue:

> When growth is consumption-led, we would expect Centre Right governments as well as Centre Left governments to respond to economic downturns by stimulating domestic consumption. When growth is export-led, by contrast, we would expect governments, regardless of their ideology and the distributive interests of their core constituencies, to pursue more restrictive macroeconomic policies, designed to boost cost competiveness.[5]

In other words, whether for developed or developing societies, an export-led growth strategy in an economic downturn is more likely to result in cuts to wages and social conditions in order to boost exports by cheapening their labour and other input costs. By contrast, a consump-tion-led strategy would defer immediate pain by boosting household

---

2 Lucio Baccaro and Jonas Pontusson, 'Rethinking Comparative Political Economy: The Growth Model Perspective', in special edition of *Politics & Society*, vol.44, no 2, 2016, p.181.
3 *Ibid* p.186.
4 See discussion of Fordism in my companion book *Capitalism Versus Democracy.*
5 *Ibid*, p.201.

disposable income either through tax cuts and more available credit, thus producing later pain in the form of higher government and household debt that would eventually need to be reduced by imposing austerity policies. Boosting consumption via higher wages and government expenditure (rather than more credit and tax cuts) could also be adopted but this would require rejecting neo-liberal growth strategies. Actually, in the recent period of stagnant wage growth, even many neo-liberals in OECD countries reluctantly advocate moderate wage growth to stimulate consumption-led growth.

Other authors associated with the Varieties of Capitalism School (VoC) have challenged Baccaro and Pontusson[6] and argue that they ignore the important role played by fiscal, monetary and general macro-economic policies in establishing 'drivers' of growth, for example, the role of currency and interest rate policies in sustaining employment and investment.[7] One could also contend that Baccaro and Pontusson ignore policies designed to boost productivity and innovation as ways of increasing consumption and exports. In fact, I would go further than this and argue that delineating countries according to one or another of the growth models is fraught with serious problems and misconceptions as most countries adopt more than one 'driver' of growth.

In Chapter Seven, I will discuss the major problems associated with using VoC analysis to establish the connection between welfare states and 'climate states'. For the moment, it is important to note that the VoC approach has been too focused on the 'economy' in the narrowest sense at the expense of social and cultural relations. As for environmental issues and climate breakdown in particular, this has been overwhelmingly ignored.[8] It is remarkable, and also a damning indictment of VoC analyses, that in 2016, VoC analysts such as Baccaro, Pontusson, David Hope, David Soskice, Cathie Jo Martin and Wolfgang Streeck could all debate the merits of different political economic growth models without even a single mention of the relationship between growth and environmental crises.[9]

It is also a pity that Baccaro and Pontusson's notion of political economy is far too economistic. Political movements and coalitions rarely

6   See Michael Piore, 'Varieties of Capitalism Theory: Its Considerable Limits', *Politics & Society*, vol.44, no 2, 2016, pp.237-41; Cathie Jo Martin, 'Economic Prosperity is in High Demand' in *Ibid*, pp.227-35 and Wolfgang Streeck, 'Varieties of varieties: "VoC" and the Growth Models', *Ibid*, pp.243-47.

7   David Hope and David Soskice, *Ibid*, pp.209-226.

8   See Glenn Fieldman, 'Financialisation and ecological modernisation', *Environmental Politics*, Vol. 23, No. 2, 2014, pp.224–242.

9   See L. Baccaro and J. Pontusson, op.cit., with responses by Hope, Soskice, Martin, Piore and Streeck.

come together over economic questions like which growth model they will champion or oppose. Instead, various domestic and international social, institutional and cultural issues are debated and adopted as political programs. Usually these political agendas are linked to particular economic policies. They rarely are presented as an explicit choice (to constituencies and electorates and even business coalitions) as to whether consumption-led growth is preferable to export-led growth or something else. Instead, conservative parties and candidates promote a mixture of pro-business tax cuts, reducing government regulations, tough law and order policies and reigning in public expenditure. Conversely, some anti-austerity movements in the EU may favour a wage-led growth strategy to increase consumption or aggregate demand. However, there is little unity within countries, let alone across the EU, as to whether ending austerity should be achieved by greater expenditure on public sector employment and infrastructure, or increased subsidies to private employers and consumers, or through a major shift to 'green growth' technologies and services, let alone far more radical solutions.

Baccaro and Pontusson rely on hindsight to identify which growth strategies have been adopted. As to future growth models and the question of political support from 'social blocs', this is largely guesswork based on assessing which policies particular segments of social classes have supported in the past. Crucially, Baccaro and Pontusson, as well as others in the 'drivers of demand growth' debate, say nothing about how the fortunes of 'social blocs' are often determined by specific electoral systems. Leaving aside authoritarian regimes, their economistic analyses ignore the important fact that the UK and the US have the most undemocratic of electoral systems (based on 'first past the post' simple majorities) allowing governments to be elected with as little as 20 to 25% of the total eligible vote. One could well ask whether the neo-liberal wave under Thatcher and Reagan could ever have been executed in its harshest forms if these electoral systems had been more democratic.[10]

---

10 Most EU governments constrained by fairer electoral systems (apart from some like France) and different 'social blocs' did not immediately follow the US and UK to the same extent in the initial years of the neo-liberal fight for ascendancy. This was also true in Australia with a more representative electoral system. The conservative Fraser government (1975-1983) was divided over neo-liberalism and feared militant labour movement opposition to neo-liberal policies; it therefore did not imitate Thatcher and Reagan. Ironically, it was the trade union movement (including prominent Communist-led unions) in a short-sighted suicide pact with the 1983 Hawke Labor government (supported by business groups) that formed a corporatist 'social bloc' to implement neo-liberal policies. After Labor was defeated in 1996, the more Right-wing Howard government and the business community no longer needed union support as the major neo-liberal restructuring had been accomplished. The former large and militant union movement is now a severely weakened political force.

One of the political lessons about 'social blocs' is that if electoral systems are manipulated to implement unpopular 'growth models', then the consequences for sustaining unity within the 'bloc' are often negative. This is even truer for macro-economic policies that are imposed undemocratically such as the 'Washington Consensus' or EU austerity policies. The outcome is not just opposition to economic policies but also deep disillusionment with and political mobilisation against the very institutional structures of the EU, IMF and other unelected organisations.

Apart from the widespread neglect of environmental issues, there is also something quite archaic about the gender blind nature of many political economic debates. These need to be fundamentally reformulated if conceptions of alternative societies are to be founded on quite different equitable principles. One glaring blind spot is the almost complete absence of social reproduction from the 'drivers of growth' debate. Most male economists ignore care and social reproduction and their vital roles in determining the level of consumption, productivity and most other aspects of capitalist growth. Take, for example, the relationship between the inability of a majority of households in OECD countries to survive financially without two incomes and the devaluing of care and lack of policies to support women and men who do not want to commercialise care arrangements. Currently, we have a narrow debate over the high costs of private child-care or aged care versus cheaper public sector care services, rather than a broader debate about reorganising paid work and care in contemporary societies. Women still shoulder a disproportionate burden of care and domestic labour while also working in paid jobs.[11] Consumption-led growth strategies that prioritise credit-fuelled private consumption over the need to increase and transform publicly funded care services and income support to households, are recipes for neglect and future political conflict. Yet, we learn little from conventional political economic debates as to what a more socially just economy of care would look like or the character of the 'social bloc' necessary to champion substantial reforms than those devised by existing male-dominated concepts of 'drivers of growth'.

My other central point in drawing attention to these narratives is that the majority of Keynesians, post-Keynesians, neo-liberals or orthodox Marxists continue to spend a great deal of energy debating 'drivers of growth' but ignore or minimise the fact that *it is 'growth' itself* which

---

11 For an analysis of the role of care and how it is still largely devalued, see Julie Stephens' book *Confronting Postmaternal Thinking: Feminism, Memory, Care*, Columbia University Press, New York, 2012 and Nancy Fraser, 'Contradictions of Capital and Care', *New Left Review*, no.100, 2016, pp.99-117.

cannot continue in its old forms without disastrous environmental consequences. Despite decades of publicity about the climate emergency and the need to protect finite natural resources and fragile eco-systems, the vast majority of policy makers have failed to register, let alone integrate into their models, how environment crises will affect the viability of all future growth strategies. The political coherence of any existing 'social bloc' will be profoundly shaken and possibly dissolved once climate breakdown and the impossibility of maintaining old forms of aggregate demand begin to register with policy makers, businesses, unions and households. The high probability that ecological modernisation goals such as decoupling will only be achieved in relative terms, rather than absolutely, is denied or carelessly deferred as a problem to be left for future decision-makers. Little surprise that the 'drivers of growth' debate is so myopic, neglectful and backward looking.

Abandoning Traditional Consumption-led Strategies

If, as many observers have noted, consumerism has replaced religion as the 'opium of the masses', then what does it mean socially, culturally and politically, to be anti-consumerist? Since the late nineteenth century, it has been common for both the Right and the Left to attack consumerism as vulgar materialist activity that is inferior to lofty spiritual and artistic pursuits. Even Hitler, following Nietzschean themes, contrasted vulgar philistine America with German and European cultural superiority. Accordingly:

> [T]he German Reich has two hundred and seventy opera houses
> — a standard of cultural existence of which they over there have
> no conception. They have clothes, food, cars and a badly constructed house but with a refrigerator! This sort of thing does not
> impress us... To sum it up, the Americans live like sows—in a
> most luxurious sty![12]

The leading philosopher to endorse Nazism, Martin Heidegger, also declared that Europe's beleaguered fortress of culture was caught in a pincer movement driven by Bolshevism from the East and American capitalism from the West.[13] At the same time, imprisoned Italian

---

12 Quoted by Ishay Landa, *Fascism and the Masses: The revolt Against the Last Humans, 1848-1945*, Routledge, New York, 2018, p.305.

13 *Ibid*

Communist leader Antonio Gramsci was arguing that American Fordism – the engine of assembly line mass production and consumption – would threaten the old European bourgeoisie with their antiquated family-based businesses and political culture. Similarly, Adorno, Horkheimer and other Frankfurt School exiles living in America, decried the 'culture industry' (Hollywood and other media) for manipulating the working class and the masses with its 'manufactured' debased cultural and ideological content.

What is the relevance of discussing these old philosophical critiques of consumer culture? In recent decades, green movements have added their voices to Right and Left attacks on consumerism. Some greens critique consumerism as a form of empty and dangerous materialism that is destroying Gaia or the mother spirit of all earthly life. Others try to justify sustainability in secular terms by showing how capitalist production is tied to the promotion of unsustainable debt-fuelled consumption. I have argued in this book that the barriers to growth and 'consumption' mean quite different things to poor people living in developing countries than to the majority of affluent people in OECD societies. Sweeping critiques of consumerism that are not connected to crucial issues of how to achieve social justice within countries and between countries do not advance our understanding of consumption and 'culture'. If the pro-market discourse about the absolute decoupling of economic growth from nature says little or nothing about social justice, then similarly, many of the anti-capitalist supporters of degrowth fail to specify and clarify which parts of daily consumption should be reduced or maintained (see later discussion).

How things change. Philosophically, from being a critique of fascism and consumer capitalism, paradoxically, Adorno's elitist cultural critique as also Deleuze's Left Nietzschean radicalism[14], has been taken up by Alt Right figures such as Richard Spencer, Aleksandr Dugin and Nick Land[15] in order to attack liberal and Left movements as well as supposedly 'effeminate', debased consumer cultures. Economically, there is also a change in attitude from the Keynes of the 1930s ('high culture' aficionado of the Bloomsbury set as well as contemporary of Heidegger, Adorno, Gramsci) to the preoccupation with consumption by present day neo-Keynesians and post-Keynesians.

The failure to seriously incorporate environmental factors into the 'drivers of growth' debate is even more evident when considering how

---

14 Andrew Culp, *Dark Deleuze*, University of Minnesota Press, Minneapolis, 2016.

15 Ibid, p.415; also see Harrison Fluss and Landon Frim, 'Behemoth and Leviathan: The Fascist Bestiary of the Alt-Right '*Salvage*, no.5, 21 December 2017.

policy-makers currently frame the enormous issue of consumption-led growth strategies. Whether Left or Right, all seem obsessed with increasing aggregate demand. Neo-liberals and other conservatives desire to increase demand at levels that do not simultaneously increase inflation or generate speculative bubbles resulting in a financial crisis. They especially oppose higher government debt flowing from an increased demand that is produced by public sector social expenditure. Left-wing analysts and labour movement critics of austerity also want higher consumption, particularly aggregate demand that is fuelled by wage-led growth and higher public expenditure in order to cut unemployment.

I give qualified support to those promoting greater aggregate demand via expenditure on 'social state' goods and services and infrastructure, such as public housing, health, education, transport and other community services. However, this emphasis on public consumption, as opposed to private consumption of privately produced goods and services is desirable only as long as public expenditure is not used to underpin undesirable outcomes. This is a crucial qualification, as these negative outcomes could include forms of employment and consumption that are environmentally damaging, or that consolidate social inequality, increase anti-democratic bureaucracy and destructive military power. Regrettably, there are many trade unionists and liberal social democrats who prefer traditional 'mixed economies' characterised by a dominant private sector and a subordinate but better-funded public sector. In this traditional model, boosting public sector expenditure and services is promoted as performing a dual role, namely, more employment and public services while simultaneously stimulating private sector employment, production and consumption via a mixture of government expenditure and more household consumption.

We have long seen advocates of greater public goods and services show little or no concern for the finite quality of natural resources. As a short to medium-term measure, increasing aggregate demand may end neo-liberal austerity but with policies that are environmentally unsustainable. Instead of scaling back on capitalist consumerism and explicitly promoting degrowth or ecologically, non-dangerous 'good growth' as I will later discuss, many centre/Left parties want improved public services without any fundamental decrease in the consumption of private consumer goods. Even more explicitly Left campaigners are little better. Over the past two decades, for example, Left-wing European Economists for an Alternative Economic Policy in Europe (a mixture of Keynesians, post-Keynesians and Marxists) have released an annual manifesto which contains many valuable policy suggestions and criticisms of dominant neo-liberal policies. Notably, only a few token references are made to environmental sustainability.[16] It is understandable that the main focus of these alternative strategies is on combatting austerity policies in the EU that have produced decades of unemployment, uneven growth and increased racism. Nonetheless, how long can Left-wing economists avoid offering alternatives policies to dominant forms of consumption, that is, subscribing to an uncritical advocacy of increasing aggregate demand?

Post-Keynesian policies are thus mainly geared to restoring 'full-employment capitalism', albeit with a greater welfare state. Despite the positive support given by post-Keynesians and Marxists to renewable energy, for many sections of the broad Left, environmental issues are considered little more than supporting measures to combat climate change or protecting various ecological habitats. While such support is not to be underestimated, only a minority of the Left are grappling with the implications of a systemic integration of environmental and political economic processes. Consequently, we are yet to read many Left policy analysts rejecting conventional material growth strategies. Once we allow for political differences with neo-liberals over the share of income going to labour as opposed to capital, and also the level of domestic taxation and expenditure on social policies, labour movement approaches to environmental sustainability are barely distinguishable from business support for ecological modernisation, that is, promoting decoupling, the 'circular economy' and so forth.

To rethink consumption-led growth strategies would entail *abandoning* long-held beliefs in Keynesian and post-Keynesian emphases on the importance of increasing conventional forms of *aggregate demand*. Redistribution of wealth and income is certainly very important. Nonetheless, one of the biggest challenges facing both reformers and radicals is how to shift the economic priorities of a large number of countries away from their high dependence on consumption-led growth. As employment in manufacturing has declined in most OECD countries, the broad service sector has taken on responsibility for a higher proportion of GDP in terms of employment, value added and consumption. Is the private production and consumption of services self-generating without manufacturing exports and natural resources exports? Many argue that capitalist growth could continue as long as the export of services such as tourism, financial and property services, retailing, aviation transport, intellectual property, education and health services as well as other new digital economy services keep expanding. What is ignored is

---

16 See European Economists for an Alternative Economic Policy in Europe, *The European Union: The Threat of Disintegration – EuroMemorandum 2017*, www.euro-memo.

that the viability of the domestic production and consumption of these largely private sector services could be seriously disrupted by the need to reduce carbon emissions. Tourism, aviation and shipping, retailing and hospitality and food production are all likely areas to be affected by the urgent need to cut fossil fuel use and reduce affluent consumption of non-renewable resources.

The assumption that services can grow indefinitely and fill the gap left by manufacturing ignores the finite limits to current forms of private service sector expansion. The prospect for numerous developing societies is particularly bleak as each competes for tourists or is unable to generate sufficient consumption-led growth due to unemployment, low wages and high debt levels. A similar crisis could envelop most EU member countries should the EU stagnate or possibly even disintegrate, leaving each member state to engage in competitive currency devaluations. This strategy may or may not generate domestic growth via exports. Deindustrialisation and cross-border value chains mean that gone are the days when it was much easier for countries to boost local manufacturing at the expense of imports. Without substantial domestic changes to existing public-sector expenditure priorities, currency devaluations would not necessarily encourage environmental sustainability. Currency devaluations would, however, reduce the standard of living for low and middle-income people by adding significantly to the cost of essential consumer imports.

In order to change the role of consumption-led growth, it is necessary not only to recognise the new political economic conditions, but also to go beyond familiar debates between Left and Right. I will briefly identify some of these new conditions before returning to them in this and later chapters. First, consumption is closely related to unemployment, austerity, and the central issues of democracy versus capitalism on the one hand and democracy versus the environment on the other hand. The shift from the consumption of goods and services produced by public sector enterprises to more privatised and less standardised consumer products is a familiar trend that is central to present-day reliance on capitalist consumption-led growth. Consumer power is highly individualised unless mobilised as citizen-consumer collective power against certain products or companies. Citizen power on a range of issues is usually only effective as collective action.[17] It is the allure and ideology of individualistic private 'choice' that makes environmental policies such as degrowth so unpopular.

---

17 See Wolfgang Streeck, 'Citizens as Customers', *New Left Review*, no.76, July-Aug 2012, pp.27-47.

Nevertheless, developments within global capitalism since the 1940s have rendered important aspects of Keynes and Kalecki's analyses seriously dated. One significant change is that national governments have lost control of the political 'business cycle' due to the reduction of barriers on imports and especially the inflow and outflow of capital. When governments in developed capitalist societies try increasing aggregate demand through stimulus policies, this does not necessarily lead to full employment as Keynes and Kalecki had hoped. Instead, higher consumption usually fuels imports rather than just local production and local employment. Developing low and middle-income capitalist societies are also constrained in their ability to increase employment because of high dependence on imports and foreign capital, poor infrastructure, and lack of highly-skilled workforces that usually take decades to build through education and training.

Of central importance is not just the issue of whether service sectors can grow or sustain high levels of employment. What is also at stake is whether national economies largely dependent on capitalist consumption-led growth are viable, without the resulting balance of payments crises and the related inability to service ballooning debt and increased unemployment. Will they need to return to much higher tax rates such as those that prevailed in OECD countries prior to the 1970s? Neo-liberal policy-makers rule out a return to higher pre-1970s tax rates, unless forced to do so. They also do not place much hope in strong economic growth in the next decade. Given low to stagnant growth rates and the demographic trend of ageing populations, policy options such as slashing social security entitlements for both pensioners and young unemployed are very risky politically. Other neo-liberal possibilities to minimise escalating debt include various indirect taxes on household savings or reducing the budgetary cost of public services. All of these policy options become much harder when revenue from consumption-led growth strategies start to become incompatible with pressures to cut carbon emissions and prevent eco-system breakdown.

As already mentioned, changing trends in consumption in affluent OECD countries has seen an increase in expenditure on holiday travel, leisure activity and eating out at the expense of stagnant or decreasing purchases of other consumer goods. This is not to be confused with degrowth but it does signal two important aspects of the future implications and character of consumption-led growth in capitalist societies. First, the retail sector is one of the largest employers in developed capitalist countries. The closure of many retail outlets and the move to online sales is part of the general threat of labour-saving trends to wage-led growth as the traditional driving force leading to increased aggregate demand. Moreover, the prospect of driverless cars roaming urban streets with consumer goods to show residents in their own homes, potentially threatens further decline in employment. Second, the shift to expenditure on hospitality services puts additional downward pressures on wages in these low-pay sectors. It also highlights the centrality of food production and consumption to any conception of how to achieve post-carbon democracies, as I have discussed in the previous chapter.

Today, a new vicious cycle is at play. Since the 1970s, central banks have abandoned full employment policies and governments cannot control the 'business cycle' domestically because they have surrendered monetary policy (such as interest rates) to central banks which are not answerable to electorates. In the Eurozone, national governments have lost much control to the European Central Bank and EU Commission, thus severely limiting their ability to counter austerity policies. Even business journalists such as Alan Kohler recognise the post-Keynesian world we live in when he observes crudely, that politics is a sideshow, as central banks run the global economy and Silicon Valley governs society.[18]

Also, the major increase in service sector employment in developed capitalist societies and a corresponding decline in manufacturing sector employment has profoundly affected the attitude of governments to consumer spending. In the 1940s, Kalecki argued that the "fundamentals of capitalist ethics require that 'you shall earn your bread in sweat'—unless you happen to have private means."[19] Hence, he believed that subsidising mass consumption was much more violently opposed by business and their experts than even public investment. It is true that attacks on the unemployed and welfare recipients as 'parasites' or 'slackers' supposedly avoiding paid work, remains a popular cry among conservative businesses, politicians and voters. Nonetheless, Kalecki's views on consumption are also quite dated in the context of stagnant or low growth economies.

There is tremendous pressure on governments by particular business lobbies to stimulate consumer spending via income tax cuts. Businesses are divided between those wanting to cut welfare entitlements and others fearing the impact of such policies on consumption and political stability. One example of this is the large number of unemployed middle-aged and older workers over the age of 45 in many OECD countries, who

---

18 Alan Kohler, 'Central banks still run the show', *The Australian*, 24 December, 2016.

19 Michal Kalecki, 'Political Aspects of Full Employment', *Political Quarterly*, no.4, October 1943, p.326.

continue to be reclassified on 'disability' and other benefit categories, thus disguising real unemployment levels and sustaining consumption while defusing potential political conflict. Across developed capitalist societies, there are now three generations of former workers and potential new workers (parents, children and grandchildren) who, since the 1970s, have not worked in cities and regions after deindustrialisation blighted their fate and the fate of their communities.

Kalecki was correct, however, to argue that without sustained full employment government attempts to stimulate private investment and mass consumption would prove increasingly ineffective over time, simply because there was a limit to the number of tax cuts and interest rate cuts that could be given. Since 2008, the relative ineffectiveness of central bank policy of zero and negative interest rates to generate a sustained 'jobs and household consumption recovery' in most of Europe and elsewhere is a case in point. In the meantime, neo-liberals have changed their tune from the 1970s and 1980s when they feared protracted 'stagflation' (inflation combined with stagnation). Now, despite modest economic recovery after a decade of difficult economic conditions, high inflation has not eventuated as conservatives feared, and policy-makers are still terrified of stagnation and deflation (falling prices and wages). Little or nothing continues to be done about mass unemployment and under-employment. Contemporary voters fear unemployment and hate austerity measures but there is a lack of overwhelming electoral support to combat the debilitating consequences of either unemployment or precarious work. Rather, today, racism and hostility to refugees and foreign workers flourishes in countries regardless of modest or high official unemployment and under-employment. Voters are deeply divided over imported foreign labour and free labour mobility that employers use as a cost-cutting, disciplining measure, not only in highly exploitative low-pay sectors, but increasingly in skilled and professional employment as well.

Any replacement of conventional consumption-led growth with degrowth in the name of sustainability, will need to simultaneously deal with financialisation – the dominant system that drives credit provision (essential for consumer spending) and diverts resources away from social goods and services, as well as away from investment in new sustainable infrastructure and technologies. Without tackling financialisation, there is little hope of a fundamental change to existing conservative and damaging public policies.

Definancialisation: Possible Reforms That Avoid Economic Collapse?

Existing consumption-led drivers of growth have been closely tied to the removal of controls over cross border capital flows and the massive growth of financial derivatives since the 1980s. Prominent organisations such as the IMF endorsed national capital controls up until the 1970s. Despite recognising that capital liberalisation policies were inefficient and risky, the IMF succumbed to neo-liberal ideology and heavily promoted anti-Keynesian liberalisation policies from the 1980s onwards.[20] In Chapter One I discussed why Left analysts see financialisation as characterised by the disproportional power of financial institutions and their significant share of profits compared with non-financial business sectors. The relative absence of profitable investment outlets in traditional non-financial sectors has witnessed the massive increase of corporate investment in financialised services and activities. This growth of profitability in financial products continues to shape household and business consumption, production and employment. It simultaneously fuels high indebtedness and electoral opposition to increased taxes, thereby constraining public expenditure on social goods and services as well as tackling eco-system crises.

The 'unchaining' of capital[21] has resulted in what Leonard Seabrooke and Duncan Wigan (following Andrew Leyshon and Nigel Thrift[22]) describe as the disjuncture between territorially fixed government fiscal systems and fluid financial systems. "The mobility of capital and its ability to switch asset identity and jurisdictional home has raised the spectre of a permanent schism between the location of value creation and the geographical allocation of profits and wealth."[23] In other words, new 'Global Wealth Chains' permit financial corporations to not only create multiple new products and services for businesses and wealthy individuals, but also to operate across national jurisdictions for the purpose of wealth creation and tax minimisation. Advocates of 'green growth', or socialist and

---

20 See Jeffrey M. Chwieroth, *Capital Ideas: The IMF and the Rise of Financial Liberalization*, Princeton University Press, Princeton, 2010. Chwieroth analyses the internal struggles within the IMF between the 'gradualists' and the 'big bang' policy advocates over the implementation of capital liberalisation.

21 See Dick Bryan, Michael Rafferty and Duncan Wigan, 'Capital unchained: finance, intangible assets and the double life of capital in the offshore world', *Review of International Political Economy*, Vol. 24, No. 1, 2017, pp.56–86.

22 Andrew Leyshon and Nigel Thrift, *Money/Space: Geographies of Monetary Transformation*, London, Routledge, 1997.

23 Leonard Seabrooke and Duncan Wigan, 'The governance of global wealth chains', *Review of International Political Economy*, vol.24, no.1, p. 2.

green critics of market globalisation have called for 'definancialisation', 're-embedding the economy', 'de-globalisation' and other such controls over the power of finance institutions. Critics link financialisation to environmentally destructive credit-fuelled consumption, the extensive misallocation and abuse of financial resources, and the perpetuation of deep social inequalities. Given the interpenetration of financialisation with a broad range of everyday socio-economic practices and eco-system degradation, the burning issue is not 'why' definancialisation, but rather 'how' to achieve this necessary objective with minimal negative fallout and without socially disastrous consequences. In short, can definancialisation be achieved within capitalist societies or is this ambition highly unrealistic?

Financialisation is a multi-headed beast that cannot be countered with just one type of policy response. Take for instance, capital flows and monetary policy. Reimposing capital controls can be done either across the board or for selected investment areas and public services, especially those involving key strategic industries in the private and public sectors of nation states that need regulation or protection. Some large countries, such as China, already exercise capital controls, while Japan and the US have the power to impose government controls over capital flows. Within the EU, co-ordinated controls over financial capital would be necessary even if the Euro were abandoned. Most national governments have the formal power to impose capital controls. The key issue is whether they are strong enough to counter the debilitating socio-economic consequences and political opposition that would most likely flow from a poorly prepared strategy to regain control over financial practices. As we shall see in relation to degrowth strategies, any country that is unable to 'delay' or 'deflect' international demands for 'adjustments' to its national currency and to its trade deficit and fiscal policies will lose control over its domestic policy goals – whether social or environmental.

Corporate opposition to definancialisation could also lead to domestic disruption and hardship flowing from investment strikes, a possible fall in trade, currency runs and devaluations, and a shortage of international purchasers of government bonds necessary for budget stability and domestic expenditure. While capital controls are essential, it would take a very strong and determined electorate to support any government facing hostile domestic and international business and political opposition, including the possibility of economic sabotage and violent confrontation (as we have already seen in some Latin American countries). Any government that failed to keep unemployment low or maintain socio-political stability, through increased public employment and services, would reduce its capacity to definancialise especially in the context of a free electoral system where the erosion of popular support could result in political defeat at the next election. In addition, capital controls could be highly unpopular if people also faced widespread shortages of imported goods and severe restrictions on their ability to travel overseas, given the likely tightening of readily available foreign currencies and the depreciation of their own currency. All these likely negative consequences could have a greater chance of being managed and tolerated, however, if a clear majority of people were democratically committed to definancialisation and the necessity of new social and environmental values.

Even non-radical analysts recognise the trilemma of monetary policy in the age of globalisation. After the collapse of the Bretton Woods system of pegged exchange rates in 1971, only two out of the following three objectives are deemed possible: national policies to defend living standards; free capital flows; and stable exchange rates. To secure standards of living and stable exchange rates, capital flows have to be controlled.[24] This is especially true for small and medium sized countries that have less ability than large economic powers to resist international financial pressures and pursue their own national agendas. It is why advocates of a democratised European Union (in contrast to the neo-liberal policies of the EU Commission and European Central Bank) desire progressive EU-wide capital controls to protect rather than penalise member states. However, the opposite has occurred. Floating currencies across the world have neither delivered control over capital flows nor protection for national standards of living. Hélène Rey attributes this outcome to the way global financial cycles are essentially determined by the influence of the policies of the US Federal Reserve and other large central banks which affect interest rates and currencies *across* the globe.[25]

In a world where the large central banks are often at odds with one another, any national government attempting to determine its standard of living will have to deal with the financial effects of global crossfire on their own currency and monetary policy, unless they can somehow secure that elusive (and perhaps illusory) phenomenon called 'national independence'. The problem is that no government can fully protect itself against global currency speculation unless it retreats to secluded

---

24 See Thomas Kalinowski, *Regulating International Finance and the Evolving Imbalance of Capitalisms since the 1970s*, MPIfG Discussion Paper 11/10, Max Planck Institute for the Study of Societies, Cologne July 2011.

25 Hélène Rey, *Dilemma Not Trilemma: The Global Financial Cycle and Monetary Policy Independence*, National Bureau of Economic Research, Cambridge, 2015, Working Paper 21162.

196

autarky. According to economist Mehrdad Payandeh, the explosion of currency futures markets in recent decades is a sign of how exchange rates and capital movements "do not mirror trade flows and the economic development of the currency zones in question. They have decoupled from developments in the real economy. Therefore, companies and market participants are obliged to cover themselves against exchange rate fluctuation by resorting to currency futures markets."[26]

There is no doubt that part of the massive growth of financial products is due to all sorts of hedging and other forms of protection. The larger question is: what is the 'real economy'? Advocates of definancialisation must deal with the demise of the traditional distinction between 'the real economy' ('High Street') and 'Wall Street' (or its equivalent in other leading G20 countries). This distinction is only partially accurate and mainly applies to a former era when productive or industrial capital was dominant. Stock markets and all forms of equities and financial transactions are one step removed from businesses and employment in the various nominally designated non-financial sectors of national economies. Yet, such is the integration and veritable size of profits, employment and income directly and indirectly related to contemporary financial institutions (for example, property, equities, pension funds), that no capitalist economy could escape unscathed by any serious downturn or dramatic scaling back in the fortunes of the financial services sector.

Take the giant derivatives market or 'weapons of mass destruction' as Warren Buffet called them in 2002. The Bank for International Settlements reported in December 2015 that outstanding derivatives were US$697.5 trillion[27] while others estimate the sum total of all futures contracts, options, warrants, swaps and other types of derivatives to be US$1.2 quadrillion or an astronomical $1,200 trillion.[28] Whatever the real figures, derivatives now play a constitutive role in everyday life.[29] It is not just home mortgages that are packaged and sold as derivative contracts, but health insurance, credit card debt, gym membership and countless other transactions that households, businesses and governments enter into as part of their consumption, production, servicing and capital raising activities.

---

26 Mehrdad Payandeh, 'Outline Of A New World Currency System', *Social Europe*, 6 March 2018.

27 Figure cited in 'ISDA Research Note: Derivatives Market Analysis: Interest Rate Derivatives', *International Swaps and Derivatives Association*, New York, July 2016, p.11.

28 Jeff Desjardins, 'All of the World's Money and Market's in One Visualization', visualcapitalist, 17 December, 2015.

29 See Edward LiPuma, *The Social Life of Financial Derivatives: Markets, Risk, and Time*, Duke University Press, Durham, 2017.

During Marx's time, the joint stock company permitted shareholders to own stock without being the direct owners of company assets. Stockholders owned exposure to the performance of capital rather than owning the means of production. As leading analysts of derivatives, Dick Bryan and Michael Rafferty note that asset backed securities and other derivatives have taken this process a step further.

Capital as a social relation involves relations of control and the extraction of a surplus from workers. But derivatives challenge our understanding of this depiction. What do we make of a form of capital that involves ownership of exposures to the performance of means of production, but not necessarily ownership of the means of production themselves? This is what derivatives entail, and in so doing they blur our conceptions of finance and production. Perhaps the power of capital comes increasingly not just from ownership of corporate assets, but also from the capacity to shift financial and other risks onto people.[30]

In the absence of fixed values and exchange rates, a debate has recently developed over whether derivatives perform an informal role or measure for international business contracts and exchanges similar to the role performed by the Gold Standard in the pre-1930 period of floating currencies.[31] Leaving aside the role of national currencies and derivatives, it is clear that financialisation and responses to it will continue to be highly politically divisive. Since 2008, rather than controlling and definancialising their economies, leading G20 countries have actually become more dependent on the health of finance capital and equity markets through quantitative easing and other government support. It is no accident that governments have used trillions of dollars to uphold the value of real estate, share markets, infrastructure and other assets vital to the financial sector. This subsidy through quantitative easing and other measures is at the expense of public services, wages and household income.

Hence, the sheer scale and centrality of financial activity to wealth creation necessitates a redefinition of the 'real economy'. According to business consultancy firm Bain and Company:

---

30 Dick Bryan and Michael Rafferty, 'Financial Derivatives as Social Policy Beyond Crisis', *Sociology*, vol.48, no.5, 2014, pp.890-91. Derivatives now help to conceptualise and organise social relations. For example, "The pricing of electricity and the fees on credit cards, and indeed the business model on which many of the services are delivered, is driven not by the costs of service provision, but by a calculation of the required competitive rate of return on the bonds issued on the basis of electricity bills and credit card debt, and so forth." P.898. Also see their earlier book *Capitalism with derivatives: a political economy of financial derivatives, capital and class*, Palgrave Macmillan, New York, 2006.

31 See for example, Tony Norfield, 'Derivatives, Money, Finance and Imperialism: A Response to Bryan and Rafferty', *Historical Materialism*, vol.21, no.2, 2013, pp.149-168.

The rate of growth of world output of goods and services has seen an extended slowdown over recent decades, while the volume of global financial assets has expanded at a rapid pace. By 2010, global capital had swollen to some $600 trillion, tripling over the past two decades. Today, total financial assets are nearly 10 times the value of the global output of all goods and services. ... Moreover, as financial markets in China, India and other emerging economies continue to develop their own financial sectors, total global capital will expand by half again, to an estimated $900 trillion by 2020 (measured in prevailing 2010 prices and exchange rates). More than any other factor on the horizon, the self-generating momentum for capital to expand—and the sheer size the financial sector has attained—will influence the shape and tempo of global economic growth going forward.[32]

The astronomical figures and the big variation in total figures here partly depend on whether the analysts include derivatives (up to $1,200 trillion) as financial assets, or primarily count only government and corporate bonds, shares and other non-derivatives financial assets. This is a grey area, as some bonds and equities are de facto packaged derivatives sold as debt. Precise figures are difficult to establish by international regulatory authorities. Even if these estimates are exaggerated, the substantive point of the disproportionate size of financial assets compared to the sum total of all goods and services produced is that they will continue to have a major impact on the future character of capitalist societies, unless they are controlled and reduced in size.

Joseph Schumpeter argued that banks within capitalist societies played a similar role to central planners in a socialist economy because in capitalist economies, entrepreneurs needed bank finance to innovate production processes and bring new goods to the market. Existing finance institutions importantly, are much more than de facto administrative central planners. Today, they are not just facilitators but integrally involved in all aspects of investment, production and consumption, in other words, they are a central part of contemporary 'real economies'. More telling is that contemporary capitalism is no longer characterised by the strict division between financial institutions and non-financial businesses or fractions of finance, industrial, commercial and agrarian capital (in Marxian terms). Financial institutions still dominate financial activity but they have encountered new competition. Today, corporations

---

32 Bain Macro Trends Group, *A World Awash in Money: Capital Trends Through 2020*, Bain & Company, Inc, New York, 2012, p.3.

in automobiles, social media, retailing, power generation, telecommunications and other industries all have their own financial divisions that provide consumer credit, compete with banking and insurance products, arrange derivatives in emissions trading markets and so forth. In short, financialisation as everyday practice transcends the banking sector, while money creation in the form of credit provision reduces government creation of money (printed money) to a small percentage of total money supply in many economies.

Critically, Schumpeter's assumption about the vital role played by finance in funding innovation has long become its opposite, namely, a major obstacle of social and green innovation. Contemporary shareholders are too dependent on the continuation of short-sighted financialisation practices. Any rapid and major decline in the disproportionate profits earned by the financial sector, compared with other industry sectors, would in itself lead to profound economic instability characterised by falling shares and property prices, crises in pension funds, rising unemployment and falling consumption. In 2016, conservative economist Martin Feldstein argued that if inflated equity prices in the US returned to historic average prices, this would entail a loss of 35%, thus wiping more than $US7.5 trillion off the $US21 trillion value of equities held by households, with even greater losses by pension funds.[33] Accordingly, asset price drops and falls in consumption would lead to a major recession or depression.

Now imagine the additional scale of the economic depression if sweeping definancialisation were implemented without corresponding alternative policies to soak up the economic damage. The finance sector is not only pivotal but *is* the 'real economy' in large capitalist societies such as the US where it has increased its proportion of total corporate profits from less than 10% in 1948 to over 30% in recent years (after reaching more than 40% prior to 2007).[34] Through financial products, services and investments, the finance sector earns more than the manufacturing sector but employs far fewer people than manufacturing did at its peak prior to the 1980s. Moreover, the finance sectors of other G20 countries are closely integrated with the US financial sector and many finance sectors earn more than their respective national manufacturing sectors.

If the pre-1950 financial institutions that Schumpeter so admired

---

33 See Martin Feldstein, 'What Could Go Wrong in America?', *Project Syndicate*, 26 October 2016.

34 For figures see Jordan Weissmann, 'How Wall Street Devoured Corporate America' *The Atlantic*, May 5, 2013. Also see Robin Greenwood and David Scharfstein, 'The Growth of Finance', *Journal of Economic Perspectives*, vol.27, no.2, 2013, pp.3-28 and Costa Lapavitsas and Ivan Mendieta-Muñoz, 'The Profits of Financialization', *Monthly Review*, July-August 2016 for analyses of the changing role of finance in the largest economy of the world.

have gone the way of the dodo, it might be possible to argue that the incredibly concentrated and powerful role of finance capital makes it easier to bring about major reform or revolution. This belief harks back to 1910 when Marxist, Rudolph Hilferding argued:

> The socializing function of finance capital facilitates enormously the task of overcoming capitalism. Once finance capital has brought the most important branches of production under its control, it is enough for society, through its conscious executive organ – the state conquered by the working class – to seize finance capital in order to gain immediate control of these branches of production.[35]

If only class conflict and political strategy were so simple and so easy today. The Great Financial Crisis of 2007-8 did, however, leave many banks vulnerable to nationalisation. A third of European banks are still in a state of severe weakness.[36] This opportunity to begin the definancialisation of OECD economies was sadly missed. It is a path that continues to be rejected, as political leaders are either too timid or oppose any move to take firm control of finance sectors. Despite the fear of another major financial crisis, very little reform of the banking system has occurred since 2008. Criminal behaviour has largely gone unpunished (or with very light penalties) and highly risky practices have been modified rather than eliminated. Large banks have grown larger and despite minor regulatory changes and crisis 'stress tests', no fundamental change has been made to the pre-2008 central role of financial institutions in contemporary societies.[37]

Apart from capital flow controls and significant changes to banking regulations, any process of definancialisation would have to also involve changes to both the type of assets held as well as the role played by pension funds in domestic and international economies. In 2017, pension funds in just 22 countries held a conservatively estimated \$US41.355 trillion in equities, bonds, cash and other assets.[38] These figures do not

---

35 Rudolph Hilferding, *Finance Capital: A Study of the Latest Phase of Capitalist Development*, 1910, English translation by Morris Watnick and Sam Gordon, Routledge & Kegan Paul, London, 1981, p.367.

36 See IMF, *Global Financial Stability Report Press Conference – 2016*, October 5, 2016.

37 See Stephen Bell and Andrew Hindmoor, 'Are the major global banks now safer? Structural continuities and change in banking and finance since the 2008 crisis', *Review of International Political Economy*, vol. 25, no.1, 2018, pp.1-27.

38 See, Willis Towers Watson and Thinking Ahead Institute, *'Global pension funds asset study 2018'*, February 4, 2018, thinkingaheadinstitute.org

include all the large holdings in government-run pension schemes or those pension funds for which there are poorly reported holdings. Of crucial significance is the heavy involvement of pension funds in share markets and bond markets. Anglo countries hold between 45% and 50% of their assets in equities, whereas countries such as the Norway, Spain, Austria and Turkey hold between 40% and 56% in bonds and bills.[39] There is also a significant variation in bonds and shares held by pension funds in foreign as opposed to domestic bonds and shares. Definancialisation would first necessitate a political struggle in order to require pension funds to gradually divest and decrease equities holdings over a ten to twelve-year period (about 2% to 2.5% per year) from 50% to 25% or less without causing a mass sell-off on global markets as funds lowered their exposure to highly risky share markets. Even a twelve-year phase-in would put pressure on pension funds to meet their income obligations to retirees and quite likely cause share markets to initially enter sustained negative or bear territory. It is the scale of shares sell-off that would determine the degree of potential economic downturn or even collapse.

One way of countering the likelihood that a shift out of equities markets would cause an economic recession, would be if pension funds increased their non-corporate bond holdings and more capital was freed from financialised investments and channelled away from equities and into social investment bonds, green infrastructure bonds and other less speculative public investment. This would have the effect of simultaneously securing retirement income and boosting employment. Depending on the country, the ratio of pension fund holdings of private corporate bonds could also be gradually reduced in favour of increased public bond holdings in local city, regional and national governments and statutory bodies. Across the globe, non-financial sector corporate bonds had grown to $US 11.7 trillion by 2017, with up to 40% of these corporate bonds rated just above junk bond status and constituting a worrying risk of default.[40] All the more reason why pension funds should begin transitioning to more secure forms of public investment and away from corporate bonds. Moreover, a degree of definancialisation could be gradually accomplished by switching capital resources away from existing profitable but damaging, risky and distorting deployment by private financial institutions. This would also help transform and alleviate the indebtedness and very heavy reliance of households and businesses on

---

39 See OECD, *Pension Markets in Focus 2017*, OECD, Paris, 2017.

40 Susan Lund et al, *Rising Corporate Debt: Peril or Promise?*, McKinsey & Company Global Institute, June 2018.

all forms of private financial services by allocating more capital for social and environmental needs, services, employment and sustainability.

The long neglect of investing in public housing by numerous governments is a prime example of how well-targeted definancialisation measures could simultaneously counter the epidemic of homelessness due to unemployment, mental illness and substance addiction, high rents and property speculation – a process that in recent decades has been largely driven by the culture of consumption and asset-growth financialisation. We should also be aware that the relationship between credit and consumption preceded contemporary financialisation. In the US, non-mortgage credit was used to purchase about 60% of durable goods and 85% of cars in the 1950s and early 1960s. Credit and poverty were perceived differently in OECD countries as either usury and hence condemned by both Churches and the Left, or as welfare support because it enabled low-income people to obtain goods.[41] In the U.S, the liberalisation of lending laws and credit growth was greatly facilitated in the 1980s by the relaxation of state usury laws following the Marquette case in 1978.[42] Analysts such as Susanne Soederberg have also identified the close relationship between credit and the 'poverty industry' in developed and developing societies. A range of practices such as payday loans, student debt, micro-finance and housing loans exacerbate 'debtfare' while still earning lucrative profits.[43] Definancialisation would therefore necessitate a combination of tighter regulation on credit, targeted income supplements and the provision of public social goods and services to reduce the predatory activity of loan sharks and finance businesses.

Regulations requiring pension funds to reduce their exposure to share markets could be supplemented by closing tax loopholes and tax incentives geared to speculative property and share market investments. Many countries have watered down their capital gains taxes in recent decades thereby enabling substantial profits to be made in non-productive investments such as property, derivatives, short-term share turnover and many other financial transactions. Careful tax reform could selectively implement penalties on financialised gains while providing carrots for private investors to switch to socially and environmentally beneficial long-term investment. These proposed tax reforms are not to be confused with

---

41 Gunnar Trumbull, *Consumer Lending in France and America: Credit and Welfare*, Cambridge University Press, New York, 2014.

42 *Ibid*, p.9.

43 Susanne Soederberg, *Debtfare States and the Poverty Industry: Money, Discipline and the Surplus Population*, Routledge, London, 2015.

revenue raising measures such as the Tobin tax on financial transactions. The Tobin tax would not definancialise economies even though it could raise revenue from financialisation.

What are needed are more stringent regulations on financial practices such as limiting the amount of credit generated by banks and other corporations and forbidding them to create money. Substantial government subsidies to private financial institutions should also be eliminated and reforms enacted that reduce the proportion of financial institutions' assets that can be held in the form of derivatives or other risky assets.[44] Apart from setting credit limit targets, the quality of financial transactions could be scrutinised through new and independent European and other international credit ratings agencies. These new agencies could replace the discredited private credit agencies that gave triple AAA ratings to Ponzi schemes that collapsed in the 2008 crisis. Mathew Lawrence of the London Institute for Public Policy Research recommended that a major redirection of financial resources could be enacted in leading global centres of financialisation such as the UK where up to 90% of outstanding bank loans have gone to other financial transactions and institutions or for property deals, instead of to more productive sectors and social investment.[45] Progressive governments could also by-pass constitutional and political obstacles to nationalisation by establishing government owned banks to compete with major private banks. These new banks would provide loan and deposit facilities guaranteed by central banks, thereby enabling households and small businesses to obtain cheaper interest rates and bypass the dubious and high-cost practices generated by the existing finance sector.

As to finance and environmental crises, the highly negative impact of financialisation on global warming and on the possibility of finding solutions to this crisis is partly recognised by financial institutions themselves. In 2015, leading financial institution Citibank estimated that the world could save $1.8 trillion over the next 25 years if it adopted energy efficiency and renewables. Otherwise climate change would cost $44 trillion (the combined GDP of the US, China and the EU in 2015) if dangerous emissions were not prevented.[46] Similarly, several years ago, the Bloomberg New Energy Report (2014) on 55 developing countries in Asia, Africa, Latin America and the Caribbean showed that renewable

44 Mathew Lawrence put forward these and other recommendations in *Definancialisation: A democratic reformation of finance*, Institute for Public Policy Research, London, September, 2014.
45 *Ibid*, chapters 3 and 4.
46 See Karin Rives, 'Citibank: How Investments in Clean Energy can Save Trillions', *The Energy Collective*, October 12, 2015.

energy was now cheaper to adopt than fossil fuels.[47] It is important to recognise the way financialisation undermines decarbonisation by enabling corporations to purchase carbon emission offsets rather than reduce their own emissions. Converting carbon into 'gold' is thus a familiar process of marketing derivatives that financial institutions have also unacceptably applied to social necessities like health, housing and other essential sectors.

Although there is a developing appetite among corporations and small and medium businesses for investment in 'green growth', the crucial factors will be whether the rate of 'green transformation' is fast enough and what the quality and nature of future private and/or government subsidized investment will likely be. Prior to 2008, the European Union was the global pacesetter in decarbonisation. However, the 2015 European Fund for Strategic Investment showed that of the proposed investment projects in member states valued at 1,409 billion Euros, less than half (€624bn) could be classified as low carbon, while the share of renewable energy generation made up just 10% of the total, and energy efficiency projects a tiny 5% of future projects.[48]According to Climate Tracker, if all the national decarbonisation commitments made at COP21 in Paris in 2015 were fulfilled, the world will be still on track for a disastrous increase in temperatures of between 2.7C and 3.6C by 2100.[49]

It is well known that financial incentives can range from government financial assistance for 'green' R&D, fostering the growth of renewable energy schemes by subsidizing households and businesses to switch to solar and other renewables, or changing tax rates for depreciation in order for businesses to abandon fossil fuels and adopt renewables and energy intensive technologies.[50] Using financial carrots also covers the mobilisation of financial resources to construct desperately needed infrastructure in both developed and developing countries.[51] However, one

---

47 See BNEP, 'Climatescope 2014 – Global study Shows Clean Energy Activity Surges in Developing World', *Bloomberg New Energy Finance*, New York, October 28, 2014 and Silvio Marcacci, 'Renewables Now Cheaper Than Fossil Fuels In Developing Countries', *The Energy Collective*, November 6, 2014.

48 figures cited by Bela Galgoczi, 'After COP21: The EU Needs to Revise its Climate Policy Targets', *Social Policy*, 18 February 2016.

49 'Climate pledges will bring 2.7°C of warming, potential for more action', Climate Tracker, 8 December 2015.

50 Xavier Timbeau, 'Green Depreciation and European Recovery', *Project Syndicate*, June 4, 2015.

51 For example, see African Development Bank, Asian Development Bank, European Bank for Reconstruction and Development, European Investment Bank, Inter-American Development Bank, International Monetary Fund and World Bank Group, *From Billions to Trillions: Transforming Development Finance Post-2015 Financing for Development: Multilateral Development Finance,* April 2, 2015.

of the major problems with market-based financial carrots to promote emissions reductions is that very little finance goes to unprofitable green infrastructure and services or to those necessary environmental projects that are opposed by businesses for a range of narrow market interests.

The annual Global Landscape of Climate Finance reports track all facets of national and international government, private and joint financial investments in mitigation, adaptation and other aspects of funding concerned with global warming. [52] Although increased funding is going into various climate projects, they remain grossly inadequate. Importantly, various analysts such as Stephen Spratt have distinguished between 'light green' and 'dark green' environmental agendas.[53] Major financial corporations and international funding bodies such as the World Bank prefer 'light green' market projects, such as funding infrastructure that is orientated to 'green growth'. Non-market schemes to protect fragile ecosystems are classified as 'dark green' and have low priority with the finance sector. There is also a serious lack of finance for anti-high material consumption agendas such as degrowth 'transition towns' and communities that combine 'dark green' values with 'red' social justice policies. These are seen to run counter to prevailing financialisation processes and market values.

It is disastrous that banking and general financial systems in capitalist countries fail to fund desperately needed social production and services yet find little difficulty in generating enormous sums for all kinds of speculative financial products and activities. These same financial institutions are largely geared to funding short-term 'light green' projects (because of their attractive rates of return on investments) but are reluctant to fund more open-ended or unprofitable long-term 'dark green' transitional forms of decarbonisation and environmental protection.[54]

The finance sector in most countries is so environmentally irresponsible, that even many 'light green' infrastructure projects, especially in developing countries, are desperately short of necessary funding to the tune of over US$1 trillion per year.[55] Very importantly, it has also been

---

52 These detailed reports from 2011 to 2017 are issued by the Climate Policy Initiative and are available online climatepolicyinitiative.org.

53 Stephen Spratt, 'Financing Green Transformations', in Ian Scoones, Melissa Leach and Peter Newell (eds), *The Politics of Green Transformations*, Earthscan/Routledge, 2015, ch.10.

54 *Ibid.*

55 See Amar Bhattacharya, Mattia Romani and Nicholas Stern, *Infrastructure for development: meeting the Challenge*, Centre for Climate Change Economics and Policy and Grantham Research Institute on Climate Change and the Environment in collaboration with Intergovernmental Group of Twenty Four (G-24) Policy Paper, June 2012. For an overview of the major obstacles to financing renewable energy, see Greenpeace International, Global Wind Energy Council and Solarpower Europe, *Energy (R)evolution A Sustainable World Energy Outlook 2015*, Hamburg, 2015, ch.4.

calculated that the financial cost of various forms of renewable or even non-renewable energy is not related primarily to the energy used, but rather to the financial cost of long-term loans (for twenty to thirty year periods) that financial institutions are prepared to fund. For example, low-cost loans averaging 3% interest to stable countries such as Germany versus 12% plus for Greece and numerous unstable developing societies.[56] This is just one small example of the disastrous long-term consequences of financialisation.

As to the relationship between definancialisation and 'green growth', the possibility of implementing a progressive decarbonisation of economies depends on the pace of change and the scale of economic transition. When neo-Schumpeterians Mariana Mazzucato and Carlotta Perez, call on governments to re-regulate and 'definancialise the economy',[57] it is clear that any government pursuing a simultaneous combination of 'definancialisation' and 'green growth' will encounter massive opposition from powerful financial corporations. What Mazzucato and Perez propose is necessary and significant, but these desirable reforms unfortunately clash with corporate needs to sustain credit-fuelled consumption and indebtedness. Meanwhile, fellow neo-Schumpeterian 'green growth' advocate, Michael Jacobs, recently presided over the neo-Keynesian Institute for Public Policy Research's 2017 'Commission on Economic Justice' report. The IPPR report simultaneously promotes the 'entrepreneurial state' and definancialisation while praising the City of London for making 'a significant contribution' to the British economy.[58] This is either wishful thinking or a deliberately myopic avoidance of measures to curb the City of London which continues to be one of the prime movers of global financialisation. While the report acknowledges how the City has exposed the UK to financial crises, it prefers cosmetic solutions to recommending major forms of definancialisation, such as those proposed by Mathew Lawrence in an earlier 2014 IPPR report as discussed above.

In short, the existing funding of 'green growth' makes dangerous climate change a strong possibility. Given the profitability of finance sector investment in all kinds of non-green financial instruments and sectors, the current rate and scale of green investment will remain too

---

56 Michael Grubb, 'Delivering the energy transition in theory and practice', *Presentation to the Melbourne Sustainable Society Institute*, University of Melbourne, December 7, 2016, also see climatestrategies.org.

57 M. Mazzucato and C. Perez, *Innovation as Growth Policy: the challenge for Europe*, Science Policy Research Unit, Working Papers Series, University of Sussex, July 2014.

58 See IPPR, *Time for Change: A New Vision for the British Economy – The Interim Report of the IPPR Commission on Economic Justice*, IPPR, London, 2017, pp.88-89.

low, too slow and too 'light green'. Moreover, the finance sector is preoccupied with profitable infrastructure ventures rather than unprofitable safeguarding of natural habitats. 'Green growth' advocates such as Nicholas Stern, Jeffrey Sachs and others are confident that a successful low-carbon strategy can attract sufficient funding. But the figures tell a different story of massive shortfalls in required global green investment. Projected green financial investment would have to escalate dramatically in the next 10 to 20 years, as it is certainly far too little to prevent dangerous climate breakdown, let alone achieve comprehensive absolute decoupling of economic growth from a range of finite natural resources.

Little wonder that simultaneously preventing dangerous asset bubbles while diverting large financial sums into 'green growth' and social expenditure requires very significant changes to both the degree and form of state intervention, levels of state intervention that existing political leaders currently reject. Any political strategy of definancialisation will of necessity involve staged targeting of financial practices, financial products and financial assets. This would thus entail not only the end of neo-liberalism but also a new international monetary regime that could not, if global instability and depression were to be avoided, be a return to a modified Bretton Woods Mark2. Creating a new domestic and international architecture could not be achieved without pressures on governments coming from mass political mobilisation. Governments could also participate in co-ordinated political intervention to facilitate the shift of private financial allocation of funds way from existing forms of wealth creation (such as many undesirable forms of credit provision to the corporate and household sectors).

Currently, definancialisation assumes either a limited reform-orientated set of goals or else a radical version that targets the dominance of private finance institutions and hence, the continued viability of capitalism. Even reforms to adopt versions of 'sustainable capitalism' remain quite unacceptable to large sections of business. Take, for example, a scenario where definancialisation gradually reduced national finance sectors by up to two-thirds, or returned them to their former size in 1950. The consequences of such a dramatic change would threaten the growth rates and profit rates of most capitalist economies. A rapid rate of definancialisation would instigate degrowth by restricting credit to non-finance sector businesses and households associated with current forms of production and consumption. Household and individual consumption that is highly dependent on credit purchases would stagnate at best and plummet at worst. This could precipitate a major depression unless alternative jobs were created.[59] Even 'green growth' infrastructure and other green investment would only take up part of the slack caused by radical definancialisation. At the very least, a much larger local and national public sector would be necessary to counter the economic slump and credit restrictions on individual and household consumption. Crucially, in non-authoritarian systems, any significant change between the size and role of private and public sectors would be impossible without a major shift in prevailing political and cultural values and practices.

Finally, the potential political divisions over any implementation of definancialisation policies are not clear cut. Large sections of the electorate and small and medium businesses may welcome greater regulation and restructuring of financial institutions if the curbing of financialisation prevented another major financial crisis and led to lower costs such as cheaper loans, as well as more funding and support for production, services and home loans. However, many businesses, households and individual consumers would also strongly oppose sweeping definancialisation, if reform measures led to serious economic downturn resulting in unemployment, bankruptcies and depressed conditions.

A vicious cycle now governs capitalist societies. The more that political reforms to combat inequality, poverty and climate breakdown necessitate extensive definancialisation measures, the more that definancialisation reforms threaten government tax revenue and socio-economic stability should curbs on financial practices precipitate a major recession. This vicious cycle is the contemporary version of the old dilemma of what constitutes the limits of 'sustainable capitalism' or 'civilised capitalism'. Each generation over the past two hundred years has been warned that capitalism is incompatible with a welfare state, or with full employment, or with equality for women and non-whites or other such proposed reforms, even though there is still a long way to go for these reforms to be fully realised. Could it be that definancialisation is similar and that major measures will hurt segments of finance capital but not lead to the collapse of capitalism? Or are there distinct limits to definancialisation beyond which not just finance corporations, but the very character and growth of contemporary finance-led capitalism is substantially threatened? Although quite different to definancialisation, the same is true of competing notions of degrowth. Do these notions simply challenge wasteful consumption, or explicitly confront and undermine the prevailing neo-liberal and social democratic market notions of 'sustainable capitalism'?

---

59 Jackson, Victor and Naqvi, op.cit., argue that a model of finance and credit can be theoretically developed for a stationary economy that is not dependent on debt-fuelled growth – although they acknowledge that it doesn't reflect the political economy of the real world (p.27).

Degrowth: Making Capitalism Sustainable or Anti-Capitalist Strategy?

Historically, there have been many cultural and political manifestations of anti-capitalist industrial and commercial development over the past two centuries. Note the fact that a particular current of nineteenth century populists/Slavophiles admired the Russian village or communal 'Mir' as an indigenous self-governing socio-political unit that was superior to what they saw as Western capitalist industrialism and cultural decadence. This tradition survived and was resurrected during late Soviet times by people like Alexander Solzhenitsyn. Similarly, Mahatma Ghandi advocated abstemious self-control combined with self-sufficient 'Village Republics' (Gram Swaraj) rather than Western industrialisation as the solution to India's problems. Today, we have come full circle. What marks the contemporary degrowth movement since the 1960s, is that in contrast to pre-industrial or earlier rejections of industrial capitalism (from nineteenth century Europe to twentieth century Asia), this new movement has metamorphosed into a direct reaction against the most heightened and elaborate manifestations of production and consumption. Consequently, practitioners of degrowth take many forms. Some strive for simplicity (either spiritual or secular) and wish to 'disengage' from, as well as stop the rate of growth of dominant practices and values of consumer capitalism. Others champion only those parts of modern technology and science that are compatible with ecological sustainability and non-violent social relations. They may also advocate degrowth as a means of preventing climate chaos as well as for socio-cultural reasons to eliminate gross forms of inequality and poverty. Importantly, supporters of degrowth arrive at their position precisely because they reject business and political attempts to preserve capitalist consumerism by decoupling economic growth from the limits of nature.

Depending on whether advocates arrive at their position from a socialist, radical ecological or spiritual and anti-commercial perspective, there is no uniform notion of degrowth. A certain proportion of residents in eco-villages, transitional towns or urban communes have detached themselves from ongoing external political struggles over unemployment, wages and social conditions while others are heavily involved in all kinds of anti-capitalist actions. Although eco-socialists oppose corporations and neo-liberal government policies, it is not uncommon for other degrowthers to say little about private property or a radical redistribution of wealth even though they are anti-consumerist and anti-growth. Instead, emphasis is placed on elaborating positive alternative forms of food production and communal living, or reduced consumption in non-communal urban settings.

Just as decoupling economic growth from natural finite resources is a broad concept, so too, degrowth has a range of political advocates that go under various names. Since the 1960s and 1970s, theorists such as Kenneth Boulding, Ivan Illich, E. F. Schumacher and Nicholas Georgescu-Roegen have warned about incessant growth and have promoted 'convivial tools,' 'small is beautiful' and the idea of the 'steady state'. In recent years, one of the founders of the renamed 'degrowth movement', Serge Latouche, proudly proclaimed that degrowth is a project of the political Left because it is inspired by socialism and is based on a radical critique of capitalist industrialisation and the narrow materialist values of the consumer economy.[60] Yet, degrowth is also associated with proponents of market-based co-operatives, and 'small-is-beautiful' business alternatives to big corporations that are far from socialist. Also, different types of radical and moderate greens favour low growth, no growth, or a mixture of growth sectors and non-growth sectors in a 'steady-state'. Only a minority favour a radical post-industrialism – a de-industrialised world of self-sufficient communes based on simplicity.[61]

In contrast to the radical Accelerationists discussed in the previous chapter, many advocates of degrowth wish to 'decelerate' capitalist technological development and growth. However, some supporters of degrowth share with post-capitalist utopians the belief that there is not the same degree of environmental limit on intellectual and cultural development in the 'immaterial' intellectual economy (aside from restrictions imposed by corporate digital rentiers, as well as the enormous environmental problem of the production of digital hardware). The massive growth of mobile phones, computers and other e-waste has reached a staggering 44.7 million tons annually, of which 40% is now produced in Asia, even though affluent Australia and New Zealand account for the highest level of per capita waste.[62] Only 20% of e-waste is currently

---

60 Serge Latouche, 'Can the Left Escape Economism?', *Capitalism Nature Socialism*, no.1, 2012, pp.74-78. In the US, Left progressives such as Gus Speth champion post-growth social change, see James Gustave Speth, 'Beyond the Growth Paradigm', *Great Transitions Initiative*, March, 2011. For an international survey of eco-socialist movements and theories, see Hans Baer, *Democratic Eco-socialism as a Real Utopia: Transitioning to an Alternative World System*, Berghahn, New York, 2018.

61 For an overview of the variety of degrowth advocates and movements, see Federico Demaria, et.al, 'What is Degrowth? From an Activist Slogan to a Social Movement', *Environmental Values*, 22, 2013, pp.191-215.

62 See C. P. Baldé, V. Forti, V. Gray, R. Kuehr and P. Stegmann, *The Global E-waste Monitor – 2017*, United Nations University (UNU), International Telecommunication Union (ITU) & International Solid Waste Association (ISWA), Bonn/Geneva/Vienna, 2017.

recycled, meaning that without a dramatic increase in 'circular economy' recycling, even growth in digital-based 'immaterial services' could be limited in the future. However, other aspects of socio-cultural knowledge (the arts and sciences) and caring services can grow and become democratised, as long as restrictive hierarchical controls by governments and corporations are removed.

In short, degrowth advocates include: a) those who oppose multi-national corporations and prefer local small businesses or self-managed workers' collectives, participatory planning and community-based co-operatives; b) those who desire a moneyless economy such as barter or networks of self-sufficient 'transition towns' and communes emphasising lifestyles based on radical forms of simplicity; and c) others who want degrowth implemented by national, regional and local governments in an economy characterised by a large and diverse public sector and a restrained or subordinated private sector, that is, an emphasis on public goods and services over private production and consumption.[63]

Martin Weiss and Claudio Cattaneo, for example, have surveyed the growing literature and many facets of degrowth movements that is impossible to do justice to here.[64] Although most supporters of degrowth can overwhelmingly be located on a progressive green or Left spectrum, a distinct minority of intolerant racists and reactionaries combine ecological degrowth issues with conservative politics, including a preoccupation with strict population controls or excluding non-white or non-Christian refugees and immigrants.[65] By contrast, most of the various degrowth movements and theorists emphasise the crucial importance of wellbeing, social justice and respect for nature, co-operation rather than competition, and peaceful co-existence. Degrowth is unintelligible as a pure economic theory if stripped of its moral, political and social critique of the destructive impacts of incessant capitalist growth on individuals, communities and ecological habitats.

---

63   For a range of degrowth movements and values see Gar Alperovitz, James Gustave Speth and Joe Guinan, *The Next System Project: New Political-Economic Possibilities for the 21ˢᵗ Century*, March 2015; Ted Trainer, 'The Degrowth Movement From the Perspective of the Simpler Way', *Capitalism Nature Socialism*, no.2, 2015, pp.58-75; Special Issue on Degrowth, *Journal of Cleaner Production*, 38, 2013; Samuel Alexander, 'Introduction to Prosperous Descent', *The Simplicity Collective*, May 20, 2015 and 'What is Degrowth? Envisioning a Prosperous Descent', *The Simplicity Collective*, November 2, 2015; Juliet Schor and Craig Thompson (eds.) *Sustainable Lifestyles and the Quest for Plenitude: Case studies of the New Economy*, Yale University Press, New Haven, 2014.

64   Martin Weiss and Claudio Cattaneo, 'Degrowth – Taking Stock and Reviewing an Emerging Academic Paradigm', *Ecological Economics*, Vol. 137, 2017, pp.220-30.

65   See Andrew Sutter's discussion of the many degrowth currents absent from Giacomo D'Alisa, Federico Demaria, Giorgos Kallis (eds.), Degrowth: A Vocabulary for a New Era in his review in *Ecological Economics*, vol.140, 2017, pp.275-76.

I also share the belief that capitalist economies are environmentally unsustainable and destroy social wellbeing. However, this does not mean that we can ignore some of the problems associated with alternative policies articulated under the general umbrella of degrowth. From a sympathetic perspective I will outline some of the obstacles to degrowth policies and visions that need to be addressed if alternatives to incessant growth are to become feasible. While it would be intellectually dishonest to ignore some of the weaknesses and political contradictions evident in degrowth theory, it is not my intention to devalue or dismiss many of the insights, practices and socio-cultural values offered by degrowth movements. The central issue is not whether degrowth is necessary, but rather the kind, rate and scale of degrowth, and how to prevent counter-productive socio-economic and political instability.

Key Political Economic Debates Over Degrowth

Some advocates of degrowth recognise that it is an ugly term that has outgrown its usefulness and prefer a range of alternatives such as 'well-being', 'human flourishing', 'good growth', 'post-growth' and so forth.[66] Degrowth is also confusing to many people because its supporters oppose only those aspects of capitalist economies that deplete and destroy natural resources. They do, however, desire 'good growth' or economic growth and employment in a range of areas such as organic food production or care work, public transport, health, education and cultural/leisure activity that promote wellbeing, strengthen communities and use minimal natural resources. It is also confusing and unclear what is to degrow. For instance, economist Kate Raworth queries: "Are we talking about degrowth of the economy's material volume – the tonnes of stuff consumed – or degrowth of its monetary value, measured as GDP? That difference really matters, but it is too rarely spelled out."[67]

As a broad movement, degrowth is divided between practitioners who largely attempt to live a daily life of reduced and alternative consumption and production, and theorists who develop macro-ecological economic models about how degrowth societies could challenge capitalist growth and make post-growth societies feasible. Lukas Hardt, Daniel O'Neill, J. Mikael Malmaeus and Eva C. Alfredsson have surveyed various ecological economic models to see how these post-growth theorists deal with

---

66   See Kate Raworth, 'Why Degrowth has out-grown its own name', *From Poverty to Power*, Oxfam, December 1, 2015.

67   *Ibid.*

major issues such as the monetary system, employment, trade, inequality, changing lifestyle and so forth.[68] I will now focus on some key issues raised in these important macro political economic debates.

The Ideal of the 'Steady-state'

First, it is important to assert that the overall socio-political goal of degrowth has to be distinguished from the notion of a 'steady state'. One can support degrowth, for example, without assuming that constantly changing socio-economic and political conditions can ever reach a state of equilibrium. Just as neo-classical economics aims for the market fiction of general equilibrium between supply and demand, so too, a number of ecologists are guided by the illusion of a 'steady state'. Leaving aside for the moment all the serious problems of the compatibility of a 'steady-state' with capitalism, it is entirely unclear whether a 'steady-state' equilibrium is achieved annually, or over a particular period, or not at all. How will a 'steady state' be measured and will growth or degrowth targets in particular local, national or international sectors of the economy require democratic approval each time or will these targets be imposed by planning departments? Are 'steady-state' goals applied to just individual national economies, or to all countries in the international system? How are these to be achieved globally if, for example, only half the governments (whether parliamentary governments or authoritarian regimes) or some other proportion of all countries agree to 'steady-state' practices and the rest pursue unsustainable production and consumption? Crucially, are these post-growth economies post-capitalist or still largely capitalist 'mixed economies' with a larger public sector than a private sector? Will taxes or production penalties be imposed on businesses or on public sector industries if they exceed growth rates? These are just a few of the many important political and socio-economic questions in urgent need of clarification.

Herman Daly's model of a 'steady state economy' for the US may be politically radical due to the very conservative nature of American politics. However, it is predominantly a modified capitalism with progressive environmental policies. Daly describes it as being closer to Sweden or Switzerland. These are hardly examples of countries with low

---

68 Lukas Hardt and Daniel W. O'Neill, 'Ecological Macroeconomic Models: Assessing Current Developments', *Ecological Economics*, vol.134, 2017, pp.198-211 and J. Mikael Malmaeus and Eva C. Alfredsson, 'Potential Consequences on the Economy of Low or No Growth – Short and Long Term Perspectives', *Ecological Economics*, vol.134, 2017, pp.57-64.

consumption rates. Moreover, the 'steady state economy' is characterised as a mixed economy whereby the government imposes a cap-trade-auction system for businesses that forces them to limit their use of basic resources thus decreasing the overall rate of depletion of natural resources. The 'steady state' also features new ecological taxes, regulates trade and capital flows, definancialises the economy and reduces the ratio of income to 100 to 1 while also stopping advertising as a tax deduction to discourage consumption.[69] Daly would like to break private monopolies and have a society based on small businesses or the self-employed, the public sector and cooperatives. However, an income ratio goal of 100 to 1 is still a massive form of income inequality that also leaves the private corporate ownership of wealth virtually untouched. Importantly, the 'steady-state' is devised for national economies because Daly is opposed to world government. I share his concern about the practical difficulties and frightening bureaucracy of a world government. Given the absence of world government, how can 'steady state' goals to limit natural resources use and other vital measures be implemented? This is one of the crucial questions left unanswered by 'steady state' advocates.

Degrowth and Inequality

It is unclear how degrowth applies to the 20% to 40% of the population in affluent OECD countries comprising all those on welfare benefits, or who are underemployed and/or employed on low incomes. A 'steady state economy' which permits growth in immaterial services but reduces material resources growth would still need to increase or redirect material production in order to provide infrastructure and goods such as adequate housing for the poor and homeless. It would also need a major redistribution of wealth if poverty and inequality were to be drastically reduced. As for degrowth in low and middle-income developing societies where more than four billion people exist on daily incomes which are a meagre fraction of those enjoyed by affluent people in OECD countries, disagreement prevails. Some argue that degrowth should also apply to the 'global South' if these developing countries are not to imitate the growth economies of the 'North'. But like many others in the degrowth movement, Herman Daly warns that it is unacceptable to preach to the global poor before first stopping overconsumption in developed

---

69 See Daly and Czech, *op.cit.* and H. Daly, 'From a Failed Growth Economy to a Steady-State Economy' *The Solutions Journal* vol.1, no.2, 2010, pp.37-43.

capitalist societies.[70]

Apart from general agreement that aid from developed countries is needed, there is no consensus on how much growth in developing countries, in order for billions of poor people to emerge from extreme poverty, is compatible with a safe climate or a global 'steady-state' world. In 2004, Herman Daly and Brian Czech argued that the GDP of a 'steady state economy' should be no bigger than $US10.6 trillion for the United States and $US32 trillion for the world.[71] At that time, US GDP was $US12.275 trillion and world GDP was $US43.607 trillion so that Daly and Czech sought just over 13% degrowth in the GDP of the US but double the reduction globally at 26% degrowth. Daly and Czech were either treating the US too softly, given that it was by far the largest and most wasteful economy in the world at the time, or their notion of degrowth was arbitrary without any logical assessment of the global use of natural resources. By 2017, US GDP had grown by more than 57% (in nominal terms) to $US19.285 trillion and world GDP had expanded by more than 78% to $US77.779 trillion, including the phenomenal growth of GDP in China which grew from just $US1.942 trillion in 2004 to $US12.263 trillion in 2017 – a more than sixfold increase.[72] Despite this massive increase, the dilemma facing advocates of degrowth is that China still has hundreds of millions of very poor people, as do numerous other countries. A global 'steady-state' either requires a rate of degrowth in the US and other developed countries far in excess of the 13% suggested by Daly, or a much larger redistribution of wealth that is far greater than envisaged by 'steady-state' advocates.

In fact, degrowth and its antecedent movements have long been identified as 'rich country' socio-political movements supported by affluent people who seek qualitative 'post-material growth' in their spiritual and cultural life as well as ending the abuse of the environment. As such, a disproportionate focus is on Western affluent societies with little analysis of how degrowth could apply to the vast majority of the global poor. Despite the much lower per capita material footprint of most people in China and other developing countries (leaving aside their substantial and growing affluent minorities), these countries have driven between 67% and 80% of global economic growth since the year 2000.

---

70 See discussion of Latouche and Daly in John Bellamy Foster, 'Degrow or Die?, *Red Pepper*, November 2010.

71 See Herman Daly and Brian Czech, 'In My Opinion: The steady state economy – what it is, entails, and connotes', *Wildlife Society Bulletin*, no.2, 2004, pp.598-605.

72 All figures for GDP taken from '2017, Economic Statistics and Indicators' *Economy Watch, 17 March 2018*.

Hence, the trilemma of degrowth is as follows. Firstly, how to simul-taneously reduce material production and consumption in affluent OECD countries without negatively affecting their own low-income populations. Secondly, how to also ensure that countries with very large poor populations such as China and India do not fuel wasteful con-sumption in North America, Europe, Japan and Australia at the expense of their own desperately poor populations. And thirdly, how to achieve a so-called global 'steady-state' if the highly populous developing countries are now the *engines of global growth*, despite developed OECD countries continuing to disproportionately use more finite natural resources? Do degrowth policies in developing countries require the reduction of export-dependent growth, thereby possibly exacerbating existing rates of inequality and poverty? Or do these countries switch heavily to domestic redistribution or 'good growth' based on the growth of the 'social state', as I will examine in the next chapter. Writers such as María Páez Victor observe that development in Latin American countries is not seen as mere economic growth but is inseparable from imperialist extractivism and exploitation.[73]

National Models in an Integrated World

Environmental economists such as Tim Jackson, Peter Victor and Ali Naqvi attempt to build on Herman Daly's 'steady-state' economics by developing their own model of a degrowth economy.[74] While they show at a theoretical level that degrowth does not result in greater inequality as critics have argued, the problem is that like Daly, Jackson, Victor and Naqvi ignore the realities of the capitalist world where the 'national economy' has almost become a fiction. As an open economy, imports and exports in the UK, for example, constitute 61% of GDP.[75] Most national governments may be responsible for revenue collection, expenditure allocations, welfare, environmental and social laws, but have far less control over material production and capital flows that largely affect revenue and expenditure. The 'steady state' or 'prosperity without growth' models provide inadequate answers about the 46% to 80% of production and trade in goods and services (depending on different

73 María Páez Victor, 'Questioning Sustainability in Latin America', in Peter Victor and Brett Dolter (eds.), *Handbook on Growth and Sustainability*, Edward Elgar, Cheltenham, 2017.
74 Jackson, Victor and Naqvi, *Towards a Stock-Flow Consistent Ecological Macroeconomics*, WWW-forEurope, Working Paper no.114, March 2016.
75 Desmond Cohen. 'Economic sovereignty: A Delusion', *Social Europe*, 12 September 2017.

reports and calculations) that now constitute part of global value chains overwhelmingly operated by multi-national corporations.[76] Hence, the 'steady-state' national model is a castle in the air that bears little relationship to contemporary capitalist economies. The engines of these economic processes are corporations that are based on the integration of multiple resources, intermediate and semi-finished manufactures and other component elements which are simultaneously resourced, produced, assembled and traded across a number of regions and countries. This is not to deny that 'steady state' advocates could aim to drastically reduce exports and imports over a period of years and return to predominantly national economies. But this radical restructuring would entail major political confrontations with businesses and workers, given that it would require a fundamental reorganisation of production, employment and consumption.

Finance and lower growth

Jackson and Victor have confronted one of the major arguments about the viability of any post-growth system, namely the inherent connection between the need for continued growth in order to service interest payments on debt. Take away growth, so the argument goes, and the capitalist system would collapse, due to the impossibility of constantly repaying interest on all forms of consumer and business debt. Jackson and Victor have modelled various hypothetical situations and processes in order to show that this argument or forecast about finance is wrong.[77] The problem is that their model is only a model and hence inadequate to predict the highly volatile nature of domestic and international capitalism. For instance, let us focus on the issue of definancialisation, discussed earlier in this chapter. As I have mentioned, despite the difficulties it is possible to phase-in various definancialisation measures. However, requiring pension funds to switch from equities to other less risky investments is a serious challenge and could trigger a major sell-off of shares and economic collapse. Also, switching from current forms of investment and financialisation products is not equivalent to degrowth.

---

76 See United Nations Conference on Trade and Development (UNCTAD), *World Investment Report 2013: Global Value Chains: Investment for Trade and Development*, United Nations, Geneva, 2013. However, the 2016 UNCTAD *Trade and Development Report*, p.118 cited 46% of intermediate merchandise trade as part of GVCs which may still add up to much higher percentages once finished goods and services are also taken into account.

77 Tim Jackson and Peter Victor, 'Does credit create a 'growth imperative'? A quasi-stationary economy with interest-bearing debt', *Ecological Economics*, vol.120, 2015, pp.32-48.

Although hostile to degrowth, finance analyst Damir Tokic makes some important points that cannot be ignored. As he puts it:

> ...any early indication of the degrowth scenario (long-term negative growth followed by infinite flat growth) would cause the stock market to crash, which would trigger further deleveraging and a vicious cycle of deflation. As a result, the economy would implode, which essentially makes degrowth (gradual decline in the size of the economy) unsustainable. However, the combination of regulatory, fiscal, and extraordinary monetary policy responses to the economic implosion is likely to eventually stabilize asset prices, boost inflation, and trigger a new long-term growth cycle, which essentially makes the ecological goals of the steady-state economy unachievable. Thus, our views on degrowth are similar to those of the critics of degrowth who argue that degrowth is environmentally ineffective, socially and politically unfeasible, and economically inefficient.[78]

One can agree with Tokic's analysis of the negative impact of degrowth on stock markets while disagreeing with his argument about the environmental ineffectiveness of degrowth. It does not automatically follow that after a collapse, governments would renew present-day forms of environmentally unsustainable production and consumption; they could also possibly opt for even more sustainable post-capitalist forms of socio-economic activity. Nonetheless, the numerous criticisms of degrowth, point to the need for advocates of degrowth to strengthen their explanations – not through abstract models but through political economic strategies and policies – outlining how they will deal with any political transition from growth to post-growth.

Instead, degrowth is still largely caught in the phase of economic and cultural critique of growth regimes. An example would be Kate Raworth who builds on the work of Daly, Jackson, Victor and others to develop a model of the 'doughnut economy', which George Monbiot exaggeratedly hails as the work of the 'Keynes of the 21st Century'.[79] Consisting of outer circles made up of the earth's planetary boundaries or 'life support system' (Rockström) and inner rings of society, economy, household, state and market, Raworth manages to integrate environment and

---

78 Damir Tokic, 'The economic and financial dimensions of degrowth', *Ecological Economics*, vol.84, 2012, pp.49-56.

79 George Monbiot, 'Finally, a breakthrough alternative to growth economics – the doughnut', *The Guardian*, 12 April, 2017.

socio-economic factors in very suggestive ways.[80] Yet, like Daly, Jackson and others, her critique of growth economics has *no politics*. Given it is couched in such general terms, it would be difficult to know where to locate it politically. In other words, the 'doughnut' is neither a political economic analysis of particular nation states (as it stipulates no transitional fiscal, monetary or other policies), nor is it a global strategy that is explicitly anti-capitalist. It outlines seven guidelines that are admirable, but as with other contributions in this genre of fusing environmental, human rights and social justice development goals, Raworth sidesteps all the difficult issues of how to actually transform capitalist political economies.

Illuminating visual diagrams are no substitute for mass political movements or answers to how these political movements can sustain support from millions of citizens once degrowth or 'post-growth' strategies make employment in existing material growth sectors unviable. This is a dilemma that no analyst can solve in theory. However, one can be guaranteed of failure if deep-seated illusions are held about a possible smooth transition to a 'doughnut economy'. Helping people redefine their existing notions of economics is very important. Regrettably, major social change will most likely be bitterly resisted and will probably involve the use of violence by those with wealth and power who have the most to lose.

Degrowth within capitalism?

I am very sympathetic to the fundamental aim of abandoning and curbing incessant growth proposed by Daly, Jackson and other 'steady state' ecologists. The problem is that what they propose remains unconvincing. This is the case with both the end goal of a 'steady state' economy and the means by which these proposals could be implemented within capitalist societies that are interdependent and highly geared to incessant growth. As a neo-Keynesian, Daly is strongly opposed to the free flow of capital, labour and immigration and instead of globalisation, advocates a return to 'national economies'.[81] Marxists such as Richard Smith have lambasted Daly and Jackson because the anti-growth school of

---

80 Kate Raworth, *Doughnut Economics: Seven Ways to Think Like a 21st-Century Economist*, Penguin Random House, London 2017. Raworth has expanded her earlier work including *A Safe and Just Space for Humanity*, Oxfam Discussion Paper, February 2012.

81 See Herman Daly, *Beyond Growth: The Economics of Sustainable Development*, Beacon Press, Boston, 1996.

ecological economics *denies* the elementary rules for capitalist reproduction. Their project of a new 'steady state' eco-capitalism, Smith argues, is just a fuzzy unworkable capitalist utopia which "rests on the assumption that capitalist economic fundamentals are not immutable, that growth is "optional", and thus dispensable."[82] Other radical environmentalists such as Sam Alexander and Ted Trainer, who argue from the position of a self-managed communal form of simplicity, also believe that degrowth is not a viable transitional strategy within capitalism.[83] It is not just that degrowth is incompatible with the logic of incessant capitalist growth, but that the strategy of establishing one new transition town or commune after another is too slow, too little and too ineffective in the long run.

While Smith makes many valid points about why degrowth and 'steady-state' strategies as currently outlined by environmentalists are incompatible with financialised capitalism, paradoxically, his strategy for sustainability is just as utopian. For how can one pursue an eco-socialist political strategy given the absence of very large radical movements in many countries? Even if there were mass revolutionary parties ready to take power, Smith's solutions risk appearing little more than empty revolutionary slogans – a rhetoric that is common to those who prefer absolute and sweeping demands rather than considered radical action. It is worth quoting at length some of Smith's solutions to incessant capitalist growth, as he articulates a commonly held Marxist position that often lacks a political differentiation between end goals and transitional strategic practices. Accordingly, Smith proclaims the need to:

1. Put the brakes on out-of-control growth in the global North – retrench or shut down unnecessary, resource-hogging, wasteful, polluting industries like fossil fuels, autos, aircraft and airlines, shipping, chemicals, bottled water, processed foods, unnecessary pharmaceuticals, and so on. Abolish luxury goods production, the fashions, jewelry, handbags, mansions, Bentleys, yachts, private jets etc. Abolish the manufacture of disposable, throw away and "repetitive consumption" products. ...

2. Discontinue harmful industrial processes like industrial agriculture, industrial fishing, logging, mining and so on.

---

82 Richard Smith, 'Beyond growth or beyond capitalism?' *World Economics Review*, issue 53, 2010, p.31.

83 See Ted Trainer, 'The Radical Implications of a Zero Growth Economy', *real-world economics review*, no.57, 2011 and Samuel Alexander, Introduction to 'Sufficiency Economy', *The Simplicity Collective*, August 11, 2015.

3. Close down many services – the banking industry, Wall Street, the credit card, retail, PR and advertising "industries" built to underwrite and promote all this overconsumption. ...

4. Abolish the military-surveillance-police state industrial complex, and all its manufactures as this is just a total waste whose only purpose is global domination, terrorism and destruction abroad and repression at home. We can't build decent societies anywhere when so much of social surplus is squandered on such waste.

5. Reorganize, restructure, reprioritize production and build the products we do need to be as durable *and shareable* as possible.

6. Steer investments into things society *does* need like renewable energy, organic farming, public transportation, public water systems, ecological remediation, public health, quality schools and other currently unmet needs.

7. De-globalize trade to produce what can be produced locally, trade what can't be produced locally, to reduce transportation pollution and revive local producers.[84]

If Smith is being more than deliberately provocative, then his proposals betray an inadequate understanding of how to bring about sustainable social change. First, it is not the 'North' which alone engages in 'out-of-control growth'. Developing countries have accounted for between 67% and 80% of global growth in the first two decades of the twenty-first century compared with stagnation and recession in America, Europe and Japan. The second point to note is that shutting-down polluting industries, luxury goods and the financial sector, retailing, advertising and Wall Street is tantamount to shutting down capitalism, not a transitional strategy. Perhaps there is no need to fear depression levels of unemployment, starvation and social chaos if a handful of revolutionaries think they can reorganise everything from their armchairs. Thirdly, Smith's proposals for alternative, socially useful employment, investment, production and trade are all good and necessary. However, these cannot be implemented overnight and therefore would need to be prioritised, phased-in and above all, require the mass political and cultural support of millions of people who would have been left shattered by the shutdown of their capitalist enterprises and income. Fourth, abolishing the military-industrial complex becomes a rhetorical pronouncement, as it assumes that the repressive-surveillance apparatuses do not shut down this revolution before it even gets started.

---

84 Richard Smith, 'Capitalism and the destruction of life on Earth: Six theses on saving the humans', *real-world economics*, no.64, 2013, p.141.

In other words, Smith wants a sustainable post-capitalist society without any clear theory of how to transform not one, but at least most of the G20 state apparatuses in major capitalist countries that account for 80% of global production and consumption. Is this to be done electorally, or through establishing a revolutionary structure of 'dual power' alongside existing state institutions, or through radical self-managed workers councils and self-sufficient communes, or does he have other proposals in mind? In the meantime, Smith's demand to abolish industrial mining, processed food and industrial food production would have most of the citizens of the new post-capitalist societies starve or be convulsed by food riots. Closing all industrial mining would result in a lack of the resource materials necessary for the production of durable and useful goods. At the very least, it will take a minimum of ten to twenty years for sufficient organic food on decontaminated soils, plus reduced meat consumption and so forth to develop as alternatives to existing polluting and chemically-based industrial food industries, as I have discussed in Chapter Four. While I endorse Smith's end goals of sustainability, I shudder at the idealist naivety of his list of demands that lacks a plausible politics of how an alternative society could become a reality, not to mention how it could remain viable within the unequal world that we confront today.

It should be remembered that Richard Smith criticised Daly's works and also Tim Jackson's 2009 first edition of *Prosperity Without Growth*. In the 2017, second edition of his book, Jackson attempts to counter critics such as Smith by rejecting as dangerous those who preach revolution and wish to demolish all old institutions and start anew.

> The spectre of a new barbarism lurks in the wings. Constrained for resources, threatened with climate change, struggling for economic stability: how long could we maintain civil society in such a world if we have already torn down every institutional structure we can lay our hands on?[85]

Crucially, Jackson also acknowledges radical critics by conceding that his proposals for a post-growth economy "are totally incompatible with the 'casino capitalism' or the 'consumer capitalism' that has characterised the richest economies in recent decades."[86] He adds an important caveat

---

85 *Ibid* p.186.

86 Tim Jackson, *Prosperity Without Growth: Foundations for the Economy of Tomorrow*, Second Edition, Routledge, London, 2017, p.222. A broad range of radicals such as Noam Chomsky and Naomi Klein as well as prominent international greens, social democrats and even the British monarchy in the form of a preface by Prince Charles have endorsed the book.

that "this is not the same thing as saying that we have arrived at the end of capitalism entirely."[87] Much hinges on the definition of 'capitalism' according to Jackson. Nevertheless, this 'definitional problem' hardly helps overcome numerous facets of corporate and state power – both geared to satisfying demands for increased shareholder value either through export-led or consumption-led growth – with both business and political leaders fearful of stagnation and deflation.

Unresolved Questions and Issues

Jackson and Smith represent the widespread impasse facing all advocates of an alternative to unsustainable capitalism. The answers they provide are far from satisfactory but the debate and the generation of ideas is crucial. One cannot deny Jackson's significant contribution to public debates on the urgent need to rethink the meaning of prosperity and why the trajectory of existing capitalist societies is disastrous. Even though Smith's policy solutions are utopian, I believe that Jackson and Daly fail to answer Smith's persuasive radical critiques of the incompatibility of degrowth with capitalism. A more fruitful discussion between ecological economists, green movement activists and radical critics of capitalism is to work through the unanswered questions posed by Jackson himself. "What happens to employment," Jackson asks, "when material consumption is no longer expanding? What happens to inequality as conventional growth rates decline? What can we say about financial stability when capital no longer accumulates? What happens to the public sector in the face of declining aggregate demand?"[88] A cooperative policy dialogue could focus on what aspects of definancialisation and degrowth could be achieved that may well fall far short of the end goals of socialism or the 'steady state', but nonetheless help to substantially reduce environmental unsustainability, inequality and other unacceptable features of contemporary capitalist societies.

One way of furthering a dialogue over degrowth and capitalism is to focus on what austerity, consumption and the relationship between national and global processes mean when considering alternatives to dominant economic and social practices. It is not enough to engage in general moral critiques of consumerism, as if these will help explain the level of degrowth that is needed to maintain eco-system sustainability. Although necessary as preliminary arguments, far too many books and

---

87 *Ibid.*
88 *Ibid*, p.174.

articles by advocates of degrowth barely advance beyond the numerous cultural, psychological and social and ecological health reasons why incessant growth should be rejected. In contrast to unplanned recessions caused by market capitalism, Sam Alexander sees degrowth as a transition away from capitalism involving 'planned economic contraction'.[89] Alexander does not elaborate sufficiently on how this 'planned contraction' is to be accomplished but it is a start.

Let us take the issue of consumption. Degrowth movements may have ignited many debates about whether no-growth in material goods could be implemented locally, nationally and internationally. However, there is no agreement over what rate of degrowth in household consumption, which sectors of particular economies and which countries should degrow or be permitted to have poverty-combating growth. Angela Druckman and Tim Jackson argue that a 37% degrowth of household consumption in developed countries such as the UK could prevent global warming. [90] Yet, as Sam Alexander has pointed out, if everyone lived like those in Findhorn (the renowned eco-village in Scotland), that this would still require one and a half planet's worth of bio-capacity, as Findhorn residents fly as often as non-residents thus increasing their otherwise small ecological footprint.[91] Would degrowth mean an end to, or very severe restrictions on flying and a mass reduction in inter and transcontinental tourism?[92] German political economists, Michael Jakob and Ottmar Edenhofer take a step even further. They observe that reducing the income and consumption of affluent individuals in the US and Europe (while raising the income of the global poor) so that they equalled a global income of US$10,000 per capita would require *drastic cuts of between 70% and 80% of current affluent levels*.[93] Clearly such massive cuts in income, especially in OECD countries, is utopian, as it is well beyond the practical realm where any party could be elected on such a platform. Jakob and Edenhofer focus on income and do not, however,

---

89 Samuel Alexander, 'Planned economic contraction: the emerging case for degrowth', *Environmental Politics*, vol.21, no.3, 2012, pp.349-368.

90 Angela Druckman and Tim Jackson, 'The bare necessities; How much carbon do we really need?' *Ecological Economics*, 69, 2010, pp.1794-1804.

91 Samuel Alexander, 'If everyone lived in an 'ecovillage' the Earth would still be in trouble', *The Conversation*, June 26, 2015.

92 Given that electric planes are probably decades away, whether post-fossil fuel aviation is sustainable with biofuels is unclear given the agricultural land required to prop up current levels of tourism. On changing aviation see Robbert Kivits, Michael B. Charles and Neal Ryan 'A post-carbon aviation future: Airports and the transition to a cleaner aviation sector', *Futures*, 42, 2010, pp.199-211.

93 See Michael Jakob and Ottmar Edenhofer, 'Green growth, degrowth, and the commons', *Oxford Review of Economic Policy*, vol.30, no.3, 2014, p.451.

discuss changing the mix between monetized incomes and social wage goods and services provided publicly. This will be further examined in the next chapter.

Jackson also counters consumerism with mainly moral and cultural arguments calling for the redefinition of myopic individual consumption into collective wellbeing. He argues for the dismantling of complex social, institutional, advertising and other structures that create the incentives for consumerism.[94] What he does not do at a national macro level, as opposed to a household or local level, is to deconstruct consumption into its constituent elements in order to see which parts should degrow or grow.

Personal and household consumption in high-income countries now makes up between 52 and 70 per cent of total GDP. Household consumption actually accounts for a higher percentage of GDP in many poor countries because they lack developed manufacturing and service industries.[95] Conversely, some high-income countries such as Norway have large fossil fuel industries that take up a higher percentage of GDP, despite households having very affluent high consumption rates. In giant middle-income economies such as China, the emphasis in recent decades on heavy industry producer goods and investment in infrastructure and exports has meant that personal consumption is only now starting to account for a greater share of GDP. Statisticians in OECD countries classify consumption as consisting of durable goods such as cars, appliances and furniture, non-durable goods (lasting less than a year) such as fuel, food and clothing, and services ranging from financial, telecommunication and health services to hospitality and tourism. In leading consumer countries such as the US, services now account for 55% to 60% of personal consumption. As a proportion of total US GDP, there has been a dramatic shift in consumption patterns from durable goods (which accounted for 40% of GDP in 1968) to services which now constitute more than 46% of GDP.

Why should these elementary facts about the different component elements of consumption be important to advocates of degrowth? If fuel and food constitute the bulk of non-durable goods, then devising ways to transition a society away from-fossil fuels and away from chemically based agribusiness food production and meat consumption may well

---

94 Tim Jackson, 'Beyond consumer capitalism: foundations for a sustainable prosperity' ch.23 in Peter Victor and Brett Dolter (eds.), *Handbook on Growth and Sustainability*, Edward Elgar, Cheltenham, 2017.

95 See 2015 figures provided by World Bank in 'Household consumption, percent of GDP by country, around the world', *The Global Economy.com*

help reach sustainability targets. Similarly, the level of imports, such as machinery, mineral resources, metals, component parts and fully assembled products as opposed to local production, will be crucial to assessing how the mix and the volume of durable consumer goods consumption can be changed. Finally, the massive growth in all kinds of services as a proportion of household and personal consumption must itself be subdivided into private sector and public provision of services.

In short, each political movement that advocates degrowth in different countries would have to calculate and campaign on how the specific allocation of resources, level of imports and forms of private and public provision affected durable and non-durable goods as well as services. If specific degrowth targets were to be met, proponents of this approach would also have to specify how the profile and content of trade with other countries as well as capital flows would need to be altered. Without this knowledge, all strategies of degrowth will continue to be vague generalisations with few specific goals for reducing particular forms of production and consumption or increasing the provision of more socially useful goods and services.

It is difficult to avoid using the broad concept 'consumption' as a short hand term despite it containing quite different elements such as durable goods or services. The same is true of 'austerity' as an all-encompassing concept that covers quite different types of policies and measures. Hungarian economist László Andor has discussed the different definitions of austerity made by political economists in recent years.[96] Some use it to describe government expenditure cuts or the 'consolidation' of fiscal policies leading to unemployment. Others use austerity to describe cuts to wages and prices to restore competitiveness in the private sector. There is also the notion of austerity applied to reducing the budget deficit which does not always mean immediate cuts to public employment, pensions and services but a reduction in the rate of increased expenditure over the coming years. From a different perspective, derivatives analysts, Dick Bryan and Michael Rafferty are concerned to go beyond focusing on the negative consequences of austerity normally featured in social democratic and radical critiques of neo-liberal fiscal and social policies since 2008. They argue that:

> ... ordinary people are being incorporated into finance in important new ways, not just as consumers, or even as borrowers, but also as payers of fixed streams of income for a range

---

96 László Andor,'Austerity: From Outrage to Progressive Alternatives', *Social Europe*, 22 January 2018.

of debt and non-debt services and goods. They are, thereby, the base of a growing range of underlying assets of financial securities, and ... the state is leading that incorporation, ...and recasting the household not just as workers and consumers but as an 'asset class.' It is not the universal experience of finance and debt for the household, but it is emergent. This perspective opens up a quite different way of thinking about the relationship between money, finance and class. It also opens up quite a different politics, targeting not just a moral and economic critique of hardship, but opportunities to challenge the new role being demanded of households in securing financial stability.[97]

What have the different notions of austerity to do with degrowth? First, it is important for degrowth advocates to stipulate which parts of national fiscal and monetary policy they wish to restructure. Will cuts to existing government expenditure and subsidies for businesses in environmentally unsustainable durable and non-durable goods result in austerity as employment, income and wages are cut in these sectors? How will cuts to military R&D, weapons procurement and recurring expenditure on military personnel, affect growth or austerity in the related civilian sectors of particular economies? Definancialisation measures are also very closely tied to aspects of austerity. If Bryan and Rafferty are correct about the way households are being converted into risk stabilising income streams for financial institutions, how can financial crises be avoided in policies that definancialise households but yet insure that their homes and durable goods are not repossessed or their employment and income negated?

Neo-liberal austerity has been widely criticised by many political movements. There is also a popular image of degrowth as 'green austerity' that will attack and cut ordinary people's standard of living. If degrowth advocates are to counter these popular images of being lumped into the same boat as neo-liberal austerity, then greater differentiation of degrowth policies are needed. Jackson and others argue that a new set of neo-Keynesian policies by governments can counter both neo-liberal cuts to public services and instability caused by future restructuring of unsustainable private production and consumerism. As I will go on to argue, states can play a vital role in providing alternative basic services, employment and general wellbeing. However, the dilemma over the rate of definancialisation and degrowth remains pivotal to the difference

---

97 Dick Bryan and Michael Rafferty, 'Reframing austerity: financial morality, savings and securitization', *Journal of Cultural Economy*, vol.10, no.4, 2017, pp.339-355.

between feasible transition and socio-economic collapse. Jackson argues that:

> Dismantling consumer capitalism doesn't look easy. Overthrowing it precipitously could drive us even faster along the road to ruin. But incremental changes on their own are unlikely to be enough.[98]

This is the inescapable political dilemma facing all radicals and reformers. There can be no return to the old military Keynesianism of the 'warfare/welfare state' prevalent in OECD countries. Similarly, social democratic post-Keynesian policies of countering austerity by increasing conventional aggregate demand (especially through wage-led growth) is still largely 'pre-environmental' as it is prioritises unsustainable economic growth. Jackson recognises many of the key aspects of the 'conflicted state' that must simultaneously ensure economic growth and foster the transition to a post-growth economy. Given that Jackson himself says there is as yet no developed macroeconomics of the post-growth society,[99] questions remain about how this political juggling act could be accomplished. This is a major task that will require substantial development in coming years.

As to long-term political strategies, it is reckless to think that the tens of millions living in megacities such as Tokyo, Shanghai, Cairo, Lagos, Mexico City or São Paulo, let alone a future global population of 9 to 16 billion people can be organised into horizontal small, face-to-face communities without any vertical co-ordinating, planning and distributive state institutions.[100] The world is in dire straits and it is the height of irrationalism to believe that stateless societies could flourish and deliver desperately needed degrowth policy solutions for billions of people. Just as dominant market notions of decoupling fail to convince on how businesses will sustain growth in the face of finite limits to natural resources, so too, various proposals for eco-communes and eco-villages will only ever constitute a very tiny part of any future solutions.

---

98 Tim Jackson, *Prosperity Without Growth, Second Edition*, p.185.
99 *Ibid*, p.174.
100 See for example, Frank Fischer, *Climate Crisis and the Democratic Prospect: Participatory Governance in Sustainable Communities*, Oxford University Press, New York, 2017, who analyses the dire crisis of climate change but advocates small eco communities as the political solution without any deep discussion of the obstacles such a vision would encounter from existing political economic institutions and social forces.

Conclusion

In this chapter I have attempted to show why both neo-liberal and post-Keynesian drivers of growth are no longer adequate to the current circumstances and need to be abandoned. I have also examined how definancialisation and degrowth are so closely related to one another even though many advocates of curbing financialisation do not support degrowth. Both degrowth and definancialisation are seen as either feasible transitional strategies within capitalist societies or utterly incompatible. Despite agreeing with many of the reasons why degrowth and definancialisation are extremely difficult to implement in contemporary capitalist societies, the situation is far from impossible. If we are not to surrender to a fatalistic passivity and helplessness in the face of unlikely revolutionary forces, then we must continue to tackle those aspects of socio-economic and environmental radical reform that are not only feasible but also urgently needed. In the following chapter, I will discuss social policies, income and work and their roles in the possible transition to a post-growth society.

6

Beyond Income Solutions

These days there seems to be an endless stream of material about the universal basic income (UBI) in the print, electronic and digital media. This discussion can tend to be highly generalised, confined to predictions that robots will destroy jobs and the desirability or not of a 'post-work' society. More targeted debates are concerned with propositions about a post-carbon economy (which may still be geared to growth) or a post-growth sustainable society. Even though we live in a world connected by global markets, it is important to note that most of these alternative imaginaries tend to be Eurocentric or American scenarios that pay lip-service to the profound problems of social inequality and poverty in less developed countries. This is not to deny the specific regional debates over social development in Latin American countries or in those Asian and African countries that permit dissenting policies to be aired. Within OECD countries there tends to be a division between sustainable development theorists and activists desperately concerned about global poverty, and most other reformers and radicals in affluent capitalist societies who give insufficient thought to these global issues. If global capitalist industrialisation and growth is incompatible with sustaining finite environmental resources, how can alternative income solutions to inequality and poverty be achieved?

In the previous chapter, I argued that the feasibility of definancialisation and degrowth strategies depends on mass popular support for increased state intervention in the form of regulatory policies and the provision of services and employment to counter the potentially high level of economic instability that would flow from radical reform agendas. I also suggested that any policy program for definancialisation and degrowth must have a social agenda that indicates how income, work and a broad range of social policies complement rather than contradict radical reform strategies. This chapter will therefore identify and evaluate these alternative policies, especially those related to income. I will begin with prevailing minimum wage and living wage campaigns. These are difficult enough in OECD labour markets, let alone in low and middle-income countries. Income and employment are also crucial to social mobility. Hence, it is necessary to discuss how changing work processes, levels of education and employment enhance or undermine social stability and mobility. Once these factors are analysed in detail and taken into account, it becomes clear that the implementation of a UBI is counterproductive to reform or radical programs that aim to enhance social security and social freedoms in the midst of what some describe as a new phase of market globalisation.

The Limits of Minimum Wages Strategies

Overcoming poverty relies on non-income strategies that foster new forms of social solidarity, co-operation and the prevention of escalating environmental crises – practices and values that individual-based income schemes cannot achieve. Yet, far too many advocates of the UBI or other basic income schemes display an inadequate appreciation of how existing minimum wage rates affect potential UBIs. Aiming for particular levels of national or supranational minimum wages entail quite different political economic obstacles and calculations to those of UBI schemes. Employers usually pay wages while a UBI will be financed from revenue collected mainly from workers and consumers or from businesses. Raising minimum wages can also have quite different social and political consequences compared with a UBI – affecting the rate of unemployment, weekly hours worked and the monetary value of either the minimum wage or the proposed UBI, as I will go on to argue.

Providing a 'living wage' as opposed to a minimum wage (that is often less than a living wage) to all low-paid workers within affluent regions such as the US and the EU would require major political struggles, not to mention spreading these wage rates to the whole world. Take the US as a starting point. With less than 7% of all workers in the dominant private sector unionised, little wonder there is such disparity between workers in US states in 2018. Several Southern states such as Alabama and Mississippi have no minimum wage, while various Northern and Western states pay $9-$11 per hour. In recent years, large states such as New York and California agreed to raise the minimum hourly wage to $13-$15 between 2018 and 2023 while many states continue to pay half this at $7.25 per hour (the Federal minimum rate). Over 42% of all paid workers in America receive less than $15 per hour which puts them at, or close to the poverty level. Workers on hourly rates rather than salaries are more likely to be women, non-whites, those under 25 with lower education living in particular areas such as the South or exploited in low-wage sectors such as hospitality in all US regions.[1]

If the official minimum wages in different American states reveal significant levels of inequality for the lowest paid, the wage disparities in the EU are far worse. The difference between official national minimum wages is more than six times, from 9 to 11.55 Euros per hour (France, Belgium, Netherlands, Luxembourg) right down to as little as 1.57 to 2.5 Euros per hour in Bulgaria or Romania. In between these are the other groups of countries on between 2 to 4 Euros and 4 to 8 Euros per hour.[2] Some EU countries have industry sectoral wage rates determined by bargaining and independent tribunals. Young people can vote if 18 or older but receive less income in EU countries if younger than 21 to 25.[3] Wage income, however, is only one important factor that determines standards of living. The other critical elements are social welfare, housing, health care, child-care, transport and the cost of utilities such as heating and electricity. Here, some EU countries are more generous than states in the US and also provide these services to non-citizen workers living outside their home countries.[4] Conversely, there are a minority group of US states which have lower relative levels of poverty than various Southern and Eastern EU countries.[5] Importantly, France and Nordic countries spend over 30% of GDP on social policies, while the US, UK, Ireland and Eastern European countries preside over greater poverty because they spend only 20% or less of their national GDP on social welfare.[6]

---

1   For figures see Characteristics of Minimum Wage Workers, *US Bureau of Labor Statistics*, Report 1054, April 2015.

2   *Benchmarking Working Europe 2018*, ETUI, Brussels, 2018.

3   See Eurofound, *Statutory minimum wages in the EU 2017*, Dublin, 2017.

4   For a survey of inequalities across the EU such as household disposable income, wage inequalities, level of welfare state amelioration of inequality and so forth, see Carlos Vacas-Soriano and Enrique Fernández-Macías, *Income inequalities and employment patterns in Europe before and after the Great Recession*, Eurofound, Luxembourg, 2017.

5   See comparative analysis in Michael C. George, *European America: The Effect of Underreported Transfer Benefits on Cross-National Poverty Analysis*, SSRN, March 2017.

6   For EU figures, see Maria Alessandra Antonelli and Valeria De Bonis, 'How Do European Welfare States Perform?' *Social Europe*, 19 July, 2017.

The differences between national minimum wage rates and how they are determined becomes highly relevant to any future attempt to arrive at a EU-wide minimum wage. Trade unions in Austria, Italy and Nordic countries, for instance, are strongly opposed to an EU-wide minimum wage, as they fear their members' wage rates and collective bargaining power will be reduced. In countries such as the Netherlands, the median wage is much higher than the highest wage in Eastern and Southern European member states and any attempt to apply the highest rate would be strongly resisted by employers in low-wage regions of the EU. Just to arrive at a EU determination of a minimum wage that is about 40% to 60% of the median wage in each member state, poses significant political hurdles in times of austerity and high unemployment. Such a median wage solution (championed by social democrats[7]) would be an improvement for many very poor workers but it would be a far cry from a decent EU-wide living wage that raised Romanian or Portuguese workers to standards of living enjoyed by employees in Sweden, France or Luxembourg.

Therefore, the political struggle to raise minimum wages in the US, EU and other developed capitalist countries must be situated within dramatically different global wage and regulatory conditions. Conscious of international competitive pressures on businesses, divided European trade union movements (more preoccupied with their own defensive national struggles) have failed to demand or win EU-wide legislation combatting a raft of poor conditions and wages associated with precarious labour.[8] The goal of a 'social Europe' based on equalising wage rates and working conditions has long been bitterly fought against by many business groups and sections of the union movement, even if it were introduced in stages over a five to ten year period. What are the potential benefits of such a desirable objective? First, it could shift power back to labour movements including part or all of the power they lost to employers in the past forty years. Second, regained labour power would thereby affect struggles over other non-wage component elements of a progressive 'social Europe' such as pensions and a raft of social welfare goods and services.

Equalising wage rates across the EU would not just alter the relative profitability and strength of different industry sectors within the EU, but also affect cross-border labour mobility and unemployment rates. However, if achieving a standard EU-wide 'living wage' is currently

---

7   See for example, Daniel Seikel, 'A Social and Democratic Europe? Obstacles and perspectives for action', Working Paper no.207, *Hans Böckler-Stiftung*, December 2016.

8   Gerhard Bosch, 'After Brexit: Prioritising A Social Europe', *Social Europe*, 24 January 2017.

remote, the prospect of mass support in most EU member countries for a European UBI is positively utopian.

Globally, it is important to note that more than half of all workers in developing countries are not covered by official minimum wage rulings. Secondly, where developing countries do have minimum wages, there is widespread non-compliance and abuse of workers' rights – a condition also familiar in developed capitalist countries. Thirdly, many developing countries may have minimum wage laws but these do not apply to workers in large informal sectors.[9] Fourthly, the International Labour Organization monitors international wage rates and the 'social wage' across the world.[10] The problem with the ILO is that it promotes social justice and labour rights but is internally divided between union and business representatives. Hence, it is torn between fighting against modern slavery and for decent jobs while seeking the creation of more jobs, many of which it knows are poor jobs. It is not just the massive inequality between labour and capital. The ILO documents that the top 1% to 10% of wage and salary earners in developed capitalist countries earn between 8 and 22 times more than the lowest-paid workers, an important factor in preventing worker's political solidarity. These levels of inequality and political disunity are replicated in developing countries.[11] As a supporter of 'green growth', the ILO is also caught between the United Nation's pro-market agenda and the realisation that many jobs classified by businesses as 'green growth' jobs are not compatible with a sustainable environment.

Focussing on improving the minimum wage can distort the real level of income inequality as it often obscures the proportion of people who do not even earn a living wage, as defined according to vastly different criteria depending on whether one is working in Chad or Columbia, Morocco or Mongolia. Market fundamentalists abhor campaigns for 'living wages' and attribute low wages in developing countries to low productivity. Instead, some free marketeers even argue that in developing countries, people "need more sweatshops rather than fewer."[12] Productivity is not an irrelevant factor, but it becomes a shameful and ruthless excuse to avoid even the slightest level of wage justice for those who perform most of the labour and make most of the profits enjoyed by their employers.

---

9   See Thomas Gindling, 'Does increasing the minimum wage reduce poverty in developing countries?', *IZA World of Labor*, May 2014.

10 International Labour Office, *Global Wage Report 2014/15: Wages and income inequality*, International Labour Organization, Geneva, 2015.

11 ILO, *Global Wage Report 2016/17 Wage inequality in the workplace*, International Labour Organization, Geneva, 2016.

12 Art Carden, 'Why Are Wages Low in Developing Countries?', *Mises Institute*, 12 January, 2008.

The garment, textile and footwear industry in twelve developing Asian countries employ over 43 million workers, more than three times the size of the total US workforce employed in all manufacturing sector industries. Of this massive workforce, up to 75% are women, except in India and Pakistan, where more males are employed because of greater discrimination against women.[13] The Clean Clothes Campaign continues to struggle to provide a living wage for garment workers in the six largest Asian producer countries where garment workers are paid much less than workers in other exploitative industries. Based on estimates of eating a necessary 3000 calories per day, plus housing, health and other living costs, the Campaign compared minimum wages with the bare living wage needed to keep workers and their families above a level of appalling poverty. On recent figures, Malaysia's minimum wage was the highest at 54% of the living wage, followed by China on 46% of the living wage, Indonesia on 31%, India 26%, Cambodia on 25% and Sri Lanka and Bangladesh at the bottom on a mere 19% of their national living wage.[14] These exploited workers officially work up to 48 hours per week and many are actually forced in several countries to work up to 16 hours per day, as well as suffer from having their wages stolen, underpaid and so forth.

While the exploitative conditions suffered by mainly women garment workers are widely known, less attention is given to the fact that these conditions are more or less pervasive in many other industry sectors and in most other developing countries from Nicaragua to Lesotho. What is not as well recognised is that given the slow rate of wage increases, it would take 122 years to reach current levels of a living wage.[15] However, since 2015-16, new waves of worker militancy in countries such as Cambodia and Bangladesh have demanded increased minimum wages. The responses of employers and governments across Asia have ranged from protracted negotiations to mass sackings and repression of striking workers by police. Whether workers in low-wage countries can save their jobs while winning campaigns for living wages is now a battle fought beyond national borders by manufacturers playing off workers in one country against other impoverished workers in another.

The introduction of robotics is an additional threat to manufacturing

---

13 Phu Huynh, 'Developing Asia's garment and footwear industry: Recent employment and wage trends', International Labour Organization Asia-Pacific Garment and Footwear Sector Research Note Issue 8, October 2017.

14 Jeroen Merk Clean Clothes Campaign, *Living Wage Report 2014*, Asia Floor Wage Alliance, New Delhi, 2014; Also see their 'Living Wage versus Minimum Wage' figures, 17 October 2013.

15 *Ibid*, p.22.

sector workers and in particular, threatens the traditional pathway of catch-up growth based on rural agricultural workers moving to urban factories. At this stage, the debate over the threat of robotic automation and artificial intelligence (AI) to jobs in OECD countries is largely academic and inconclusive. Not so in China. The Chinese province of Guangdong employs over 40 million workers in manufacturing, or significantly more than the total number of manufacturing workers in all 28 EU countries. In response to a combination of shortages of labour, numerous militant unofficial wildcat strikes and the successful campaigns of workers gaining higher wages, the provincial government in Guangdong is investing approximately US$154 billion to increase robotics in manufacturing with the goal of automating 80 per cent of its manufacturing production by 2020.[16] It is unclear what proportion of existing workers will lose their jobs given labour shortages in certain industries. However, with weak union movements in many countries, plus the constant cheapening cost of robotics, workers are caught in an invidious situation of either suffering malnourishment on sub-living wages or seeing many jobs abolished. Despite governments having the power to protect workers by regulating the introduction of robots, few, if any, exercise this power.

Raising the minimum wage from a fifth or a quarter of the living wage in many developing countries therefore requires long and very difficult militant campaigns. As for a global minimum wage, this may appear a desirable goal but is most unlikely to win global support from workers in developed countries such as those who strongly oppose even an EU-wide minimum wage. In a world divided by massive wage and income disparities, equalising global income is morally defensible but politically utopian. The obstacles within the next twenty years to winning a global minimum wage, even one aimed at achieving a third or half of average wage rates in affluent OECD countries, are so monumental that nothing short of world revolution would be required. Importantly, even a future world revolution would have to deal with significantly reduced levels of total available paid work if current automation trends escalate. This is another crucial reason why wage and income levels, important as they continue to be, should not form the principal basis of future living standards. In an emerging world where existing relations between work and income as well as the relation between material affluence and environmental resources are unsustainable, workers need new sources of support beyond wages to guarantee adequate standards of living.

---

16 Sputnik news, 'China Builds City's First All-Robot Factory Replacing Human Workers', Sputniknews.com, 5 June 2015.

Crumbling Pillars of Social Mobility

In the years 2012 to 2018, conservative estimates by the ILO put global unemployment in the range between 192 and 201.1 million people,[17] with an additional 1.4 billion people working in what is classified as 'vulnerable' or extremely precarious, low-paid employment. Once we add underemployment to the mix, which is much higher than official unemployment figures, total global levels of people in all three categories exceed 2 billion or more than a third of the world's working age population of 15 to 67. The situation for women is far worse. Paid employment participation rates for women are significantly lower globally, and particularly bad in South Asia, North Africa and the Middle East where they are up to 58% lower than for men.[18] Children under the age of 15 are also widely exploited in many developing countries. So far, the destabilising consequences of the enormous number of jobless or insecure people has been politically contained due to the wide variations between countries of participation rates of people in paid work, as well as the cushioning effect of social welfare, especially in most OECD countries. Very importantly, the total number in vulnerable or precarious employment includes quite different social groups, as I will outline below. The crucial question is whether the political 'containment' of diverse social groups can continue for decades to come. Will global warming, automation, low growth/stagnation and urbanisation in developing countries (such as uprooting female agricultural labour and swelling urban unemployment) make existing crisis-management policies ineffective and redundant?

Take the increasingly widespread and polarised debate about robotics and artificial intelligence. Pessimistic analysts warn that half of existing jobs will be abolished while optimists believe that millions of new jobs (as yet unspecified) will be created by technical innovations. Silicon Valley corporations,[19] free market technological utopians and assorted post-capitalist radicals such as 'fuck work' anarchists or 'post-work' Accelerationists welcome mass automation through robotics or AI. By contrast, since the 1970s, social democrats and labour movements have promoted different alternatives to deindustrialisation, such as maximising

---

17 See two reports by the ILO: *World Employment and Social Outlook: Trends 2017* and *World Employment and Social Outlook: Trends 2018,* International Labour Organization, Geneva, 2017 and 2018.

18 *World Employment Social Outlook: Trends for Women, ILO, Geneva, March 2018.*

19 Jathan Sadowski, 'Why Silicon Valley is embracing universal basic income', *The Guardian*, 22 June, 2016.

school retention rates and post-secondary education in universities or technical training institutes to facilitate millions of 'knowledge-economy' jobs based on upgrading low-skilled jobs to highly skilled cognitive jobs. Neo-liberals, social democrats and 'green growth' innovators have long mouthed now familiar clichés about 'social inclusion', life-long education and retraining for multiple jobs over a working life. Meanwhile, global inequality continues to rise.[20]

Despite the 'knowledge economy' based on the techno-sciences and the digital economy remaining the dominant macro socio-economic paradigm, full-time secure jobs have declined in large areas of services. The failure of the 'knowledge economy' model as the panacea to mass unemployment was evident well before the crisis of 2007-8. [21] Unfortunately, it is clear that yet another study or report on automation will not determine whether the fear of machines stealing people's jobs is exaggerated or underestimated. It will take at least another ten to twenty years to clarify how businesses and governments will apply the latest technological advances. James W. Cortada in his three-volume study of sixteen industries in the US from 1950 onwards, showed how the application of digital technology transformed different industries in far from uniform speeds.[22] Change will certainly come at a faster rate than in the previous sixty years. Regardless of which industry or country, it is the political struggles in labour markets and trade and product markets that will determine the scale and rate of technological change, as it ever has been in history.

What is clear, however, is that creeping or rapid automation has already undermined decades of liberal social democratic policies based on upgrading low skilled to high skilled jobs via mass education. In fact, six decades of social integration and generational mobility via mass education is largely exhausted in OECD countries. For political reasons, this does not mean that funding for mass education systems will dramatically

---

20 For the EU see the studies in *Inequality in Europe*, Social Europe, Friedrich-Ebert Stiftung and Hans Böckler Stiftung, 2017; and for the world see Facundo Alvaredo, Lucas Chancel, Thomas Piketty, Emmanuel Saez, Gabriel Zucman et al. *World Inequality Report 2018*, World Inequality Lab, Paris, December 2017.

21 As a developed capitalist country, Australia is a good example of how policy makers began speaking a new language called 'knowledge economese' by the 1980s. See my critique of the 'knowledge economy' in *Zombies Lilliputians and Sadists: The Power of the Living Dead and the Future of Australia*, Curtin University Press and Freemantle Arts Centre Press, 2004, part 2.

22 James W. Cortada, *The Digital Hand: How Computers Changed the Work of American Manufacturing, Transportation, and Retail Industries*, vol.1, 2004; *American Financial, Telecommunications, Media and Entertainment Industries*, Vol.2, 2006; and *American Public Sector Industries*, vol.3, 2008, all three volumes published by Oxford University Press, New York.

decline or that societies are on the verge of collapse. Yet, it does mean that the four pillars of liberal capitalist mixed economies, mass education, full-time employment, growing household consumption and the public provision of services over the life cycle – from child care to aged care – are now severely stressed or crumbling in many countries.

For over thirty years, social analyses have focused on how the 70/30 society of comfortable workforces on the one side, versus marginalised people and the underemployed or low-wage workers on the other side, is eroding political and institutional stability. Most OECD countries are characterised by high structural unemployment among youth and to a lesser extent in the over 45s. Those in middle-aged demographic groups are particularly worried about their children's futures and their own employment prospects in the two decades prior to retirement. In most OECD countries, the former affluent and briefly stable lifecycle of education, work, raising a family and eventual retirement that characterised social life from the late 1940s to the late 1970s is either being disrupted or is now beyond the reach of growing but substantial minorities. By contrast, most developing countries have been unable to replicate the same patterns and degrees of social mobility flowing from the pre-1980s private and public institutional pillars formerly evident in developed OECD countries. Under the current domination of private ownership and global markets, it is most unlikely that developing countries will ever achieve the mid to late twentieth-century standards of living enjoyed by majorities in the West.

Significantly, many policy-makers across the world are ill prepared for the fact that the erosion of the old pillars of consumer capitalism is already underway. Many fail to grasp adequately the consequences of this trajectory. Those who think that a UBI can be a substitute for the now weakened pillars of social integration are unrealistic. Income is merely one pillar that cannot carry the weight of other important social and political relations and necessities.

In contrast to corporate dreams of decoupling economic growth from nature, high levels of automation in the form of the robotics and the digitalisation of information are fully realisable given the exponential growth in networked computation, AI software development and other technology. There is no denying the desire of many businesses to implement labour-saving technology at the right price. However, everything hinges upon actual political struggles around its implementation. For instance, governments could face major revenue shortfalls affecting a raft of expenditure programs if high levels of debt-driven household consumption become unsustainable due to ever-higher levels of unemployment or low-paid work. Those promoting innovation as the saviour of capitalist societies (see Chapter One), are either blinkered optimists or have managed to convince policy makers into believing that labour-saving technology could create sufficient high skilled 'knowledge jobs', whether for tens of millions of low-paid and marginalised surplus populations in developed countries, or for hundreds of millions of poorly educated people in developing countries. Nonetheless, policymakers continue to promote variations of the 'knowledge economy' model in OECD countries. They persistently ignore that this social democratic alternative to neo-liberalism began to pre-maturely die more than two decades ago. It is unclear whether it will be superseded by a new phase of digitalised, insecure hyper-exploitative capitalism, or by increased provision of more secure public and private employment. Even preventing an escalation of hyper-exploitative capitalism through greater regulation of the 'gig economy' will not of itself create sufficient full-time reasonably paid 'knowledge economy' jobs. That would require a major restructuring of capitalist economies in order to try to soak up surplus labour.

Hence, the dilemmas keep multiplying that face both neo-liberal policy-makers and all those advocating a range of anti-neo-liberal 'green new deal' or revived social democracies. Whether to fight for decent jobs and minimum wages or opt for UBI schemes is confusing for crisis managers who remain divided on the issue of whether or not a UBI can sustain social integration via the provision of sufficient household income needed for mass consumption. Currently, capitalist societies depend on individual and household consumption which accounts for approximately 52% to 70% of the GDP of the top G20 countries, and also because it helps drive future capital investment without which capitalist markets would stagnate and decline. Regardless of whether or not automation drastically slashes future employment, it is clear that mass consumption and production cannot be sustained at current levels if decoupling economic growth from the finite limits of natural resources fails to materialise, or if decarbonisation is too slow and inadequate to prevent the destruction of a safe climate.

American sociologist Randall Collins exemplifies the pessimistic focus on increasing educational 'credentialism' combined with automation.[23] Whereas it took almost 200 years to destroy traditional blue-collar working class jobs through mechanisation, the computerised displacement of 'middle class' labour, Collins argues, is proceeding at a much, much

---

23 See Randall Collins, 'The End of Middle-Class Work: no more escapes' in Immanuel Wallerstein, Randall Collins, Michael Mann, Georgi Derlugian and Craig Calhoun, *Does Capitalism Have a Future?* Oxford University Press Oxford, Oxford, 2013 pp.37-70.

faster pace.[24] He concurs with his co-contributor Immanuel Wallerstein who sees the terminal crisis of capitalism occurring between 2030 and 2045.[25] Collins places the crisis around 2040 when structural unemployment will reach 50%, and 70% not long after that. He also assumes that once capitalist markets run out of new peripheral areas of the world to conquer, the struggle for profitability within the 'core' assumes terminal transformation. Accordingly:

> An unemployment rate of 10% is painful, by American standards; 25% (found in crisis economies) is big trouble, but it has been sustained in the past. But when unemployment reaches 50% of the work-capable population, or 70%, the capitalist system must come under such pressure – both from under-consumption and political agitation – that it cannot survive. If we think such unemployment rates are unimaginable, let us imagine again, through the lens of technological displacement of all categories of work by electronic machinery.[26]

Collins and others[27] who project catastrophic scenarios flowing from robotics succumb to technological determinism and ignore the high likelihood of countervailing Right or Left political repercussions within major OECD countries, especially should unemployment rise to between 15% and 20%, let alone to between 50% and 70%. Trade unions and business groups are also increasingly preoccupied with automation,[28] but often do not consider options beyond conventional policy frameworks.

All assumptions about the socio-political consequences of automation are guesswork. Nobody knows whether it will lead to less than 5% of jobs being fully automated (McKinsey Global Institute[29]) or as high as 70% of existing jobs as Collins and others prophesise. Job destruction by robots

---

24 Collins, p.57.

25 Wallerstein, 'Structural Crisis, Or Why Capitalists May No Longer Find Capitalism Rewarding' in *Does Capitalism Have a Future?*

26 Collins, p.58.

27 See for example, Carl Benedikt Frey and Michael Osborne, *The Future of Employment: How Susceptible Are Jobs to Computerisation?*, Oxford Martin School, Oxford University, 17 September 2013 or Erik Brynjolfsson and Andrew McAfee, *The Second Machine Age: Work, Progress, and Prosperity in a Time of Brilliant Technologies*, W. W. Norton, New York, 2014.

28 See for example, Christophe Degryse, *Digitalisation of the economy and its impact on labour markets*, Working Paper 2016.02, European Trade Union Institute, Brussels, 2016; CEDA, *Australia's future workforce?*, Committee for Economic Development of Australia, Melbourne, 2015.

29 James Manyika et al, *Harnessing automation for a future that works*, McKinsey Global Institute, January 2017.

only leads to rising unemployment levels if no new jobs – no matter how bad – fail to emerge. We also know that millions of workers in terribly precarious jobs have not so far risen up in protest, as there is no inherent connection between radical political consciousness and low-paid work or unemployment. Indeed, in many instances, precarity seems to immobilise rather than mobilise. Yet, this political passivity may come to an end, if and when millions of formerly secure workers are also threatened.

While developing countries have the lawless spheres of the 'informal sector' where anything goes, developed countries are witnessing their own violations of traditional employer/worker relations. Much sociological and political analysis deals with all kinds of social precarity, especially how new jobs in developed capitalist countries are following the poor conditions of insecure work in developing societies.[30] So far, the rise of precarious jobs has been far from uniform across all sectors of industry, let alone across OECD countries. Also, the 'informal sector' and 'precarity' are very loose concepts that often encompass diverse social groups – from peasants or street vendors right through to university educated workers in casual jobs – that have little social, cultural and class relations in common apart from their precarious work. The rate of increase in precarious work varies between countries and will depend in future on national labour market legislation, levels of unemployment and other factors. Even in those countries where precarious employment is not very high, it is the public fear of 'precarity' that immobilises workers and spurs employers into cutting conditions. Politically, in countries with weak unions, it is difficult to unite insecure workers in diverse industries and forge successful oppositional movements. Labour and globalisation analyst Ursula Huws calls the plethora of new work conditions, 'logged labour', and argues that the old twentieth century paradigm of work is dissolving:

> In this new model, workers are increasingly managed via online platforms, monitored indirectly and expected to produce measurable outcomes. Their work is 'logged' in three distinct senses: it is cut up into standard, quantifiable components; it is subjected to continuous surveillance and monitoring; and it requires the worker to be connected to an online platform in order to obtain work. In a curious paradox, work is increasingly formalised even

---

30 See Jan Breman, 'A Bogus Concept?' *New Left Review*, no.84, 2013, pp.130-138, a review of Guy Standing, *The Precariat: The New Dangerous Class*, and Standing's response 'Why the Precariat is not a 'bogus concept', *Open Democracy*, 4 March, 2014; also see various contributors to special issue 'Politics of Precarity: Migrant Conditions, Struggles and Experiences', *Critical Sociology*, vol.42, nos. 6/7, 2016.

while it becomes less predictable and more precarious, with workers having to resubmit themselves repeatedly for employment, funding, promotion or inclusion in a particular team, and required to respond at short notice to unpredictable demands for work.[31]

Most discussion of automation focuses on job prospects. Far less is devoted to analysing how a combination of low growth and increasing automation disrupts the decades-long relationship between education and social reproduction that underpins political economic stability. With the old models of work rapidly dissolving, the shape of labour markets, social welfare systems and the hopes of families for their children's education and upward social mobility will undoubtedly generate much fear and anxiety. Notably, this does not necessarily mean that most jobs will become precarious because, as I have argued, this will depend on the level of struggle within particular national and local labour markets.

During the twentieth century, education was the 'sacred cow' that promised social mobility and prosperity. By 2001, after decades of neo-liberal globalisation, analysts preoccupied with the narrow concept of education as 'human capital' such as World Bank analyst Lant Pritchett, collated cross-country figures for the decades after 1960 and concluded that, "on average, education contributed much less to growth than would have been expected..."[32] Pritchett attributed the reasons for the poor outcomes in economic growth from investment in education, to a range of specific national differences such as a mismatch between skills needed and education provided. In other countries, the 'pirate effect' prevailed, that is, newly acquired skills benefited private individuals' remuneration but the larger social impact of expenditure on education was socially wasteful or counterproductive.[33]

Today, Pritchett's critique of the poor 'return on investment' in education has been taken further by neo-liberal policymakers. Defenders of the market now attack the old concept of education as 'human capital' underpinning the 'knowledge economy'. However, neo-liberals attack it not because it is a narrow, instrumental and impoverished notion of education. Rather, this old concept of education as 'human capital' is being questioned for two basic reasons: firstly, it is no longer the pathway to

---

31 Ursula Huws, 'Logged labour: a new paradigm of work organisation?', *Work organisation, labour & globalisation*, vol.10, no.1 2016, p.7.

32 Lant Pritchett, 'Where Has All the Education Gone?', *World Bank Economic Review*, vol.15, no.3, 2001, pp.367-391.

33 *Ibid*, p.387.

growth in developing countries; and secondly, it is an over-costly invest-ment burden in all countries given the unfolding impact of automation on jobs.

Ricardo Hausmann, Director of the Center for International Devel-opment at Harvard University, is typical of those who use Pritchett's work to advance a case against education as the route to economic growth:

> In the 50 years from 1960 to 2010, the global labor force's average time in school essentially tripled, from 2.8 years to 8.3 years. This means that the average worker in a median country went from less than half a primary education to more than half a high school education. How much richer should these countries have expected to become? In 1965, France had a labor force that averaged less than five years of schooling and a *per capita* income of $14,000 (at 2005 prices). In 2010, countries with a similar level of education had a *per capita* income of less than $1,000. In 1960, countries with an education level of 8.3 years of schooling were 5.5 times richer than those with 2.8 years of schooling. By contrast, countries that had increased their education from 2.8 years of schooling in 1960 to 8.3 years of schooling in 2010 were only 167% richer. Moreover, much of this increase cannot possibly be attributed to education, as workers in 2010 had the advantage of technologies that were 50 years more advanced than those in 1960. Clearly, something other than education is needed to generate prosperity.[34]

Hausmann and others are not arguing that education has no ben-efits. But in capitalist societies where most neo-liberal policymakers have lacked a strong commitment to adequate public expenditure on education in the first place, let alone social equality, it is unclear what they propose as a replacement of mass education and its role in the maintenance of social stability.

Currently, there is conflict between those who believe that mass edu-cation is a 'poor investment' and a range of reformers and radicals who favour the introduction of a broader general education instead of narrow vocationally orientated curricula. This is complicated by technocratic approaches that stress the need for different types of technical, non-rou-tine education and training as a counter to or complement of robotics. As Alexander Sidorkin asks: "How do we convince kids to come to

---

34 Ricardo Hausmann, 'The Education Myth', *Project Syndicate*, May 31, 2015.

school, if in the future, there will be no employment for all or even most of them? If we lose the use of the preparation for work discourse, what will motivate children to stay in school and apply effort to learning?" [35]

One thing is certain, greater automation will escalate the politics of education. It offers new political opportunities to those who champion the decommodification of education so that it is not narrowly geared to vocational training. Disastrously, it also unleashes the dogs of inequality as Right-wing policymakers campaign to cut educational expenditure on the grounds that mass job destruction by robotics and AI makes it wasteful public expenditure. Right-wing critiques of education expenditure will only gain legitimacy if education policy is completely divorced from the larger picture, namely, the fundamental need to challenge the massively uneven global distribution and control of wealth between countries and within countries.

Social democratic supporters of a 'knowledge economy' are caught between these twin poles: the narrow concept of education as 'human capital' and Right-wing critiques of mass education as 'wasteful expenditure'. There is a familiar scenario played out in most OECD countries. Social democratic reformers have argued for decades that measures such as allocating more resources to early childhood development, increasing high school retention rates and targeting disadvantaged children and families will increase social mobility, lessen the need for expenditure in the criminal justice system and help reduce inequality. This model of social change depends on education being accorded a central role. However, marketeers no longer rely so heavily on educated 'human capital'. This will shake the faith of liberal social democrats who have long believed in education and innovation as the remedies to all sorts of economic and social ills.

The reality is that investing in 'human capital' and educational credentialism have both passed their 'use-by' date in a context where the educated global surplus labour population is growing without the usual 'rewards' – jobs and social mobility. It is the failure of social democratic parties and labour movements to fully recognise that the old pillars of social integration are crumbling that leads to calls for piece-meal reforms and greater social expenditure on education. Once again, we witness a familiar naïve faith in a 'civilised capitalism'. What the social democratic faith in the 'knowledge economy' ignores is that various capitalist industries are in a new phase where profits are squeezed. Hence, the reluctance of businesses and governments to deliver large numbers of

---

35 Alexander M. Sidorkin, 'Education for Jobless Society', *Studies in Philosophy and Education*, vol.36, no.1, 2017, p.11.

relatively well-paid jobs or as was the case more than forty years ago, to fund social security. Moreover, given the demands of businesses for further tax cuts, greater social expenditure is not possible without major and more intense political struggles to restructure tax systems as I will go on to discuss.

Any conception of the role of education and labour markets, of the level of waged and unwaged income, of technological change in the midst of pervasive global poverty and unemployment depends on the way welfare states in developing societies plus older ones in OECD countries deal with the multitude of current and future environmental and socio-economic challenges.

With the new digital platforms and automation, it is now widely accepted that many of the largest corporations only employ a fraction of workers compared to former industrial giants in earlier decades.[36] More telling is the estimation by mainstream policy analysts that robotics and higher productivity will mean that within twenty to thirty years, total global output of manufactured goods could be produced by as little as 3% to 5% of the world's workers. Just as the combination of capital-intensive agriculture and the rise of manufacturing and services witnessed the reduction of agricultural labour to between 2% to 3% of workers in developed capitalist countries, so too, a similar pattern is now occurring globally within the main centres of manufacturing. If you told peasant farmers over 100 years ago that infinitely more food could be produced with only 2% of the workforce, you would not have been believed. The dislocation of agricultural labour during the nineteenth and twentieth centuries unfolded over many decades. If rapid automation of manufacturing expels millions of current workers over two or three decades, the transitional socio-political consequences could be dramatic should alternative paid work or a major extension of the 'social state' fail to materialise. I am not arguing that mass automation will displace 40% or 50% of workers within a decade. However, a 'knowledge economy' model of social mobility and integration is based on a minimum 15 to 20 year four-stage educational process – from early pre-school to elementary, high and post-secondary learning and skill acquisition. Although schools constantly tell students and parents to prepare for a transformed labour market, few parents of children entering learning facilities today will find a recognisable labour market by the time students exit educational institutions in 2040 or shortly later.

Currently, the vast majority of workers in more than half the large

36 See for example, Adair Turner, 'The Skills Delusion', *Project Syndicate*, 12 October, 2016.

G20 economies are employed in the services sector rather than manufacturing, mining, construction and agriculture. If labour shedding in services replicates the historical experiences of agriculture and manufacturing in coming decades, then governments will truly confront challenges without historical precedent. Decision-makers in developed OECD countries will at least face the enormous challenges of dealing with surplus under-employed or unemployed workers with various levels of welfare services already in place, inadequate though they may be. Most developing countries have no such developed welfare structures in place. Not only will they have to abandon future plans to solve unemployment through industrialisation, but also these poor countries will desperately require massive aid from the developed world in order to prevent major socio-political crises far in excess of what has already occurred in previous decades.

Will proponents of 'green growth' succeed in building green sustainable infrastructure and urban renewal in developing countries as an alternative to mass channelling of agricultural workers into factories? Politically, current prospects for 'green growth' in G20 countries range from moderately hopeful to bleak. Internationally, no such major green development and employment strategy is feasible without the significant political change required to provide massive assistance from wealthy countries and the diversion of financial resources away from existing profitable financialisation practices and other business activities.

Even if total global manufacturing employment is reduced to about 5% and routine service sector employment slashed, many analysts still refuse to acknowledge that there will be a tsunami of mass unemployment in the future. Familiar arguments usually cite the unlikely replacement of most non-routine cognitive, emotional caring labour or skilled technical jobs.[37] Others claim there is still a lack of clear data showing that new technology substantially increases productivity in *all* industries.[38] It is also argued that 'cobots' programed to work co-operatively with humans

---

37 See Michael Chui, James Manyika, Mehdi Miremadi, 'Where machines could replace humans – and where they can't (yet)', *McKinsey Quarterly*, McKinsey & Company, July 2016, pp.1-16; David H. Autor, 'Why Are There Still So Many jobs? The History and Future of Workplace Automation', *Journal of Economic Perspectives*, Vol.29, no.3, 2015, pp.3-30 and Joel Mokyr, Chris Vickers, and Nicolas L. Ziebart, 'The History of Technological Anxiety and the Future of Economic Growth: Is This Time Different?' *Journal of Economic Perspectives*, Vol.29, no.3, 2015, pp.31-50.

38 Bart Van Ark, 'The Productivity Paradox of the New Digital Economy', *Conference Board and International Productivity Monitor*, 2016. Also, Gill Pratt, 'Is a Cambrian Explosion Coming for Robotics?', *Journal of Economic Perspectives*, Vol.29, no.3, 2015, pp.51-60, lists eight technical barriers (such as computation power, electronics storage power, etc.) that still need to be overcome before automation really takes off.

rather than fully autonomous robots, plus a shortage of workers due to ageing populations or the cheaper cost of low-paid workers are all likely to counter alarmist predictions of mass unemployment.

We may not know the character of future labour markets but capitalist growth and technological innovation has already failed to provide work globally for the ILO's very conservatively estimated 200 million unemployed; nor has it provided decent full-time jobs for the more than 1.4 billion low-paid, insecure global workers. To add to major global concerns, automation could possibly wipe out more jobs in developing countries than in developed capitalist societies. World Bank President, Jim Yong Kim, said in 2016 that "World Bank data has predicted that the proportion of jobs threatened by automation in India is 69 per cent, 77 per cent in China and as high as 85 per cent in Ethiopia."[39]

In Chapter Two, I discussed fears of pro-market globalisation policy-makers that we had reached 'peak trade' and that the 'end of the liberal order' was at hand due to populist and nationalist movements championing protectionist policies.[40] Paradoxically, despite the decline of international trade and the rise of anti-globalisation populists, market analysts such as Richard Baldwin also argue that we are entering a new 'wilder' phase of globalisation that will give more power to businesses compared with earlier forms of globalisation.[41] As robotics become much cheaper and information technology develops far greater capacity than present connectivity, Baldwin believes businesses will increasingly deploy 'telerobotics' and 'telepresence'. These new tendencies do not depend on the expansion of traded goods. Rather, by moving ICT offshore instead of outsourcing whole factories and product lines as in previous decades, the new phase will see low paid workers in developing countries operating 'telerobotics' to do all kinds of manual and routine jobs in manufacturing and services in developed countries. An example is low-paid hotel cleaning in London performed by much lower-paid workers in India who operate telerobots, thus saving businesses very much higher wage costs if they had paid workers in London or in other developed capitalist countries. Similarly, exported 'telepresence' communication technology is predicted to make obsolete many white-collar service jobs through 'life-like' visual communication screens (advanced 'Skypes').

39 Speech by World Bank President Jim Yong Kim, 'The World Bank Group's Mission: To End Extreme Poverty', Washington, October 3, 2016.

40 See for example, Robert Kuttner, *Can Democracy Survive Global Capitalism?*, W. W. Norton, New York, 2018.

41 Richard Baldwin, *The Great Convergence: Information Technology and the New Globalization*, Harvard University Press, Cambridge, 2016.

Notably, nationalist populist movements and trade unions, according to Baldwin, will be powerless to stop these new forms of globalisation through tariffs and other protectionist legislation, short of stopping the internet and other international telco exchanges.[42] Manufacturing jobs have gone, he argues, and will not return; and now it is the turn of routine service sector jobs. One cannot protect jobs, says Baldwin, but one can protect workers. The burning question that market analysts such as Baldwin do not answer, is how can this be done in a context of 'wild globalisation' when even solid growth in capitalist societies no longer delivers previous levels of job creation? Short of revolution or social upheaval, political and business leaders will be forced to adopt new measures to sustain aggregate demand, especially household and individual consumption, otherwise the consequences could well be deflation and depression. Such consequences may make the recession of the past decade look mild by contrast.

As to radical technological utopians and others on the Left, the 'precariat' now play a similar role to the 'proletariat' in traditional revolutionary socialist political campaigns and imaginary hopes. Cultural analyst Sabine Hake has shown through a detailed study of German Socialist and Communist writings, theatre and film that the 'proletarian dream' was the political imaginary that functioned as a substitute for the real historical working class or the 'masses' that were made up of quite different and complex socio-economic and cultural elements.[43] When Marx and Engels published the Communist Manifesto in 1848, the industrial proletariat were a small minority of total rural and urban workers. They never grew to become a majority of all workers in the next 150 years, despite the complex segments of the working class (manufacturing, service sector and others) constituting the largest part of developed capitalist societies. Similarly, today, many conceive the 'precariat' as a new emerging class even though most workers in capitalist societies have always been employed in insecure jobs. There are few cultural, political or socio-economic values or characteristics shared by all who come under the precariat umbrella.

While a majority of employed workers are not yet in the underemployed, very casualised 'precariat', there is no doubt that exploitative, insecure, new 'logged labour' and other erosions of full-time, work conditions have grown in recent decades. Also, in a period when many

---

42 Richard Baldwin interview with Eshe Nelson, 'Brace yourself: the most disruptive phase of globalization is just beginning', *Quartz*, 7 December, 2016.

43 Sabine Hake, *The Proletarian Dream: Socialism, Culture, and Emotion in Germany 1863-1933*, De Gruyter, Berlin/Boston, 2017.

workers have ceased supporting social democratic and communist parties and now vote for Right-wing nationalist/populist parties or candidates, even greater radical hopes are vested in the 'precariat'. Like the earlier 'proletarian dream', a socio-political narrative and agenda has emerged based on the speculative notion that most workers will become members of the 'gig economy' or 'precariat' in the near future. This threat of 'precarity' drives either the social democratic demand to protect 'gig economy' workers or a radical utopian agenda that links precarious work and automation to political demands for a UBI or 'Fully Automated Luxury Communism' and other visions of the 'post-work' society. Therefore, it is particularly necessary to critically evaluate UBI schemes as they are currently conceived.

Disputing Universal Basic Income

Given widespread fear over the future lack of jobs, debates over various universal basic income schemes are very common these days. Remarkably little has changed in the discussion of UBI schemes since the 1960s and 1970s, except that the revival of interest in recent years has led to more experiments in restricted basic income (rather than universal income) pilot trials from Finland to Uganda.[44] A broad range of advocates across the political spectrum – ranging from Hayekian libertarians and Silicon Valley entrepreneurs right through to socialist radicals, feminists, and green advocates of degrowth – all champion a variety of UBI schemes. One can distinguish the following main differences between numerous UBI proposals:[45]

44 For details of pilot schemes conducted by governments and NGOs see *Basic Income Earth Network (BIEN)*, basicincome.org. However, Francine Mestrum, 'The Alternative Facts of the Basic Income Movement', *Social Europe*, 16 February, 2017, criticises BIEN for not revealing that all these pilot schemes are not universal schemes but rather highly qualified provision of income to people in need or who are unemployed and so forth. Also, the Finnish trial will be abandoned at the end of 2018 because of strong opposition to it.

45 For bibliographies and a sample of discussions of UBI schemes during the past thirty years see: Karl Widerquist, José A. Noguera, Yannick Vanderborght and Jurgen De Wispela (eds), *Basic Income An Anthology of Contemporary Research*, Wiley Blackwell, Oxford, 2013; Philippe Van Parijs, '*Basic Income: A Simple and Powerful Idea for the 21ˢᵗ Century*', Basic Income European Network, VIIIth International Congress, Berlin 6-7 October, 2000; Michael Tanner, 'The pros and Cons of a Guaranteed National Income', *Policy Analysis, Cato Institute*, May 12, 2015; Jurgen De Wispelaere and Leticia Morales, 'The stability of basic income: a constitutional solution for a political problem?' *Journal of Public Policy*, July 2015, pp.1-25; Sean Healy et al. 'Basic income – Why and How in Difficult economic Times: Financing a BI in Ireland', *Social Justice Ireland*, Paper for BIEN Congress, Munich, 14 September, 2012; Daniel Raventós, *Basic Income: The Material Conditions of Freedom* translated by Julie Wark, Pluto Press, London, 2007; Katie Cruz, 'A feminist case for Basic Income: an interview with Kathi Weeks', *Critical Legal*

Firstly, there is the model of cost-cutting, anti-public sector proposals mainly put forward by free market policy analysts. Minimal UBI payments or tax credits would substitute for a plethora of social welfare payments thereby saving money on public administrative personnel and a range of social welfare state services.

The second model is a guaranteed 'adequate' income (GAI) set 20% to 50% above particular national definitions of poverty so that individuals and families could escape the social consequences of deep-seated poverty and income insecurity. This would be very expensive and cost much more than total expenditure outlays on welfare payments. Importantly though, these GAI proposals reject cutting other aspects of the social welfare state so that a GAI or 'adequate' UBI would directly challenge low-paid jobs and require a massive boost in tax revenue to fund.

Thirdly, there are restrictive or open universal basic income schemes. The main differences here relate to whether only citizens of a particular country are eligible, or whether all non-citizen residents in a nation, or all people living in member states of the EU (including or excluding refugees from outside the EU), or ultimately, whether every adult in the world should receive a UBI.

Fourthly, schemes with multiple criteria are being proposed. Some UBI schemes would pay all children lower rates if under the age of 18 or 16; others would pay all individuals in a household separately regardless of co-habitation ties, or one income per household according to cost of living for sole or multiple parents, number of dependents and so forth. Eligibility also differs as to whether people earning above a certain income threshold should have their UBI payments clawed back via the tax system, and whether recipients of a UBI will be limited to people under pension age or will receive the UBI in addition to an aged pension or other public benefits such as child support, housing rent support, unemployment support, food and energy subsidies and so forth. Left versions of this, such as those in the international Basic Income Earth Network (BIEN), generally favour a UBI as a supplement to other entitlements whereas Right-wing proposals advocate minimalist alternatives to existing welfare, plus work tests.

Finally, political and cultural divisions exist between those who

---

Thinking, 22 August, 2016; Alice Fabre, Stephane Pallage and Christian Zimmermann, *Universal Basic Income versus Unemployment Insurance*, The Institute for the Study of Labor (IZA) Bonn, Paper no.8667, November 2014; Nick Srnicek and Alex Williams, *Inventing the Future*, chs. 5 and 6; Marc de Basquiat, 'Towards a Universal Basic Income in France: elements for a debate', *generationlibre.eu*, 16 January 2016 and Marko Kovic, 'The universal basic income: Benefits, pseudo-problems and real problems' ZIPAR Discussion Paper Series, Volume 1, Issue 2. Zurich 2017.

support a UBI as a minimal backstop to prevent social instability arising from mass job destruction, and radical anti-capitalists who see the UBI as fostering political and industrial militancy once the threat of loss of income is removed. Environmentalists believe a UBI will also help lower consumption and production, once higher income from paid work ceases to be a necessity. Culturally, the minimalists tend to see little change in capitalist culture except that crime, boredom and addiction will increase and probably require significantly extra policing alongside the UBI. By contrast, the moderates wish to improve income support in a reformed 'civilised capitalism' or 'green capitalism' while the maximalists wish to break the 'work fetish'. They see the flowering of new co-operative, caring social relations, especially helping to break traditional patriarchal and unequal gendered domestic labour roles, plus the flourishing of creative individuals in the 'post-work' society. Radical schemes thus conceive the UBI as a strategic launching pad for the transition to post-capitalism.

Most of the disputes over UBI schemes relate to cost, eligibility and social and political consequences if an initial minority without paid work evolves into a 'post-work' majority. As to proposals for a global UBI (Srnicek and Williams[46]), or even a global minimum wage (Fredric Jameson[47]), these are so utopian that they betray little understanding of the political obstacles to overcoming global inequalities. Currently, many governments have the capacity to introduce austere UBI schemes or targeted basic income rather than universal payments. These would not threaten the work ethic or move us into the 'post-work' society by tempting large numbers to leave their unpleasant jobs. Such a UBI might possibly prevent starvation but could hardly be called a progressive or humane innovation, except in those countries totally lacking basic income payments for the unemployed and the destitute. For example, in the 2018 Italian election, the Five Star Movement proposed that any Italian citizen over 18 and not in work, with an income or pension below the poverty line, would be eligible for the basic income of 780 Euros per month. Those of working age would have to make the commitment to spend at least two hours a day looking for work and would lose the 'citizen's income' if they refused to take one of the first three jobs offered to them – hence, more a form of unemployment income rather than an unconditional UBI. As for more generous, reform-orientated UBI schemes, these are proposed in many countries with minimal

46 Srnicek and Williams, op.cit., p.188.
47 'Fredric Jameson: People are saying "this is a new fascism" and my answer is – not yet! Interview with Filip Balunovic', *Lefteast*, 4 November, 2016.

consideration of potential multiple side effects and complications flowing from such schemes.

The 'Magic Pudding' of Capitalist Revenue and Transfer Systems

As a magical cure-all, UBI schemes are supposed to underpin and immunise consumer capitalism and also post-capitalist socialist and green societies against the forthcoming tsunami of unemployment caused by robotics. Yet, the task of designing and funding UBI schemes so that they can simultaneously serve the incompatible and competing interests of business, the poor and unemployed, let alone be the foundation of individual income in new post-capitalist societies, not only defies political reality but is fundamentally contradictory.

Like all forms of public provision in capitalist societies, any UBI scheme will depend on the dominant political culture and national taxation system framing eligibility criteria and funding capacity. Regardless of the proportion of tax to GDP (for example, higher tax ratios collected in some Nordic countries and France or low tax ratios in various Anglo-American countries, Japan and most developing countries), we must never forget that the bulk of total direct tax revenue or indirect taxes such as consumption, sales and other taxes are collected from wage and salary earners and consumers. Leaving aside rampant corruption and the black economy, in most countries large corporations and small to medium businesses account for no more than 10% to 25% of revenue collected. In fact, many businesses are able to legally pay no more than zero to 10% of whatever the official national company tax rate applies (due to all kinds of deductions and offshore arrangements). The liberalisation of capital flows has resulted in the proverbial 'race to the bottom' with governments pressured to slash tax rates on businesses and high-income individuals. Additionally, in all those countries with contributory social welfare and retirement systems, it is often employees who indirectly pay for the majority of social welfare insurance and their own pension schemes as businesses and governments are able to pass on their share of the costs in the form of higher prices, government charges and interest rates on higher unfunded deficits.

The fundamentally profound injustice of sources of revenue in capitalist societies are often overlooked or unrecognised by many supporters of proposed UBI schemes. In other words, transfer schemes or 'welfare states' as they are better known, have always been predominantly based

on the transfer of income from wage and salary workers to other dependent members of their own class in need of health care, education and
other public goods and services. What is new about UBI schemes is that
wage earners and other consumers are supposed to fund additional and
very expensive income schemes from a social base that is going to be further torn apart by increased mass unemployment and precarious work.
Defending UBI schemes, Robert Lechte argues that a UBI "is a transfer
program, not spending: the overall net cost is therefore zero, a net tax
cut for all but the rich."[48] But where do the hundreds of billion of dollars
come from in order to be then transferred to recipients of the UBI?
If not from taxpayers or increased annual debt, does the government
simply print the money each year without fear of inflationary pressures
and the devaluation of the currency? It is never fully explained how this
'magic pudding' of ever-replenished revenue or unlimited sources of
newly created money (no matter how many bites one takes) could be
sustained. I will discuss other proposals for funding UBI schemes from
non-workers shortly.

Historically, there have always been political divisions over how social
assistance should be provided. Christian and other forms of charity were
rejected because they made the giver feel better but stigmatised the poor.
In a period of growing inequality, it is no accident that billionaires are
depicted as heroes in the media while essential social reform languishes.
The struggles during the twentieth century to provide social rights were
in direct opposition to charity and the so-called 'deserving poor'. The
right to social protection benefits were either paid to recipients directly
from taxation revenue or in the form of social insurance contributory
schemes. There is also the 'social dividend' or investment in future generations model. Social dividends tend to penalise the current generation
until sovereign investment funds or other sources of the social dividend
grow in size and are able to distribute benefits. In those OECD countries
where retirees have no entitlements from private pension funds or public
social insurance schemes, current pensions are approximately 25% or
less of average wages. It needs to be underlined that many UBI proposals
are less than half of existing pensions and this means that they would be
below the poverty line.

It is calculated that modest UBI schemes will cost hundreds of billions
of Euros or dollars extra in various countries,[49] approximately double

---

48 Robert Lechte, Letter to Editor, *The Age*, April 9, 2018.
49 For example, 2017 French Socialist Party presidential candidate Benoit Hamon's modest UBI
    was estimated to cost between 300 and 400 billion Euros – see Lucy Williamson, 'France's
    Benoit Hamon rouses Socialists with basic income plan', *BBC News*, 24 January 2017; Gigi

to quadruple the total expenditure outlays on existing welfare state expenditure depending on the amount of UBI payment. Most radical proponents of UBI see the cost of UBIs partly coming from getting rid of burdensome welfare bureaucracies and the integration of welfare and tax systems. A certain amount of savings could be made on reducing current welfare policing costs (without succumbing to ruthless cuts to services) and from a more systematic integration of tax systems and welfare payments. But these budgetary savings would be heavily outweighed by the additional enormous cost of the UBI. Also, regressive taxes such as consumption or value added taxes constitute sizeable proportions of total revenue collected and the burden falls most heavily on low and middle-income households and individuals. Increasing consumption taxes to pay for a UBI would compound the regressive character of taxation and increase inequality.

In recent decades, there has been an erosion of social solidarity fuelled by Right-wing individualist ideology. This has been evident in calls by younger generations and childless individuals and couples demanding governments cease penalising them by preferential expenditure on children, the aged and families. UBI schemes will exacerbate social divisions and opposition from those forced to pay for millions who don't engage in paid work. Even though all workers will also supposedly receive basic income payments, it is almost certain that most governments will claw back these payments via taxation once total paid work income and UBI payments exceeds a designated level. After excluding retired people, children, the disabled and unemployed, the employment participation rate in many countries varies from less than 60% to 70%. Economist John Quiggin calculates that in the initial years, a very modest restricted guaranteed minimum income (GMI) of about 20% of average wages (less than most OECD pensions), rather than a universal payment for all, as advocated by Philippe von Parijs and many others, could be funded by tax increases on wage earners of an additional 5%.[50] However, once the employment participation rate fell below 50% of work able adults (as more workers opt out of paid work), taxes would have to increase by 10% or more.

Quiggin believes that a restrictive GMI rather than a UBI is economically feasible but not politically sustainable in the current political climate. However, he goes on to argue that:

Foster, 'Universal basic income: the dangerous idea of 2016' *The Conversation*, 27 December, 2016, calculates that an income of AUD$20,000 to 19 million adult Australians would cost AUD$380 billion or double the total of the present welfare system.

50 John Quiggin, 'Guaranteed minimum income: how much would it cost? (updated)', *Crooked Timber*, 5 August 2012.

A shift of 10 per cent of national income away from working households might seem inconceivable, but of course that's precisely what's happened in the US over the last twenty or thirty years, except that the beneficiaries have not been the poor but the top 1 per cent. So, if that money were clawed back by the state, it could fund a UBI at no additional cost to the 99 per cent.[51]

What Quiggin highlights is the very significant political change needed to simply turn the clock back to restore the income taken by corporations and wealthy individuals from ordinary households, let alone funding a more generous UBI.

Despite mass unemployment in Spain, *Podemos* dropped a modest UBI from its 2015 platform after realising that it would cost an unaffordable 14.5% of Spain's GDP – a burden that would largely fall on workers. In 2016, Hilary Clinton also considered campaigning for a very modest UBI funded from carbon taxes and oil taxes but eventually dropped the proposal because it required raising "enormous sums of money".[52] In the UK, a very meagre UBI (equivalent to the current Jobseekers Allowance level of £73.10) would cost almost £250 billion per year (approximately 13% of total UK GDP), or 31% of the current UK government budget.[53] Others have proposed more radical solutions to fund UBI schemes. For example, rather than taxes on businesses, economist Yanis Varoufakis proposes legislation be enacted requiring that "a percentage of capital stock (shares) from every initial public offering (IPO) be channelled into a Commons Capital Depository, with the associated dividends funding a universal basic dividend (UBD). This UBD should, and can be, entirely independent of welfare payments, unemployment insurance, and so forth, thus ameliorating the concern that it would replace the welfare state…"[54]

Although appealing, Varoufakis' proposal has a range of deficiencies. First, the number of IPOs in any one country (let alone the whole EU) would be insufficient to cover the hundreds of billions of Euros or dollars necessary to pay a modest UBI. Second, and very importantly, unless there was binding international legislation, new IPOs could evade national legislation and register in another country with

---

51 *Ibid.*

52 See Dylan Matthews, 'Hilary Clinton almost ran for president on a universal basic income', *Vox,* 12 September, 2017.

53 See figures in Social Prosperity Network Report, *Social prosperity for the future: A proposal for Universal Basic Services,* Institute for Global Prosperity, UCL, London, 2017, p.22

54 Yanis Varoufakis, 'The Universal Right to Capital Income', *Project Syndicate,* 31 October, 2016.

minimal regulations over capital and hence deliver zero or minimal dividends for a UBI. Third, it would take years to build a Commons Capital Depository which would still provide unreliable income for UBI recipients, given that it would be subject to the fluctuating fortunes of international markets such as recessions and low growth. Fourth, there is the question of whether the UBI would be funded by dividends from fossil-fuels ventures, military-industrial and other companies practicing dangerous activities or by exploiting low-paid workers domestically or internationally. It would be important to exclude all these immoral business practices, however, this would reduce considerably the dividends available to fund a UBI.

Another proposed source of revenue for a UBI would be using money from tax havens. Regardless of whether one supports a UBI or not, the enormous amounts of money in tax havens have rendered 20th century national tax systems ineffective for 21st century needs and this loophole should be closed. Funds in tax havens vary from Gabriel Zucman's estimate of US$7.6 trillion to Sara Dillon's use of the Tax Justice Network's estimate of between US$20 and US$30 trillion.[55] Annual tax evasion estimates range from US$500 to US$650 billion with developing societies losing 6-13 per cent of total revenue compared with OECD countries losing 2-3 per cent.[56] Depending on the analyst, the US alone loses between US$35 and US$200 billion annually.[57] Unfortunately, even the upper annual amount is only a small fraction of the cost per year of a UBI in a large G20 country, let alone the cost of a global UBI. A case in point would be a very austere UBI in America of US$10,000 per annum. While this is still well below the US poverty line, it would cost a prohibitive US$2.7 to $3 trillion annually.[58]

---

55 See Gabriel Zucman, *The Hidden Wealth of Nations: The Scourge of Tax Havens*, Translated by Teresa Lavender Fagan, University of Chicago Press, Chicago, 2015 and Sara Dillon, *Tax Avoidance, Revenue Starvation and the Age of the Multinational Corporation*, Research Paper 16-18, Suffolk University Law School, 13 December 2016.

56 Alex Cobham and Petr Jansky, *Global distribution of revenue loss from tax avoidance: Re-estimation and country results*, United Nations University-Wider, Working Paper 2017/55, March 2017.

57 Cobham and Jansky calculate the higher amount while the lower amounts are estimated by Jane H. Gravelle, 'Tax Havens: International Tax Avoidance and Evasion' Congressional Research Service, Library of Congress, January 15, 2015. One of the reasons for the discrepancy in figures is that tax evasion can take different forms and is not equivalent to all lost revenue going to tax havens. Also see The Statement of Principles of the *Independent Commission for the Reform of International Corporate Taxation*, June 2015, which estimates over US$100 billion is lost annually by developing countries due to corporate transfer pricing and other tax evading practices.

58 Figures quoted by Richard McGahey, 'Universal Basic Income and the Welfare State', October 2016, published in Jose Antonio Ocampo and Joseph Stiglitz (eds), *The Welfare State Revisited*, Columbia University Press, New York, 2018.

Recouping all funds in tax havens would certainly assist in partially funding UBI schemes in many countries for a year or so but other much more sustainable and substantial tax levies on businesses would be desperately needed. Most UBI proposals are envisaged as national schemes. However, without co-ordinated international regulatory intervention, nations would have great difficulty closing tax havens and would not be able to fund national UBI schemes. Other legislation to recoup money in tax havens would also need to include the break-up of the four large international accounting firms – Deloitte, PWC, KPMG and Ernst & Young – that audit 98 per cent of corporations with annual turnover of US$1 billion or more. Without this and other definancialisation regulatory measures, no effective combined assault on tax evasion is likely to succeed.[59]

Various proposals have also been floated such as taxing robots and rentiers. It is difficult to assess the amount of revenue that could be raised from taxing robots, simply because we do not have any idea how much automation will actually be implemented. If businesses were taxed for each robot at the minimum rate of taxes paid by displaced workers, there would be little incentive to replace human labour unless machines were more productive and much cheaper to buy than paying low-wages to workers. Businesses that regarded any new national tax rates on robots to be too high might simply go offshore to lower tax regimes and/or implement investment strikes to undermine the higher tax regime.

The same applies to rentiers (Uber, Google, Facebook, AirBnB and so forth) who directly employ relatively few full-time workers while utilising all kinds of 'logged labour' and skimmed revenue from various digital platforms. Breaking the rentiers' control is essential to lower prices or make digital goods and services free. It is most doubtful, however, that the source of revenue from this progressive action could come anywhere close to funding a UBI. One could, nonetheless, envisage all kinds of new taxes on financial rentiers such as taxes on financial transactions, property, land and also on fossil fuels. If businesses were actually forced to pay higher tax rates to cover the cost of a UBI (without cuts to other welfare goods and services), this could only be possible if massive political struggles were successful. Given the scale of the political battles needed to raise extremely high levels of additional taxation required for such austere UBIs, why expend so much political energy on UBI schemes that may do so little to combat poverty and inequality?

---

59 See Michael West, 'Oligarchs of the Treasure Islands', www.michaelwest.com.au 11 July 2016.

Complications Arising From UBI Schemes

Any UBI funded by workers or by businesses and wealthy individuals is politically complicated on its own. It becomes even more complex when we look at the side effects of any new scheme on existing retirees (or imminent retirees) as well as on non-citizens. Many UBI advocates tend to be young and do not confront the problem that one third of the population will be over 60 within thirty years in developed countries and over twenty per cent in developing societies. Within OECD countries, it would be very difficult politically to implement UBI schemes that threatened to reduce more generous pension payments or deny these payments to workers within 10 years from retirement. Hence, a transitional retirement system might need to be upheld alongside a UBI for at least forty years until these pensioners die. Also, very expensive but more 'generous' UBI schemes that were at, or slightly above the poverty line, would encourage workers to leave paid work thereby unintentionally weakening the viability of national and private pension funds needed to continue paying retirement pensions. The lack of economic growth in recent years has already placed serious stress on the solvency of many pension funds, a situation that would only deteriorate if a UBI contributed to the labour participation rate declining below fifty per cent.

As for non-citizens, any UBI that is compassionate towards migrants and refugees would need to consider cross-border people movements. Most countries are not part of a supranational bloc and therefore would have to deal with their own domestic non-citizens. Combatting racism is a major global challenge that can be overcome or minimised with determined and appropriate leadership and policies. However, the very expensive cost of a UBI would seriously undermine the financial capacity of governments to provide vitally needed aid to refugees as well as international aid to desperate countries which are the major sources of global migration. Some see the Mediterranean as the new Rio Grande in coming decades. Demographic pressures are dropping in Latin America and North America. However, the growing populations in Sub-Saharan Africa and parts of the Middle East who are affected by wars, problem-ridden economies and climate change could drive a new wave of cross-border people movements, especially into Europe.[60] A supranational UBI within the EU would be almost politically impossible given the divisive levels of racism and intolerance shown in member states.

---

60 See Gordon Hanson and Craig McIntosh, 'Is the Mediterranean the New Rio Grande? US and EU Immigration Pressures in the Long Run', *Journal of Economic Perspectives*, Vol.30, No.4, 2016, pp. 57-82.

An EU-wide minimum wage benchmark and comparable 'social state' benchmarks in all countries would need to precede any UBI scheme. Otherwise, it would be extremely difficult to ensure that an EU-wide UBI actually supplemented wellbeing rather than exacerbated poverty. Proposals by the Unconditional Basic Income Europe movement of a Euro-dividend or UBI of 200 euros a month[61] is so low as to be little more than a cruel joke, given the high cost of living. The notion that one begins with a small UBI payment and campaign to increase it to an adequate payment is illusory, as evidenced by the fact that this has rarely happened, even with government aged pensions, or that any major increase has taken between 70 to 120 years.

As for the more than five billion people living in countries without adequate pensions or unemployment income safety nets or nation-wide welfare services, the institutionalisation of UBI schemes paying a third to half of the austere UBI proposed in affluent OECD countries would still require additional tax revenue or foreign aid totalling trillions of dollars annually. For a number of years, we have seen governments in Mexico, Brazil, Iran and some African countries pay cash transfers rather than a UBI to poor families, some in return for ensuring school attendance, immunisation against diseases and other requirements.[62] The Indian government's 2016-17 Economic Survey proposed a targeted UBI, to minimise existing misallocation of funds and corruption. However, this would be a replacement for most food, fuel and other subsidies going to the poor rather than an additional and more generous payment.[63] If existing payments-in-kind fail to reach millions due to corruption, how will a UBI be paid if most Indians do not have a bank account? Moreover, this absolutely meagre income equivalent of just 90 British pounds, not a month but *per year*, to 75% of the poorest people (not even a universal income), would have cost about 5% of India's GDP if funded without cutting other goods and income subsidies. The 'magic pudding' solution fails to answer how countries economically weaker and poorer than India could fund a UBI, without massive foreign aid.

To sum up, the strongest arguments by advocates of UBI schemes concern the desire to end the humiliation and degradation of human beings as well as the policing of the unemployed and others on welfare

---

61 Francois Denuit, 'Choosing An Ambitious Social Europe Via a Euro-Dividend', *Social Europe*, 5 June 2017.

62 Philip Alston, 'Universal Basic Income as a Social Rights-Based Antidote to Growing Economic Insecurity' in Katharine G. Young (ed.), *The Future of Social Rights*, Cambridge University Press, (forthcoming), available at SSRN, 29 November 2017.

63 See *Economic Survey, 2016-17*, Government of India Ministry of Finance Department of Economic Affairs, Economic Division, January, 2017, pp.173-195.

benefits by government agencies and outsourced private contractors. Also, there is an urgent need to end exploitative, precarious low-paid jobs which people are forced to take in order to survive. The weakest arguments for UBIs relate to the question of how to raise and sustain the excessive revenue needed from either capital or labour just to deliver quite austere, sub-poverty or poverty level income schemes. Politically, the major problem remains one of how to mobilise workers to support a *two-tiered society* based on those who do not perform paid work living off remaining workers who are required to pay higher taxes and face threats to the funding of their social services and pensions. Given the prohibitive cost of even a sub-poverty-level UBI, how can such a scheme generate the positive flowering of a powerful alternative, co-operative and creative culture within less than one or two generations? As most of the workers and business people funding the taxes for a UBI are precisely those immersed in the practices and ideology of competitive, individual-istic consumer capitalism, would the political tensions between the two cultures not make the UBI too divisive, too explosive and unsustainable?

Universal Basic Services: Decommodification and Inequality

Crucially, inequality is not solely due to labour markets but is also due to the overall public provision (or lack of provision) of a wide range of social goods and services, from housing and health services to other necessi-ties of everyday life. All expenditure by governments must be evaluated according to which segments of society bear the major cost of expend-iture and whether this expenditure subsidises business profits and the unequal accumulation of private wealth or is directed towards providing non-market social goods, services and income. Moreover, it is also neces-sary to assess whether expenditure is heavily directed towards destructive purposes (military budgets, environmental resource exploitation) or is ori-ented to sustainable environmental practices, conflict resolution and aid to poor, less developed countries. It is no surprise that state revenue and expenditure in capitalist societies is predominantly geared to reproduc-ing inequality and an irrational market system. Unfortunately, currently proposed UBI schemes will only perpetuate market individualism and national and global inequality, despite the hopes of many of its advocates for the contrary. This will be an affect of prioritising the mobilisation of very scarce public revenue for the satisfaction of *individual* choice over the desperate need to alleviate deep-seated poverty and social injustice.

Ideological individualism (in the guise of an anti-capitalist UBI) is also a feature of the leadership of some anti-neo-liberal parties. For example, Katja Kipping, a prominent member of Germany's Die Linke Party, expresses the individualism embodied in a UBI when she argued: "The old left wanted control over the means of production, the new left wants control over their own lives."[64] One can understand the desire to be free from the compulsion to work in alienating jobs or not be policed by bureaucratic welfare states. However, it is a fundamental illusion to think that a UBI will give people 'control over their own lives' when their basic income will be so very low that they will not be able to purchase goods and services in a market society over which they have minimal or no control. UBI schemes are therefore regressive because they help perpetuate the inequality of the whole social system. Equally importantly, they are both very ineffective ways to combat the widespread lack of social goods and services as well as being very divisive politically.

If the level of political mobilisation necessary to bring about a UBI were ever to emerge, a far more effective and progressive social and political agenda than a UBI has long been advocated in the form of extensive 'social state' goods and services. Extending and transforming 'social states' is important, not just because it strengthens social support for those in need, but also because it is necessary to vigorously counter the numerous policing tests (behavioural modifications) and exclusionary practices of 'coercive paternalism' that neo-liberal welfare policy makers have implemented in recent decades.

As mentioned earlier, income is only one of several socio-economic and environmental pillars underpinning social formations. If one wishes to simultaneously reduce inequality and also lay the transitional conditions for a post-carbon democracy or a post-growth society, it is important not to lose sight of all those aspects of everyday life that can be provided in non-income forms. Minimal determinants of the quality of life – a clean and healthy environment or communities and regions free from domestic and communal violence or war – cannot be provided by income alone, unless one lives in expensive gated enclaves or can afford to escape to safer and ecologically cleaner countries. And even high-income households are characterised by domestic abuse of women, whether partners, wives or domestic servants.

Instead of a UBI, the provision of UBS or 'universal basic services' could be much more radical and redistributive.[65] Existing welfare ser-

---

64 Quoted by Karl Widerquist, 'Basic Income's Third Wave' Georgetown University, Fall 2016, works.bepress.com/widerquist/74.

65 See *Social prosperity for the future: A proposal for Universal Basic Services*, Institute for Global Prosperity, UCL, London, 2017.

vices provide inadequate coverage of the basic needs of a significant segment of the population in developed capitalist countries. For a fraction of the cost of a meagre UBI, free public transport, housing, food, health, energy, education and other cultural and social services could be provided to low income people – whether of working age (with or without dependent children) or retirees. Each country would work out what basic services are needed and how best to deliver them in the least bureaucratic and complex manner. Raising the standard of living of the bottom 30% to 40% of the population in non-consumerist forms would go very much further to reducing poverty and disadvantage than any over-costly UBI.

By contrast, most developing societies have either no welfare states or rudimentary 'social states'. Add the fact that hundreds of millions lack decent housing, running water, electricity, connected sewage and other basic infrastructure, and one begins to get a sense of why a UBI is an extremely expensive luxury that could well be spent on other necessities that will not be provided by income alone, both in developing and developed countries. As for income, cash payments are necessary for those without any income, particularly in poor countries. Unlike a universal payment regardless of need, it is well established that targeting income assistance to women in developing societies is a much more effective way to alleviate family malnourishment and lack of basic necessities. Even though models of the 'extended family' are slowly being replaced in some developing societies (due to urbanisation, lower fertility rates and the marketisation of socio-economic life), many people still hold communitarian values based on religious and cultural care values. Consequently, a UBI could be more politically divisive than in OECD countries.[66] In the medium term, instead of governments paying an individualistic UBI, a fairer and more sustainable solution would be to assist whole communities to develop the provision of basic utilities and infrastructure, housing, communal work projects and so forth. This could dramatically help transform the living conditions of billions of very poor people.

Each society must be evaluated according to whether it has a 'floor' below which all people may not sink, and also whether it has a 'ceiling' that guards against excessive accumulation of private wealth at the expense of most other members of society. During the past decade, a range of United Nations agencies have proclaimed their commitment to a 'Social Protection Floor' that provides access to essential services, social transfers in cash or in kind to ensure income and food security,

---

66 See Ali Hassan Mughal et al, 'A Communitarian Alternative Solution to the Pension Crisis', *International Journal of Political Theory*, Vol.1, no.1, 2016, pp.28-48.

as well as the protection of human rights. Articulating these important values is one thing, actually delivering 'social floors' is another matter. Some OECD societies once had rudimentary 'floors' (rather than equality) that applied to most citizens but which were eroded by neo-liberal policies in recent decades. The vast majority of developing countries do not have any nation-wide universal state provided 'floors' to protect against widespread malnutrition, disease and general poverty. China, the market model of massive development, has numerous state and private welfare schemes riddled with employer corruption and the society still lacks a comprehensive, government–run universal, non-enterprise based and non-communal provision of welfare.[67] It continues to spend far less on social protection services relative to OECD countries and presides over very large inequalities within cities and between urban and rural populations.[68]

In the former Soviet Union and other Communist countries, limited social welfare, health care, housing and other services were provided by the state-owned enterprise or collective farm employing people. On the one hand, rent, utilities, public transport fares and other public services were cheap. However, aside from mass human rights abuses and shortages of public goods and services, this was a very restrictive, work-oriented or 'productivist' welfare system. Once these Soviet enterprises were closed or privatised after the collapse of Communism, numerous people were left without adequate social services or retirement income. The same will happen in China if state-owned enterprises are closed or sold and the national government fails to institute a comprehensive social safety net or 'floor'.

I would argue that the lesson is that all capitalist societies, let alone any future post-capitalist society, must have universal provision of social goods and services that protect people from both the fluctuating fortunes of markets or the fragile conditions of self-sufficient green communities as well as the effects of predicted dramatic climate events and crises. Crucially, diverse social needs cannot be met without democratically controlled and restructured state institutions. Some former Communist countries as well Nordic social democracies were once closer to having 'ceilings' that limited (with minor exceptions) very extreme forms of private income and wealth. There is no country that exists today with a 'ceiling' that puts a bar on the obscene accumulation of private wealth by hundreds of billionaires. UBI schemes will have no impact on the lack of 'ceilings' and will fail to provide adequate 'floors' other than the high

---

67 See survey in 'China's social security system' *China Labour Bulletin*, Hong Kong, 2017.
68 See 'China Systematic Country Diagnostic', World Bank, Washington, 2017, ch.2.

political probability of austere, sub-poverty level income. Similarly, the funding of comprehensive, non-income 'social wage' goods and services is not possible unless there is a parallel campaign to impose 'ceilings' and higher taxes on private wealth, at the very minimum. The same is true of the need to regulate working conditions by imposing maximum work hours beyond which workers cannot be exploited.[69]

Many also erroneously believe that a UBI decommodifies labour and welfare in that it uncouples income from paid work and welfare work tests. However, this decommodification could only be financially sustainable if the vast majority of workers continue to perform commodified wage labour and businesses pay taxes. As for the transition to post-capitalist societies, radicals such as Mason, Srnicek and Williams and assorted Accelerationists posit a fundamentally flawed transitional political strategy based on a UBI and the development of a zero marginal cost society (free of capitalist rentiers like Uber). Those who believe that the zero marginal cost society is compatible with a UBI are mistaken. In a hypothetical capitalist or post-capitalist society where goods and services are free or near free, it is clear that governments will suffer from a massive loss of tax revenue and therefore be unable to fund UBI schemes. In my view, demanding *full unemployment* (Srnicek and Williams) is a seriously flawed politics; wishful dreaming that rests on a fantasy about the fiscal system. Moreover, it is out of touch with most of us, especially workers, who fear unemployment and poverty-level UBI schemes. Similarly, those advocates of degrowth who see UBI schemes underpinning the flowering of green communes have little understanding of the fiscal constraints of national state apparatuses. A society that is required to find tax revenue for UBI recipients living in communes (that could, in the green imagination, hypothetically grow to between 20% and 50% of the population) is unsustainable. Given that little or no tax revenue will flow from supposedly largely self-sufficient communes, the impossible tax burden on non-commune workers or businesses could result in major political conflict.

By contrast, a social and political strategy that increases the decommodification of multiple spheres of society is much more socially and culturally progressive than an individual-based strategy focusing solely on income. It is utopian to imagine that capitalist growth would eventually equalise income between those on less than US$2 per day and others on US$50 plus per day. Even mainstream economist, Jeffrey Sachs, argues that most contemporary economists advocate policies

---

69 Matthew Dimick, 'Better than Basic Income? Liberty, Equality, and the Regulation of Working Time *Indiana Law Review*, Vol. 50, No. 473, 2017 pp.473-517.

divorced from any moral consideration. They simply do not care, he argues, about global poverty or that six million children die every year in a world where global income is over US$125 trillion and a tiny 1%, or over $1 trillion in aid per annum, could help alleviate global poverty.[70] If, however, anti-neo-liberal political forces become powerful in coming years, they could multiply by fivefold Sachs' annual 1% and demand the implementation of a strategy that aims for much greater equalisation of living conditions over a period of ten to twenty years. While there is no quick solution here, providing 'social wage' goods and services for poor countries and marginalised people in developed societies is both feasible and indispensable to socially just, future societies. One should not underestimate the political difficulty of this objective, as most countries fail to give anywhere near 1% of GDP in foreign aid, let alone more than 4% or 5%. Poverty alleviation is also much more than increasing foreign aid. It should not be forgotten that the G20 countries account for about 84% of global GDP yet some of its members such as India, China, Indonesia, Brazil and South Africa have almost half of the world's poorest people. If poverty reduction were to become a serious goal, these countries would have to alter significantly their domestic expenditure priorities.

Currently, non-waged income and services in OECD countries provided by national and local public sectors account for between 20% and 30% of household income and consumption, depending on the country concerned as well as location in or out of labour markets and levels of low to high wages.[71]Moreover, at present, this very important part of household consumption is largely provided by bureaucratised welfare state agencies. There is, unfortunately, very little public awareness that extending state provision of public goods and services could be done by entirely different forms of decentralised, community-based organisations and agencies that are centrally funded but more sensitive and organisationally responsive to local, grass-roots needs. An initial socio-political strategy could aim to both transform the structures of the 'social state' as well as increase non-income goods and services to households to a level between 40% and 60% of household and individual needs. The increased delivery of a whole range of social necessities – from housing, energy, public transport, health, education and care services through to food subsidies, cultural activities and other needs – would not only

70 Jeffrey Sachs, *Economics and the Cultivation of Virtue*, Three lectures at the London School of Economics on February 13, 14 and 15, 2017.

71 See Christoph Hermann, 'The public sector and equality', *Global Social Policy*, vol.16, no.1, 2016, pp.4-21.

increase the decommodification of social life much quicker than a UBI, but also generate employment and tax revenue.

A 'social state' strategy also addresses multiple problems simultaneously. UBI supporters claim that it would help reduce the workweek by giving workers bargaining power with employers. This would only be partially true in the politically unlikely event of governments raising massive revenue to fund a UBI above the poverty level. Even then, a UBI would be much lower than wages and many would still be afraid of losing their jobs. Instead of mass unemployment due to robotics and other forms of automation, a much more effective political demand would be *the government as employer of last resort*.[72] Along with others, I have argued for this option since the 1980s.[73] This decades-old demand would immediately eliminate unemployment and underemployment and yet, unlike UBI schemes, generate taxation revenue as the former unemployed paid taxes on their wages. For example, in the US it was recently calculated that giving secure jobs to 15 million unemployed and underemployed people would cost US$750 billion compared with $2.7 trillion for a below-poverty UBI.[74] A job guarantee would also act as an economic stimulus in times of recession, whereas a UBI would do little or nothing to counter an economic downturn.

The economist Hyman Minsky desired to help low income people and influenced many American advocates of a job guarantee such as L. Randall Wray. While a strong critic of laissez faire economics and the contemporary financial system, it is vital to remember that Minsky was not a radical, had little or no environmental consciousness and wanted primarily to stabilise capitalism.[75] By contrast, the concept of a job guarantee can be developed as part of a radical strategy. Local and regional public sectors and community organisations could determine how to deploy workers to deliver a wide range of care services, housing and social and environmental infrastructure, paid for by revenue collected by

---

72 Versions of this demand have been made for decades. See for example, Philip Harvey, *Securing the Right to Employment: Social Welfare Policy and the Unemployed in the United States*, Princeton University Press, Princeton, 1989; William Mitchell and L. Randall Wray, 'In Defense of Employer of Last Resort: a response to Malcolm Sawyer,' *Journal of Economic Issues*, vol. 39, no.1, 2005, pp.235-245; Pavlina R. Tcherneva, *Beyond Full Employment: The Employer of Last Resort as an Institution For Change*, Working Paper no.732, Levy Economics Institute, Bard College, September 2012.

73 See manifesto by Joe Camilleri, Peter Christoff, Boris Frankel, Rob Watts and John Wiseman, *New Economic Directions for Australia*, Centre for Australian Social Policy Analysis, Coburg, 1989, p.36.

74 See Mark Paul, William Darity Jr. and Darrick Hamilton, 'Why We need A Federal Job Guarantee, *Jacobin*, 4 February, 2017.

75 Hyman P. Minsky, *Stabilizing an Unstable Economy*, 2nd edition McGraw Hill, New York, 2008.

the national government. Importantly, mindless labour such as digging and re-filling holes and other forms of time 'fill-in' public work for the unemployed (still visible in some countries) would be rejected. This type of mindless work has long been deliberately designed by governments to avoid competing with private sector provision of goods and services. Instead, new community-deliberated social priorities would service real needs, enhance local democracy and provide meaningful employment.

Crucially, a job guarantee or work provided by the government as 'employer of last resort', would *not* be compulsory, as is commonly the case with many existing 'welfare to work', job retraining and job search schemes. Rather than existing penalties and policing of the unemployed, the work guarantee could be implemented in conjunction with phased reductions in the length of the workweek. Unlike an individualistic UBI payment, it would foster organised community forms of solidarity. Various similar options have been advocated in recent decades. One option would be to voluntarily employ all those wishing to work full-time on the same conditions applying to all other public sector employees. Another option is that all unemployed and underemployed people could be employed on half to two thirds fractional employment with corresponding wages and conditions enjoyed by full-time employees. These fractional continuing jobs would still pay well above a UBI and provide secure employment (instead of precarious work) to the individuals concerned. It would also provide vital services and infrastructure to the general public, as well as tax revenue to help fund this additional public sector employment. Moreover, with unemployment eliminated, governments could begin reducing full-time work by one or two hours each year so that full-time public employment declined to between 20 and 25 hours a week over a decade and fractional work hours declined on a pro-rata basis as well. Given the renewed strength of labour movements under conditions of full-employment, such a policy would put great pressure on many private sector employers to match public sector hours and conditions.

In the medium-term future when high productivity and total goods production will only require 3% to 5% of the global workforce, Keynes' famous 1930 dream of a 15 hour workweek for 'our grandchildren by 2030' might still come true, even though probably delayed by a decade or two.[76] It will also have to be an entirely different reduced working week and lifestyle to the one Keynes envisaged, as his society was based on a pre-environmentalist notion of abundance rather than resources scarcity.

---

76 John Quiggin, 'Prospects of a Keynesian utopia', aeonmagazine.com, 27 September 2012, believes that the 15 hour week is possible but will take an extra 30 years to be realized in 2060.

Rethinking the Culture of 'Post-Work' Individualism

No society, especially a post-capitalist society, can maintain social harmony and integration, let alone communal solidarity, if large minorities choose to reject shared responsibilities. The French socialist Paul Lafargue's argument in *The Right to be Lazy* (1883) remains a powerful critique of the 1848 workers' demand of 'the right to work'. Sacrificing one's life performing unnecessarily long work hours in alienating jobs is rightly criticised. The revolutionary Left has long argued that the abolition of wage slavery rather than full employment is the goal of an emancipatory politics. Nonetheless, using this old anti-capitalist slogan to justify a 'post-work' society based on a UBI is not only an illusion but also not a viable foundation for a post-capitalist society or post-growth democracy. Capitalist societies are based, as Marx put it, on the freedom of individuals to collide with one another in the pursuit of private interests. However, an alternative society will always be short of resources and require social co-operation to share work and protect against environmental destruction and social scarcity.

While the revolutionary Left has long argued that the abolition of wage slavery rather than full employment is the goal of an emancipatory politics, this objective will remain utopian without world revolution.[77] The same also applies to the promise of a generous UBI within capitalist societies without the requisite and sustainable fiscal resources and political solidarity. By contrast, a job guarantee scheme could reduce the workweek to 20 hours or 15 hours eventually and liberate people to enjoy greater personal leisure time and enable them to participate in community activities. It will not, however, constitute a completely 'post-work' society because no world of 'post-work' could function (except in the utopian imagination) without any labour. The goal instead is to alleviate and transform existing wage labour conditions and income for the approximately 40% of the paid workforce in OECD countries (and much higher percentages in developing societies) that suffer from low wages and highly exploitative conditions.

Also, a UBI is unlikely to transform unequal gender relations or herald a new ethics of care where men and women share the intimate, emotional and material work of caring for the vulnerable (infants, children, the sick, disabled and frail elderly). We are reminded of liberal feminists who believed that gender inequality would disappear when women

---

77 See David Calnitsky, 'Debating Basic Income' *Catalyst*, vol.1, no.3 2017, pp.63-92. Like many others, Calnitsky discusses the UBI without any clear or persuasive explanation of how such a scheme could be funded, especially if a majority of workers opt for an exit from wage slavery.

became economically independent and entered the paid workforce in large numbers. Unfortunately, gender based domestic violence and all other forms of discrimination and inequality still flourish. Just as the old socialists believed that overthrowing private ownership would give rise to non-sexist, non-racist and other egalitarian values, so too, a new economism is associated with UBI schemes that attribute the emergence of a non-sexist and non-racist culture as well as an ethics of care out of a miserly basic income. Contemporary debates by women reveal that they are divided over the UBI. Some see it as facilitating greater support for new mothers and single parents.[78] Others see it doing little to end sexism and racism.[79] In the early 1970s, Mariarosa Dalla Costa, Selma James and Silvia Federici were prominent in campaigning for 'wages for housework'.[80] This demand focussed on the hidden unpaid work that women carried out for capitalists by nourishing and reproducing the 'variable capital' or labour power that husbands, sons, brothers or fathers performed in factories and other workplaces. Leaving aside its problematic reduction of care to a narrow monetary value, the demand for 'wages for housework' was effectively a radicalising non-negotiable demand, as the total cost to the capitalist state was seen by its advocates as unaffordable. By contrast, a UBI is conceived by its supporters as financially feasible within capitalist societies and often lacks the explicit and older anti-capitalist agenda of Dalla Costa, Federici and James. Ironically, both 'wages for housework' and UBI schemes succumb to the power of capitalist commodification by reducing work to mere income and production, thereby stripping care and paid work of its richer and more meaningful personal and social values.

In contrast to a UBI, or versions of 'wages for housework', the strategy of developing a comprehensive 'social state' has an explicit and vested interest in nurturing a culture of co-operation and care, of respect and recognition of individual and social needs. Overcoming the gendered division of labour in paid and unpaid labour requires not just the obvious cultural changes in dominant male values and behaviour but very importantly, the material provision of new increased care services that end the isolation and ease the burden on women through social funding and a profound change in community priorities. The

---

78 Petra Bueskens, 'Mothers And Basic Income: The Case For An Urgent Intervention', *New Matilda*, 23, February, 2017.

79 See Tracey Reynolds, 'Black Women, Gender Equality and Universal Basic Income, *Compass*, 27 January, 2017; also see contributions by Jane Lethbridge, Ruth Lister, Barb Jacobsen and other women as part of the *Compass* debate on the UBI.

80 Mariarosa Dalla Costa and Selma James, *The Power of Women and the Subversion of the Community*, 2nd edition. Falling Wall, Bristol, 1973.

voluntary reconfiguration of domestic residential space, or the pooling and enhancement of communal resources to reflect different needs and stages of the life cycle as well as help integrate different generations (currently living isolated lives) are a few examples that go well beyond the capacity of a very limited UBI or 'wages for housework'.

If the provision of increased 'social state' goods and services helps shift household priorities away from the current need to consume privately provided consumption goods and services, then securing incomes through publicly funded employment could further challenge consumer capitalism. Public employment through 'employer as last resort' will help decommodify larger areas of paid labour by freeing them from the constraints of labour markets as well as decommodifying services. Lack of housing has always been a prime cause of poverty. The increased provision of community designed public housing (not the soulless housing estates that blight the horizons of cities) as well as urban renewal though sustainable energy, transport and 'green cities', are all familiar objectives achievable through the social provision of goods and services rather than destructive speculative private property investment.

However, the development of an enlarged 'social state' is advocated without any of the illusions associated with the steady-state goals espoused by many advocates of degrowth. Above all, there is no delusionary hope that a major extension of the 'social state' will be compatible in the long-term with a profitable capitalist system. On the contrary, it would be unrealistic fantasy to think that any strategy that significantly extends the decommodification of labour and everyday social necessities is not a threat to markets and financialisation. The latter thrive precisely on the commodification and privatisation of all spheres of life, in short, practices and values that are antithetical to a 'social state'. One only has to think of why neo-liberals launched concerted attacks on social welfare states from the late 1970s, namely, to halt and wind back tax revenue as a growing percentage of GDP. Without supportive political mobilisation, any new extension of the 'social state' would also encounter major opposition from business groups eager to prevent decommodified 'social state' allocations increasing as a proportion of existing economies and social relations.

Instead of illusory degrowth notions of conflict-free transitions to a sustainable 'steady-state', the strategy of extending 'social states' is politically premised on the recognition that in most developed capitalist countries they will be strongly resisted by businesses and significant sections of employees opposed to higher taxes or a reduced workweek. Political opposition will also arise from those nationalists opposed to substantial international aid to poor countries or from conservatives who reject governments providing jobs and greater social welfare. If so, why pursue such a contentious strategy? One could equally ask: what are the alternatives? Little foresight is required to see that we are moving into a volatile future where unemployment or low-paid precarious jobs will increase due to automation and heightened global competitive pressures. Industrialisation for all developing societies is both a fanciful and an undesirable solution to inequality. Even 'green growth' solutions will provoke resistance and are likely to prove ineffective in preventing an increase in global warming or in generating a new wave of long-term sustained growth in trade and employment. Of course, as we have seen, near stagnant, crisis-ridden conditions can last for years as they have in previous decades.

One cannot predict whether campaigns to extend the 'social state' succeed globally or perhaps only in some nations or not at all. What can be guaranteed, however, is that the fortunes of electoral majorities in developed countries affected by corroding 'social pillars' are increasingly interconnected to the much lower standards of living of billions living in developing societies. Without more significant state intervention to extend social 'floors' and impose new 'ceilings' on private wealth like ending tax havens, redirecting resources to fund the global poor and placate increasingly worried electorates in OECD countries, political instability will most likely escalate.

The crucial point is that social inequality cannot be overcome with a single policy or strategy whether in the form of a UBI or an extended 'social state'. Rather than provide a UBI to all, regardless of wealth and income, a number of analysts have investigated combining a basic income with a guaranteed job depending on each country's level of pensions, unemployment benefits and level of unemployment and job precarity.[81] As an intermediary social policy strategy this may be feasible for the short term if the combined basic income and job offer only goes to the bottom 15 to 40% in order to first reduce poverty by eliminating unemployment and underemployment. However, exclusionary and discriminatory political, social and cultural practices, as well as economic exploitation and environmental degradation all require extensive radical overhaul of existing institutional structures and decision-making. While the task has to begin somewhere, it is important to recognise that in any transition to post-capitalist societies, a UBI will be a major distraction and do little to alter existing inequalities or provide a secure foundation for a post-capitalist, environmentally sustainable society.

---

81 See Felix FitzRoy, 'Basic income and a public job offer: complementary policies to reduce poverty and unemployment' *Journal of Poverty and Social Justice*, online 17 March 2018.

Conclusion

I have argued in this chapter that a UBI is highly divisive philosophically, culturally and politically. As a social policy, no UBI can guarantee positive or negative outcomes because it largely depends on how individuals use their income within the context of a divisive politics over how it will be funded. By contrast, a 'social state' strategy removes the guesswork associated with a UBI, especially the negative implications of selfish or atomised individualism. It is a forward-looking strategy that is directly tied to combatting inequality and poverty, providing the essential material necessities that enable individuals and communities to exercise their freedoms through social co-operation. Individuals may or may not set goals for themselves. No such luxury is available to societies, unless we are happy to see the continued negative social and environmental consequences of societies drifting and stagnating for decades. Without a 'social state' strategy we are left with crisis-ridden capitalist societies or the utopian dreams of individual abundance in a world of scarcity.

Most welfare systems and UBI proposals in OECD countries mirror one another. Existing government social welfare systems are geared to individual or family cases that professional social workers, educationists, psychologists, or the criminal justice system manages. The heavy concentrations of unemployed and marginalised populations in geographical rural or urban spaces are largely left without adequate help because most existing welfare systems are geared to individual symptoms and fail to implement sweeping structural reforms to eliminate the common social causes of suffering and disadvantage. So too, with UBI schemes. The moment that social reformers recognise that social malaise cannot be solved by income alone, the larger problem of how to fund the transformation and delivery of adequate social programs begins to dwarf any notion of the UBI as a magic bullet. It is therefore high time that the illusory promises of individualist income schemes were abandoned.

Conclusion: Capitalism Versus Sustainability

This book has strongly critiqued and challenged current thinking on ways to make capitalism sustainable. It has also vigorously analysed a range of different proposals on how to move towards a post-capitalist future. The aim has been to bridge the political and theoretical chasm, or 'analytical apartheid' that characterises so much socio-economic policy, on the one side, and environmental analyses on the other. Consequently, the preceding chapters have discussed some of the problems inherent in the solutions to socio-economic and environmental crises put forward by theorists, decision-makers, policy analysts and activists. These include the religious faith of defenders of the market in technological innovation and the continued promotion of export-led industrialisation as the solution to poverty and inequality in low and middle-income developing countries.

It is a standard claim made by defenders of utopian thinking that there would be no progress without imaginative ideas to spur action. This may have been true in the past but is only partially valid today. One could equally argue that it is contemporary utopian thinking in both its technological and political-economic forms that is undermining the chances of radical policies succeeding by distracting attention away from the many types of practical and urgent action needed to combat major socio-economic and environmental crises. This is not an argument in favour of conventional small incremental change strategies – although all improvements, no matter how small, are welcome. The pressing crises we face today, especially dangerous environmental crises, no longer permit the luxury of ineffective old and very slow evolutionary social change models that are still promoted by mainstream parties.

Throughout this book I have critiqued pro-market utopian proposals, such as the absolute decoupling of economic growth from nature, as well as anti-capitalist utopian images of a zero marginal cost society or UBI schemes that promise illusory incomes for all in a so-called 'post-work' society. All these proposals are utopian because they are unrealisable or unsustainable regardless of whether there is a capitalist or post-capitalist society. Near zero marginal cost can be achieved for some products as can the *relative* decoupling of growth from nature in particular industries, due to new technologies and productivity gains. But these potential or actual developments are not to be confused with the unavoidable and inevitable costs – whether natural or social, and whether counted in monetary terms or in expended labour – built into the production of key necessities such as food or producer goods and resources, minerals, machinery and the like.

These reservations aside, I strongly support many radical changes to society that conservative defenders of capitalism might call 'utopian'. The test of a utopian idea is not whether particular policies and practices are opposed simply because they threaten the existing socio-political order. An idea or policy is deemed utopian because the proposals are impractical or unrealisable even after all obstacles in the form of existing unequal power, wealth, property and hostile political cultural attitudes have been overcome or transformed. If a 'post-work' society is merely another name for a new society based on the phased reduction of waged labour to 15 to 20 hours per week (so that people have more free time to enjoy new interests or develop more caring social relations), rather than the end of all paid work, then this goal is certainly quite feasible. It only appears 'utopian' to businesses and political defenders of existing capitalist labour market conditions or to hostile and fearful workers still immersed in the dominant work culture. One can definitely struggle for a shorter working week without subscribing to the divisive and illusory proposals of a UBI that is envisaged not as a meagre income supplement, but an income that will supposedly eventually replace paid work for most people.

American Marxist sociologist Eric Olin Wright has subverted the concept of utopia by focusing on 'real utopias'. These are not traditional unattainable utopias but ways of organising society that are either already practised in elementary forms, or else political economic processes that are quite realisable given appropriate changes in political power. Discussing the four main ways 'to be an anti-capitalist in the twenty-first century'[1],

---

1   Eric O. Wright, 'How To Be an Anticapitalist Today', *Jacobin*, 2 December, 2015.

Wright rules out 'smashing capitalism' and 'escaping capitalism'. The first is a product of the anger of living in deeply unequal and destructive capitalist societies. Not only is this unlikely, given the weakness of tiny revolutionary movements confronting existing repressive state appara- tuses today, but also that violence and non-democratic methods would pervert rather than produce an emancipatory post-capitalist society. Likewise, 'escaping capitalism' as Wright recognises, remains a very lim- ited option that applies only to a few individuals who can 'drop out' and live 'off the grid'. Intentional communities and co-operatives of volun- tary simplicity may challenge commodity capitalism, but at present, this mode of life is hardly an option for the vast majority of people, especially those raising children and trying to survive on a daily basis.

The only strategies that Wright sees as feasible are 'taming' or 'erod- ing' capitalism. 'Civilising' or 'taming' capitalism cannot prevent all the harms caused by capitalism but it can help deal with many symptoms such as unemployment, inadequate health care, housing and social ser- vices. Eroding capitalism is different from revolution, in that people can engage in activity and create various institutional responses that extend the sphere of non-capitalist public practices. Hence, Wright concludes:

> If you are concerned about the lives of others, in one way or another you have to deal with capitalist structures and insti- tutions. Taming and eroding capitalism are the only viable options. You need to participate both in political movements for taming capitalism through public policies and in socioeconomic projects of eroding capitalism through the expansion of emanci- patory forms of economic activity. We must renew an energetic progressive social democracy that not only neutralizes the harms of capitalism but also facilitates initiatives to build real utopias with the potential to erode the dominance of capitalism.[2]

Within the context of a conservative, violent American society, Wright's choice of options is logical and realistically radical, although he says little about post-growth ecological sustainability. Even in Europe, Australia, Canada and New Zealand that have a history of more extensive social democratic and labourist traditions, the fantasy notion of 'smashing' or 'escaping' capitalism also apply. As to dozens of low and middle-income developing societies, the struggles against a variety of authoritarian capitalist regimes often result in violent repressive action against liberal

---

2   *Ibid*

democratic movements, let alone against socialist revolutionaries.

In OECD countries, Wright also argues that even 'eroding' capitalism is far-fetched unless combined with 'taming' capitalism. Although he makes a number of persuasive points, like many social scientists, Wright is attracted to ahistorical typologies. The reality is that it is often only with hindsight that we can tell whether particular policies or practices that we thought were 'taming' capitalism actually turned out to be 'eroding' capitalism. Take, for instance, the neo-liberal reaction from the 1970s onwards against increased social services and spaces of decommodification. Conversely, policies and practices that were seen at the time as 'eroding' capitalism proved to be merely 'taming' or reinvigorating capitalism. Another stark example would be the absorption of some of the 1960's cultural and political critiques of capitalism into new modes of management.[3]

Importantly, anti-capitalist political strategies are extremely difficult to apply if there is no clear political terrain in which to realise these goals. As Chairman Mao put it: 'It is no use preaching socialism unless you have got a country to practise it in.'[4] The same could also apply to 'green growth', degrowth or post-growth. Mao's axiom downplays the fact that it is first necessary to preach social change goals before social movements can implement these objectives. However, one needs more than just a country, but also much clearer national and supranational institutional structures and policies to achieve these goals. In this concluding chapter I will therefore discuss the role of state institutions and their relation to the various socio-economic and environmental proposals analysed in previous chapters.

The Impossibility of Radical Reforms Without State Institutions

There are significant differences between how political movements see 'the state' and how environmental policy academics and political economists analyse state institutions. Many activists tend to confuse elected governments with state institutions. This overlap does occur in some countries where political parties occupying office for long periods tend to fuse into 'party-state' machines. Party officials and appointees from

3   Luc Boltanski and Eve Chiapello, *The New Spirit of Capitalism*, trans.by Gregory Elliott, Verso, London, 2005.

4   Quoted by Gregory Elliott, *Ends In Sight: Marx/ Fukuyama/ Hobsbawm/ Anderson*, Pluto Press, London, 2008, p.120.

the business sector or social institutions favourably disposed to the ruling government tend to occupy informal and formal positions of power in departments, statutory bodies, public media organisations, educational, legal, military and other key institutions. These appointees often remain entrenched in state apparatuses long after the ruling party has been removed from office. Extra parliamentary social movements and protest groups often live in the hope that street protests, media campaigns and petitions will lead to change via sympathetic government or opposition party support. At the same time, even naïve or hopeful campaigners recognise their lack of power in comparison to corporate lobbyists and political donors.

During the 1970s and 1980s, neo-Marxist theorists of the capitalist state (myself included) downplayed the role of conspiracies and the focus on members of the 'power elite' as being of very limited use in explaining the more complex roles and structures of states in reproducing capitalist relations. Emphasising the everyday indispensable roles performed by state institutions on behalf of capitalist classes – regardless of the social backgrounds of the office holders or their membership of 'elite circles' – remains extremely important. However, the scale of corruption and the flagrant and crude exercise of power over whole governments or individual politicians by corporate leaders and other key players have increased in recent decades. It is therefore important not to overlook how neo-liberal attacks on state regulations have legitimised and incentivised abuses of power and extensive corruption. Reversing this market culture will not be easy without mass political campaigns by ordinary citizens to 'take back' state institutions – public institutions that they actually never ever fully controlled prior to the era of neo-liberalism.

Generally, contemporary mainstream political leaders and businesses that wish to decouple economic growth from nature have no need to reconceptualise state institutions. But they do need stringent government controls over corruption and watered-down decoupling practices if the technical goal of overcoming the natural limits to growth is not to become tokenistic. One only has to look at how neo-liberals, social democrats, green liberals and authoritarian statists such as the Chinese government are all hoping that decoupling innovation strategies will actually work. Here lies one of the central political paradoxes of 'sustainable capitalism'. On the one hand is the minimalist approach, namely, the belief in market forces unleashing innovation without significant state regulatory controls or the need for major social reforms to combat inequality and poverty. On the other hand, is the reality of capitalist practices (evident among both corporations and small businesses) of the need to cut corners, profit maximise and place eco-systems second to these considerations. Without widespread regulatory enforcement of rigorous environmental and social standards, voluntary market self-regulation renders absolute decoupling utterly impossible. For every enterprise or government that takes policing of resources use, production standards and consumer eco footprints seriously, there will continue to be plenty of others more committed to disregarding environmental and social needs. Weak state institutions unable to 'tame capitalism' or strong states committed to incessant growth are a double recipe for future disasters.

For quite different reasons, socialist revolutionaries who wish to overthrow 'the state' fail to spend enough energy thinking about how existing state institutions, roles and functions could be reformed. Apart from a minority of socialists who develop alternative state planning models and schemes to create community care structures, most activist opponents of capitalism only have vague and elementary notions of the specific roles and functions that state institutions will have to play in any transition to post-capitalism. Likewise, intentional communities disengaged from conventional political processes, contribute little in the form of macro-political economic analyses. Their focus is primarily on community institutions operating outside state institutions at the local face-to-face level.

This leaves two other broad and amorphous socio-political groups most concerned with state institutions. The first group are reform-orientated policy analysts, unions, mainstream environmentalists, NGOs, mainstream parliamentary parties and one-party regimes, as well as assorted technocrats, businesses and supranational agencies – all promoting variations of 'green growth'. Key linkages within this group range from the preoccupation with climate policy and ecological modernisation even though a significant proportion do *not* share more wide-ranging concerns about connecting environmental reforms with socio-economic issues such as inequality, poverty and civil liberties.

By contrast, the second group are very critical of capitalist societies and embrace radical greens, heterodox political economists, eco-socialists, local and national degrowth movements, and anti-market globalisation organisations concerned about low-income societies and indigenous communities. They are divided between those who emphasise local and regional alternative pathways (many of which are outside state institutions), and others who stress the need for new national and supranational state institutions and policies.

Both the first group and many in the second assume that either 'green growth' or a post-growth future will only come about with the full involvement of state institutions at local, national or supranational levels. To clarify my own position, it is important to identify the strengths and weaknesses of each group and what could be adopted from each, as part of a strategy towards constructing post-neo-liberal or post-capitalist futures.

a. 'Green growth' or 'sustainable capitalism'

In Chapter One, I analysed the neo-Schumpeterian advocates of 'green growth' such as Mariana Mazzzucato, Carlota Perez and Michael Jacobs who argue that we need to 'rethink the state' in order to 'rethink capitalism'.[5] In recent years, 'green growth' social democratic and 'Third Way' approaches have been visible at national and supranational levels within the EU as well as at international levels through organisations such as the Global Commission on the Economy and Climate. Depending on the organisation or the policy analyst, some are closer to neo-liberal positions in advocating hybrid public/private solutions to environmental infrastructure, innovation and social services delivery models. Others promote traditional or new social democratic public-sector solutions and state regulation to achieve administrative and ecological modernisation. Then there are those unconcerned about democracy and equality who favour the application of technocratic and administrative solutions.

Many advocates of 'green growth' combine neo-Keynesian macro-economic policies, with neo- as well as post-neo-liberal ideas about using state institutions to achieve green social and eco-system objectives. In fact, much of this pro-market strategy is geared to deploying state fiscal, monetary and social investment strategies in order to achieve 'sustainable and inclusive growth'. It is a strategy primarily focused on curbing the excesses of free markets and modernising capitalism rather than replacing these social formations.

One major problem here is that depending on the audience, 'green growth' advocates present ambiguous or contradictory arguments to conflicting constituencies. Business groups are targeted by emphasising technocratic reforms that minimise the distance between new agendas and existing neo-liberal policies. Also, ambitious state-run national agendas to strengthen future national and global competitiveness via modernisation are legitimised by being put under the 'green growth'

---

5   See policy contributions in Michael Jacobs and Mariana Mazzucato (eds.) *Rethinking Capitalism: Economics and Policy for Sustainable and Inclusive Growth.* Wiley-Blackwell and The Political Quarterly, Oxford, 2016.

umbrella. Other advocates of 'green growth' promote an alternative agenda for sweeping post-neo-liberal socio-economic and environmental reforms that tap into widespread critiques of inequality, poverty and environmental destruction. The twin Janus faces of 'green growth' reform means that one is never quite sure if eco-modernisers are mainly looking backwards in order to persuade hostile business and government policy-makers, or forwards in order to deal with environmental and socio-economic crises in a non-market manner.

As I have argued in Chapter One, there are several main weaknesses to the neo-Schumpeterian notions of 'green growth'. First, there is still a heavy preoccupation with capitalist growth even though it is dressed up in ecologically modernised clothing. The model of the interventionist 'entrepreneurial state' rightly insists that taxpayer's funds should shape and direct R&D rather than leave private businesses to overwhelmingly benefit from public support. However, the prioritisation of 'value creation' (through innovation) over old social democratic 'redistribution' is so very close to the neo-liberal 'trickle down' effect that it will leave inequality largely untouched. Second, neo-Keynesian policies that help definancialise economies and improve desperately needed public services are to be welcomed. Nonetheless, the advocates of 'green growth' naively believe that they can control the 'business cycle' and are silent about the earlier historical failures of Keynesian policies to prevent major recessions. Third, they also say little on how they will deal with extensive forms of exploitation and inequality at the global level. Fourth, the neo-Schumpeterians say nothing about the 'welfare-warfare state' and how state funding of innovation needs to be shifted away from its heavy involvement in military R&D following more than a century of wars and militarisation. It is as if 'green growth' can flourish in the 'civilian economy' which is supposedly unaffected by the 'dark side' of innovation and imperial conflicts. Finally, there is a very heavy emphasis on top-down policy-making geared to 'enlightened' business and political leaders rather than building mass-based political movements from below.

Overall, 'green growth' strategies offer a number of valuable social and environmental reforms when compared to conservative, fossil-fuelled businesses and Right-wing parties presiding over ecological and social crises. Those advocates of 'green growth' closer to reform-orientated social democracy, for instance, make important political allies in the struggle to change present-day conservative societies. Nevertheless, the positive qualities of 'green growth' reforms are outweighed by the illusory and often benign images of capitalist reality that have been outlined earlier. Given the absence of large radical social change movements, it is understandable why 'green growth' political strategists believe that their moderate policies may be the only feasible pathway to reforms in a number of powerful G20 countries. In fact, they do not claim that the 'rational innovative state' will bring about socialism or the 'post-growth society'. Rather, the old objective of 'civilising capitalism' is now re-envisaged in the twenty-first century as the improbable goal of 'sustainable capitalism'.

Although the social democratic neo-Schumpeterians are to be supported in their opposition to Right-wing free marketeers and climate sceptics, these advocates of 'sustainable capitalism' fail to link their campaign for rapid decarbonisation to the need for far greater reform of socially destructive market practices. Hence, there is a high probability that their overall programs are quite likely to be beneficial in the short-to-medium run, but by merely deferring or ameliorating rather than tackling deep-seated problems, may end up being far worse for humanity and species biodiversity in the long term.

b. Post-growth alternatives

If those supporting 'green growth' veer between neo-liberals, on the one side, and Left social democrats and greens on the other, many advocates of post-growth also swing between displaying affinities with either social democrats or with radical greens and socialists. This is not surprising as post-growth and 'steady-state' supporters come from either radical green and socialist movements or have Keynesian and post-Keynesian backgrounds, as is the case with political economists Tim Jackson and Herman Daly. As I have discussed, Jackson, Daly and others emphasise the crucial role that state institutions will have to play, once degrowth policies are implemented by governments, in providing 'counter-cyclical' fiscal support and employment. They argue that states need to develop a range of interventions, to counteract and cushion the negative socio-economic impacts flowing from new policies that require private businesses to scale back on their use of natural resources. Governments must also ensure that the unsustainable social logic of consumerism is not left to individual choice or voluntary community action.[6] A post-growth society is also contingent upon not accepting existing rigid definitions of the capitalist state and capitalism. Jackson and other degrowthers work with a notion of contemporary capitalism as a system that is based on

---

6   Tim Jackson, *Prosperity Without Growth*, p.203.

multiple forms of ownership. This notion is much more pliable than Marxist arguments about the non-negotiable need of capitalist enterprises for incessant growth and the accumulation of capital.

My position is that both Jackson and orthodox Marxists are partially correct. Marxists are right to argue that growth is not a dispensable option for businesses. While Jackson needs to clarify and develop his argument about state institutions, his analysis is also persuasive. In support, I believe that there are no rigid or clearly defined boundaries or definitions of capitalist mixed economies (of state and private sectors) applicable to all countries that specify the size and activity of public sector institutions or the sources of state revenue and expenditure priorities. Within this politically defined 'grey area', much reform can be implemented with mass political support, as indicated by historical variations in tax and social services as a proportion of GDP in different capitalist countries. What will determine future roles for state institutions will be the balance of domestic political forces within particular countries and the ability of reform-orientated governments to 'delay' or 'deflect' external attempts to impose monetary and trade 'adjustments' that disrupt or terminate domestic reform agendas. This is discussed in detail in Chapter Two.

We cannot know *a priori* what privately owned enterprises or those controlled by governments, pension funds and other shareholders will, or will not do. These reactions depend on the specific health or fragility of particular capitalist enterprises and industries, and their capacity to live with, or their determination to resist, higher taxes and new social and ecological reform measures. It should never be forgotten that 'capitalism' is a generic term that exists in diverse forms in different countries. In contrast to the Varieties of Capitalism analysts who focus mainly on economic processes in the narrowest of terms and ignore vital environmental and socio-cultural relations and processes, I argue that contemporary capitalist countries are not purely 'economic' systems. Rather, they are complex social and cultural systems whose boundaries overlap or intersect with eco-systems and investment, production, distribution, administration and consumption practices. No so-called capitalist 'economy' can maintain a profitable existence without all the numerous subsidies and unpaid costs borne by state institutions and unpaid domestic care labour and large numbers of people performing voluntary social labour, not to mention the use and abuse of so-called 'free' natural habitats. This is also precisely why the possibility of any post-growth strategy will have to be fought culturally and politically over the future direction taken by state institutions and households. Ultimately, however, any radical restructuring that threatens the growth and

profitable survival of most capitalist enterprises will produce major political conflict. The outcome of this conflict will determine whether state
supported post-growth practices are modified or completely stopped, or
whether business forces fail to get their way and society ceases to remain
capitalist.

Without new comprehensive socio-economic and environmental
state roles to redefine socio-economic activity, there is no possibility of a
post-growth society. Jackson argues that we need the following:

> ... a positive, dynamic role for a 'progressive State'. One which
> is attentive both to changing social conditions and to the under-
> lying needs of its citizens. One which collaborates actively in the
> design of the good life. One which is inclusive and considerate.
> One which invests vigorously in the common good. One which
> is entrepreneurial and innovative. ...In short, the progressive
> State is not just the instrumental means for ensuring social and
> economic stability in a low-growth environment. It is the basis
> for a renewed vision of governance. It is the foundation for a
> lasting prosperity.[7]

While I agree with most of these points, there are a number of confusing and conflicting arguments in Jackson's strategies for a redefined,
post-growth state. For example, one contradiction is that any state that
becomes 'entrepreneurial' within the context of capitalist societies (and
here Jackson explicitly endorses Mariana Mazzucato's 'entrepreneurial
state'[8]) in my view will also abandon degrowth, as it will compete with
or become involved in capitalist growth strategies. Also, Jackson presents
mixed messages about state institutions. In a paper written on the green
economy at community level with Peter Victor, they outline a whole
series of suggestive local organisations such as worker and producer
co-ops, non-profits, self-employed ventures, solidarity markets and barter
exchanges, covering everything from finance, food production, community currencies, to the provision of energy, health, education, housing
and cultural activities.[9] What is notable in this vision of the local 'green
economy' is the complete absence of any role for state institutions. It is
not that most of these community organisations are incompatible with
local, regional or national and supranational state institutions. But there

---

7   *Ibid,* p.209.
8   *Ibid,* p.193.
9   Tim Jackson and Peter Victor, *Green Economy at Community Scale*, Metcalf Foundation, Toron-
     to, November 2013.

is no conception offered by Jackson and Victor about how the funding and operation of local services, especially employment, education, health and finance are connected to larger national state institutions.

The vital missing link of how new state institutions co-exist with, and also support, co-ordinate and regulate the plethora of community level organisations is crucial for several reasons. First, given Jackson's emphasis on the central role of national governments in the transition to a post-growth society, we must know how local communities will thrive and survive. In a society that could deteriorate quickly into a great depression if capitalist enterprises are forced to cut growth and there is no coun-tervailing increase in state expenditure and employment, just what are the connections between local and national processes and institutions? Second, local stateless communities, transition towns and eco-villages continue to be utterly politically and economically insignificant. It would be a miracle if they ever grew to a size where they constituted a major threat to capitalist growth regimes. Jackson and Victor, like so many advocates of alternative socio-economic organisational forms, make the extraordinary leap from tiny isolated community experiments to a new national and international political economy, all without outlining how the local and the national and supranational will function in the future.

Nonetheless, Jackson concedes the need for higher levels of state governance to manage 'common pool resources' such as the oceans, the climate and the money system.[10] He supports a variation of Minsky's notion of 'government as the employer of last resort' to counter aggres-sive capitalist cost-cutting in order to stabilise an unstable economy. He also supports state regulation to definancialise the economy, such as measures to control credit-fuelled consumption.[11] Given these state-ini-tiated policies, how will local employment or 'community currencies' fit in with national budgetary expenditure priorities and national and inter-national monetary systems? How can the local 'commons' be managed so that national and international environmental sustainability criteria and human rights and civil liberties are safeguarded?

This brings me to my next point about the local and how to factor in the larger national and the international. Advocates of post-growth either appeal to all those constituencies that favour stateless, self-suf-ficient communities, or else recognise that in a world of profoundly unequal natural and socio-economic resources, it is state institutions that will need to redistribute resources and provide vital co-ordinating and regulatory roles. Self-regulating market societies have *never* existed

---

10 Tim Jackson, *Prosperity Without Growth*, p.192.
11 *Ibid*, p.208.

and as it is clear, lightly regulated markets continue to produce human misery and ecological catastrophes. Therefore, we cannot naively support a new post-growth world where each community organisation is only answerable to its local members or constituents. This is a recipe for widespread failure due to abuse or conflicts between privileged and deprived communities with social and class divisions, despite the well-intentioned desires of existing or future participants. Hence, the need for Jackson and others to spell out how the crucial connections between a variety of local organisations and the mutual needs of both locals and non-locals can be democratically pursued. In a pluralist post-growth democracy where a variety of values and practices bloom, it is not enough to have an economic and institutional plan of how the local community interacts with the national and international. Without a prevailing general moral commitment to care for and help others, to share resources and skills with strangers, scarcity will inevitably lead to conflict and undermine the sources of good will.

c. Neither 'green growth' nor degrowth

Standing between supporters of 'green growth' and degrowth are a range of post-Keynesian and Marxist critics of neo-liberal capitalism. Many are still trapped in a pre-environmental consciousness and either favour anti-austerity policies based on increasing aggregate demand (through wage-led growth and household consumption) or else believe that overthrowing capitalist hegemony will somehow inevitably solve all social and environmental problems. Others support various technological utopian solutions and eco-socialist policies but do not endorse degrowth strategies, either because they mistakenly associate this solely with radical green simplicity (an austere lifestyle rejected by a majority of the working class), or because they still view economic growth as absolutely necessary to solving inequality.

Political economist Ian Gough comes from a neo-Marxist background and belongs to a minority of radical economists who devote considerable energy to examining the relationship between social welfare and environmental policies. His recently published book *Heat, Greed and Human Need*[12] was written at approximately the same time as this book. While Gough covers some of the territory I have traversed in previous chapters, he employs quite a different methodology. Gough presents an important

---

12 Ian Gough, *Heat, Greed and Human Need: Climate Change, Capitalism and Sustainable Well-being*, Edward Elgar, Cheltenham, 2017.

argument about the role of states in resolving existing environmental and social welfare problems that is highly pertinent to 'green growth' and degrowth. He veers between neo-Marxist critique and social democratic reform, standing mid-way between 'green growth' and degrowth.

Gough argues that supporters of 'green growth' are preoccupied with the eco-efficiency of production and rates of decarbonisation but pay little attention to the essential links between patterns of consumption and greenhouse gases.[13] Advocates of 'green growth' also fail to prioritise reducing social inequality or to address how changes to consumption and decarbonisation could be implemented in a socially egalitarian manner. Yet, although sympathetic to the objective of post-growth, Gough regards degrowth as a political non-starter because it is incompatible with capitalism and is rejected by too many constituencies. All social reform agendas, he argues, whether social democratic, green or eco-socialist, depend on tax revenues generated by capitalist growth regimes. How then can governments raise sufficient revenue while challenging the very mode of production and consumption that would result in massive economic disruption flowing from degrowth? He concludes that the "only sure ways to provide security of income in a post-growth society will be to tax or socialise a substantial part of private wealth" and moreover, "to avoid a devastating impact on material living standards it will be necessary to question and partially dismantle a defining feature of capitalism – the private ownership of the means of production."[14]

Given that capitalist countries have presided over multiple crises like the falling share of wages in national income, mass unemployment, cuts to the funding of adequate public services and early signs of dangerous climate breakdown, Gough proposes a three-stage transitional strategy for sustainable wellbeing. Stage one is 'green growth' that drives the 2015 Paris agenda of renewable energy and decarbonisation. He then proposes an intermediate stage of 'recomposed consumption' that will require "new top-down 'eco-social policies', to tax high-carbon luxuries, ration carbon at the household level, and socialise new areas of consumption."[15] This second stage will also require 'upstream prevention' by governments acting across environmental, social and economic domains of public policy such as health service provision.

Gough's aim of 'recomposing consumption' is designed "to develop a safe 'consumption corridor' between *minimum* standards, allowing every individual to live a good life, and *maximum* standards, ensuring a

13 *Ibid*, p.198 and Chapter Three.
14 *Ibid*, p.181.
15 *Ibid*, p.198.

limit on every individual's use of natural and social resources."[16] In other words, this intermediate stage would require the development of new eco-welfare states at national levels. All kinds of citizen and government discussions about combatting hyper-consumption, plus a suite of tax measures, penalties on advertising and other policies would facilitate and complement the move to the stage of 'recomposed consumption'. Once these two stages were developed and successfully applied, it would be easier to transition to the third stage of post-growth necessary for a socially just and sustainable post-capitalist society.

I agree with many of the sharply observed insights provided by Gough, as his book is one of the better analyses of the twin socio-economic and environmental crises of capitalism. There are, however, several areas that could be strengthened to become a more powerful argument for necessary social change. Take, for example, 'recomposed consumption'. Gough provides insufficient discussion of how the component elements of consumption – durable goods, non-durable goods and services – could be reconfigured not just in terms of minimising carbon emissions but also very importantly in achieving a broader form of resources sustainability. This is something I have tried to address in Chapter Five. On the positive side, it is possible to see a 'recomposed consumption' based on households and individuals changing their patterns of consumption with the assistance of state institutions. The 'safe consumption corridor', to minimise carbon emissions, could be achieved if governments boost the social state, that is, provide universal basic services to achieve what Gough calls 'upstreaming prevention'. Carbon emissions from non-durable household consumption, such as transport fuel and food production, could also be significantly reduced through greater provision of non-fossil fuelled public transport and non-chemical based local food production. The same is true of other aspects of consumption, namely, the need for a qualitative reappraisal and possible reduction of the many services used by households that constitute the third part of consumption currently provided by private businesses. Some of these services are not carbon-intensive or wasteful, while others in retailing, financial services, private health, information technology and hospitality are based on highly exploitative low-paid labour, unnecessary over-supply and monopoly capitalist rentier platforms geared to excessive fees and rampant tax avoidance.

Many of these durable and non-durable goods are imported and would affect trade and capital flows. Gough and 'steady-state' advocates

16 *Ibid*, pp.197-98.

while aware of necessary international political economic changes to trade, capital flows, tourism, labour migration flows and value chain processes beyond the nation state, largely fail to spell these out. There are also some parallels between Gough's three-stage transition and the old orthodox Marxist 'stages' of history – feudal, capitalist and socialist – which humanity would have to go through in order to reach communism. The controversial old question was always whether the socialist revolution would only come after the bourgeois revolution and would it occur within one nation or internationally? These are debates that polarised socialists over one hundred years ago. The same is now happening in relation to sustainability – whether 'green growth' or post-growth. Do countries have to go through the 'green growth' stage before they can implement 'recomposed consumption', or can these strategies be implemented simultaneously?

In fact, the weakest part of Gough's three-stage transition relates to his reliance on the seriously flawed and historically obsolete notion of different types of states used by the Varieties of Capitalism School (VoC). Gough, Jackson and many 'green growth' advocates are fully aware of the global ramifications of carbon emissions. Yet, when it comes to 'recomposing consumption' and developing new 'eco-social states', their analyses are confined to the UK, EU or OECD countries. Gough sees the best chance of developing a new 'eco-welfare state' in those 'social democratic' welfare states and 'coordinated market economies' such as Sweden or Germany rather than in 'liberal market economies' of the US, Canada, Australia and his own country – the United Kingdom. Currently, this argument seems vaguely plausible except for two crucial factors. First, that the VoC model is parochial and obsolete and second, that the academic ideal types of 'welfare state' and 'climate state' or 'environmental state' are misleading ways of understanding contemporary capitalist countries and what is needed to develop social change policies.

Misconceptions of 'Environmental States' and Post-Growth Strategies

Far too many social welfare analysts in developed capitalist countries still adhere to variations of Gosta Esping-Andersen's 'Three Worlds of Welfare' (Scandinavian 'social democratic', Anglo-American 'liberal' and various European conservative or 'corporatist' countries such as

Germany).[17] Since the 1980s, neo-liberal practices have merged with old social democratic welfare institutions in Scandinavian countries. Although still characterised by significantly different levels of social expenditure, the 'Three Worlds' have moved closer in the direction of fused practices characterised by varying degrees of neo-liberalism, as well as earlier social democratic or corporatist and conservative practices overlapping or combining with neo-liberal marketising incursions. In Germany, Austria and other countries with welfare based on former conservative religious notions of the family and the role of women, market liberalisation has eroded these conservative and corporatist social conditions without providing extensive egalitarian wage and other forms of equality for women.

Importantly, none of the European 'welfare states' engages in significant or explicit decommodification practices that threaten market dominance. Instead, welfare budgets remain much higher in France and Scandinavian countries compared with Anglo-American countries, but there is a much more conscious policy to complement and adopt market practices rather than to create larger decommodified spheres in key social care, education and other services. Crucially, Esping-Andersen's models were developed in a world where the Atlantic countries were the leading centres of capitalism. The 'Three Worlds' are inapplicable to southern European countries, as well as to former Communist countries in Eastern Europe. By 2002, Esping-Andersen recognised that his earlier 'Three World' model was unrepresentative and belonged to an earlier historical phase of capitalism. At the height of neo-liberalism and 'Third Way' policies, he called for a 'new welfare state' that is child centred, provides security for the aged and is women-centred.[18] Family, state and market are three pillars of welfare in OECD countries. However, the old family welfare policy geared to the male bread winner is obsolete, he argued, given the mass entry of women into the paid labour market, high youth unemployment and the demand for both child-care and quality education for children to boost their 'life chances'. Esping-Andersen also believed that major changes within markets and cuts to state taxes, privatisation and so forth, necessitated a reappraisal of how market, family and state functioned as 'pillars' in the new political economic climate in Europe. Within a few years after his call for a new welfare state, Esping-Andersen's proposed reforms were rendered inadequate in a Europe

17 Gøsta Esping-Andersen, *The Three Worlds of Welfare Capitalism,* Princeton University Press, Princeton, 1990.
18 Gøsta Esping-Andersen with Duncan Gallie, Anton Hemerijck, and John Myles, *Why We Need a New Welfare State,* Oxford University Press, Oxford, 2002.

suffering from the Great Recession and years of austerity.

For all Esping-Andersen's positive emphasis on the need for a new child and women-centred welfare state that also raised security for the aged as a high priority, this model was largely cocooned in Europe. First, Esping-Andersen and the VoC analysts are too narrow in their approach to contemporary market societies. Their frameworks are incapable of understanding how the non-existent, weak or quite different forms of welfare provisions and services function in the growth centres of global capitalism, especially leading Asian capitalist countries with enormous populations. It is Latin American, African and Asian countries where the family and extended kinship structures are often the main or only 'pillar' of welfare, despite large numbers of women performing paid work. Asian countries now account for a growing part of global production and consumption within the context of quite different cultural and political traditions such as the widespread absence of parliamentary democracy and poorly developed state provision of social security. Second, these Euro-centric analyses do not say anything about crucial environmental issues and how decarbonisation or 'sustainable capitalism' affects the future of a socially just welfare system, as well as sustainable incomes and public services.

Any 'green growth' or post-growth political strategies involving state institutions cannot afford to rely on old and narrow models that ignore or exclude the momentous global historical changes occurring in developing societies. Yet, the Atlantic-orientated, pre-environmentalist VoC school continue to use typologies similar to Esping-Andersen's, and focus primarily on 'liberal market economies' and 'co-ordinated market economies' (CME). Interestingly, China has more 'coordinated market' activity than any European country with this CME label attached. However, China is excluded because it is not a parliamentary democracy while Austria is considered to be fine as a CME even though it has authoritarian neo-fascists in government.

The VoC approach is also influential with various environmental academics (including Gough and Jackson) who primarily focus on EU countries and write in journals such as *Environmental Politics*.[19] Emerging out of the global political disputes over decarbonisation policies, these academics argue that a 'climate state', 'green state' or 'environmental state' – the name changes from author to author – is emerging just like the 'welfare state' did a generation or two ago. None believe that

---

19 See Andreas Duit, Peter H. Feindt and James Meadowcroft, 'Greening Leviathan: the rise of the environmental state?', *Environmental Politics*, vol.25, no.1, 2016, pp.1-23 and in the same issue Ian Gough, 'Welfare states and environmental states: a comparative analysis', pp.24-47.

these new 'environmental states' are large enough or powerful enough at the moment to put environmental needs above collective business needs. But could they become so in coming years?

I do not have space here to discuss the numerous problems associated with these ideal types of the 'environmental state'. Rather, I wish to discuss the political implications of such a misleading approach in understanding the character and structural roles of state institutions. One can readily accept the growth of numerous government policies, agencies and forms of regulation related to natural resources, decarbonisation and all kinds of urban environmental issues. However, all these government departments, agencies and laws do not add up to a coherent 'environmental state' any more than a range of departments, pensions, laws, taxes and other activities constitutes a 'welfare state'. It is common to use the term 'welfare state' as a shorthand term to describe disparate policies and practices ranging from government benefits categories, public housing, health, employment, education and training or child care, right through to aged care, energy and food subsidies as well as some elements of the criminal justice system. Each one of these diverse segments evolved in a more or less ad hoc manner over many decades due to public campaigns, workers' struggles, business agendas, competing electoral promises and so forth. Rather than coherent but distinct 'three worlds of welfare', the opposite is the case. It is impossible to find a set of local and national state institutions and elected governments in each OECD country that do not preside over widespread inconsistencies characterised by jealously guarded and conflicting departmental cultures and policies, tax regulations, old and new benefits entitlements, legal statutes and numerous other areas of 'welfare management' and socio-economic policy. Importantly, the administrators and policy-makers within local and national state institutions are not equivalent to an individual subject that acts and speaks with one voice.

It is true that social democratic or liberal and conservative governments have tried to shape and impose a coherent political logic on the totality of these services. Yet, the electoral turnover of governments in most countries (other than long-serving social democratic governments in Nordic countries prior to the 1990s) has resulted in hybrid policies or various entrenched institutional practices that were too difficult to comprehensively overhaul and systematise. Even theorists of the so-called new 'environmental state' such as Sweden's Andreas Duit, acknowledges that the preceding level or character of a country's 'welfare state' or democracy has not determined the main structural character of the various 'environmental states'.[20] This is important because it undermines the hopes of Gough, Jackson and others that social democratic and 'coordinated market economies' will be more likely to lay the foundations for post-growth state institutions.

The reality is that it is misleading to categorise any individual country's set of state apparatuses according to whether it is a 'welfare state' or an 'environmental state'. Some countries are clearly more favourably disposed than others in regard to implementing renewable energy and protecting their environments. In the 1950s and 1960s, many social democrats believed that the 'welfare state' could lead to the evolution of capitalism into socialism once the market had been sufficiently curbed and 'civilised'. Since the 1980s, neo-liberal governments have shattered these social democratic illusions by trying to ensure (but not always succeeding) that all OECD countries only provide very limited non-market solutions to people in poverty or suffering from disadvantage. Yet, those who label new state activities the 'environmental state' hope that they will eventually grow in size and power to be able to prioritise environmental values over market interests, just like they imagined was once supposedly the case for the social democratic 'welfare state'.

If we look at the major policies of a country like Germany, a state that the 'environmental state' theorists admire as a leader or model, the overall picture is far from attractive or promising. It is true that Germany has developed renewable energy through its *energiewende* and support for global decarbonisation and ecological modernisation.[21] But seeing Germany's relationship to Europe and the world primarily through its 'climate state' policies is partial at best and illusory at worst. Instead, Germany's environmental policies are far outweighed by its role as the main enforcer of punishing austerity measures in the Eurozone that have caused social pain for tens of millions. Part of Germany's export-driven capitalist accumulation is aided by its marketing of ecologically modernised products. Yet, environmental issues come second to its intimate dealings with authoritarian and proudly illiberal regimes. Germany's main trading partners are the illiberal Visegrád group (Poland, Hungary, Czech Republic and Slovakia) followed by authoritarian China, anti-environmental Trump-led America and Germany's EU neighbours such

---

20 Andreas Duit, 'The four faces of the environmental state: environmental governance regimes in 28 countries', *Environmental Politics*, vol.25, no.1, 2016, pp. 69-91.

21 Robyn Eckersley, 'National identities, international roles, and the legitimation of climate leadership: Germany and Norway compared', *Environmental Politics*, vol.25 no.1, 2016, pp. 180-221.

as France, Austria and the Netherlands.[22] In other words, becoming an 'environmental state' can be a narrow and costly objective if it goes hand in hand with either imposing social injustice domestically and within the EU, or championing trade well ahead of any concern for anti-democratic and unsustainable growth practices in key trading partners across the world.

Instead of seeing countries through the 'rose tinted' lens of either the 'environmental' or 'welfare state', it is necessary to not lose sight of quite contradictory actual and potential state roles and relations: on the one hand, environmental sustainability and welfare social justice practices that clash with some or many business practices and institutional objectives; on the other hand, the inseparable relationship between strictly limited environmental policies as well as welfare benefits and services that either complement capitalist production or do not threaten dominant market relations.

What stands out is that all capitalist societies with complex state institutions simultaneously pursue anti-welfare and anti-environment policies that contradict and make a mockery of other state departments and agencies in the same country pursuing environmental and social justice objectives. For instance, if we use the logic of theorists of the 'environmental state', then why not call most of the large G20 countries 'warfare states' as they spend far less on the environment than they do on all kinds of military forces, R&D, intelligence agencies and budgetary outlays that foster cognate industries devoted to military production and exports. Also, why not simply call them 'capitalist states' (as Marxists do) given that state institutions devote a majority of national fiscal resources and administrative activity to protecting, subsidising and facilitating every facet of the material and immaterial needs of private enterprise through a multitude of agencies and departments – a significant part of which is cleaning up the social and environmental mess caused by markets.

However, states do not just steer and intervene in the so-called external 'economy'. Almost forty years ago, I criticised both liberals and Marxists for creating artificially rigid divisions between 'the state', 'civil society' and the 'economy'.[23] Everything does not belong to either 'ideological state apparatuses' or 'repressive state apparatuses', as the old Althusserians use to proclaim. While it is necessary to distinguish between public

---

22 *Foreign Trade Ranking of Germany's trading partners in foreign trade 2017*, Statistisches Bundesamt (Destatis) 23 March 2018, p.2.

23 See my analysis 'On The State of The State: Marxist Theories After Leninism', *Theory And Society*, Vol.7 Nos.1 and 2, 1979, pp.199-242 and *Beyond the State? Dominant Theories and Socialist Strategies*, MacMillan, Basingstoke, 1983, ch.2.

and private sectors, these 'boundaries' are fluid and state institutions have long been part of 'the economy' and 'civil society'. This can be seen in the employment of millions of workers, the operation of state-owned enterprises, the role of states as generators of aggregate demand through the provision of social income, joint partnerships with businesses in public/private ventures, cultural organisations and media. One should also add state investments in infrastructure, education, health and pharmaceutical industries, R&D, the militarised sector and environmental and urban heritage protection for tourist industries. Hence, the notion of a separate 'environmental state' or 'welfare state' is only superficially valid if viewed through the lens of the interconnection between environmental and welfare activities with everyday business and social practices.

On the positive side, the very centrality of state institutions, in all facets of everyday production and consumption means that changing and extending state institutions could also lay the foundations for the shift to a post-growth society, if mass support for this agenda is mobilised. A sympathetic government could certainly nurture self-managed collectives and other forms of participatory democratic communities at local and national levels. But it would be illusory to think that these horizontal 'collaborative commons' could become the dominant form of institutional relations and meet the desperately needed redistribution of globally scarce environmental and material resources. There is much that is attractive in anarchist, self-managed socialist, green self-sufficiency and other models of grass roots critiques of the abuses perpetuated by hierarchical state apparatuses. Nevertheless, one does not need to defend the deficiencies and undemocratic character of existing parliamentary and authoritarian political administrative institutions to recognise that the sheer scale and complexity of national and global problems are too large to be resolved predominantly at local level. Importantly, insofar as revolution is a mirage and millions of people will need to vote on whether they support the reorganisation of society into self-managed cooperatives or 'commons', the prospect of any such transition in the next twenty years in countries with free elections is remote at best.

Global Crossroads: Post-Carbon Capitalism or Post-Growth Sustainability

I will leave an analysis of the social groups and classes likely to support or oppose a post-growth society to my companion book *Capitalism Versus Democracy*. In the meantime, any local or national pathway to post-growth sustainability that ignores uneven and volatile global conditions is bound to either fail or be buffeted by external developments and conflicts. Gough's three-stage transition, for example, may not develop beyond stage one at the national level, let alone globally. It is clear that in major authoritarian countries like China and Russia, or deeply divided countries such as India, the US, Brazil or Nigeria, the very notion of stage two ('recomposed consumption') is, for the medium-term future a non-starter. The same is true for most countries when it comes to radical forms of degrowth. The obstacles in many countries to any transition to a radical grass roots democratic model seem to be of little concern to proponents of self-management or green self-sufficiency who can appear more pre-occupied with utopian face-to-face relations at the local level. If we rule out the dystopian nightmare of a single world government, this still leaves eco-socialists and a variety of green reformers with the difficult problem of alternative decision-making institutions. Are we to have federations of local councils in combinations with national and supranational state institutions, or national governments with internationalist values, or mixtures of national and supranational regional institutions like a democratised EU? There are certainly numerous proposals of alternative models to replace existing EU institutions. However, although it is currently very important both economically and politically, the undemocratic European Union is, nonetheless, too weak to set global agendas, even if other countries wished to follow its model. Beset with numerous crises and, with less than 450 million (after Brexit), it is seventeen times smaller than the current world's population of 7.6 billion. Even in purely market terms, the EU, like the US and Japan, continues to lose global market share to new regional powers.

Hence, both VoC models of European capitalist countries and mainstream analysts of future 'emergent markets' are too narrow and unreliable foundations for either 'sustainable capitalism' or a post-capitalist, post-growth future. For example, former chairman of Goldman Sachs Asset Management, Jim O'Neill (who coined the term 'BRICS' in 2001) subsequently coined another term, the 'Next-11' (South Korea, Mexico, Indonesia, Turkey, Iran, Egypt, Nigeria, the Philippines, Pakistan, Bangladesh, and Vietnam) to describe those most populous countries likely to emerge as leading capitalist countries. O'Neill acknowledges that these countries have little in common and despite having a combined population of 1.5 billion that is larger than either China's or India's, their collective GDP equals only half that of China.[24]

---

24 Jim O'Neill, 'The "Next Eleven" and the World Economy', *Project Syndicate*, 18 April, 2018.

I mention O'Neill's list as typical of the numerous market forecasts regularly produced by business consultancy firms all seeking to identify the next generation of growth countries after Brazil, Russia, India, China and South Africa (who have hardly all turned out to be economic success stories). If mainstream analysts are preoccupied with identifying new and future engines of growth, many progressive social change advocates are still largely focussed on familiar but parochial American and European types of capitalism.

However, the crises of unsustainable capitalism are probably going to be far more consequential in developing societies where the bulk of the world's population resides. Remember, that rapid industrial development over the next 20 to 30 years is a 'future' much closer than most people imagine it to be. We must not confuse the old 'limits to growth' scenarios, such as 'peak oil', with the far more destructive consequences on eco-systems of potential high-consumption lifestyles for an additional five to seven billion people. The old 'North' and 'South' models need to be abandoned given that middle-income countries, especially in Asia and some Latin American and African countries, are exceeding OECD growth rates, carbon emission rates, inequality rates and environmental destruction rates. Far greater differentiation needs to be made between low and middle-income countries that particularly suffer from unequal trade rules, rapacious commodities extractivism, labour exploitation and other negative conditions, and those ascending industrialising countries of the so-called 'South' that exploit other weaker 'Southern' countries just like their developed OECD capitalist counterparts.

In 1999, Wolfgang Sachs wrote an influential work on 'sustainable development' as an oxymoron. Critiquing the concept of endless growth and the exploitation of the poor countries of the 'South' by the rich countries of the 'North', Sachs argued that "both the crisis of justice and the crisis of nature suggest looking for forms of prosperity that would not require permanent growth. For the problem of poverty lies not in poverty but in wealth. And equally, the problem of nature lies not in nature but in over-development."[25] While I agree with most of Sachs' critique of capitalist models of development that destroy environments, the notion of 'sustainable development' should not be abandoned just because the World Bank and other ideologists of the market distort its meaning. Ultimately, 'development' is compatible with a post-growth

---

25 Wolfgang Sachs, 'Sustainable Development and the Crisis of Nature: On the Political Anatomy of an Oxymoron' in Frank Fischer and Maarten Hajer (eds.) *Living with Nature: Environmental Politics as Cultural Discourse,* Oxford University Press, Oxford, 1999, p.41.

society if social justice is to be attained. Post-growth advocates are opposed to incessant industrial growth and wasteful consumerism but are not opposed to the possibility of poor countries developing their essential services and infrastructure. Unfortunately, in the absence of mass radical movements, 'green growth' models are currently probably the most likely strategies that are politically viable, even though they are grossly deficient. These strategies may aim to raise several billion people up to the unsustainable affluent lifestyles enjoyed by majorities in OECD countries. But even this environmentally dangerous objective will fail unless advocates of 'green growth' also seriously embrace the goal of ending major forms of inequality – an objective that most businesses oppose. However, if 'green growth' does more than simply make capitalism run on green energy, and provides running water, electricity, sewage and other essential services, then these minimalist objectives will be a welcome achievement.

Crucially, there is no way that the earth's life support systems will cope with the further industrialisation of most low and middle-income countries geared to the rate of export-led development as has already occurred in North East Asian countries. Without an alternative form of limited industrialisation orientated to providing green infrastructure, housing and sustainable cities (rather than unsustainable and highly exploitative capitalist export-led commodity production and manufacturing), there is no hope for a sustainable earth. This new objective of limited green industrialisation must be combined with the provision of universal basic services and a 'recomposed consumption' for both developing societies and OECD countries. Failure to transform the composition of the three elements of affluent consumption (durable goods, non-durable goods, and services) in both developed capitalist countries and amongst the growing middle-classes in middle-income countries (who will soon be numerically greater than all people in OECD countries) spells ecosystem catastrophe further down the track.

Leaving aside post-growth prospects for the moment, the future development of 'green growth' sustainable democracies particularly rest on domestic politics within six powerful countries: China, the US, India, Japan, Germany and Russia which account for more than 60% of global greenhouse gas emissions. It is not that political action in most other countries is irrelevant or inconsequential. Far from it. Yet, it does mean that some or all of the six countries mentioned have a disproportionate influence on crucial areas, whether military, environmental, financial and general economic growth and stability. Although five of these countries are nominally representative parliamentary democracies, it is difficult to predict in which direction they will move and the extent of domestic reforms, let alone radical reforms that they may embrace. The paradox of China is that, as a 'command capitalist' authoritarian system it is able to push through major decarbonisation and modernisation programs. This is not the case for neighbouring India, which as a chaotic parliamentary democracy appears either incapable of, or too divided to implement. Being the country with the world's largest population, India's fragile eco-systems plus international pressures will require significant domestic policy changes regardless of which government is in power.

The Chinese Communist Party (CCP) with almost 90 million members (most of them managers, officials and business people) is light years away from the 'vanguard party of the proletariat'. It rules through a combination of the iron fist and limited forms of local democracy and social media criticism as well as consultative processes. This helps ensure that the Party's administrative structures are in touch with grass roots sentiments, thereby letting 'steam out' for better managerial purposes. The Chinese Communist leadership regards Gorbachev's 1980s democratisation reforms as a major mistake. Unless there is a profound economic crisis leading to the erosion of Communist power, it is therefore difficult to imagine that the CCP will embark on large-scale internal democratisation. Without internal Communist Party democratisation, one should not discount the possibility that any turbulent challenges from other domestic socio-political forces demanding, for example, a pluralist democracy, could result in civil war at worst, or American-style political paralysis at best. This is because democratisation could unleash deregulated market forces in the absence of large countervailing socialist and green parties. If greater regional divergences increase, combined with rising unemployment, social conflicts and disunity, all could make recent localised domestic unrest and wild cat strikes look like a picnic.

One of the authoritarian legacies of Soviet Communism is that the political culture in most post-Communist countries in Central Asia and Eastern Europe continues to be marked by conservative capitalist regimes – from Kazakhstan, Russia and the Ukraine to Poland, Hungary and the Balkan states – that practice a range of illiberal, racist, and socially intolerant and regressive policies. For China to further move in this direction would be a disaster for both the Chinese people and the world as a whole. The major challenge for democracy movements in China is to develop strategies that do not imitate failed market policies and institutions in other countries. If a mass democratic movement succeeds in getting the authoritarian CCP to abandon its repression and abuse of human rights, yet increases its regulation of private and state-owned businesses so that wealth is more equitably distributed, working conditions improved and destructive environmental practices drastically curbed, this will indeed be an alternative that helps transform China in the direction of a more democratic post-carbon society. As to post-growth, there is virtually no chance that this goal could gain legitimacy in China in the next decade or two given that even lower 2 to 3% annual rates of growth (normal for OECD countries) could cause serious domestic turbulence.

The US may be an old 'democracy' but it has been hamstrung by domestic political gridlock for decades. Unable to rejuvenate its problem-plagued cities and dilapidated infrastructure and underfunded public services, or solve high degrees of violence and deep-seated racial and other political cultural divisions, 'American democracy' is saddled with an archaic constitution that neither permits full democratic representation nor efficient government. As a global powerhouse, US domestic social and political economic problems fuel international military, economic and environmental crises and especially international gridlock. Nearly all major global crises – whether global warming, poverty and inequality, militarisation, or financial and economic support for highly negative corporate practices – are made much harder to resolve given American veto power and refusal to act as a co-operative rather than an obstructionist and interventionist global power.[26] It is not that Japan, China, India, Russia and the EU are acting in a selfless altruistic manner on these key crisis issues. However, the constantly re-elected very conservative American Congress and successive administrations actively block or disrupt progress for a range of vested domestic and international reasons.

While social democratic policies have gained increased support due to the campaigns of Bernie Sanders and others, the transition to 'green growth' social democracy (let alone post-growth) will face enormous obstacles to overcome deeply embedded conservative institutional structures. Conversely, the paradox of America is that it has the economic resources, technological know-how and creative talents to lead the world in innovative social and environmental reforms. Also, progressive ideas such as 'government as guaranteed employer for all' are already becoming popular as mainstream policies. The diversity of American society – from reactionary socio-political groups and regions to significant reform-orientated and culturally and environmentally aware populations – means that future developments are much less predictable

26 For an analysis of international gridlock, see Thomas Hale, David Held and Kevin Young, *Gridlock: Why Global Cooperation is Failing When We Need It Most*, Polity Press, Cambridge, 2013.

than indicated by the present-day political climate of the Trump era. It therefore remains an open question as to whether America will remain trapped in a backward looking political culture or finally breaks decades of gridlock and begins delivering domestic and international progressive change.

The significant replacement of fossil fuels by renewable energy in the next ten to twenty-five years could be a positive game changer. However, for oil and gas powers such as Russia, Saudi Arabia, Iran, Iraq, Nigeria and others, the consequences could range from manageable crises to political breakdown. We do not know how decades of conflict, especially in the Middle East, will be resolved once oil and gas lose their strategic importance in world military and economic affairs. Will US external and domestic policies change for the better once the fossil-fuel lobby loses its domestic and international leverage power, or will economic crises and political conflict inside Russia and Middle Eastern countries unleash a new wave of civil wars, terrorist threats and mass waves of refugees? Apart from the Saudis and others investing in non-fossil fuel sectors, there appears to be little or no forward planning to prepare fossil-fuel exporting countries for the disruptive domestic and international consequences that will follow any transition to renewable energy. Given these circumstances, policy analysts and social change movements must be prepared for the potentially major geo-political shocks that could flow from a far from smooth and problem-free transition away from fossil fuels. Unless democratic movements succeed in bringing about change, the authoritarian governments and their fossil-fuel corporate allies have little incentive in these countries to abandon their current base of political, economic and military power.

Meanwhile, both Germany and Japan share characteristics of being major exporting powers, albeit with different levels of dependence on fossil-fuel resources. Because their military ambitions were shaped by their defeat as former fascist powers, there is a propensity for these powers to use their economic weight rather than military capacities. Dependent on the American military umbrella, both Germany and Japan are caught between American rivalry with China and Russia. Although Japan has a large defensive military, preventing an outwardly re-militarised Japan will be crucial for regional peace in Asia. Despite containing oppositional green and other reform movements, Germany and Japan are both conservative societies that help counter radical reform movements in Europe and Asia. Germany's persistent blockage of anti-neo-liberal reforms within the EU is particularly short-sighted and could well result in the collapse of the Euro and the break-up of the EU, should the next financial crisis exacerbate internal European divisions. Given the strong possibility that export growth will stagnate or significantly decline in coming years, Germany and Japan face the difficult options of either clinging to old fiscal practices or undertaking major domestic socio-economic reforms. The implications for the EU and globally of any such move away from highly conservative policies by Germany and Japan will be crucial for the possible development of democratic post-growth agendas. Japan is not integrated into a supranational state, as is Germany. Hence, it is more likely that its domestic politics will be more immune to external political pressures. Germany's political culture is also much more favourably disposed to decarbonisation and will probably remain a leader in this area despite its conservative fiscal and monetary policies.

Since the collapse of the Bretton Woods system in 1971, there has been no international coordinating treaty of comparable power. Opponents of neo-liberalism have either retreated to Left and Right forms of protectionist/nationalist policies or failed to fill the policy vacuum left by Bretton Woods. Yet, a post-carbon and post-growth world cannot fall back on self-sufficient local communes or dangerous nationalist competitive mercantilism if the world is to avoid devastating crises. We need solutions to the following imbalances and problems:

First, authoritarian regimes currently control significant amounts of fossil fuels[27] but 'democracies' like the US resist international treaties. Oil and gas production is closely tied to both government and corporate corruption and the widespread violation of environmental safety standards. Furthermore, military expenditure and deployment is closely related to the preservation of existing energy sources and geo-political power. Post-carbon capitalist societies are possible without democratic governments. But no secure post-carbon democracies are possible in a world divided between authoritarian and democratic regimes unless countries defuse and de-escalate the current level of militarisation in preparation for the transition to a post-carbon world.

Second, financial capital and assets are heavily concentrated in the US, Europe, China and Japan but many low and middle-income developing countries desperately need capital to resolve their massive socio-economic and environmental problems. Most corporations and governments in developed capitalist countries currently have a vested interest in maintaining the status quo. The inability of developing countries to decarbonise and improve living conditions, or develop essential green infrastructure and limited industrial capacity (primarily for domestic needs rather than

---

27 See David Victor, David Hults and Mark Thurber (eds.) *Oil and Governance: State-Owned Enterprises and the World Energy Supply*, Cambridge University Press, Cambridge, 2012.

export industries), is a costly tragedy that developed capitalist countries cannot perpetuate indefinitely. The longer it takes for a new more comprehensive 'Bretton Woods' Mark Two to emerge that will facilitate international fiscal and monetary co-operation and vital assistance to weaker countries, the higher the likelihood that post-carbon transitions will be painful and very ugly processes in many countries.

Third, conventional economic growth and commodity production and consumption will continue destroying eco-systems in coming years but these dominant processes are ultimately unsustainable. Although extremely difficult, preventing disastrous climate breakdown has only an outside chance of success. Even if governments succeed in limiting global temperatures to 1.5°C or 2°C, avoiding climate chaos is in no way equivalent to achieving economic sustainability. No new national or international models of generating environmentally sustainable income and domestic social cooperation have emerged to cope with the inevitable crises that will follow in coming years once existing levels of trade and production are forced to be scaled back for environmental reasons. As I have argued, leading corporations and governments strongly favour absolute decoupling of growth from nature as a means of avoiding necessary and fundamental social change. Advocates of post-growth will need to further develop domestic and international policies that show how new forms of production, consumption and employment are possible in the highly likely eventuality that absolute decoupling of economic growth proves to be a mirage. Unfortunately, 'post-growth' movements are divided in their alternative policies between those market utopians who believe in 'sustainable businesses' (a modified capitalism without corporations) and others who advocate post-growth as post-capitalist social formations.[28]

---

28 See, for example, *The Post-Growth Alliance* (postgrowth.org) which already has fifty affiliated organisations and think-tanks from different countries committed to developing alternative social, economic and environmental policies, as well as practical sustainability measures for everyday living. While producing many valuable contributions, there are fundamental differences between the affiliated organisations in terms of their political priorities and their emphasis on either grass roots solutions or national and international interventions, as well as the degree to which they are anti-capitalist. For instance, The Post-Growth Institute is committed to not-for profit businesses rather than non-market models for the future. Its definition of post-growth economics is controversial. Accordingly, "Post-growth can be distinguished from similar concepts and movements (such as degrowth and steady state economics) in that it seeks to identify and build on what is already working, rather than focusing on what is not. Post-growth advocates try to encourage, connect and further develop already existing ideas, concepts, technologies, systems, initiatives, and actions. In this way, "post-growth" does not specify the answer to the limits-to-growth challenge, as "steady state economics" and "degrowth" attempt to do, but rather, seeks to understand and address this challenge from an evolving complex systems perspective." Clearly, this definition harbours market illusions about capitalism that would not be acceptable to other advocates of post-growth such as proponents of anti-capitalist degrowth.

Fourth, in order to tackle poverty and inequality through the creation of adequate caring services and employment, the definancialisation of skewed economies must include necessary international tax agreements and capital controls without which domestic reform agendas will be weakened or undermined. Should feared levels of job-destroying automation eventuate on a scale much larger and quicker than technological optimists currently deny, a concerted effort to close tax-havens, streamline international tax rates, reform domestic sources of revenue and generate new forms of income will all become imperative. For many years, there has been a great disparity in the levels and range of taxes collected by different governments that are owed to them – from as low as 10% to as high as 95%. Hence, the degree of corruption or legal loopholes tolerated in many countries all affect the ability to fund new social programs, particularly the ability of governments to act as 'employer of last resort'.

Fifth, outside the EU, there are currently no strong movements in the Asia-Pacific region, Latin America or Africa pushing for countries to establish socio-economic, cultural and environmental agreements and supranational political structures, other than narrow market-orientated trade pacts. Within the EU, the Left are divided between those who wish to break up the EU and others who want deeper EU-wide democratisation. Most national trade union movements, centrist social democratic parties and Right-wing conservative parties no longer articulate coherent and widely appealing visions of the good life. Instead, much of their energy is consumed by short-term electoral strategies or defensive industrial relations campaigns. Globally, the possibility of constructing post-carbon 'green growth' or post-growth democracies requires medium to long-term vision and planning. In a world where democratic decision-making could become confined to a small number of countries, and where borders could be closed, where political economic walls are erected and cultural intolerance flourishes, it may be quite possible to successfully decarbonise energy usage, but such countries would be the antithesis of a post-carbon or post-growth democracy.

Sixth, it is crucial for all those desiring egalitarian, environmentally sustainable and socially just societies not to become restricted and inward looking. New ways of protecting the vulnerable, enhancing living standards and protecting endangered habitats must be found without closing down international connections and retreating to parochial futures. Currently, as I have discussed, most of the models of degrowth or 'steady state' economies are local or national. Herman Daly, for example, is typical of those preoccupied with the national when he proclaims:

> Cosmopolitan globalism weakens national boundaries and the power of national and subnational communities, while strengthening the relative power of transnational corporations. Since there is no world government capable of regulating global capital in the global interest, …it will be necessary to make capital less global and more national.[29]

It is true that market globalism weakens many local communities. But it is an illusion to think that capitalism or the transition to post-capitalism will be able to continue if it is confined to the nation-state. More importantly, it is parochialism rather than cosmopolitanism that has long been the enemy of democracy and social justice. Without accepting the necessity of international connections and socio-economic processes, inward looking nationalism becomes a recipe for unsustainability and failure. Challenging disastrous forms of capitalist rule is not an either/or task of pursuing domestic democratising reforms or an international and cosmopolitan set of goals. Closing off one or the other option is a guarantee that both will fail. Just as one cannot have socialism in one country, so it is impossible to have strong post-carbon and post-growth democracies within just one nation-state. Whatever new political organisations and programs emerge, these will struggle to attract mass support unless they prioritise security and care. Prevalent notions of 'security' focus primarily on keeping populations safe from terrorists and unidentified military threats. Yet, in an age of increasing social dislocation and fearfulness, security must be redefined and take centre stage as the need to keep people safe from the lack or loss of jobs, or the lack or loss of income, housing, health and other essential conditions necessary for social and individual wellbeing.

Concluding Comments

I strongly support many of the values and objectives outlined by post-growth advocates. It is, however, not a minor quibble to raise critical questions about the respective democratic controls, power sharing, or relationship between local decision-making and non-market national planning of vital activities. The provision of everything from medicines and infrastructure, right through to essential services and hundreds of other needs cannot all be resourced or produced at the local level or even

---

29 Herman Daly, *Beyond Growth: The Economics of Sustainable Development*, Beacon Press, Boston, 1996, p.111.

at national level. If post-growth societies are to have a chance of success, it is first necessary to have at least some minimal idea of how highly integrated socio-economic relations and resources can be altered. Perhaps it is necessary in theory to 'disaggregate' and assess numerous key elements needed to keep a country running reasonably smoothly. Social change activists in each city or locality could begin the preparation of alternative policies by undertaking a 'stocktaking' or assessment of what can be funded, produced and organised in each local community and what human and natural resources will need to be provided by national state institutions or imported from other countries. Most people in the world will not have an immediate choice as to whether they wish to belong to a smaller local or national community or larger supranational entities such as the EU. The important thing is to guard against delusions of national self-sufficiency that are often fuelled by misconceived parochialism or dangerous nationalist political values. A difficult balance between preserving local eco-systems and contributing to international co-operation to assist those countries lacking resources will have to be negotiated.

I have argued for policies such as the major expansion of the 'social state' – of services that could generate employment, improve wellbeing and possibly result in a smaller ecological footprint if higher employment does not simply fuel the conventional aggregate demand for private consumer goods. Such a decommodifying strategy would increase the size of new public-sector activities through combinations of decentralised local cooperatives and other publicly funded community organisations linked to national and supranational institutional structures. At the moment, no such shift to increased levels of community-based and nationally and internationally provided public consumption would be politically possible or sustainable without a dramatic change in cultural values and political consciousness all aimed at altering priorities in both personal consumption and larger resource allocation. Without redefining what is meant by 'welfare' as well as the conventional roles and structures of existing public sectors, the debate over social justice and sustainability will remain bogged down by conservative notions of the relations between taxation, debt and growth.

It is common these days to hear advocates of radical change declaring that we need new positive narratives about the benefits of an alternative society rather than just focusing on crises and creating more fear and anxiety. I support these positive scenarios and their equivalents in developing countries that encounter far more desperate conditions than affluent countries. While I leave the discussion of political organisations and social change agents to the companion book *Capitalism*

Versus Democracy, a few brief preliminary words are necessary. There is a danger that positive counter-narratives against neo-liberalism will prove ineffective if these 'imagined futures' promote either an unattainable stateless utopia based upon abundance and unlimited freedom, or the delusion that one can retreat to the embedded 'national' but historically obsolete capitalism of the pre-1970s. Instead of reviving the past, it is imperative that social change activists develop new models of organising and administrating local and national public institutions, new fiscal and monetary policies, new objectives of delivering care and other essential services domestically and internationally.

It may be stating the obvious, but it is essential to reiterate this once again: short of revolution or enlightened despotism, the finest and most elaborate political manifestos are only as good as the support they can muster from nervous and conflicted electorates – populations simultaneously eager for solutions to their deteriorating conditions, yet frightened of the insecurity of the 'unknown' that social change will unleash. This insecurity is directly related to the crucial fact that no government around the world (or mainstream opposition parties) are currently either fully aware or well prepared for the multiple challenges flowing from the impending conflicts that will be caused by escalating environmental crises, unsustainable production and consumption, transformed labour markets and the inadequate nature of social security systems. Many now realise that doing nothing is far more dangerous to social and environmental wellbeing than struggling to replace failed and broken political economic policies and institutions. We will never get an ideal new system. But we are certainly able to construct societies that are infinitely better than the ones we live in at the moment.

Future social change movements will need to be based on a new form of radicalism that abandons utopian illusions and confronts the eco-system constraints within which we must all survive. Free-marketeers, technocrats, social democratic Keynesians, Marxist technological utopians and assorted authoritarian statists all share something in common – they either still refuse to fully recognise environmental limits or dream of artificially extending these limits through absolute decoupling techniques. Sadly, it is only a minority of anti-capitalist post-growth movements that have recognised that future societies must radically rethink the future of growth. One thing is certain, the new world will look very different to the present world as a consequence of either the convulsions caused by unsustainable growth, or as a result of attempts to restructure existing dominant practices and institutions. The 'fictional expectations' that guide our present action may turn out to be different to what we hope and wish for. Yet, this should not deter us from having clear socio-political goals. Better to attempt to shape the future than remain passive victims of hostile forces. James Baldwin said it well when he pointed out during the difficult years of black civil rights struggles: "Not everything that is faced can be changed but nothing can be changed until it is faced."[30]

---

30 Baldwin's quotation spoken in Raoul Peck's 2016 film, *I Am Not Your Negro*.

Abridged Bibliography

Acemoglu, D. and Robinson, J. *Why Nations Fail: The Origins of Power, Prosperity, and Poverty*, Crown, New York, 2012.

\--------- and Verdier, T. *Can't We All Be More Like Scandinavians? Asymmetric Growth and Institutions in an Interdependent World?*, Massachusetts Institute of Technology Department of Economics, Working Paper Series, Paper 12-22, August 2012.

Aden, N. 'The Roads to Decoupling: 21 Countries are Reducing Carbon Emissions While Growing GDP', *World Resources Institute*, Washington, April 5, 2016.

Adorno, T.W. 'Spengler after the Decline' in *Prisms* trans. by Samuel and Shierry Weber, London 1967

\--------- '*Was Spengler Right*', *Encounter*, January 1966, pp.25-28.

Aglietta, M. 'America's Slowdown', *New Left Review*, 100, July/August 2016, pp.119-29.

Akaev, A. and Korotayev, A. 'Global Economic Dynamics of the Forthcoming Years: A Forecast', *Structure and Dynamics*, vol.10, no.1, 2017, pp.1-23.

Alexander, S. 'Planned economic contraction: the emerging case for degrowth', *Environmental Politics*, vol.21, no.3, 2012, pp.349-368.

\--------- 'What is Degrowth? Envisioning a Prosperous Descent', *The Simplicity Collective*, November 2, 2015.

\--------- Introduction to 'Sufficiency Economy', *The Simplicity Collective*, August 11, 2015.

\--------- 'If everyone lived in an 'ecovillage' the Earth would still be in trouble', *The Conversation*, June 26, 2015.

Alperovitz, G., Speth, J.G. and Guinan, J. *The Next System Project: New Political-Economic Possibilities for the 21ˢᵗ Century*, March 2015.

Altieri, M. and Toledo, V. 'The agroecological revolution in Latin America: rescuing nature, ensuring food sovereignty and empowering peasants', *The Journal of Peasant Studies,* Vol. 38, No. 3, July 2011, 587–612.

Alvaredo, F. et al, *World Inequality Report 2018*, World Inequality Lab, Paris, December, 2017.

Altvater, E., Moore, J. et.al. *Anthropocene or Capitalocene?: Nature, History, and the Crisis of Capitalism,* PM Books, Oakland 2016.

American Petroleum Institute, 'Natural Gas and the US Model for 'Decoupling', *Energy Tomorrow Blog*, April 12, 2016.

Anderson, P. 'Editorial Renewals', *New Left Review*, 1, Jan-Feb, 2000, pp.5-24.

Atkinson, A. B. *Inequality What can be Done?*, Harvard University Press, Cambridge, 2015.

Baccaro, L. and Pontusson, J. 'Rethinking Comparative Political Economy: The Growth Model Perspective', in special edition of *Politics & Society*, vol.44, no 2, 2016, pp. 175-207.

Baldwin, R. interview with Nelson, E. 'Brace yourself: the most disruptive phase of globalization is just beginning', *Quartz*, 7 December, 2016.

Bank for International Settlements, *Monetary Policy: inching towards normalisation*, Basle, 25 June, 2017.

Baran, P. and Sweezy, P. *Monopoly Capital*, Monthly Review Press, New York, 1966.

Bauwens, M. and Iacomella, F. 'Peer to Peer Economy and New Civilization Centered Around the Sustenance of the Commons' in Bollier, D. and Helfrich, S. (eds), *The Wealth of the Commons: A World Beyond Market & State*, Levellers Press, Amherst, 2016.

--------- and Onzia, J. 'A Commons Transition plan for the City of Ghent', *Commons Transition*, 8 September, 2017.

Beckert, J. *Capitalist Dynamics: Fictional Expectations and the Openness of the Future*, MPIfG Discussion Paper 14/7, Max Planck Institute for the Study of Societies, Cologne, March 2014.

--------- *Imagined Futures Fictional Expectations and Capitalist Dynamics,* Harvard University Press, Cambridge, 2016.

Bell, S. and Hindmoor, A. 'Are the major global banks now safer? Structural continuities and change in banking and finance since the 2008 crisis', *Review of International Political Economy*, vol. 25, no.1, 2018, pp.1-27.

Benson-Armer, R., Noble, S. and Thiel, A. *The consumer sector in 2030: Trends and questions to consider*, McKinsey & Company, December 2015.

Birtchnell, T. Urry, J., Cook, C. and Curry, A. *Freight Miles: The Impacts of 3D Printing on Transport and Society*, Lancaster University, 2013.

Block, F. 'Swimming Against the Current: The Rise of a Hidden Developmental State in the United States', *Politics & Society*, Vol. 36 No. 2, June 2008, pp. 169-206.

-------- and Keller, M. 'Where do innovations come from?' in F Block and M Keller (eds), *State of Innovation: The US government's role in technology development*, Paradigm, New York 2010.

Borjas, G. 'Immigration and Globalization: A Review Essay', *Journal of Economic Literature*, vol. 53, no. 4, December 2015, pp. 961-74.

Böröcz, J. 'Global Inequality in Redistribution: For a World-Historical Sociology of (Not) Caring', *Intersections East European Journal of Society and Politics*, vol.2 no.2, 2016, pp.57-83.

Bourne, J. K. *The End of Plenty: The Race to Feed a Crowded World*, WW. Norton & Co, New York, 2015.

Bowman, A. et al. 'Central Bank-Led Capitalism?', *Seattle Law Review*, vol.36, 2013, pp. 455–87.

Boyer, R. 'The Present Crisis. A Trump for a Renewed Political Economy', *Review of Political Economy*, Volume 25, Number 1 January 2013, 1–38.

Bridgestone Group, 'Looking Ahead to the World in 2050' *Bridgestone Group Environmental Report 2015*.

Bryan, D. and Rafferty, M. *Capitalism with derivatives: a political economy of financial derivatives, capital and class*, Palgrave Macmillan, New York, 2006.

-------- 'Financial Derivatives as Social Policy Beyond Crisis', *Sociology*, vol.48, no.5, 2014, pp.887-903.

-------- 'Reframing austerity: financial morality, savings and securitization', *Journal of Cultural Economy*, vol.10, no.4, 2017, pp.339-355.

-------- and Wigan, D. 'Capital unchained: finance, intangible assets and the double life of capital in the offshore world', *Review of International Political Economy*, Vol. 24, No. 1, 2017, pp.56–86.

Buendía, L. and Palazuelos, E. 'Economic growth and welfare state: a case study of Sweden', *Cambridge Journal of Economics*, vol.38, 2014, pp.761-777.

Bueskens, P. 'Mothers And Basic Income: The Case For An Urgent Intervention', *New Matilda*, 23, February, 2017.

Burlamaqui, L. and Kattel, R. 'Development as leapfrogging, not convergence, not catch-up: towards schumpeterian theories of finance and development', *Review of Political Economy*, vol.28, no.2, 2016, pp. 270-288.

Carolan, M. *The Real Cost of Cheap Food*, Routledge Earthscan, London, 2012.

Carrington, D. 'Global pollution kills 9m a year and threatens survival of human societies', *The Guardian*, 20 October 2017.

--------- 'Earth has lost half of its wildlife in the past 40 years, says WWF', *The Guardian,* 1 October 2014.

Catephores, G. 'The Imperious Austrian: Schumpeter as Bourgeois Marxist', *New Left Review*, May/June 1994, pp.3-30.

Chandy, R. K. and. Tellis, G. J. 'The Incumbent's Curse? Incumbency, Size, and Radical Product Innovation', *Journal of Marketing*, July 2000, pp.1-17.

China Labour Bulletin, 'China's social security system', *China Labour Bulletin,* Hong Kong, 2017.

Christoff, P. (ed.) *Four Degrees of Global Warming*, Earthscan/Routledge, London, 2013.

--------- 'The promissory note: Cop21 and the Paris Climate Agreement', *Environmental Politics*, vol.25, no.5 2016, pp.765-787.

Chui, M. Manyika, J. Miremadi, M. 'Where machines could replace humans – and where they can't (yet)', *McKinsey Quarterly*, McKinsey & Company, July 2016, pp.1-16.

Cobham, A. and Jansky, P. *Global distribution of revenue loss from tax avoidance: Re-estimation and country results*, United Nations University-Wider, Working Paper 2017/55, March 2017.

Cohen, D. 'Economic sovereignty: A Delusion', *Social Europe*, 12 September 2017.

Colebrook, C. *Measuring What Matters: Improving the indicators of economic performance*, IPPR Commission on Economic Justice, London, April 2018.

Coursinavos, J. 'Political aspects of innovation', *Research Policy*, vol. 38, 2009, pp. 1117–1124.

--------- *Cycles, Crises, Innovation: Path to Sustainable Development – a Kaleckian-Schumpeterian Synthesis*, Edward Elgar, Cheltenham, 2012.

Coyle, D. *GDP: A Brief but Affectionate History*, Princeton University Press, Princeton, New Jersey, 2014.

Crouch, C. 'Privatised Keynesianism: An Unacknowledged Policy Regime', *British Journal of Politics and International Relations*, Vol. 11, 2009, pp.382–399.

Cuboniks, L. *Xenofeminism A Politics for Alienation*, laboriacuboniks.net 2015.

D'Alisa, G. Demaria, F. and Kallis, G. (eds.), *Degrowth: A Vocabulary for a New Era*, Routledge, London, 2014.

Dalla Costa, M. and James, S. *The Power of Women and the Subversion of the Community*, 2nd edition. Falling Wall, Bristol, 1973.

Daly, H. *Beyond Growth: The Economics of Sustainable Development*, Beacon Press, Boston, 1996.

--------- and Czech, B. 'In My Opinion: The steady state economy – what it is, entails, and connotes', *Wildlife Society Bulletin*, no.2, 2004, pp.598-605.

Davidson, R. 'Between Como and confinement: Gramsci's early Leninism', *Marxist Left Review*, no.14, Winter 2017.

Davies, R. *Public enemies: the role of global public goods in aid policy narratives*, Development Policy Centre Discussion Paper 57, Australian National University, March 2017.

Development Alternatives Group and Wuppertal Institute, *Decoupling Growth from Resource Consumption*, Backround Paper to 2nd Indo-German Expert Group Meeting on Green and Inclusive Economy, New Delhi, 3-4th February, 2014.

Dillon, S. *Tax Avoidance, Revenue Starvation and the Age of the Multinational Corporation*, Research Paper 16-18, Suffolk University Law School, 13 December 2016.

Dobbs, R. et al. *Poorer than their Parents? Flat or Falling Incomes in Advanced Economies* McKinsey & Co Global Institute, July 2016.

Dølvik, J. Fløtten, T. Hippe J. M. and Jordfald, B. *The Nordic model towards 2030 A new chapter?* trans. by Walter Gibbs, Fafo, 2015.

Duit, A. Feindt, P. and Meadowcroft, J. 'Greening Leviathan: the rise of the environmental state?', *Environmental Politics*, vol.25, no.1, 2016, pp.1-23.

Duit, A. 'The four faces of the environmental state: environmental governance regimes in 28 countries', *Environmental Politics*, vol.25, no.1, 2016, pp. 69-91.

Eckersley, R. *The Green State: Rethinking Democracy and Sovereignty*, The MIT Press, Cambridge, 2004.

--------- 'National identities, international roles, and the legitimation of climate leadership: Germany and Norway compared', *Environmental Politics*, vol.25 no.1, 2016, pp. 180-221.

Edward, P. and Sumner, A. *'The Geography of Inequality: Where and by How Much has Income Distribution Changed Since 1990?'*, Centre for Global Inequality, Working Paper 341, September 2013.

Enriquez, L. Smit, S. and Ablett, J. *Shifting tides: Global economic scenarios for 2015–25 Are we in for a bumpy ride? How bumpy? And for how long?* McKinsey Insights, September 2015.

Esping-Andersen, G. *The Three Worlds of Welfare Capitalism*, Princeton University Press, Princeton, 1990.

--------- and Gallie, D. Hemerijck, A. and Myles, J. *Why We Need a New Welfare State*, Oxford University Press, Oxford, 2002.

Esteva G.and Escobar, A. 'Post-Development @ 25: on 'being stuck' and moving forward, sideways, backward and otherwise', *Third World Quarterly*, May 2017.

Eurofound, *Statutory minimum wages in the EU 2017*, Dublin, 2017.

European Economists for an Alternative Economic Policy in Europe, *The European Union: The Threat of Disintegration – EuroMemorandum 2017*.

European Trade Union Institute, *Benchmarking Working Europe 2018*, ETUI, Brussels, 2018.

Fastenrath, F. Schwan M. & Trampusch, C. 'Where states and markets meet: the financialisation of sovereign debt management, *New Political Economy*, vol.22, no.3, 2017, pp. 273-293.

Feldstein, M. 'What Could Go Wrong in America?', *Project Syndicate*, 26 October 2016.

Ferguson, P. 'The green economy agenda: business as usual or transformational discourse?' *Environmental Politics*, Vol. 24, No.1 2015, pp.17-37.

Fischer, F. *Climate Crisis and the Democratic Prospect: Participatory Governance in Sustainable Communities*, Oxford University Press, New York, 2017.

FitzRoy, F. 'Basic income and a public job offer: complementary policies to reduce poverty and unemployment', *Journal of Poverty and Social Justice*, online 17 March 2018.

Food and Agriculture Organisation, '*The State of Food and Agriculture 2017, In Brief*', Food and Agriculture Organization of the United Nations, Rome, 2017.

Foroohar, R. 'We've Reached the End of Global Trade', *Time*, 12 October, 2016.

Foster, J. B. 'The Political Economy of Joseph Schumpeter A Theory of Capitalist Development and Decline', *Studies in Political Economy*, no.15, Fall 1984, pp.5-42.

--------- 'The Long Ecological Revolution, *Monthly Review*, November 2017.

Frankel, B. *The Post Industrial Utopians*, Polity, Cambridge, 1987.

--------'Beyond Labourism and Socialism: How the Australian Labor Party Developed the Model of New Labour', *New Left Review*, no.221, 1997, pp.3-33.

-------- *Beyond the State? Dominant Theories and Socialist Strategies*, MacMillan Press, London 1983.

-------- 'On The State of The State: Marxist Theories After Leninism', *Theory And Society* Vol.7 Nos.1 and 2,1979, pp.199-242.

Frase, P. 'By Any Means Necessary', *Jacobin*, Issue 26, Summer 2017.

-------- *Four Futures: Visions of the World After Capitalism*, Verso, London, 2016.

Fraser, N. 'Contradictions of Capital and Care', *New Left Review*, no.100, 2016, pp.99-117.

Frey, C. B. and Osborne, M. *Technology at Work The Future of Innovation and Employment,* Citi GPS: Global Perspectives & Solutions, Oxford Martin School, February 2015.

Fücks, R. *Green Growth, Smart Growth: A New Approach to Economics, Innovation and the Environment*, with an Introduction by Anthony Giddens, Anthem Press, London, 2015.

Garfinkel, I. and Smeeding, T. 'Welfare State Myths and Measurements', *Capitalism and Society*, vol.10, no.1 2015, pp.3-26.

Geier, K. et al. 'How Gender Changes Piketty's 'Capital in the Twenty-First Century', *The Nation*, August 6, 2014.

Giddens, A. in conversation with Fücks, R. 'We Need a Radicalism of the Centre', Heinrich Böll Stiftung, The Green Political Foundation, 3 May 2010.

-------- *The Politics of Climate Change*, Polity Press, Cambridge, 2009.

Gill, I. S. and Kharas, H. *The Middle-Income Trap Turns Ten*, World Bank, Policy Research Working Paper 7403, August 2015.

Global Financial Integrity, the Centre for Applied Research at Norwegian School of Economics, et al. *Financial Flows and Tax Havens: Combining to Limit the Lives of Billions of People*, Washington DC, 5 December 2016.

Global Footprint Network, 'August 13th is Earth Overshoot Day this year', footprintnetwork.org, 26 October 2015.

Gordon, R.J. 'Is US Economic Growth Over? Faltering Innovation Confronts the Six Headwinds', NBER Working Paper No. 18315. August 2012.

-------- *The Rise and Fall of American Growth: The US Standard of Living Since the Civil War*, Princeton University Press, Princeton, 2016.

Gore, A. *The Future: Six Drivers of Global Change*, Random House, New York, 2013.

Gorz, A. *Farewell to the Working Class: An Essay on Post-Industrial Socialism*, trans.by Michael Sonenscher, Pluto, London, 1982.

Gough, I. *Heat, Greed and Human Need: Climate Change, Capitalism and Sustainable Wellbeing*, Edward Elgar, Cheltenham, 2017.

Government of India Ministry of Finance Department of Economic Affairs, Economic Division, *Economic Survey, 2016-17,* January, 2017.

Graeber, D. 'On the Phenomenon of bullshit Jobs', *Strike! Magazine*, August 17, 2013.

Guangyuan, M. 'How the Fortune 500 List Perfectly Mirrors China's Distorted Economy', *Epoch Times*, August 1, 2016.

Haagh, L. ' Basic Income and Institutional transformation, *Compass*, 24, February 2017.

Habermas, J. *Towards a Rational Society: Student Protest Science and Politics* translated by Jeremy J. Shapiro, Beacon press, Boston, 1971, ch.6.

Hake, S. *The Proletarian Dream: Socialism, Culture, and Emotion in Germany 1863-1933*, De Gruyter, Berlin/Boston, 2017.

Hale, T. *Design considerations for a registry of sub- and non-state actions in the UN Framework Convention on Climate Change*, Blavatnik School of Government, Oxford, 24-February 2014.

Hale, T. Held, D. and Young, K. *Gridlock: Why Global Cooperation is Failing When We Need It Most*, Polity Press, Cambridge, 2013.

Hall, P. and Soskice, D. 'An Introduction to Varieties of Capitalism' in Hall, P. and Soskice, D. (eds.), *Varieties of Capitalism: The Institutional Foundations of Comparative Advantage*, Oxford University Press, Oxford, 2001, pp.1–68.

Hamilton, C. *Requiem for a Species*, Earthscan/Routledge, London 2010.

Hansen, A. 'Economic Progress and Declining Population Growth', *The American Economic Review*, Vol. 29, no. 1, March 1939, pp. 1-15.

Hansen, J. et al. 'Young people's burden: requirements of negative co2 emissions' *Earth System Dynamics*, 8, pp.577-616, 2017.

Hanson, G. and McIntosh, C. 'Is the Mediterranean the New Rio Grande? US and EU Immigration Pressures in the Long Run', *Journal of Economic Perspectives*, Vol.30, No.4, 2016, pp. 57-82.

Harvey, D. *Seventeen Contradictions and the End of Capitalism*, Profile Books, London 2014.

Hausmann, R. 'The Education Myth', *Project Syndicate*, May 31, 2015.

Hawken, P. (ed.), *Drawdown The Most Comprehensive Plan Ever Proposed To Reverse Global Warming*, Penguin Random House, New York, 2017.

Heemskerk, E.M. and Takes, F.W. 'The Corporate Elite Community structure of Global Capitalism', *New Political Economy*, vol.21 no.1, 2015, pp.98-118.

Hellebrandt, T. and Mauro, P. *The Future of Worldwide Income Distribution*, Peterson Institute for International Economics, April 2015.

Helm, D. *The Carbon Crunch: How We're Getting Climate Change Wrong – and How to Fix It*, Yale University Press, 2012.

--------- *What should oil companies do about climate change?*, Energy Futures Network, Paper No.9, 26th February 2015.

Hepburn, C. and Bowen, A. 'Prosperity with Growth: Economic growth, climate change and environmental limits', *Centre for Climate Change Economics and Policy*, LSE, Working Paper no.109, October 2012.

Hermann, C. 'The public sector and equality', *Global Social Policy*, vol.16, no.1, 2016, pp.4-21.

Hilferding, R. *Finance Capital: A Study of the Latest Phase of Capitalist Development*, 1910, English translation by M. Watnick and S. Gordon, Routledge & Kegan Paul, London, 1981.

Hirst, P. and Zeitlin, J. 'Flexible Specialisation versus Post-Fordism: Theory, Evidence and Policy Implications', *Economy and Society*, Vol. 20 no. 1, February 1991, pp.1-55.

Horkheimer, M. 'The Jews and Europe' *Zeitschrift für Sozialforschung*, December 1939, reprinted in Stephen Bronner and Douglas Kellner (eds), *Critical Theory and Society: A Reader*, Routledge, New York, 1989.

Hoy, C. and Sumner, A. *Gasoline, Guns, and Giveaways: Is There New Capacity for Redistribution to End Three Quarters of Global Poverty?* Center for Global Development, Washington DC, Working Paper 433, August 2016.

Hutton, W. 'Litvinenko's murder shows why Putin's Russia will never prosper', *The Guardian*, 24 January 2016.

Huws, U. 'Logged labour: a new paradigm of work organisation?', *Work organisation, labour & globalisation*, vol.10, no.1 2016, pp.7-26.

Hynes, H. Patricia *Taking Population Out of the Equation: Reformulating I=PAT*, Institute of Women, North Amherst, 1993.

International Labour Office, *World Employment Social Outlook: Trends for Women, ILO, Geneva, March 2018.*

--------- *World Employment and Social Outlook: Trends 2018*, International Labour Organization, Geneva, 2018.

Intergovernmental Panel on Climate Change, *Climate Change 2014 Synthesis Report*, WMO and UNEP, Geneva 2015.

International Energy Agency, *World Energy Outlook 2017*, OECD/IEA, Paris, November 2017.

International Monetary Fund, *Global Financial Stability Report Press Conference – 2016*, IMF, October 5, 2016.

--------- *Global Trade: What's Behind the Slowdown?*, International Monetary Fund, October 2016.

International Resource Panel, *Decoupling Natural Resource Use and Environmental Impacts From Economic Growth*, United Nations Environmental Programme, March 2011.

Institute for Public Policy Research, *Time for Change: A New Vision for the British Economy – The Interim Report of the IPPR Commission on Economic Justice*, IPPR, London, 2017.

Jackson, T. *Prosperity Without Growth: Foundations for the Economy of Tomorrow*, Second Edition, Routledge, London, 2017.

--------- and Victor, P. and Naqui, A.A. *Towards a Stock-Flow Consistent Ecological Macroeconomics*, WWWforEurope, Working Paper no.114, March 2016.

--------- and Victor, P. *Green Economy at Community Scale*, Metcalf Foundation, Toronto, November 2013.

Jacobs, M. and Mazzucato, M. (eds.) *Rethinking Capitalism: Economics and Policy for Sustainable and Inclusive Growth*, Blackwell, Oxford, 2016.

Jacobs, M. 'High Pressure for low emissions: How civil society created the Paris climate agreement', *Juncture*, IPPR, London, 14, March 2016.

Jakob, M. and Edenhofer, O. 'Green growth, degrowth, and the commons', *Oxford Review of Economic Policy*, vol.30, no.3, 2014, p.447-468.

Jameson, F. in Zizek, S. (ed.), *An American Utopia: Dual Power and the Universal Army*, Verso, London, 2016.

--------- interview with Balunovic, F. 'Fredric Jameson: People are saying "this is a new fascism" and my answer is – not yet!', *Lefteast*, 4 November, 2016.

Kahn, H. and Weiner, A.J. *The Year 2000: A Framework for Speculation on the Next Thirty Years*, Macmillan, New York, 1967.

Kalecki, M. 'Political Aspects of Full Employment', *Political Quarterly*, no.4, October 1943, pp.322-330.

Keane, B. 'Silliest neoliberal poll champions brutal regimes', *Crikey*, 28 September 2017.

Keane, J. *The Life and Death of Democracy*, Simon & Schuster, London, 2009.

Keith, D. Wagner, G. and Zabel, C. 'Solar geoengineering reduces atmospheric carbon burden', *Nature Climate Change*, September 2017.

Keynes, J. M. *The General Theory of Employment, Interest and Money*, Macmillan Press, London, 1936.

Khazan, O. 'A Shocking Decline in American Life Expectancy', *The Atlantic*, 21 December 2017.

Kiely, R. 'The Last Refuge of the Noble savage? A Critical Assessment of Post-Development Theory', *European Journal of Development Research*, vol.11, no.1, June 1999, pp.30-55.

Kivits, R. Charles, M. and Ryan, N. 'A post-carbon aviation future: Airports and the transition to a cleaner aviation sector', *Futures*, 42, 2010, pp.199-211.

Klein, N. *This Changes Everything: Capitalism vs the Climate*, Simon & Schuster, New York 2014.

Kleinknecht, A. Mandel, E. and Wallerstein, I. (eds.), *New Findings in Long-Wave Research*, Macmillan, Basingstoke, 1992.

Komesaroff, M. *Make the Foreign Serve China: How Foreign Science and Technology Helped China Dominate Global Metallurgical Industries*, Centre for Strategic and International Studies, March 2017.

Kovic, M. 'The universal basic income: Benefits, pseudo-probems and real problems' ZIPAR Discussion Paper Series, Volume 1, Issue 2. Zurich 2017.

Krippner, G. *Capitalizing on Crisis: The Political Origins of the Rise of Finance*, Harvard University Press, Cambridge, 2011.

Krugman, P. 'Secular Stagnation, Coalmines, Bubbles, and Larry Summers', *New York Times* blog November 16, 2013.

Kuznets, S. 'Economic Growth and Income Inequality', *American Economic Review*, vol. 45 March, 1955, pp. 1–28.

Lachapelle, E. MacNeil, R. & Paterson, M. 'The political economy of decarbonisation: from green energy 'race' to green 'division of labour', *New Political Economy*, vol.22, no.3, 2017, pp.311-327.

Landa, I. *Fascism and the Masses: The revolt Against the Last Humans, 1848-1945*, Routledge, New York, 2018.

Lapavitsas, C. and Mendieta-Muñoz, I. 'The Profits of Financialization', *Monthly Review*, July-August 2016.

Latouche, S. 'Can the Left Escape Economism?', *Capitalism Nature Socialism*, no.1 2012, pp.74-78.

Lawrence, M. *Definancialisation: A democratic reformation of finance*, Institute for Public Policy Research, London, September, 2014.

Layfield, D. 'Turning carbon into gold: the financialisation of international climate policy, *Environmental Politics*, vol.22, no.6, 2013, pp.901-917.

Lister, R. 'Coming off the fence on UBI?', *Compass,* 20 January 2017.

Mackay, R. and Avanessian, A. (eds), *#The Accelerationist Reader*, Falmouth, Urbanomic, 2014.

Magdoff, F. and Foster, J. B. 'Stagnation and Financialisation: The Nature of the Contradiction', *Monthly Review*, May 2014.

Maliranta, M. Määttänen N. and Vihriälä, V. 'Are the Nordic countries really less innovative than the US?', VoxEU.org. 19 December 2012.

Malmaeus, J. M. and Alfredsson, E.C. 'Potential Consequences on the Economy of Low or No Growth – Short and Long Term Perspectives', *Ecological Economics*, vol.134, 2017, pp.57-64.

Martin, C. J. 'Economic Prosperity is in High Demand', *Politics & Society*, vol. 44, no. 2, 2016, pp.227-35.

Marx, K. *Preface to a Contribution to the Critique of Political Economy*, Selected Works Volume One, Moscow 1950.

--------- *Capital A Critique of Political Economy, Volume One*, translated by B. Fowkes, Penguin and New Left Review, Harmondsworth, 1976.

Mason, P. *PostCapitalism; A Guide to Our Future*, Allen Lane, London, 2015.

Mathews, J. *Greening of capitalism: how Asia is driving the next great transformation*, Stanford University Press, Stanford, 2015.

--------- *Global Green Shift*, Anthem Press, London, 2017.

Mathur, A. and Turner, A. 'Why Renewables Are Not Enough', *Project Syndicate*, May 11, 2016.

Mazzucato, M. *The Entrepreneurial State Debunking Public vs. Private Sector Myths*, Anthem Books, London, 2013.

--------- and Perez, C. *Innovation as Growth Policy: the challenge for Europe*, Science Policy Research Unit, Working Papers Series, University of Sussex, July 2014.

--------- *Mission Oriented Research and Innovation in the European Union: a problem solving approach to fuel innovation-led growth*, EU Publications, February 2018.

McKibben, B. 'Recalculating the Climate math', *New Republic*, 22 September, 2016.

McKinsey & Company, *Debt and (Not Much) Deleveraging*, McKinsey Global Institute, February 2016.

McMichael, P. *Development and Social Change A Global Perspective* Sixth Edition, Sage, London, 2017.

McMurtry, J. *The Cancer Stage of Capitalism: From Crisis to Cure*, Pluto Books, London, 2013.

Meckling, J. 'Distributional Effects, Regulatory Pressure, and Business Strategy in Environmental Politics, *Global Environmental Politics* vol.15 no.2, May 2015, pp.19-37.

--------- and Jenner, S. 'Varieties of market-based policy: Instrument choice in climate policy', *Environmental Politics*, vol.25, no.5 2016, pp. 853-74.

Milanovic, B. *Global Inequality: A New Approach for the Age of Globalization*, Harvard University Press, Cambridge, 2016.

Millar, R. J. et al, 'Emission budgets consistent with limiting warming to 1.5°C', *Nature Geoscience*, 18 September, 2017.

Mills, C. *Towards a Future Post-Capitalism: Accelerationism and its Aesthetics*, Dissertation for the Department of Visual Cultures, Goldsmiths College, University of London, 2016.

Minsky, H. *Stabilizing an Unstable Economy*, 2nd edition McGraw Hill, New York, 2008.

Mitchell, W. 'The secular stagnation hoax', *Bill Mitchell-billy-blog*, November 3, 2014.

Mol, A. 'Chinese Sustainability in Transition: Which direction to take?' *in* M. Redclift and D. Springett (eds.), *Routledge International Handbook of Sustainable Development*, Routledge, New York, 2015, ch.23.

Monbiot, G. 'Insectageddon: farming is more catastrophic than climate breakdown', *The Guardian*, 20 October 2017.

--------- 'Finally, a breakthrough alternative to growth economics – the doughnut', *The Guardian*, 12 April, 2017.

Moore, J. *Capitalism in the Web of Life: Ecology and the Accumulation of Capital*, Verso, London, 2015.

Moretti, E. Steinwender, C. and Reenen, J. 'The Intellectual Spoils of War? Defense R&D, Productivity and Spillovers', emi.berkeley.edu (draft) 2014.

Negri, A. *From the Factory to the Metropolis: Essays Volume 2*, Edited by Federico Tomasello and trans. by Ed Emery, Polity, Cambridge, 2018.

Newman, J.M. 'The Myth of Free', *Social Science Research Network*, 25 August, 2016.

Nordhaus, W.D. 'A New Solution: The Climate Club', *New York Review of Books*, June 4 2015.

Noys, B. 'Futures *of Accelerationism*', academic. edu 23 October 2016.

--------- *Malign Velocities: Accelerationism & Capitalism*, Zero Books, Winchester, 2014.

O'Connor, J. *The Fiscal Crisis of the State*, St.Martin's Press, New York, 1973.

O'Connor, J. Shola Orloff, A. and Shaver, S. *States, Markets, Families: Gender, Liberalism and Social Policy in Australia, Canada, Great Britain and the United States*, Cambridge University Press, Cambridge, 1999.

OECD, *Pension Markets in Focus 2017*, OECD, Paris, 2017.

--------- *Revenue Statistics 2015*, OECD, Paris, September 17, 2015.

--------- *Towards Green Growth* OECD, Paris, 2011.

O'Neill, J. 'The "Next Eleven" and the World Economy', *Project Syndicate*, 18 April, 2018.

Ostrom, E. *Governing the Commons: The evolution of institutions for collective action*, Cambridge University Press, Cambridge, 1990.

Owen, R. Bessant, J. and Heintz, M. (eds.) *Responsible Innovation: Managing the Responsible Emergence of Science and Innovation in Society*, John Wiley, London, 2013.

Oxfam, 'An Economy for the 99%', *Oxfam Briefing Paper*, 16 January 2017.

Palley, T. *Inequality, the Financial Crisis and Stagnation: Competing Stories and Why They Matter*, Macroeconomic Policy Institute, Hans-Böckler-Stiftung, Dusseldorf, Working paper 151, May 2015.

Parijs, P. '*Basic Income: A Simple and Powerful Idea for the 21st Century*', Basic Income European Network, VIIIth International Congress, Berlin 6-7 October, 2000.

Paul, M. DarityJr., W. and Hamilton, D. 'Why We need A Federal Job Guarantee, *Jacobin*, 4 February, 2017.

Perez, C. *The new context for industrializing around natural resources: an opportunity for Latin America (and other resource rich countries)?*, Working Papers in Technology Governance and Economic Dynamics no. 62 May 2014, The Other Canon Foundation, Norway and Tallinn University.

--------- 'Finance and Technical Change: A Long-term View', *African Journal of Science, Technology, Innovation and Development*, Vol. 3, No. 1, 2011, pp. 10-35.

Phelps, E. 'Trump, Corporatism, and the Dearth of Innovation', *Project Syndicate*, 17 January, 2017.

--------- 'What is Wrong with the West's Economies?', *New York Review of Books*, August 13, 2015.

Piketty, T. *Capital in the Twenty-First Century*, translated by Arthur Goldhammer. Harvard University Press, Cambridge, 2014.

Pilling, D. *The Growth Delusion: Wealth, Poverty, and the Well-Being of Nations*, Penguin Random House, New York, 2018.

Pixley, J. *Emotions in Finance: Booms, Bust and Uncertainty*, Cambridge University Press, Cambridge, 2004, second edition 2012.

Polanyi, K. *The Great Transformation: The political and economic origins of our time*, Beacon Press, Boston 1944.

Pollan, M. *Omnivore's Dilemma*, Penguin, New York, 2007.

Pritchett, L. 'Where Has All the Education Gone?', *World Bank Economic Review*, vol.15, no.3, 2001, pp.367-391.

PWC, *The Long View: How will the economic order change by 2050?*, PWC, February 2017.

Quiggin, J. 'Guaranteed minimum income: how much would it cost? (updated)', *Crooked Timber*, 5 August 2012.

--------- 'Prospects of a Keynesian utopia', aeonmagazine.com, 27 September 2012.

Raftery, A. et. al. 'Less than 2°C by 2100 unlikely', *Nature Climate Change*, 31 July 2017.

Raworth, K. 'Why Degrowth has out-grown its own name', *From Poverty to Power*, Oxfam, December 1, 2015.

--------- *Doughnut Economics: Seven Ways to Think Like a 21st-Century Economist*, Penguin Random House, London 2017.

Rey, H. *Dilemma Not Trilemma: The Global Financial Cycle and Monetary Policy Independence*, National Bureau of Economic Research, Cambridge, 2015, Working Paper 21162.

Reynolds, T. 'Black Women, Gender Equality and Universal Basic Income, *Compass*, 27 January, 2017.

Rifkin, J. *The Biotech Century: Harnessing the Gene and Remaking the World*, Tarcher/Putnam, New York, 1998.

--------- *The Zero Marginal Cost Society: The internet of things, the collaborative commons, and the eclipse of capitalism*, Palgrave Macmillan, London, 2014.

--------- 'How Developing Nations Can Leapfrog Developed Countries with the Sharing Economy', *The Huffington Post*, 2 November, 2015.

Roach, S. 'The Courage to Normalise Monetary Policy', *Project Syndicate*, 26 September 2017.

--------- 'Global Growth – Still made in China', *Project Syndicate*, 29 August 2016.

--------- 'Another Lesson from Japan', *Project Syndicate*, 26 June 2017.

Rockström, J. et al. 'Planetary Boundaries: Exploring the Safe Operating Space for Humanity', *Ecology and Society*, Vol.14, no.2, 2009, pp.1-33.

Rodrik, D. 'Premature deindustrialization', *Journal of Economic Growth*, no.1 2016, pp.1-33.

--------- *Development Strategies for the Next Century*, Economic Commission for Latin America and the Caribbean Seminar, Santiago, Chile, 28 August 2001.

--------- *Is Global Equality the Enemy of National Equality?* January 2017, Dani Rodrik's weblog, rodrik.typepad.com.

Rosa, H. *Social Acceleration: A New Theory of Modernity*, trans.by Jonathon

Trejo-Mathys, Columbia University Press, New York, 2013.

Rundle, G. *A Revolution in the Making: 3D printing Robots and the Future*, Affirm Press, South Melbourne, 2014.

Ruta, M. and Venables, A. *International trade in natural resources: practice and policy*, World Trade Organisation, Working Paper ERSD-2012-07, March 2012.

Ruttan, V. 'Is War necessary for Economic Growth?', Clemons Lecture, Saint Johns University, Collegeville, Minnesota, October 9, 2006.

Sachs, J. *Economics and the Cultivation of Virtue*, Three lectures at the London School of Economics on February 13, 14 and 15, 2017.

Schandl, H. et.al 'Decoupling global environmental pressure and economic growth: scenarios for energy use, materials use and carbon emissions', *Journal of Cleaner Production*, 132, 2016, pp. 45-56.

Schor, J. and Thompson, C. (eds.) *Sustainable Lifestyles and the Quest for Plenitude: Case studies of the New Economy*, Yale University Press, New Haven, 2014.

Schumpeter, J. *Capitalism, Socialism and Democracy*, Harper & Row, New York, 1942, Taylor & Francis e-Library with an introduction by Richard Swedberg, 2003.

--------- 'The March into Socialism', *The American Economic Review*, vol.40, 2, 1950, pp.446-456.

Schwab, K. (ed), *New Growth Models: Challenges and steps to achieving patterns of more equitable, inclusive and sustainable growth*, World Economic Forum, Geneva 2014.

--------- *The Global Competitiveness Report 2017-2018*, World Economic Forum, Geneva, 2017.

Seabrooke, L and Wigan, D. 'The governance of global wealth chains', *Review of International Political Economy*, vol.24, no.1, 2017, pp.1-29.

Shah, S. 'US Wars in Afghanistan, Iraq to Cost $6 Trillion', *Global Research News*, Feb.12, 2014.

Sharp, G. 'Constitutive Abstraction and Social practice', *Arena*, no.70, 1985, pp.48-82.

Sidorkin, A. 'Education for Jobless Society', *Studies in Philosophy and Education*, vol.36, no.1, 2017, pp.7-20.

Sieber, A. 'How not to save the world', *International Politics and Society*, 5 April 2018.

SIPRI, 'Global Military Spending remains High at $1.7 trillion', Stockholm International Peace Research Institute (SIPRI), Solna, 2 May 2018.

Skidelsky, R. 'How Much Debt Is Too Much?', *Project Syndicate*, January 28, 2016.

Smil, V. *Making the Modern World Materials and Dematerialization*, Wiley, Chichester, 2014.

Smith, R. 'Green Capitalism: The God that failed', *real-world economics review*, no.56, 2011.

--------- 'Beyond growth or beyond capitalism?' *World Economics Review*, issue 53, 2010.

Soederberg, S. *Debtfare States and the Poverty Industry: Money, Discipline and the Surplus Population*, Routledge, London, 2015.

Solomou, S. *Phases of Economic Growth, 1850-1973 Kondratieff Waves and Kuznets Swings*, Cambridge University Press, Cambridge, 1990.

Spratt, D. and Sutton, P. *Climate Code Red*, Scribe, Melbourne, 2008.

Spratt, D. *Recount It's Time to "Do the math" Again*, nocarbonbudget. info April 2015.

--------- 'Climate Reality Check: After Paris, Counting the Cost', breakthroughonline.org.au March 2016.

--------- and Dunlop, I. *What Lies Beneath: The Scientific Understatement of Climate Risks*, Breakthrough – National Centre for Climate Restoration, Melbourne, September, 2017.

--------- '1.5°C Just a Decade Away', *Breakthrough*, April 5, 2018.

Spratt, S. 'Financing Green Transformations', in I. Scoones, M. Leach and P. Newell (eds), *The Politics of Green Transformations*, Earthscan/Routledge, 2015, ch.10.

Srnicek, N. and Williams, A. 'Accelerate Manifesto for an Accelerationist Politics', *Critical Legal Thinking*, 14 May 2013.

--------- *Inventing the Future: Postcapitalism and a World Without Work, revised and updated edition*, Verso, London, 2016.

Standing, G. 'Why the Precariat is not a 'bogus concept', *Open Democracy*, 4 March, 2014.

Steffen, W. et.al. 'Planetary Boundaries: Guiding Human Development on a Changing Planet', *Science*, January 16, 2015.

Stengers, I. *Another Science is Possible: A Manifesto for Slow Science*, trans. by Stephen Muecke, Polity, Cambridge, 2017.

Stephens, J. *Confronting Post Maternal Thinking: Feminism, Memory and Care*, Columbia University Press, New York, 2012.

Stern, N. 'The Stern Review + 10: new opportunities for growth and development' speech given at The Royal Society and London School of Economics and Political Science, Grantham Institute, 28 October, 2016.

Stirling, A. *Towards Innovation Democracy? Participation, Responsibility and Precaution in Innovation Governance*, SPRU and STEPS Centre, University of Sussex, November 2014.

Streeck, W. *Buying Time The Delayed Crisis of Democratic Capitalism* trans.by P. Camiller, Verso Books, London, 2014.

--------- 'How Will Capitalism End?', *New Left Review*, no.87, May/June 2014, pp.35–64.

Summers, L. 'The Age of Secular Stagnation: What it is and what to do about it', *Foreign Affairs*, March/April 2016.

Tcherneva, P. R. *Beyond Full Employment: The Employer of Last Resort as an Institution For Change*, Working Paper no.732, Levy Economics Institute, Bard College, September 2012.

The Global Commission on the Economy and Climate, *Better Growth Better Climate, The New Climate Economy* Washington DC, September 2014.

--------- *Seizing the Global Opportunity: Partnerships for Better Growth and a Better Climate*, Washington DC, July 2015.

The World Bank, *Poverty and Shared Prosperity 2016 Taking on Inequality*, International Bank for Reconstruction and Development/The World Bank, Washington, 2016.

Thierer, A. *Permissionless Innovation, The Continuing Case for Comprehensive Technological Freedom*, Mercatus Center, George Mason University, 2014.

Thompson, G. 'Central Banks and Fin-tech Governance in a Global Context' Draft paper for Workshop on '*The Changing Technological Infrastructures of Global Finance*', Queens University, Waterloo, Canada, May 30-31 2017.

Tokic, D. 'The economic and financial dimensions of degrowth', *Ecological Economics*, vol.84, 2012, pp.49-56.

Tomlinson, J. 'Why wasn't there a 'Keynesian revolution' in economic policy every-where?', *Economy and Society*, vol.20, no1, 1991, pp.103-117.

Trainer, T. 'Eco-modernism?', *Arena Magazine*, no.143, August-September 2016, pp.36-38.

--------- 'The Degrowth Movement From the Perspective of the Simpler Way', *Capitalism Nature Socialism*, no.2, 2015, pp.58-75.

Turner, A. 'The Skills Delusion', *Project Syndicate*, 12 October, 2016.

--------- 'Greece and Japan: A Tale of Two Debt Write-Downs', *Social Europe*, 16 June 2016.

Umpfenbach, K. et al. *How will we know if absolute decoupling has been achieved?*, Dynamix Project, European Union, September 2013.

UNEP, *Global Material Flows and Resource Productivity Assessment Report for the UNEP International Resource Panel*, United Nations Environment Programme, 2016.

United Nations Conference on Trade and Development (UNCTAD), *World Investment Report 2013: Global Value Chains: Investment for Trade and Development*, United Nations, Geneva, 2013.

--------- *Trade and Development Report 2016*, United Nations, Geneva, 2016.

Vacas-Soriano, C. and Fernández-Macías, E. *Income inequalities and employment patterns in Europe before and after the Great Recession*, Eurofound, Luxembourg, 2017.

Vansintjan, A. *'Accelerationism… and Degrowth? The Left's Strange Bedfellows'*, Institute for Social Ecology, social-ecology.org 28 September 2016.

Varoufakis, Y. *Adults in the Room My Battle With Europe's Deep Establishment*, Penguin Random House, London, 2017.

--------- 'The Universal Right to Capital Income', *Project Syndicate*, 31 October, 2016.

Vermeiren, M. *Power and Imbalances in the Global Monetary System: A Comparative Capitalism Perspective*, Palgrave MacMillan, Basingstoke, 2014.

--------- 'One-size-fits-some! Capitalist diversity, sectoral interests and monetary policy in the euro area', *Review of International Political Economy*, vol.24, no.6, 2017, pp. 929-957.

Victor, M. 'Questioning Sustainability in Latin America', in *Peter Victor and Brett Dolter (eds.), Handbook on Growth and Sustainability*, Edward Elgar, Cheltenham, 2017.

Wade, R. 'Our misleading measure of income and wealth inequality: the standard Gini coefficient', *Triple Crisis*, 6 May 2013.

--------- 'Industrial Policy in Response to the Middle-income Trap and the Third Wave of the Digital Revolution', *Global Policy*, Vol.7, no.4, 2016, p.469-480.

Wallerstein, I. et.al. *Does Capitalism Have a Future?* Oxford University Press, Oxford, 2013.

Waring, M. *Counting for Nothing: What Men Value and What Women Are Worth*, originally published 1988, second edition, University of Toronto Press, Toronto, 1999.

Watts, J. and Vidal, J. 'Environmental defenders being killed in record numbers, new research reveals', *The Guardian*, 13 July 2017.

Weiss, M. and Cattaneo, C. 'Degrowth – Taking Stock and Reviewing an Emerging Academic Paradigm', *Ecological Economics*, Vol. 137, 2017, pp.220-30.

Willis Towers Watson and Thinking Ahead Institute, *'Global pension funds asset study 2018'*, February 4, 2018, thinkingaheadinstitute.org

Wiseman, J. *Pathways to a zero-carbon economy: Learning from large scale de-carbonisation strategies*, Visions & Pathways Project, Melbourne, March 2014.

Wolf, M. 'The grasshoppers and the ants – a modern fable', *Financial Times*, 25 May 2010.

World Bank, *China Systematic Country Diagnostic: Towards A More inclusive and Sustainable Development 2017*, World Bank, Washington, February 2018.

World Economic Forum, *The Global Risks Report 2014*, 9th Edition, Geneva, 2014.

--------- *The Global Risks Report 2018*, 13th Edition, Geneva, 2018.

World Trade Organization, *World Trade Outlook Indicator*, February 2018.

Wright, E. O. 'How To Be an Anticapitalist Today', *Jacobin,* 2 December, 2015.

Wright, C. and Nyberg, D. *Climate Change, Capitalism and Corporations: Processes of Creative Self-Destruction*, Cambridge University Press, Cambridge, 2015.

Xi, J. Speech in Full to Opening Plenary at Davos, *World Economic Forum*, 17 January, 2017.

Zhang, Y. *Peak Neodymium – Material Constraints for Future Wind Power Development*, Masters Thesis, Department of Earth Sciences, Uppsala University, 2013.

Žižek, S. *Living in the End Times, Verso*, London, 2010.

Zucman, G. *The Hidden Wealth of Nations: The Scourge of Tax Havens*, Translated by T. Lavender Fagan, University of Chicago Press, Chicago, 2015.

Index

249, 261, 267, 297-301
indigenous groups 51, 76, 79
inequality 7, 18, 22, 30, 36, 38-40, 58,
    61-2, 65-6, 68-74, 76, 81-3, 85-101,
    115, 124, 129-30, 135-6, 139-40,
    144, 148, 158, 167, 173, 188, 209-
    10, 214-15, 217, 224, 231-9, 246,
    255, 259, 262-70, 273-4, 278-80,
    282, 287-8, 298-9, 301, 305
innovation, innovation-led growth
    2-4, 12-13, 17-38, 45-48, 55-62,
    65-7,101, 103-4, 108, 116-7, 127,
    129-30, 135, 137-41, 145, 150-2,
    154,158-59, 162-3, 166, 179, 181,
    183, 200, 238, 241, 246, 249, 253,
    275, 279, 281-2
International Energy Agency 119
IPCC reports 133-4
Jackson, Tim 126, 129-31, 134, 137,
    140, 209, 217-20, 223-9, 283-7, 292,
    294
Jacobs, Michael 30, 50, 53, 57, 60-1,
    207, 281
Jakob, Michael 225
James, Selma 271
Jameson, Fredric 159, 253
Japan 9, 28, 36-43, 62, 64, 69-71, 73,
    77, 81, 87, 97, 106, 111-12, 116,
    122, 144, 148, 150, 195, 217, 222,
    254, 297, 299, 301-3
job guarantee 268-70
Kalecki, Michal 47, 116-18, 121, 125,
    165, 181-2, 191-3
Kaya, Yoichi 133
Keane, Bernard 35
Keynes, John M. 2, 64, 187, 191, 219,
    269
Keynesians, neo-Keynesian and
    post-Keynesians 12, 14, 30, 35, 38-9,
    52, 65-6, 98, 116, 125-7, 180-1, 185,
    187-9, 192, 194, 207, 220, 228-30,
    269, 281-2, 287
Kharas, Homi 81-2
Kiely, Ray 79
Kim, Jim Yong 249
Kipping, Katja 263

Klein, Naomi 54, 223
knowledge economy 51, 63, 83, 129,
    141, 156, 239, 241, 244, 246-7
Kondratieff Long Waves 24-6, 55-6,
    58-9, 93, 161
Koo, Richard C. 43
Korotayev, Andrey 59
Kuznets, Simon, Kuznets Curve 91-4
labour movements 18, 76, 94, 234, 238,
    246, 269
Land, Nick 187
Latin American countries 48, 55, 62,
    75, 78-9, 82-3, 91, 93, 96, 110, 122,
    139, 150, 169, 176, 195, 204, 217,
    231, 260, 292, 298, 305
Latouche, Serge 211, 216
La Via Campesina 167, 176
Lawrence, Mathew 204, 207
Left Prometheans 115
living wage 232, 234-7
Loach, Ken 161
Magdoff, Fred 42
Magdoff, Harry 42
Malmaeus, J. Mikael 213-4
Marcuse, Herbert 160
Martin, Cathie Jo 183
Marx, Karl, also Marxian, Marxist 8, 21,
    23-4, 26, 41-2, 48, 55, 125, 155,
    158-60, 180-1, 185, 188-9, 198-9,
    201, 220-1, 250, 270, 276, 279, 284,
    287-8, 290, 295, 308
Mason, Paul 160-1, 165-6, 266
Mauro, Paolo 98-9
Mathews, John 58, 140
Mazzucato, Mariana 47, 55-61, 140 162,
    207, 281, 285
McKibben, Bill 48
McKinsey & Co 29, 38, 70, 85, 99, 145,
    202, 242, 248
Meckling, Jonas 122-3
Mélenchon, Jean-Luc 68
middle-income countries 13, 75, 78-88,
    92, 96, 98-9, 101, 108, 232, 298-99
Milanovic, Branko 90-5, 97
military expenditure 45-6, 48, 87, 303
military R&D 33, 46-7, 56, 70, 228, 282